Collins Easy Learning Complete English is a handy three-in-one book: spelling, writing, and grammar and punctuation in one volume. The book is ideal for anyone who wants to improve their English. Whether you are preparing for exams, need a quick look-up guide to English, or you simply want to browse and find out more about the English language and how it works, this book gives you all the information you need in a clear and accessible format.

Grammar & Punctuation: this section begins with a clear outline of the different parts of speech, and goes on to describe their forms and uses. All the main tenses of English are explained and exemplified, with emphasis on their function in everyday English.

Next, you will find a description of different types of statement and clause, with attention given to structures such as question forms, conditionals, and reported speech.

Finally, a guide to punctuation gives you clear and up-to-date information on important topics such as the use of the apostrophe, capital letters, and full stops.

Spelling: this section uses simple explanations, backed up with examples demonstrating each point, to describe the important features of English spelling. It also points out the most difficult words to spell, and offers ways of learning these.

The section begins with an explanation of how the letters and groups of letters regularly correspond to certain sounds, and then looks at the reasons why the spelling of some words does not match the sound.

Next, it looks at recurring patterns, and rules you need to be familiar with in order to understand and predict how words are spelt.

The last part is concerned with words whose spellings are not easy to predict: it provides some practical advice on learning tricky spellings and then looks at difficult words themselves, showing why each can present pitfalls even to experienced users of English.

All of the difficult words that are examined in this section are listed in an alphabetical index at the end.

Writing: this section begins by reviewing all the things you need to know before you can write effectively. The topics covered here apply to all types of writing, and range from planning your writing to checking it at the end. Tricky issues such as how to show speech, abbreviations, and numbers are also covered. In addition, there is a comprehensive guide to style, looking at areas such as writing plain English, avoiding ambiguity and writing with the appropriate level of formality.

The second part of the writing section takes a detailed look at different types of writing, from informal emails and letters to formal essays, reports and presentations. It gives advice on structure, tone and style, with examples of good practice, as well as providing suggestions for useful words and phrases to use in your own work.

The third part deals with common mistakes, and issues that people often disagree about. Expert practical guidance is given, so you can feel confident of making the right choice whatever the situation.

The Collins corpus forms the basis of all the points covered in this book, helping us to make accurate decisions about how the English language works in today's world. Explanations are fully illustrated with examples that remain close to the corpus, occasionally with small changes made so that they can be as clear and helpful as possible.

We hope you enjoy learning about the English language and improving your skills. For more information about Collins language reference books, visit us at www.collinslanguage.com.

contents 5

1. Grammar & Punctuation

10 contents

grammar

Parts of speech

Sentences are made up of **words**. A sentence can be made up of any number of words.

> *He left us.*
> *The man in the corner lowered his newspaper.*
> *Whenever I see Tammy I worry about how I look.*
> *Until tomorrow then.*
> *Yes.*

We can put words together in many ways to make new sentences.

> *I can help you.*
> *Can I help you?*

Grammar describes how we put words together. Each word in a sentence belongs to a particular set or **class**, depending on how it is used. These classes are called **parts of speech**.

All sentences begin with a capital letter and end in either a full stop, a question mark, or an exclamation mark. When we talk about these marks, e.g. commas, semicolons, full stops, brackets, and so on, we are talking about **punctuation**.

The term **clause** is used to describe a group of words that contains a **verb**, the **subject** of that verb, and, often, some other words such as an **object**.

> *I live in Sussex.*
> *...where I live.*
> *Jessica lived in Manchester at first.*
> *He was living in Rome that year.*
> *...when he had eaten breakfast.*

A sentence can contain one or more **clauses**.

> *I can help you if you will let me.*
> *Whenever you need to talk to someone, just pop in and see*
>   *if I'm here.*

Many sentences are made up of a single clause. Single clause sentences are called **simple** sentences.

> *He arrived on Friday.*
> *My brother loves his skateboard.*

A clause always contains a **verb**.

> *run*   *walk*
> *think*   *believe*

A sentence, however, does not always have to be a clause. See p. 262 for more about clauses.

> *Certainly not.*
> *Until tomorrow then.*
> *Yes.*
> *Why?*

A **phrase** is just a **group** of words. The term is usually kept for words which go together naturally.

> *the other day*
> *my friend Henry*
> *in spite of*
> *over the hill*
> *would have been walking*

Many words can refer to one thing only or to more than one. We use the terms **singular** and **plural** for this. A more general term is **number**. Pronouns and nouns can be singular or plural in grammatical number. See p. 204.

When we want to identify the speaker or the person spoken about in grammar, we use **first person** to mean the speaker, **second person** to mean the person who is spoken to, and **third person** to mean the person who is spoken about. For example, we talk about 'first person plural' or 'third person singular'.

pronouns	singular	plural
1st person 2nd person 3rd person	I you he, she, it	we you they
nouns	the man a girl	the men two girls

A **verb** tells us about an action or a state of being. Ordinary verbs are called **main verbs**.

come	go	think
want	economize	believe

A main verb is sometimes called a 'doing word'. A special group of verbs are called **auxiliary verbs**. These can be put together with main verbs to form different tenses.

I **am** thinking.
She **has** seen the film already.
I **can** help you.
We **might** need to.

A **noun** is a word that labels a thing or an idea. Nouns are sometimes called 'naming words'.

table	book	ugliness
time	animal	thing

If we do not want to repeat the same noun in a sentence or a paragraph we can replace it with a **pronoun**. A pronoun is a word that is used instead of a noun phrase or a noun.

> Gary saw Sue so **he** asked **her** to help him.
> Ross was hungry so **he** stopped at a burger bar.

An **adjective** gives more information about a noun. Adjectives help us describe or pick out which particular thing among many is being referred to. Adjectives are sometimes called 'describing words'.

> a man   a **tall** man
> their TV   their **new wide-screen** TV
> the cat   the **fat black-and-white** cat

A **determiner** is used to point more precisely to the person, thing, or idea that is being talked about. Examples of determiners are **definite** and **indefinite articles** and **possessives**.

> **the** cat   **a** man
> **my** aunt   **their** TV

An **adverb** gives information about the way that an action is carried out or when and where it takes place.

> She ran **quickly** down the path.
> The children laughed **hysterically**.
> He lifted the box **carefully**.

Some adverbs can also be used before adjectives,

> He was a **rather** tall man.
> This cake is **quite** nice.
> It was **fairly** good.
> It's a **very** hot day.

or to introduce a sentence. Many adverbs are formed from adjectives by adding -*ly*.

> **Fortunately**, *the rain stayed away.*
> **Honestly**, *I can't help it.*

A **preposition** is one of a small group of words that can be used with nouns and verbs. Prepositions give information about position or movement.

> **on** *the bridge*   **over** *the rooftops*
> **in** *the morning*   **at** *the gates*

When a preposition is used in front of a noun, the two together do the work of an adverb.

> *He is coming* **now**.
> *He is coming* **in the morning**.
> *I found him* **there**.
> *I found him* **near the gates**.

A **conjunction** joins two or more nouns or clauses to each other. Conjunctions are sometimes called 'joining words'.

> *I went to the shop* **and** *bought some bread.*
> *I bought some bread,* **but** *I forgot to get the milk.*

Many words can act as more than one part of speech. It is not unusual for an English word to be a **noun** in one sentence and a **verb** in another sentence.

> *Jamal scored several* **runs**.
> *She* **runs** *half a mile each morning.*
> *I've been chosen for the school* **play**.
> *Christopher and Angus* **play** *golf together on Fridays.*

Parts of the sentence

Sentences consist of a number of parts, using different parts of speech. The most important parts of speech are:

- The **subject**, which is either a noun phrase (see p. 137) or a pronoun (see p. 204). Normally the subject comes before the verb phrase in a sentence.

    The girls had been swimming.
    The new teacher came in.
    They had finished.

- The **verb phrase**, which includes the main verb and which may have auxiliary verbs to go with it. See also pp. 32–91.

    The girls had been swimming.
    The new teacher came in.
    They had finished.
    She uses her skateboard quite a lot.
    Rajiv was reading a new novel.
    She is riding someone else's horse.

- The **object**, which is a noun phrase or a pronoun.

    She used her old skateboard.
    Rajiv was reading a new novel.
    Josh found it.

Not all verbs need an object. When there is one, the object normally comes after the verb phrase. Some verbs may also need an **indirect object**. See also p. 232.

    Hamish gave me a party invitation.
    Ruth gave Lauren a nice bunch of flowers.

- An **adverbial**, or **adjunct**, which is an optional part of the sentence.

This may be:

- a single word, an **adverb**.

    Suddenly, it started to rain heavily.

- an **adverbial phrase**, a group of words that functions as an adverb.

    In the morning, the sky was clear.
    You probably won't notice it after a while.

- an **adverbial clause**, a group of words including a verb, which functions as an adverb.

    I'll get some biscuits for you when I've poured the drinks.
    When I've poured the drinks, I'll get some biscuits for you.
    Mark played while Isabel sang.

Though some adverbials have a fixed position, most can be added to a sentence in several places. Any number of them can be added, limited only by the sense of the sentence.

    In the winter, the roads get very slippery.
    The roads get very slippery in the winter.

- A **complement**. With certain verbs, such as *be* and *seem*, a complement takes the place of an object. A complement can be either an adjective or a noun phrase. Complements provide further descriptive detail about the subject. See also p. 234.

    He became a doctor in 2005.
    Andrew is a motor-mechanic.
    He felt a bit silly when he realized what he'd done.
    They became good friends despite the mistake.

Direct and indirect objects

The **object** of a sentence (if there is one) normally comes after the verb phrase. Whether there is an object or not depends on the meaning of the verb. For example, if you want to talk about what someone is doing, you might say '*She is writing*' but if you want to talk about the point of the activity, you might say, '*She is writing a book*'.

> *She was riding.*
> *She was riding **her horse**.*
> *Erica was writing.*
> *Erica was writing **a letter**.*

An object that follows a verb like this is called the **direct object**.

> *Rory found **a pen**.*
> *Our cat doesn't like **milk**.*

Some verbs also have another sort of object, called an **indirect object**. An indirect object names the person for or to whom something is done. It is usually needed with verbs like *give*, *find* and *owe*. For example, with *give*, we need to name both the thing that is given and the person it is given to.

> *Mike owes **Tom** five pounds.*
> *Rob gave **me** a box of chocolates.*
> *Susan bought **her rabbit** some more food.*

Some verbs must always take a direct object, some never take a direct object; others sometimes take one and sometimes don't, depending on the meaning. When a verb has an object it is called a **transitive** verb.

> *Rowan bought **a magazine**.*
> *I don't like **rap music**.*

When it does not have an object it is called an **intransitive** verb.

> *Lynn fainted.*
> *Patrick screamed.*
> *Soon, everyone was shouting.*

Some verbs may be either **transitive** or **intransitive**.

> *Ann was reading (a letter).*
> *Kim was drawing (a picture).*

When a verb has both an indirect and a direct object it is called a **ditransitive** verb.

> *Amy owes* **Mark** *ten pounds.*
> *Stephen gave* **me** *some flowers.*
> *Katie bought* **her hamster** *a new cage.*

A direct object is needed where the meaning of the verb requires something to give it a focus. This is why we sometimes say that a direct object 'complements' a verb.

- Some verbs must have an adverbial as well as a direct object, for example to specify a place.

> *He placed* **the parcel** *on the chair.*
> *She put* **the umbrella** *in a corner.*

Verbs

Verbs are words that allow us to talk about activities, processes, states of being, and states of mind.

> This basket **holds** quite a lot.
> John **was reading** Katherine's essay.
> Fiona **is preparing** a talk for next week's class.
> Helen **feels** much happier now.
> I **forgot** that it **was** your birthday.
> Paul **owned** several old motorbikes.

Verbs can be divided into two major groups, according to the way they are used. Those in the larger group are called **main verbs**. The rest are called **auxiliary verbs**.

Verb phrase

A verb phrase can be a single word or a group of associated words.

> he **walks**
> he **is walking**
> he **had walked**
> he **can walk**
> he **has been walking**
> he **might have been walking**

When a verb phrase consists of a single word it is called a **simple** verb. Many verbs in English are made by combining an auxiliary verb and a main verb; this is called a **compound** verb.

- When we want to talk about everything to do with a verb, we use the term **verb phrase**.

Main verbs

These are the verbs that we use to indicate actions and states. Most of the verbs in English are main verbs. They are also called **lexical** verbs. Main verbs are divided or **classified** in several ways:

- according to whether they refer to **states**

> *I can really **taste** the herbs in this omelette.*
> *This scarf **belongs** to me.*
> *He **hates** losing.*
> *She always **liked** boats and sailing.*
> *I already **feel** that I **have known** you for ages.*

  or **actions**.

> *Three boys **were kicking** a ball around in the field.*
> *We **were running** across the football field.*
> *For six hours, Stuart **drove** across open desert.*

- into **regular** and **irregular** verbs according to the spelling of their forms.

> *regular: talk, talks, talking, talked.*
> *irregular: swim, swims, swimming, swam, swum.*
> *irregular: go, goes, going, went, gone.*

- according to whether or not they are followed by an object. That is, whether they are **transitive** or **intransitive**. See p. 85.

> *I can **read**.*
> *We both **read** the same newspaper.*
> *Don't **tell** me.*
> *We both **ran** away.*
> *Sue **found** a bracelet.*
> *I **saw** my best friend on Friday.*

Auxiliary verbs

These verbs are used in combination with main verbs in order to allow us to talk about different times or periods of time, different degrees of completion, and different amounts of certainty or doubt. There are several types of auxiliary verb. The **primary** auxiliaries help express time, and the **modal** auxiliaries help to express certainty and doubt. See pp. 39–78.

Tense

We use verbs to talk about actions and states. Verbs **tenses** allow us to talk about the time when the action or state takes place.

All main verbs have two **simple** tenses, the **present simple** and the **past simple**.

present simple	past simple
I walk she sings they come you bring	I walked she sang they came you brought

In these tenses the verb is used on its own without any auxiliary verbs.

English verbs also have **compound** tense forms. In these tenses the main verb is accompanied by one or both of the auxiliary verbs *be* and *have*. See p. 92 for more on tenses.

Aspect

The compound tenses of the verb express two **aspects** – **continuous** and **perfect**.

- The term **aspect** is used to talk about continuing actions versus completed actions or states. Simple tenses do not have aspect.

continuing actions	
I am walking she is singing they are coming you are bringing	I was walking she was singing they were coming you were bringing

---

> | completed actions | |
> |---|---|
> | *I have walked*
she has sung
they have come
you have brought | *I had walked*
she had sung
they had come
you had brought |

We use these compound verbs when we want to talk about:

– the continuous nature of an action (using a form of the auxiliary *be* + *-ing*). This is called the **continuous aspect**.

> *I **am** still **studying** French.*
> *He **was living** in London all that year.*
> *James **is helping out** with the children this week.*
> *Sara and Scott **were looking** for a new flat at the time.*

– the completion of an action (using a form of the auxiliary *have* + a past participle, usually *-ed*). This is called the **perfect aspect**.

> *I **have been** a teacher for four years.*
> *He **had lived** in London for a year before coming to Sussex.*
> *James **has helped out** before.*
> *Sara and Scott **had found** their flat by then.*

The two aspects of the verb can be joined so that we can talk about the duration and the completion of an action in the same verb phrase. See pp. 92–93 for more on tense and aspect.

> *I **have been studying** French for four years.*
> *I **had been living** in London for four years when I met him.*
> *James **has been helping** us this week.*

Simple tenses

Simple tenses show moments in time, timeless states, and habitual or repetitive actions.

> It **tastes** good.
> Julie **keeps** a diary.
> Adrian **went** home at midnight.
> She **heard** a strange noise in the night.
> Rob usually **walks** to school.
> Yesterday he **went** by car.

The **present simple** and the **past simple** of regular verbs are formed by using the base form of the verb. See pp. 98–101.

Continuous tenses

Continuous tenses show duration or continuity.

> It **is raining** hard this morning.
> It **was raining** when we came out of school yesterday.
> I'm **having** dinner. Can I call you back?
> He **was listening** to the radio when he heard the news.

The **present continuous** and the **past continuous** are formed from either the present or the past tense of the verb *be* + the **present participle** (or '*-ing* form') of the main verb. See pp. 102–105.

Perfect tenses

The present perfect tense shows that an action is completed but that it still has some importance in the present time.

> *Ken **has walked** all the way from the station. (...and he's tired.)*
> *He **has** never **visited** me. (...and I'm feeling neglected.)*
> *She **has missed** the train. (That's why she's not here.)*

The **past perfect** is used to talk about something that happened in a time before a particular time in the past.

> *He told us that he **had tried** it before.*
> *I **had** never **been** climbing before our activity holiday last year.*
> *She was late because she **had missed** her train.*

The **present perfect** and the **past perfect** are formed using either the present or the past tense of the verb *have* + **the past participle** of the main verb. See pp. 106–109.

Perfect continuous tenses

Perfect continuous tenses show duration, completion, and importance in the present time.

> *I **have been working** hard in the garden all day.*
> *My mother **has been helping** me.*
> *My sisters **have been riding** all day.*
> *I **had been working** in Italy that summer.*
> *Some of us **had been waiting** for two hours when the doctor appeared.*

The **present perfect continuous** and the **past perfect continuous** are formed using either the present or past tense of the verb *have* + **the past participle** of *be* + **the present participle** of the main verb. See p. 110.

Other verb forms

Other verb combinations are used for positive or negative statements, or to express degrees of time and probability.

> *Do you **like** espresso coffee?*
> *I **don't like** fried food.*
> ***Could** I **have** a coke, please?*
> *You **will be** in Edinburgh within two hours.*
> *They **will** probably **meet** us at the station.*

Types of main verb

Verbs of action

Most verbs describe an action such as *walking*, *running*, or *reading*.

> John **is running** for the train.
> Sophie **has** just **bought** a new camera.
> She **is putting on** an exhibition of her photographs.
> Robbie **has seen** the film already.

When we need a verb to describe a new activity, we can either invent a new word, or we can adapt other parts of speech.

> You can use your phone to **access** the internet.

- Action verbs can be expressed in all the tenses.

Verbs of state

Some verbs are used to talk about states of being or states of mind.

These include:

- verbs relating to the senses, e.g. *feel, hear, see, smell, taste*
- verbs relating to emotions, e.g. *adore, fear, hate, like, love, want, wish*
- verbs relating to mental activity, e.g. *agree, believe, expect, forget, mean*
- verbs relating to possession, e.g. *belong, own, possess*

> I **feel** unhappy.
> I **hate** arguments.
> These flowers **smell** gorgeous.
> Rob **wishes** he **hadn't agreed** to the plan.
> We **mean** you no harm.
> That car **belonged** to us once.

- Verbs of state are not usually used in continuous tenses. When they are used in continuous tenses, they change their meaning.

    *I'm just **feeling** to see if the bone is broken.*
    *We **were tasting** some interesting New Zealand wines.*
    *Naomi **is expecting** a baby.*

There are some uses of the verb *be* that allow you to choose between a state or an action meaning. The word used as the complement makes an important difference.

<table>
<tr><td>*Mark **is being** silly*</td><td>**but not** *Mark is being tall*.</td></tr>
<tr><td>*Oscar **is being** nasty*</td><td>**but not** *Oscar is being intelligent*.</td></tr>
</table>

The verb *seem* has a limited number of adjectives that can be used as its complement.

<table>
<tr><td>*Simon seems **happy***</td><td>**but not** *Simon seems tall*.</td></tr>
</table>

The forms of main verbs

English verbs have up to five different forms. These are:

1 the base form, e.g.   *pull*
2 the 3rd person singular,
   present simple tense, e.g.   *pulls*
3 the past simple tense, e.g.   *pulled*
4 the past participle, e.g.   *pulled*
5 the present participle, e.g.   *pulling*

- Regular verbs are all formed in the same way, by building on the **base form** (form 1). This is the form you normally find in a dictionary. Most verbs are regular.

- Irregular verbs have different forms, particularly forms 3 and 4. See p. 36.

Form 1:   The **present simple** tense has all but one of its forms the same as the **base form**.

Form 2:   When the **present simple** tense has a 3rd person singular subject, the verb is formed from the **base form** + *-s*.

Form 3:   The **past simple** is formed from the **base form** + *-ed*.

Form 4:   The **past participle** is formed from the **base form** + *-ed*.

Form 5:   The **present participle** is formed from the **base form** + *-ing*.

A special variation of the base form is the *to infinitive*. There are a number of uses of a verb where both the words *to* + the **base form** must be present.

The base form is sometimes called the 'bare infinitive'.

As mentioned above, the 3rd person singular is formed from the **base form** + **-s**. Below are the exceptions to the rule:

Verbs ending in **-o**, **-ch**, **-sh**, **-ss**, **-x**, **-z** or **-zz**: add **-es** to make the 3rd person singular, e.g.

torpedo	he torpedo**es**
catch	he catch**es**
focus	he focus**es**
push	he push**es**
miss	he miss**es**
box	he box**es**
buzz	it buzz**es**

Verbs ending in **-y** after a consonant: change **y** to **i** and add **-es**, e.g.

carry	he carr**ies**
fly	he fl**ies**
worry	he worr**ies**

As mentioned above, the present participle is made up of the **base form** + *-ing*. There are some exceptions to the rule. All verbs that contain a short final vowel in front of a final consonant double the consonant before *-ing*, e.g.

sob	sobbing
bid	bidding
flog	flogging
run	running
stop	stopping
get	getting
put	putting

Irregular verbs

Irregular verbs are verbs that *do not* form the past simple tense and the past participle by adding *-ed* to the base form.

The three main groups of irregular verbs

In Group A, the base form, the past simple and the past participle are the same:

1	the base form	*put*
2	the present simple tense	*puts*
3	the past simple tense	*put*
4	the present participle	*putting*
5	the past participle	*put*

A	bet	cut	let	set	spread
	burst	hit	put	shed	thrust
	cast	hurt	shut	split	upset

In Group B, the past simple and the past participle have the same form:

1	the base form	**buy**
2	the present simple tense	**buys**
3	the past simple tense	**bought**
4	the present participle	**buying**
5	the past participle	**bought**

B1

base form	past form	base form	past form
bend	bent	hang	hung
bind	bound	have	had
bleed	bled	hear	heard
bring	brought	keep	kept
build	built	kneel	knelt
buy	bought	lay	laid
catch	caught	make	made
find	found	say	said

Some of these verbs have alternative spellings for the past participle:

B2 The past form may be either *a* or *b*.

base form	past forms		base form	past forms	
burn	burnt	burned	smell	smelt	smelled
dream	dreamt	dreamed	spell	spelt	spelled
lean	leant	leaned	spill	spilt	spilled
learn	learnt	learned	spoil	spoilt	spoiled

In Group C, the base form, the past simple, and the past participle all have different forms:

1	the base form	*go*
2	the present simple tense	*goes*
3	the past simple tense	**went**
4	the present participle	*going*
5	the past participle	*gone*

C

base form	past forms		base form	past forms	
arise	arose	arisen	ring	rang	rung
awake	awoke	awoken	rise	rose	risen
bear	bore	borne	saw	sawed	sawn
begin	began	begun	see	saw	seen
bite	bit	bitten	shake	shook	shaken
blow	blew	blown	show	showed	shown
break	broke	broken	shrink	shrank	shrunk
fly	flew	flown	strive	strove	striven
give	gave	given	take	took	taken
know	knew	known	throw	threw	thrown
ride	rode	ridden	write	wrote	written

Auxiliary verbs

An auxiliary verb is a verb that is used together with a main verb to show time and continuity.

- *Be* and *have* are the **primary auxiliaries**. A primary auxiliary is used to construct compound tenses.

- *Be* is used to make present continuous and past continuous tenses

  *I **am working**.*
  *Rob **is using** the computer.*
  *We **were** all **wondering** about that.*
  *Kevin **was teaching** in America in 1985.*

  and also for the passive. See p. 44 for more on *be*.

  *These books **are sold** in supermarkets.*
  *Martin **was arrested** and held overnight.*

- *Have* is used to make present perfect and past perfect tenses. See p. 48 for more on *have*.

  *Stephen **has finished** fixing the car.*
  *George and Alice **have seen** the show already.*
  *Amanda **had** already **eaten** when we arrived.*
  *They **had** not **expected** to see us there.*

- *Do* is the **supporting auxiliary**. It is used in forming negatives, questions, and emphatic statements. See p. 52 for more on *do*. See pp. 92–97 for more on simple and compound verb forms.

  *I **do** not **like** sausages at all.*
  ***Do** you **like** prawns?*
  *You **do like** prawns, don't you?*

- *Will*, *may*, *might*, and the other verbs listed on pp. 53–54 are the **modal auxiliary verbs**, usually called simply, **modal verbs**. A modal verb allows us to talk about actions as possible, doubtful, or necessary.

> Charlie **will go** home on Friday.
> Charlie **may go** home on Friday.
> Charlie **could go** home on Friday.
> Charlie **must go** home on Friday.

Auxiliaries can be combined together in a single verb phrase. For example, a verb phrase may consist of a **modal** + a form of *have* + a form of *be* + a form of a **main verb**.

> I **could have been making** *a bad mistake by trusting him.*
> Sara **will have been living** *in New Zealand for 2 years next month.*
> You **must have been given** *the wrong number.*

The auxiliary verb, or if there is more than one of them, the first auxiliary verb, performs these following grammatical functions:

– It shows **tense** and is the **finite** part of the verb phrase.

> I **have** seen it.
> She **had** seen it.
> She **has** been thinking.
> She **had** been thinking.

– It shows **number** and **person** agreement with the subject.

> She **has** seen it.
> They **have** seen it.
> I **am** looking for it.
> You **are** looking for it.

– It will take any **negative** immediately after it.

> I **do not** want to do that.
> She **has not** been concentrating.

– It can come before the subject to make a **question**.

> **Do you** want to help us?
> **Have you** got a mobile phone?

Contracted forms

Auxiliaries are very often used in contracted forms. In the case of *be* and *have*, the contracted form can involve linking the subject and the auxiliary verb into a single form e.g. *I'm*, *I've*, *we'd*, *Sue's* (*Sue has* or *Sue is*).

> **We're** back!
> (**We are** back!)
> **I've** found it.
> (**I have** found it.)
> **They'd** gone when I got there.
> (**They had** gone when I got there.)
> **Tom's** here.
> (**Tom is** here.)

The contracted negative form **auxiliary** + *n't* is common with all the auxiliaries except *am*, e.g. *hasn't*, *wouldn't*, *don't*.

> She **isn't** (is not) trying.
> We **don't** (do not) live here.
> He **hasn't** (has not) seen it.
> I **can't** (cannot) come.

In standard British English, the contracted form of *am not*, when it is part of a question, is *aren't I*.

> *Aren't I going to need some matches?*
> *I'm getting a lift with you, aren't I?*

• Contracted forms are more informal than full forms. They are therefore more common in spoken English. Full forms are usually preferred in formal written English.

Auxiliaries are used in sentence tags. See p. 245 for more about sentence tags.

> *You had only just bought that carpet when the kitchen flooded,*
> ***hadn't you?***
> *It's Katie's birthday on Saturday, **isn't it?***
> *You are joking, **aren't you?***

Auxiliaries are also used to make a short addition to a statement, such as:

– a positive addition to a positive statement, accompanied by *so* or *too*.

> *I went to the park and Lucy **did too**.*
> *I loved the film, and **so did** Finlay.*

– a negative addition to a negative statement, accompanied by *neither* or *nor*.

> *My dad never eats mussels and **neither do** I.*
> *I don't want to speak to William now. – **Nor do** I.*
> *I can't understand it. – **Neither can** I.*

- Auxiliaries can be used in positive sentences to give emphasis. When they are emphatic they are never contracted.

  *You **have** made a mess!*
  *That **was** a nice surprise!*
  *I **am** proud of Katie. She's so clever.*

  In the present simple tense and the past simple tenses the appropriate form of *do* is used to show emphasis.

  *I **do** like Penny. – So do I.*
  *We **did** have a lovely time.*

  An auxiliary on its own can be used to give a short answer to a question. Whatever auxiliary is used in the question is used on its own in the answer. The main verb is not repeated. Short answers are very common in spoken English.

  Do you like avocados? Yes, I do. or No, I don't.
  Have you read anything by Michael Morpurgo?
     Yes, I have.

Be

The verb *be* is used as an auxiliary verb and it can also be used as a main verb. See p. 32.

The verb *be* is irregular. It has eight different forms: *be*, *am*, *is*, *are*, *was*, *were*, *being*, *been*. The present simple and past simple tenses make more changes than those of other verbs.

I am late.	*We are late.*
You are late.	*You are late.*
He is late.	*They are late.*

I was late.	*We were late.*
You were late.	*You were late.*
She was late.	*They were late.*

The present participle is *being*.

> *He is being very helpful these days.*

The past participle is *been*.

> *We have been ready for an hour.*

- The present simple tense forms of *be* are often contracted in normal speech. Note that the contracted form of *they are* is spelled *they're*, and not *their* which is the possessive form of *they*.

I'm here.	*We're here.*
You're here.	*You're here.*
He's here.	*They're here.*

Any form of *be* is made negative by adding *not* immediately after it. In speech, some forms of *be* also have contracted negative forms. Some of these forms emphasize the negative.

	emphasizes the negative
*I'm **not** late.* *You **aren't** late.* *He **isn't** late.* *We **aren't** late.* *They **aren't** late.* *I **wasn't** late.* *You **weren't** late.* *He **wasn't** late.* *We **weren't** late.* *They **weren't** late.*	*You**'re not** late.* *He**'s not** late.* *We**'re not** late.* *They**'re not** late.*

The major uses of *be* as an auxiliary verb are to form continuous tenses and the passive.

- **Continuous** tenses of main verbs use the appropriate form of *be*, present or past, followed by the present participle (or *-ing* form). See p. 102 and p. 110.

- The **passive** form of a main verb uses the appropriate form of *be* followed by the past participle. See p. 122.

The verb *be* is also used as a main verb. It is commonly found joining a subject to its complement.

As a **main verb**, *be* is used to talk about:

- Feelings and states. For this we use the simple tenses of the verb with a suitable adjective. See p. 92.

    *I **am delighted** with the news but he **is not happy**.*
    *She **was busy** so she **was not able** to see me.*

- People's behaviour. For this we use the continuous tenses of the verb with a suitable adjective. See p. 100.

  > *I **am not being** slow, I **am being** careful.*
  > *You **were being** very rude to your mum when I came downstairs.*

- *Be* + the **to infinitive** is sometimes used to refer to future time. This is a rather formal use, which often appears in news reports. See pp. 132–136.

  > *The Prime Minister **is to visit** Hungary in October.*
  > *The Archbishop **is to have** talks with the Pope next month.*

- *It + be*: we use *it* as a subject when we are talking about time, distance, weather, or cost. In this use, *be* is always singular.

  > *Hurry up, **it's eight thirty**!*
  > *Is it? I didn't know **it was so late**.*

  > ***It's** thirty miles to Glasgow.*
  > *Come and visit us. **It's not very far**.*

  > ***It's** cold today but **it isn't wet**.*

  > ***It's very expensive** to live in London.*

- *There + is/are* is used to talk about something existing. In this use, the form that *be* takes may be singular or plural, depending on the number of the noun, and *be* is sometimes contracted.

  > ***There's** a spare toothbrush in the cupboard.*
  > ***There was** a cold wind blowing.*
  > ***There isn't** enough petrol for the journey.*
  > ***There are** several petrol stations on the way, **aren't there**?*

To make the continuous tenses of the main verb *be* we have to use *be* twice, once as an auxiliary and once as a main verb.

> You *are being* so annoying!
> I know I *am being* silly, but I am frightened.

The question form of clauses with the verb *be* in them is made by putting the appropriate form of *be* right in front of the subject.

> *Are you* better now?
> *Is he* free this morning?
> *Was he* cooking dinner when you arrived?

Have

The verb *have* is used as an auxiliary verb

> She **has** run a lovely, deep, bubble bath.
> Katie **had** read about the concert in the newspaper.

and also as a main verb. See p. 28.

> She is **having** a bath at the moment.
> The driver has **had** his breakfast, so we can go.

The verb *have* has the forms: *have*, *has*, *having*, *had*. The base form of the verb is *have*. The present participle is *having*. The past tense and past participle form is *had*.

- The present and past forms are often contracted in everyday speech, especially when *have* is being used as an auxiliary verb.

  The contracted forms are:

have = **'ve**	I**'ve** seen the Queen.
has = **'s**	He**'s** gone on holiday.
	Ian**'s** behaved badly.
had = **'d**	You**'d** better go home.
	Ian**'d** left them behind.

The form *have* contracts to *'ve*. This can sound rather like *of*, especially after other auxiliary verbs.

> She **would've** given you something to eat.
> You **could've** stayed the night with us.
> If he'd asked, I **might've** lent him my car.

Avoid the common mistake of writing *of* in this case.

As an **auxiliary** verb, *have* is used to make the **perfect tenses** of main verbs.

The **perfect** tenses of main verbs use the appropriate form of *have*, present or past, followed by the past participle. See pp. 106–113.

> *I **have read** some really good books over the holidays.*
> *I **had seen** the film before.*

The negative of a clause containing a compound verb with *have* is made by adding *not* or another negative word immediately after the appropriate form of *have*. In speech, some forms of *have* also have contracted negative forms.

> *I **have never seen** such luxury.*
> *Rachel **had not been** abroad before.*
> *She **had hardly had** time to eat when Paul arrived.*

- present tense and past tense forms that emphasize the negative element:

*I/we/you/they'**ve not**;*   *he/she/it'**s not***
*I/we/you/he/she/it /they'**d not***

> *She'**s not** told me about it yet.*
> *We'**ve not** been here before.*
> *They'**d not** seen him for weeks.*

- present tense and past tense negative forms that are used less emphatically:

*I/we/you/they **haven't**;*   *he/she/it **hasn't***
*I/we/you/he/she/it /they **hadn't***

> *He **hasn't** found anywhere to stay this holiday.*
> *We **haven't** been here before.*
> *They **hadn't** looked very hard, in my opinion.*

As a **main verb**, *have* is used to talk about:

• states or conditions, such as possession or relationship.

– In these uses, continuous tenses are not possible. With this meaning *have* is sometimes used alone, adding only *not* to make negatives, and adding nothing to make questions.

> *I **have** something for you.*
> *We **haven't** anything for you today.*
> ***Have** you no sense of shame?*
> *The driver **has had** his breakfast, so we can go.*
> *We **had** a good time.*

It is also often used with forms of *do* to make negatives and questions.

> ***Do** you **have** a pen?*
> ***Does** she **have** my umbrella?*
> *She **doesn't have** any brothers or sisters.*
> ***Do** you **have** time to see me now?*

• *Have got* is an informal form of this main verb use of *have*, often used in speaking, especially in British English.

> *I **haven't got** any brothers or sisters.*
> ***Has** she **got** my umbrella? – Yes, she **has**.*
> *She **hasn't got** any money.*

• activities, including those such as eating, and leisure.

With this meaning of *have*, negatives and questions are formed using one of the forms of *do*.

> *He **was having** a shower when I phoned.*

*I'm **having** lunch at twelve o'clock.*
*Come and **have** a sandwich with me,*
*No thanks. I **don't** usually **have** lunch.*

*He's **having** a day off.*
***Did** you **have** a good holiday?*

Contractions and weak forms are not possible with this meaning.

Have got is not used with this meaning.

- to express obligation using *have to* or *have got to*.

*I've **got to** go now, I'm afraid.*
***Do** you **have to** leave so soon?*
***Have** you **got to** leave so soon?*

> When *have* is a main verb, it makes perfect forms like all other main verbs. This means that it is possible to use *have* twice in present or past perfect sentences, once as an auxiliary verb and once as a main verb.
>
> *We **have had** enough, thank you.*
> *They **had** already **had** several warnings.*

Do

The verb *do* is used as an auxiliary verb.

*I **do** not want it.*
*You **do** not want it.*
*He **does** not want it.*

*We **do** not want it.*
*You **do** not want it.*
*They **do** not want it.*

*I **did** not want it.*
*You **did** not want it.*
*She **did** not want it.*

*We **did** not want it.*
*You **did** not want it.*
*They **did** not want it.*

It can also be used as a main verb. See p. 32. When *do* is used as an auxiliary verb it is a **supporting verb**. Because a main verb cannot combine directly with negatives or make questions, *do* is used to support the main verb.

Don't talk!
Don't run!

It is also used to stand in for another verb to avoid repetition, as shown on p. 43.

The verb *do* is irregular. It has five different forms: *do*, *does*, *doing*, *did*, *done*. The base form of the verb is *do*. The past simple form, *did*, is the same throughout. The present participle is *doing*. The past participle is *done*.

The present simple tense *do* and the past simple tense *did* can be used as an auxiliary verb. As an auxiliary, *do* is not used with **modal** verbs.

*I **do** not want it.*
*You **do** not want it.*
*He **does** not want it.*

*We **do** not want it.*
*You **do** not want it.*
*They **do** not want it.*

I **did** not want it.	We **did** not want it.
You **did** not want it.	You **did** not want it.
She **did** not want it.	They **did** not want it.

As an **auxiliary** verb *do* is used in the following ways:

− to help make the negative and question forms of present simple and past simple tenses.

> Oh dear, I **didn't feed** the cat this morning.
> **Do** you **know** what time it is?
> **Did** Tim **pay** for his ticket last night?

− to make the negative form of a command.

> **Don't** talk!
> **Don't** run!

− to make a command more persuasive. See p. 250.

> **Do** let me see it!

− to avoid repeating a main verb in additions, commands, sentence tags, and short answers.

> They often go to the cinema, **and so do** we.

> Don't run on the road! Don't **do** it!

> You live in Glasgow, **don't** you?

> Do you play cricket? – No, I **don't**.
> Did they tell you the news? – Yes, they **did**.
> Jim likes jazz, I think. Yes, **he does**.

– in comparisons.

> *She **sings** better than I **do**.*

The positive forms of *do* cannot be contracted. In speech, the negative has contracted forms.

> *I **don't** (do not) agree with you.*
> *She **doesn't** (does not) live here now.*
> *They **didn't** (did not) buy any food.*

- present tense negative forms:
  *I/we/you/they **don't**; he/she/it **doesn't***

- past tense negative form:
  *I/we/you/he/she/it/they **didn't***

When *do* is a main verb, it has a range of meanings that includes *carry out, perform, fix,* or *provide.* It is sometimes used in place of a more specific verb.

> *I'll **do** the lawn now.*
> *(I'll **mow** the lawn now.)*
> *I'll **do** you.*
> *(I'll **punch** you.)*
> *We don't **do** coach parties.*
> *(We don't **serve** coach parties.)*

It is then used with the full range of tenses and forms. See also p. 98.

> *Are you **doing** your homework?*
> *You **have been doing** well this term.*
> *She **had done** enough, so she stopped.*
> *This **has been done** before.*

The main verb use of *do* can be used to talk about:

– habits.

> *I **do** the washing up every evening.*
> *This what I usually **do**.*

– behaviour.

> *He **did** something rather foolish.*
> *I **didn't do** anything wrong.*
> *What **are** you **doing**?*

– plans.

> *What **are** you **doing** on Sunday?*

As a main verb, *do* makes negatives and questions like all other main verbs:

– in the present simple tense with auxiliary *do*.

> *What **does** he **do** for a living?*
> ***Do** I **do** it this way?*
> *No, you **don't do** it like that at all.*

– in the past simple tense with auxiliary *did*.

> ***Did** Henry **do** it, then?*
> ***Didn't** Henry **do** it, then?*
> *He **didn't do** it, you know.*

This means that it is possible to use *do* twice in negative and interrogative sentences; once as an auxiliary verb and once as a main verb.

- As a main verb, *do* can be used with modal verbs.

  *They **will do** it for you, if you ask nicely.*
  *I **can do** it, but I **shouldn't do** it.*

Modal verbs

Modal verbs are a particular kind of **auxiliary**.

> *Look, I can do it! – Oh yes! So you **can**.*
> ***Can** I use your phone? – Of course you **can**.*
> *Do you think she **will** come? – I'm sure she **will**.*
> *I **must** get our tickets today.*

Modal verbs are used when you need to add special elements of meaning to a main verb, e.g.:

– to express different degrees of doubt and possibility about the action of the main verb.

> *I **may** not **be able** to do it.*
> *I think that I **might have caught** your cold.*
> *I **could ask** for you, if you like.*
> *You **couldn't do** it, **could** you?*

– to express degrees of future possibility, ranging from the definite future, ***will***, to the possible future, ***may***, and the conditional future, ***could***.

> *You **will be seeing** her **on Friday** at Jackie's house.*
> *I **may** be late home **tomorrow evening**.*
> *I **could bring** some more bread home with me **tonight**.*

– to request or give permission for an action to take place.

> ***May** I come in?*
> *You **can** borrow my car tonight if you like.*

– to make a prohibition, when used with a negative.

> *You **shouldn't** use this computer without permission.*
> *You **cannot** borrow my car tonight.*
> *He **must not** see this letter.*

– to speculate.

> *The weather's so bad the flight **could** be late.*
> *It **might** be all over by the time we get there.*
> *He **may** be very cross about all this.*

– to express obligation and duty.

> *I **must** give in my essay today.*
> *Helen **ought to** tell the truth.*

– to refer to typical behaviour.

> *She **can** be very kind on occasions like this.*

– to add politeness to a request which might otherwise sound abrupt.

> ***Would** you please close the door.*

– to make conditional sentences (see p. 277).

– in reported speech (see p. 283).

Modals can refer to a time range that reaches from the immediate present to some future time, so that they can all be used for future reference, especially when they are used with a time adverbial. See pp. 114–121.

> *You **will be seeing** her **on Friday** at Jackie's house.*
> *I **may** be late home **tomorrow evening**.*
> *I **could bring** some more bread home with me **tonight**.*

Some modals can refer to a time range that goes back from the immediate present to some indefinite past time. They can refer to habitual action when they are used with a time adverbial.

> *When I was little, I **would** ride my bike round and round the lawn.*

Form

Unlike other verbs, modal verbs have only one form, the **base form**, and only one tense, the present simple.

> You **will** be seeing her **on Friday** at Jackie's house.
> I **may** be late home **tomorrow evening**.
> I **might** go to visit Grandma **on Saturday**.

They do not have a **to** infinitive. They have no -**s** inflection in the 3rd person singular.

> **He will** be seeing her on Friday.
> **She may** be late home.

- Since modal verbs do not have past tense forms, you have to use other verbs to provide some of the modal meanings in the past, e.g. past necessity is expressed by *had to* instead of *must*.

> I **must** visit Auntie May today.
> I **had to** visit Auntie May yesterday.

- The modals **shall** and **will** are usually contracted to *'ll* in spoken English. All the negative forms can be contracted to form a single word such as *can't*, *won't*, *wouldn't*. These contracted forms are common in both spoken and written English.

> I will/shall = I'll
> We will/shall = we'll
> You **mustn't** say things like that, Jane.
> John **can't** come to my party.

There are other contracted forms such as *he'll*, *we'll*, *shan't*, and *they'll*, which are common in spoken English but rare in written English.

- Several verbs act as modals sometimes and as full main verbs at other times. These are called **semi-modal verbs**.

  > How **dare** he!
  > He **dared** to ask me to do his washing!
  > She **needn't** come if that's how she feels.
  > Monica **needs** a new raincoat.

Position

Modals come before any other auxiliary verb or main verb in the verb phrase.

- Modal verbs are followed by the **base form** of the verb if there is no other auxiliary verb present.

  > Yes, you **can borrow** those earrings tonight.
  > You **should try** that new restaurant in town.
  > You **must come** over again some time.

If one of the auxiliary verbs **have** or **be** follows the modal verb, the main verb will take the appropriate present or past participle form.

  > I **may have upset** him.
  > You **could have looked** for it yourself.
  > Janice **might be coming** too.
  > Sue **will have been worried** about her, I imagine.

- In negative sentences, **not** comes immediately after the modal verb and in front of all the other verbs.

  > They **may not wait** for you if you're late.
  > He **must not be** disturbed after 9 o'clock.

- *Can* cannot be combined with the auxiliary form *have*, but the negative form *can't* can be combined with *have*.

> They **can't have seen** him.   **but not** *They can have seen him.*

Can and could

Both these verbs indicate ability in some respect. The use of *could* is usual in clauses that contain a reference to past time.

> *Morag **can** speak French quite well now.*
> *I **couldn't** play chess two years ago, but I **can** now.*

> *When I was younger I **could** play tennis really well.*
> *Winston is so strong he **can** lift me right off my feet.*
> ***Can** you get up the stairs without help?*
> *You **can** come over for dinner whenever you like.*

Can and *could* are used:

– to indicate that you know how to do something.

> *Mary **can** do these sums.*
> *I **couldn't** draw very well when I was younger.*

– to show ability to do something. (Compared with *be able to*, *can* indicates ability of a more general nature that includes 'is permitted to'.)

> *When I was younger I **could** ski really well.*
> *Graham **can** run ten miles in 25 minutes.*
> ***Are you able to** walk to the car?*

– to make polite requests or to ask for permission:

Could is more tentative than *can*. (Compare with *may*, which is more formal.)

> ***Can** I borrow the car tomorrow evening, Mum?*
> ***Could** I come with you on the trip?*
> ***May** I take this book home with me?*

– to express the possibility of an action in the future, especially when the possibility is related to plans or projects. (Compare with *may*, where the possibility referred to is still uncertain and in the future.)

> *We **can** go to Paris next week since you are free.*
> *We **could** go to Paris next week if you are free.*
> *We **may** go to Paris, but it depends on our finances.*

– to express the possibility of an action in the present.

> *You **can** dive off these rocks; it is quite safe here.*
> *We **could** dive off the rocks, but we must take care.*

– to talk about actions that were possible but did not happen, using *could* + the perfect form of *have*.

> *Mary **could have stopped** the fight but she didn't.*

– using the perfect form of *have*, to speculate about actions that have recently taken place.

> *Who **could/can have broken** the window?*
> *Who **would have guessed** that they were related?*

A distinction between *can* and *could* is observed in conditionals. *Could* is used when the conditions are not met.

> *If Louisa is coming, she **can** look after the children for a while.*
> *If Helen had more money, she **could** buy a computer.*

When changing sentences from direct to reported speech *can* is usually changed to *could*.

> *Bernard said, 'I **can** do it for you, Sue.'*
> *Bernard said that he **could** do it for Sue.*

can
The negative form is: **cannot**.

> *I **cannot** understand why he did it.*

The contracted negative form is: **can't**.

> *I **can't** help it.*

could
The contracted negative form is: **couldn't**.

> *I **couldn't** help it.*

May and might

Both *may* and *might* can be used in requests and in expressions of possibility for the present and future.

> *Might I ask you your name?*

> *The weather **may/might** be better tomorrow.*
> *Craig **may/might** know his results soon.*
> *We **may/might** go to the cinema tonight.*

> *'**May** I come with you?' Nicky asked.*
> *Nicky asked if she **could** come with them.*

May and *might* are used as follows:

– *May* is used to ask permission in a more formal way than *can*.

> ***May** I have a drink, please?*
> ***May** I use your ruler? I've lost mine.*

Might is occasionally used in formal situations.

> ***Might** I suggest a different solution?*

– *May* is used to give permission, particularly when applied to *you, he, she, they* or a proper noun, to show that the speaker is allowing something to happen.

> *You **may** go now.*
> *Users **may** download forms from this website.*

– Both *may* and *might* are used to express the possibility of some future action; *might* is more tentative than *may*.

> *The weather **may/might** be better tomorrow.*
> *Craig **may/might** know his results soon.*
> *We **may/might** go to the cinema tonight.*

– *May* is often used for politeness, to make an order appear as a request; *might* is used to make the speaker more remote from the request.

> You **might** give that idea a bit more consideration.
> You **might** want to move a bit closer to the screen.

– *Might* is occasionally used when someone is trying to persuade another person to do something, perhaps with some degree of irritation. This use is a little old-fashioned.

> You **might** give me some cake too, Lucy.
> Anna, come on, you **might** tell me what he said!

• When *might* is used in a conditional sentence, the *if* clause can be in the present or the past tense. Compare with *could*. See p. 62.

> If Louisa **comes**, she **might** look after the children.
> If Louisa **came**, she **might** look after the children.

When changing sentences from direct to reported speech *may* usually becomes *could*.

> 'May I come with you?' Nicky asked.
> Nicky asked if she **could** come with them.

may
The contracted negative form is: none or **mayn't** (rare).

might
The contracted negative form is: **mightn't**.

> He **mightn't** have enough money.
> We might come and live here, **mightn't** we, mum?

Must

Must is used to express obligation, give orders and give advice. It can only be used for present and future reference. When the past is involved, you use *have to*.

Must is used:

– to express obligation.

> *All pupils **must** bring a packed lunch tomorrow.*

– to give orders firmly and positively.

> *You **must** go to sleep now.*

– to give advice or make recommendations emphatically.

> *You **must** get one of these new smoothie-makers – they're great!*
> *You **must** see 'Nim's Island' – it's brilliant.*

– to speculate about the truth of something.

> *She **must** be mad!*
> *You **must** be joking!*
> *There **must** be some mistake.*
> *Mr Robertson is here; it **must** be Tuesday.*

When this sort of statement is made in the negative or interrogative, *can* is used instead.

> *Can Mary be joking? **Can** she really mean that?*
> *You **can't** be serious!*
> *It **can't** be true!*

- *Must* can be used in the interrogative, but many speakers prefer *have to* instead.

    Must you go so soon?
    Must I invite Helen?
    Do you have to go soon?
    Do I have to invite Helen?

You can use *must* with a negative:

- to forbid someone to do something.

    *You **must not** cross when the light is red.*
    *You **must not** say things like that.*

- to talk about an event or state that is unacceptable.

    *There **mustn't** be any mistakes in your letter.*
    *The whale **must not** become extinct.*

> Note that to express the fact that you are not obliged to do something, you use *do not have to*.
>
> Compare:
>
> *You **must not** come in here.*
> *You **don't have to** come in here (if you don't want to).*

- It is necessary to change *must* to *have to* when changing sentences from direct to reported speech.

    *'I **must** fill out those forms this evening,' said Ian.*
    *Ian said that he **had to** fill out some forms.*

must

The contracted negative form is: *mustn't*.

> You **mustn't** worry so much.

Shall and will

The normal way to express simple future time in English is using the modal verb *will* followed by the **base form** of a main verb.

> The modal verb *shall* is not used very much in modern English, except in suggestions or offers of help.
>
> *Shall I help you? Shall I cook supper?*
> *Shall we go to the cinema tonight?*

Any distinction between *will* and *shall* is difficult to make in spoken English, since the contracted form, *'ll*, is used to mean both *shall* and *will*.

Shall is used:

– with questions involving *I* and *we* when the speaker is making a suggestion or offering help.

> *Shall I help you? Shall I cook supper?*
> *Shall we go to the cinema tonight?*

Will is used:

– with *I* and *we* to show intentions and to make promises.

> *Don't worry. I shan't/won't be late and Helen won't be late either.*
> *We shall/will be in touch.*
> *I shall/will try to ensure that you get a good room.*

– with *you, he, she, it,* and *they,* to give reassurances.

> *He will be well treated.*
> *You will have your money next week.*

–   to insist on something. Full forms are normally used, and are
    stressed in speech.

> You **will** do what I tell you!
> Jane **will** go to Mary's even if I have to carry her there.

–   to make polite requests and to give invitations.

> **Will** you help me look for my purse?
> **Will** you come to lunch on Friday?

–   to give orders.

> You **will** finish your work before you watch TV, **won't** you?
> Louisa, **will** you please be quiet!

–   to show that someone persists in doing something (full form with
    stress).

> Oh! Tony **will** keep jogging me when I'm trying to write!
> No wonder you feel sick. You **will** eat chocolate all day long.

–   to show prediction.

> The match **will** be finished by now.
> I think it **will** probably rain tomorrow.

will
The contracted form is: '**ll**.

> He**'ll** be home soon.

The contracted negative form is: **won't**.

> Eve **won't** speak to Harriet.

shall

The contracted form is:	*'ll*.

The contracted negative form is:	*shan't* (used mainly in British English).

> I *shan't* say a word.

Should

The modal verb *should* is used in the following ways:

– to talk about moral obligation. Compare *ought to* on p. 77.

> They **should** do what you suggest.
> People **should** report this sort of thing to the police.
> She suggested we **should** visit Aunty Irene more often.
> Rob insisted that we **should** think of others before
>   ourselves.

– to give advice or instructions.

> You **should** undo the top screws first.
> You **should** keep your credit card separate from your chequebook.

– to suggest that something follows on logically from what has just been said.

> They left here at 6 o'clock, so they **should** be home now.

– to show politeness in a conditional clause. This use is used in formal written communication.

> If you **should** decide to go, please contact us.
> **Should** you need more information, please call the manager.

• **Should** can be used with the main verb after certain set expressions such as, *it is a pity that, it is odd that, I am sorry/surprised that*. This is a more formal use than the same expression without **should**.

> It's a pity that this **should** happen.
> I was quite surprised that he **should** be doing a job like that.

- *Should* + the perfect form of the main verb can be used to express regret about something that was done or not done. Compare with *ought to*.

    *He **should have stopped** at the red light.*
    *You **should have told** me you were ill.*

- When changing sentences from direct to reported speech, *should* does not change.

    *Anna said that I **should** try to relax more.*

In formal English, *should* can be used with *I* or *we* in conditional clauses, instead of the more common *would*. This form is usually, but not always, found together with an **if** clause.

    *I **should** love to visit Peru **if I had the money**.*
    *I **should** be very cross **if they didn't give me a certificate**.*
    *We **should** hate to miss the play.*

In this sense, *would* is more common in modern spoken English.

    *I **would** love to visit Peru.*
    *I **would** be very cross if they didn't give me a certificate.*
    *We **would** hate to miss the play.*

should
The contracted negative form is: *shouldn't*.

Would

The modal verb *would* is commonly used as follows:

– to make a polite request.

> *Would you mind moving your bag?*
> *Would you give me a hand with this ladder, please?*

– to offer something politely.

> *Would you **like** some tea or coffee?*

– together with *like* as a polite form of *want*.

> *We **would like** to see Mr Brown now, please.*
> *My friends **would like** to see your garden.*

– to refer to habitual activity in the past, with the meaning of *used to*.

> *I remember Jeff; he **would** watch TV all day if you let him.*
> *Jess was a kind girl; she **would** always go out of her way to help people.*

– to show that someone persisted in an activity in the past: **would** is sometimes stressed here.

> *John **would** keep nagging at her, though I asked him not to.*
> *She **would** go on and on until I lost my temper.*

– to express and ask about probability.

> *I saw a girl at the window. Who **would** that be?*
> *Oh, that **would** be his elder sister!*

– in conditional clauses, usually together with an **if** clause.

> *I **would** have taken it if it had been available.*
> *If you offered me some more I **wouldn't** refuse.*
> *Brian **would** have phoned the police if it he'd seen the accident.*

When changing sentences from direct speech to reported speech, **will** is usually changed to **would**.

> *Anna said, 'Raymond **will** help you.'*
> *Anna said that Raymond **would** help us.*
> *James said, 'The car **won't** start!'*
> *James said that the car **wouldn't** start.*

would
The contracted form is: **'d**.

> *I'**d** have done it too, given the chance.*
> *We'**d** like to look at the garden.*
> *He'**d** be very angry if he knew about it.*

The contracted negative form is: **wouldn't**.

> *Even if he'd known about it, he **wouldn't** have been angry.*

Ought to

The use of *ought to* is similar to *should*, but it is much less frequent.

Like *should*, the verb *ought to* does not have a past form. It is only used with reference to the present and the future.

Ought to is rarely used in questions and negatives. When it is, it is confined mainly to formal styles.

In negatives, *not* comes between *ought* and *to*. In questions, the subject comes between *ought* and *to*.

> I **ought not to** have said those things to her.
> **Ought** we **to** make such a sacrifice for the benefit of future generations?

Ought to is used as follows:

– to express an obligation or an expectation that someone should do something.

> You **ought to** listen carefully.
> We **ought to** leave now.
> Lucy **ought to** go by herself.
> People **ought to** be a bit nicer to us.

– to express the likelihood of something happening.

> Annabel **ought to** be here by now.
> The journey **ought to** take about 2 hours.

– *Ought to* + *have* + **past participle of main verb** is used to express regret that something was not done or to reproach someone for doing or not doing something.

I ought to have spoken up earlier. I'm sorry.
You ought to have offered to help.
They ought to have told us what to expect.

- In questions and negatives, **should** is frequently used instead of **ought to** because it sounds more natural.

Ought I to report it to someone in authority?
Should I report it to someone in authority?
Ought we to make a start?
Should we make a start?

ought to
The contracted negative form is: **oughtn't (to)**.

Oh dear, we oughtn't to have let that happen.
Well then she ought to do something about it, oughtn't she?

Dare and need

The two verbs *dare* and *need* have characteristics of both modal verbs and main verbs. Because of this, they are called **semi-modals**. They sometimes behave like modal verbs and do not add -s to the form that goes with *he*, *she*, and *it*. That is, they have no 3rd person singular inflection. They are then followed by the **base form** of a main verb.

> *Need I say more?*
> *Dare I ask how the project's going?*

The past form *needed* is not used as a modal; *dared* is occasionally used as a modal.

The modal uses of these verbs are all **negatives** or **questions**.

> *Where will you all be today? –* **Need** *you ask?*
> *You* **needn't** *come if you're busy.*
> *Dare I suggest that we have a rota system?*
> *I* **daren't** *tell him the truth; he'll go crazy.*

Questions that are formed are often set expressions such as *Need I/you ask?*, *Dare I suggest...?* and *Need I/we say more?*

Dare and *need* sometimes behave like main verbs with -s inflection. In this case they are followed by the *to* infinitive. They can also use the auxiliary *do* and have the whole range of tenses appropriate to a main verb.

> *Louisa* **doesn't need** *to know.*
> **Does** *Paul* **need** *to go now?*
> *Paul* **needs to go**.
> **Dare to be** *different!*
> *I* **don't dare to mention** *it to him.*

When *dare* or *need* are used as modal verbs in a positive **statement**, there must be a word of negative meaning in the same clause. This word can be outside the verb phrase and may be a word with a negative sense, such as *only, never, hardly*.

> He **need only** ask and I will tell him.
> **No** sensible driver **dare** risk that chance.

As a modal verb, *dare* has forms as follows:

I **dare** not *go*.   I **dared** not *go*.
He **dare** not *go*.   He **dared** not *go*.

Dare I *do* it?
Dare he *do* it?
Daren't he *do* it?

As a main verb, *dare* has forms as follows:

I **dare to do** it.   I **do** not **dare to do** it.
He **dares to do** it.   He **did** not **dare to do** it.
He **does** not **dare to do** it.   **Does** he **dare to do** it?
He **doesn't dare to do** it.   **Doesn't** he **dare to do** it?

As a modal verb, *need* has forms as follows:

I **need** not *go*.   **Need** I *go*?
He **need** not *go*.   **Need** he *go*?
He **needn't** go.   **Needn't** he *go*?

As a main verb, *need* has forms as follows:

I **need** it.   I **need to do** it.
He **needs** it.   He **needs to do** it.
I **do** not **need to go**.   I **do** not **need to do** it.
He **does** not **need to go**.   **Does** he **need to go**?

- Either of the two forms of **dare** and **need** can be used for sentences that have much the same meaning.

   *Anna **didn't dare to jump** off the high fence.*
   *Anna **dared not jump** off the high fence.*
   *You **don't need to come** if you don't want to.*
   *You **needn't come** if you don't want to.*

Used to

The verb *used to* is a 'marginal' modal verb. Unlike the other modal verbs, it is only found in the past tense. Therefore, when it is used with *do* to make negatives and questions, the form of the auxiliary verb is always *did*.

Used to is used as follows:

– to describe an activity or a state that happened many times in the past.

> *Gerry always **used to** go for a run before breakfast.*
> *Peter **didn't use to** say things like that when I knew him.*

– to refer to an activity or state that was true in the past but is no longer true.

> *I **used to** like rock climbing when I was younger.*
> *You **didn't use to** be so stressed!*

Used to takes the following forms:

– The form *used to* is used with all subjects e.g. *I, we, you, he, she, it, they*.

> I **used to**   We **used to**
> You **used to**   You **used to**
> She **used to**   They **used to**

> *I **used to** live in New Zealand.*
> *He **used to** deliver newspapers papers but he owns the shop now.*
> *Nancy and Bill **used to** live in California.*

There are two forms for a negative:

– *did not/didn't use to*.

> *We **didn't use to** have central heating when I was a child.*
> *Alan **didn't use to** like children, but it's different now he has his own.*

– *used not to*.

> *I **used not to** be able to watch myself on TV at all.*
> *We **used not to** worry much about money.*
> *Things **usedn't to** be so bad.*

There are two forms for a question:

– *did* + **subject** + *use to* + **base form**:
e.g. *did he use to...?*

> *Did they **use to** visit you often? – Well, Mary **used to**.*

– *used* + **subject** + *to* + **base form**:
e.g. *used he to... ?*

> *Used he to play the guitar?*

• In negatives, the form with *did* is used the most. In questions, the form with *did* is almost always preferred.

The common contracted negative form is ***didn't use to***. The rarer contracted negative form is ***usedn't to***.

Do not confuse *used to* + **base form** with *be used to*
+ **present participle**, where *used to* means *accustomed
to*.

> *They lived in India for a long time, so they **are used
> to eating** spicy food.*

Phrasal verbs

A **phrasal verb** is a type of verb that is created when a main verb is combined with either:

- an **adverb**,

>| *take off* | *give in* |
>| *blow up* | *break in* |

- a **preposition**,

>| *get at* (someone) | *pick on* (weaker children) |

- or an **adverb** + **preposition**,

>| *put up with* (insults) | *get out of* (doing something) |

Type A. Verb plus adverb

Some Type A phrasal verbs have no object, i.e. they are **intransitive**. The sentence makes sense without any further addition to the verb.

> *Mary went away.*
> *Helen sat down.*
> *The students came back.*

Others do require an object, i.e. they are **transitive**.

> *We could make out a figure in the distance.*
> *He tried to blow up the Houses of Parliament.*
> *Could you put your clothes away, please?*

If the object is a **noun**, many Type A phrasal verbs will allow the adverb to come either:

– before the object,

>I **picked up** Jim *on my way home.*
>He **blew out** the candle.
>She **tidied away** her things.

– or after the object.

>I **picked** Jim **up** *on my way home.*
>He **blew** the candle **out**.
>She **tidied** her things **away**.

If the object is a **pronoun**, it must come before the adverb.

>I **picked** him **up**.
>He **blew** it **out**.
>She **tidied** them **away**.

Sometimes you can guess the meaning of these verbs from the meanings of the parts.

>to **sit down** = sit + down
>to **go away** = go + away

Sometimes you have to learn the new meanings, or use a dictionary.

>to **make up** (an answer)   = invent
>to **turn down** (an invitation)   = decline
>to **work out** (a problem)   = solve
>to **put up** (a visitor)   = accommodate

Type B. Verb plus preposition

Type B phrasal verbs always have an object. This is because prepositions always have an object.

>He *asked for* his bill.
>He *asked for* it.
>She *listened to* the doctor.
>She *listened to* her.
>They *referred to* our conversation.
>They *referred to* it.

Sometimes there are two objects – the object of the verb and the object of the preposition.

>He *asked* the waiter *for* the bill.

Type C. Verb plus adverb and preposition

Type C phrasal verbs are a combination of the two previous kinds of verb. All the parts of a Type C phrasal verb come before the object.

>We are *looking forward to* our holiday/it.
>Don't *put up with* bad behaviour/it.
>You must *look out for* the warning signs/them.

- It is sometimes hard to tell adverbs and prepositions apart, because often the same word can be both a preposition and an adverb, depending on how it is used. For further information about prepositions see p. 223.

The following are examples of the three types of phrasal verb that are explained on p. 85.

Type A

Phrasal verbs made from a verb plus an adverb may be intransitive (do not take an object) or transitive (take an object).

some phrasal verbs that do not take an object	*some phrasal verbs that do take an object*
to break down	to blow something up
to carry on	to break something off
to fall down	to bring a child up
to get about	to bring a subject up
to get up	to catch somebody up
to give up	to clear something up
to go away	to close something down
to go off	to give something up
to go on	to leave something out
to grow up	to make something up
to hold on	to pick someone up

Type B

Phrasal verbs made from a verb plus a preposition are all transitive.

to add to something	to hope for something
to agree with someone	to insist on something
to apply for a job	to laugh at something
to approve of something	to listen to something
to arrive at a place	to look after someone
to ask for something	to look for something
to believe in something	to look into something
to belong to someone	to pay for something
to call on someone	to refer to something
to care for someone	to rely on someone
to come across something	to run into someone
to deal with something	to run over something

Some Type B verbs are doubly transitive, since both the verb and the preposition can have an object.

to **add** insult **to** injury
to **ask** a grown-up **for** help
to **check** your answers **with** the teacher
to **pay** the assistant **for** your shopping
to **refer** a customer **to** the manager

Type C

Phrasal verbs with an adverb plus a preposition all take a prepositional object.

to be fed up with something	to keep away from something
to carry on with something	to look back on something
to catch up with something	to look forward to something
to check up on something	to look out for something
to come up with something	to look up to someone
to cut down on something	to make up for something
to do away with something	to put in for something
to face up to something	to run away with something
to fall back on something	to run out of something
to get on with someone	to run up against something
to get out of something	to stand up for something
to go back on something	to walk out on someone
to go in for something	to watch out for something
to break in on someone	to lead up to something

Tense

Time reference

Verb forms help us make time reference through their **tense**. Tense shows whether an action or a state took place in the past or takes place in the present.

> Jessica **works** in the post office.
> Laurence **worked** in the post office over the Christmas holidays.

There are two **simple tenses** and six **compound tenses**.

Simple tenses

The simple tenses consist of a single word.

There is a **present simple** tense

> I like
> you like
> he likes
>
> I live
> you live
> he lives

and a **past simple** tense.

> I liked
> you liked
> he liked
>
> I lived
> you lived
> he lived

The simple tenses of regular verbs

The **present tense** is the same as the **base form** of the verb, except that an -s is added to the verb when it has a noun or *he, she,* or *it* as a subject. This is called the 3rd person singular form.

> *he/she/it likes*
> *he/she/it lives*

The **past tense** of a regular verb is made from the **base form** of the verb with -*ed* (or -*d* if the verb already ends in -*e*) added. The spelling is the same for all persons.

> *I liked*   *I lived*
> *you liked*   *you lived*
> *he liked*   *he lived*

The simple tenses of irregular verbs

Most irregular verbs make the **present tense** from the **base form** of the verb just as regular verbs do.

> Present
> *I find*   *I go*
> *you find*   *you go*
> *he/she/it finds*   *he/she/it goes*

- Irregular verbs make the **past tense** in a number of different ways. Sometimes the past tense is a completely different word. See pp. 36–38 for more on irregular verbs.

> Past
> *I found*   *I went*
> *you found*   *you went*
> *he/she/it found*   *he/she/it went*

Aspect

When we use a verb, we often need to be able to refer to more than the time at which an event took place. We sometimes need to be able to refer to actions and states as completed or not completed. **Aspect** describes the way we think of verbal actions.

The **continuous aspect** is formed by using the appropriate form of the auxiliary *be* together with the *-ing* form (**present participle**) of the main verb.

We use **continuous aspect** to show that an action:

– is going on at the time of speaking.

> *I'm having dinner at the moment. Can I call you back?*
> *I know what you are doing!*
> *Look! Someone's walking around in our garden!*

– was going on throughout the time that you are referring to.

> *I was having dinner when he called.*
> *I was waiting for her when she came out of the classroom.*
> *We were driving home when we saw the accident.*

– will be going on at the time that you are referring to.

> *We're going to Turkey for a holiday next year.*
> *They're coming to us for Christmas this year.*

The **perfect aspect** is formed by using the appropriate form of the auxiliary *have* together with the *-ed* form (**past participle**) of the main verb.

We use **perfect aspect** to show that an action:

– is complete at the time of speaking.

> *I've finished the book. It was brilliant.*
> *We've enjoyed having you all to stay.*
> *Jo has borrowed the book, so I can't check now, I'm afraid.*

– was complete at the time you are referring to.

> *Oh dear; I had forgotten my promise to Aunt Jane.*
> *Sharon had lost her key, so she had to wait outside.*
> *Sue had seen the film three times already, but she didn't mind.*

It is possible to have a compound tense that shows both aspects, continuous and perfect.

> *Peter has been talking about you a lot recently.*

Compound tenses

The compound tenses are a combination of present or past **tense** (shown through an auxiliary verb) with continuous or perfect **aspect**. See also pp. 92–93.

> *I'm **doing** my homework at the moment, so I can't come out.*
> *Ben **has seen** the camera that he wants.*

> *She **was listening** to the radio in the kitchen.*
> *Sandra **had invited** all her friends.*

• The tense of the auxiliary verb shows whether the compound verb is **present** tense,

> *I'm **having** dinner at the moment; I'll call you back.*
> *We've **had** a lovely stay; thank you.*

or **past** tense.

> *We **were dancing** around the living room and singing along.*
> *Mum **had gone out** and left us some snacks.*

The choice of the **auxiliary** and the **participle** shows what aspect the verb has.

– if it is the auxiliary *be* and the *-ing* participle (the present participle), the aspect is **continuous**.

> *My brother **is having** a party tomorrow.*
> *The kids **were running** wild when we got home.*

– if it is the auxiliary *have* and the *-ed* participle (the past participle) the aspect is **perfect**.

*Jill **has walked** more than 500 miles for charity.*
*Someone **had tied up** the dog to stop it wandering off.*

These are the main compound tenses:

present continuous　　　　= present of *be* + *-ing* participle.

*Kerry **is waiting** until Jessica gets here.*

past continuous　　　　= past of *be* + *-ing* participle.

*Maria **was watching** TV when Jo called.*

present perfect　　　　= present of *have* + *-ed* participle.

*Sam **has seen** a few things that he'd like.*
*We**'ve bought** some better equipment.*

past perfect　　　　= past of *have* + *-ed* participle.

*She **had** really **believed** their story!*
*Rory **had had** enough of their silly questions.*

A compound verb can also combine both the continuous and perfect aspects, using **two auxiliary verbs** and a **main verb**. This produces the following combinations:

present perfect continuous
　= present of *have* + past participle of *be* + *-ing* participle.

*For the past two months, Zoe **has been visiting** us once a week.*
*We**'ve been trying** to finish that job since Easter.*

past perfect continuous
= past of *have* + past participle of *be* + *-ing* participle.

> *Vicky **had been hoping** for better news.*
> *I **had been travelling** all day, so I was exhausted.*

The modal auxiliaries can be used in compound tenses.

> *She **might be babysitting** for us on Friday.*
> *We **would be sitting** here for hours if I told you everything.*
> *I **may have eaten** something that disagreed with me.*
> *I expect Nayeema **will have bought** something for tea.*

They come in first position in the verb phrase, so they are followed by:

– the subject and the rest of the verb in questions.

> ***Will you be going** shopping after work?*

– the negative *not* and the rest of the verb in negative statements.

> *Marcus **may not have been** entirely truthful.*

– the subject, the negative *not*, and the rest of the verb in negative
 questions.

> ***Will you not be pushing** for that to be changed?*

If the contracted negative form of the modal is used, then it comes
before the subject and and the rest of the verb.

> ***Won't** he **be calling** on us this evening?*

> Modals are not used with the supporting auxiliary verb *do*.

See pp. 62–84 for the meanings and uses of modal auxiliary verbs.

Responses

You usually use just the first part of the verb phrase in a compound verb as the response form. That is, you use one of the auxiliary verbs. If it is a simple tense you use the supporting auxiliary *do*.

> *Do you **like** avocados? – Yes, I **do**.*

If one of the forms of *be* or *have* is the first verb in the verb phrase, then use that as the response form.

> *Has Claire been round yet? – Yes, she **has**.*
> *Was Nayeema asking for help? – Yes, she **was**.*

If a **modal** verb is first in the verb phrase, some speakers prefer to use the modal and the auxiliary form together as the response form.

> *Do you think he **might have left** the parcel somewhere? –*
> *Yes, he **might** or Yes, he **might have**.*
> *So Laurence **could be coming** with us then. – Yes, he **could***
> *or Yes, he **could be**.*

The present simple tense

Typical forms of this tense are as in:

> I know her.
> He knows her.

The present simple tense of *do* is used as the supporting auxiliary when you want to:

- ask a question,

> *Do* I know you?
> *Does* she know you?

- make a negative statement using *not*,

> I *do not* know her.
> She *does not* know you.

- or give a short response.

> *Do* you just *have* coffee for breakfast? – *Yes, I do*.

We use the present simple tense to talk about:

- habits, likes and dislikes, and things that happen regularly.

> I *like* coffee for breakfast but everyone else in my family
>   *prefers* tea.
> I *don't take* sugar in my coffee.
> What *does* Jamie *usually have* for breakfast?
> They *often go* to the cinema *on Saturdays*.
> I *don't usually watch* TV.

(When we talk about habits, we often add adverbs such as *often*, *always*, *usually*, *sometimes*, or *never*, or adverbial phrases such as *on Sundays* or *in the summer*.)

– statements of fact that are scientific truths or that are about a permanent state.

> The sun **rises** in the east.
> Birds **fly** south in the winter.
> We **live** in Scotland.

– statements that indicate the speaker's opinions or beliefs.

> I **think** he's a very good teacher.
> I **don't agree** with that at all.

– for dramatic narrative to tell a story or describe an action vividly,

> He **walks** slowly to the checkout and **puts** his bag on the counter. As the cashier **opens** the till he **draws** a gun ...

– or when giving a commentary on a sports event or public function.

> ... but Nadal **sees** it. He **runs** up to the net and **smashes** the ball.

We can also use the present simple for planned future actions with a time adverb, for example to talk about travel plans and timetables. See pp. 114–121 for more about future reference.

> The train **leaves** at 10.40 a.m. and **arrives** at 3.30 p.m.

We use the present simple in conditional sentences about real possibilities that affect the future. See p. 277 for more on conditional sentences.

> If I **lend** you my notes, I won't be able to revise tonight.

The past simple tense

Typical forms of this tense are as in:

> I *met* her.
> She *met* him.
> I *went* there.
> She *went* there.

Because the past simple consists of one word only, the past simple tense of *do*, which is *did*, is used as the supporting auxiliary when you want to:

– ask a question,

> *Did* I *meet* him?
> *Did* she *meet* him?
> *Did* I *go* there?
> *Did* it *go* there?

– make a negative statement using *not*,

> I *did* not *meet* her.
> He *did* not *meet* her.
> I *did* not *go* there.
> He *did* not *go* there.

– or make a response.

> *Did* you see Jenny yesterday? – No, I *didn't*.
> *Did* Penny phone you ? – Yes, she *did*.

We use the past simple tense to talk about:

– single actions in the past.

> He **locked** the door and **left** the house.
> I **went** out and **brought** the cat back in again.

– habitual actions in the past, often with *always*, *never*, or *often*.

> In those days I **always went** to Juliano's for lunch.
> I **cycled** in every day and that soon **made** me fit.
> I **often visited** Glasgow on business when I was in publishing.

– past actions where a definite time is mentioned. It is often used with a time expression such as *ago* or *last month*, when the action is seen as finished.

> **Some time ago** now, I **went** to America for a month.
> **Once upon a time** there **was** a king in a faraway land.
> I **saw** Roger **a little while back**.
> I **bought** the microwave **a year ago**.

– points where the main action is broken. The rest of the sentence uses the past continuous tense to describe the past activity or action.

> I was clearing out the garage when a car **came** down the drive.
> We were leaving the house when the phone **rang**.

The present continuous tense

Typical forms of this tense are as in:

> *I am winning.*
> *He is winning.*
>
> *Am I winning?*
> *Is she winning?*
>
> *I am not winning.*
> *He is not winning.*
>
> *Aren't I winning?*
> *Isn't she winning?*
>
> *Am I not winning?*
> *Is she not winning?*

Some main verbs are not normally used in the continuous in standard British English, though they may be used this way in other varieties of English. These are generally verbs about states rather than actions.

> *I am winning.*   **but not** *I am liking it.*
> *I am not winning.*   **but not** *I am not liking it.*

We use the present continuous tense to talk about:

– things that are happening now, at the time when we are talking.

> *Mum's **mowing** the lawn, and I'm **doing** my homework,*
>   *but Isabel **isn't doing** anything.*
> *The children **aren't** asleep; they're **messing about**.*
> *Come on; you're **not trying**.*

When you give a short answer to a question, it is normal to echo the auxiliary but not the main verb.

> **Are** you **waiting** for someone? – Yes, I **am**.
> **Is** Hamish **working** in the library? – No, he **isn't**.

– a temporary activity, even if it is not happening at the time when we are talking.

> I'm **studying** German at college.
> I'm **thinking** of getting a new car.

– a temporary situation in contrast to a permanent situation.

> I'm **living** in Scotland **at the moment**.
> Fiona **is working** in the stables over the holidays.

– a changing state or situation.

> My headache **is getting** better.
> The daylight **is slowly fading**.

– the circumstances under which something is generally done.

> I have to wear glasses **when I'm driving**.

– arrangements for future events along with a time adverb or phrase. See p. 114 for more on the future.

> I **am flying** to New York **next week**.

We also use it to express annoyance at a repeated action. In this case, one of the following adverbs is used with the verb: *always, forever, constantly, continually.*

> She's **always whining** about something.
> He's **forever** laughing and making silly comments.

The past continuous tense

Typical forms of this tense are as shown in:

> I was winning.   **but not** I was liking it.
> She was winning.
> They were winning.

> Was I winning?
> Was she winning?
> Were you winning?

> I was not winning   **but not** I was not liking it.
> We were not winning.
> They weren't winning.

Some main verbs are not normally used in the continuous in standard British English, though they may be used this way in other varieties of English. These are generally verbs about states rather than feelings.

We use the past continuous tense in these ways:

– with a time expression, such as *at 6p.m. yesterday*, to talk about an action that began before that time and finished after it. The exact length of time the action took is not important.

> What **were you doing** at eight o'clock last night? –
> I **was standing** at the bus stop.

– to talk about an interrupted action. Note that for the event that interrupts the action, we use the past simple tense.

> We **were** all **sitting** in our places when the bell **rang**.

– to talk about a short action that happened whilst a longer one was already taking place.

> While I **was waiting** for the bus I **dropped** my purse.

– to describe a scene in the past, especially in a story.

> It was a dreadful morning. The snow **was still falling**, the wind **was blowing**, and the cars **were skidding** on the icy roads.

The present perfect tense

Typical forms of this tense are as shown in:

> I *have finished*.
> He *has found* them.
> They*'ve finished*.
> They*'ve found* her.
> Listen! I*'ve heard* some great news; Jim*'s won*!
> They*'ve bought* a brand new car.
> You*'ve got* a nerve!

> *Have* they *finished*? – No, they *haven't*.
> *Has* Mary *arrived* yet? – No, she *hasn't*.

> I *have* not *finished*.
> He *has* not *finished*.
> Ranee *hasn't found* her bracelet yet.
> They *haven't seen* her.

The contracted forms are:

has = **'s**	have = **'ve**
has not = **hasn't**	have not = **haven't**

The present perfect tense is used to talk about events that are relevant to the present but that happened in the past. It is used to talk about an action that started in the past, without mentioning a specific time.

> Her daughter *has had* an accident.
> We *have seen* the Eiffel Tower and the Arc de Triomphe.

If the present perfect occurs more than once in a compound sentence, the second and subsequent instances of *have* can be left out.

> They *have bought* their tickets and *booked* their seats.

- We can use *just* if we want to show that the action has very recently been completed.

    > They **have just bought** their tickets.
    > He **has just finished** his homework.

    If the event did not take place you can use *never*. If you want to find out whether it took place or not, you can use *ever*.

    > **Have** you **ever been** to Greece?
    > I'**ve never done** anything like this before.

- If we want to indicate a moment in time or a period of time, we can use expressions such as *recently*, *lately*, *this morning*, *today*, or *this week* with the present perfect tense.

    > I **haven't been** to the cinema **recently**.
    > I'**ve waited a week** for your answer.

- In questions and negative sentences, the present perfect can be used with *yet*, meaning 'at the time of speaking'. In positive sentences, use *already*.

    > **Haven't** you **finished yet**?
    > **Have** you **bought** the tickets **yet**?
    > I'**ve already seen** that film.

The present perfect tense is often used to answer the question *How long...?* together with *for* to talk about a period of time, or *since* to talk about duration from a point in time.

> I **have lived** in Edinburgh **for** fifteen years.
> **How long have** you **lived** in Edinburgh?
> We'**ve had** this car **since** 2008.
> We **haven't spoken** to each other **since** the night of the argument.

The past perfect tense

Typical forms of this tense are as shown in:

> I **had misheard**.
> She **had misheard**.
> I **had finished**.
> She **had found** them.
> She**'d gone**.
> They**'d found** her.

> **Had** I **misheard**?
> **Had** it **gone**?
> **Had** Mary **arrived** before Peter told you? – No, she **hadn't**.

> I **had not misheard**.
> He **had misheard**.
> I **had not finished**.
> It **had not worked**.
> I **hadn't realized** how serious the problem was.
> They **hadn't seen** her.

The contracted forms are:

> had = **'d**   had not = **hadn't**

The past perfect tense goes one step further back into the past than the present perfect.

> **Had** you ever **seen** her before then? – No, I **hadn't**.

The past perfect tense is used to talk about:

– an action that took place in the past before something else took place.

> She **had just made** some coffee when I arrived.

- an action or state that began before another action in the past and continued up to the time of the second action and perhaps even beyond that time.

> Ashraf **had** already **known** my brother **for two years** when I met him.

• It is often used in the main clause of a complex sentence, to set the scene for a past event.

> We **had** always **wanted** to visit Canada **for a long time**, so last year we decided to go.

• It is often used with a time expression such as *always* or *for several days*.

> We **had** always **wanted** to visit Canada, so last year we decided to go.

The present perfect continuous tense

Typical forms of this tense are as shown in:

> *I have been waiting.*
> *I've been waiting.*
> *She has been waiting.*
> *She's been waiting.*

> *Have I been snoring?*
> *Has he been waiting?*
> *Have you been waiting long?*

> *I have not been waiting.*
> *She has not been waiting.*

We use the present perfect continuous tense to talk about:

– actions and states that began in the past and are still continuing at the time of speaking.

> *I have been holding this ladder for ages. When are you going to come down?*

– actions and states that began in the past and have only just finished.

> *Thank goodness you're here! I've been waiting for hours.*

– repeated actions.

> *I've been getting this magazine every week for a year.*

There is sometimes little difference between the meaning of the present perfect and the meaning of the present perfect continuous when they are used for long-term actions.

> *I **have been working** here for three years.*
> *I **have worked** here for three years.*

We usually choose the continuous form for more temporary actions or states.

> *I **have been living** in London since I left school.*

… and the present perfect form for more permanent ones.

> *I **have lived** in London since I was born.*

- We cannot use this tense with verbs such as *be*, *know*, and *like*, which are not used in continuous forms.

- We can use *for* and *since* with the continuous form in the same way as with the present perfect form. See also pp. 102–105 for more about continuous uses of the verb.

> *I **have been studying** English for three years.*
> *I **have studied** English for three years.*
>
> *I **have been living** in London since I left school.*
> *I **have lived** in London since I was born.*

The past perfect continuous tense

Typical forms of this tense are as shown in:

> *I had been waiting.*
> *I'd been waiting.*
> *She had been waiting.*
> *She'd been waiting.*

> *Had I been talking nonsense? What had I said?*
> *Had he been waiting long?*
> *Had you been expecting to meet Mary at the station?*

> *I had not been waiting.*
> *She had not been waiting.*
> *They hadn't been looking very carefully.*

The past perfect continuous tense is used to talk about an action which began before another action in the past and either:

– continued up to the time of the second action,

> *I hadn't been waiting long when a lorry drew up beside me.*

– or was completed before the second action happened.

> *I had been studying and decided to take a stroll to clear my mind.*
> *We had been cleaning the car for hours, so we stopped and had a drink.*

• The past perfect continuous is often used in the main clause of a complex sentence, to set the scene for an event.

> *I had been driving for about an hour when I heard a noise in the engine.*

- The past perfect continuous is often used to talk about a repeated action.

  *She **had been trying** to telephone her mother all day.*

  Remember that you cannot use the past perfect continuous with verbs such as *like*, which are not used in the continuous. See p. 102.

Future reference

Verb forms

English has no future tense as such. However, several forms, especially the **modal** verbs *will* and *shall*, can be used to make future reference. These forms are summarized as follows:

1 *Will/shall* + the **base form** makes the most direct form of future reference. See p. 70. The other modal verbs that express possibility make a more indirect reference to future time.

> It **will take** *several years to finish.*
> *Jean* **will look after** *the dogs while we're away.*
> *I* **shall** *simply* **tell** *her to mind her own business.*
> *We* **shall see**.

2 *Be going to* + the **base form** is used to express intention and make predictions. See p. 117.

> *He failed his exam last year; this year he* **is going to work** *harder.*
> *You'd better take the washing in; it* **is going to rain**.

3 The **present continuous tense** is used to talk about plans and arrangements in the future with a time adverb. See p. 102.

> *Sarah and Harriet* **are meeting** *at ten o'clock* **on Tuesday**.
> *I* **am flying** *to Glasgow* **on Friday**.

4 The **present simple tense** is used with a time adverb to talk about future plans which are part of a timetable or previous arrangement. See p. 98.

> *The main film* **starts** *at 2.45 p.m.*
> *We* **leave** *at 4 p.m.* **tomorrow**.

5 The **future perfect tense** (*will have* + the **past participle**) is used with a time adverb to talk about an action that will be finished at the time in the future that you are referring to. See p. 119.

> *I was hoping to meet James, but by the time I arrive he **will have gone** home.*

6 *Be about to* + the **base form** is used to talk about the very near future. See p. 120.

> *I'm sorry I can't stop and chat; I'm **about to leave** for work.*

7 The **future continuous tense** (*will be* + the **present participle**) is used to talk about future action in progress. See p. 121.

> *What **will** you **be doing** on Saturday morning? Oh, I'll **be shopping** as usual.*

8 *Be to* + the **base form** is used to talk about formal plans, especially in journalism. See p. 121.

> *The President **is to attend** an EU–Russia summit tomorrow.*

1 *will/shall*
The modal verbs *will* or *shall* followed by the **base form** of a main verb are used to express future reference.

I shall come.	*We shall come.*
or	or
I will come.	*We will come.*
You will come.	*You will come.*
She/he/it will come.	*They will come.*

Will can be used with all persons of the verb, although some speakers prefer to use *shall* in the 1st person singular and plural. See p. 70 for further details.

- The contracted form is *'ll* for both verbs, so there is no difference in informal speech.

  I'll probably be late, but I expect they'll be on time.

  The contracted negative forms are **won't** and **shan't**.

  *We **won't come**.*
  *We **shan't come**.*

- If there are two verbs in the sentence, it is normal not to repeat the modal form before the second one.

  *I **won't go** see him or **speak** to him for six months.*

We use **will** (or **shall**) for future reference in the following ways:

- to talk about future facts.

  *I **shan't see** Mary next week.*
  *I'll **be** on the plane this time tomorrow.*

- to make promises or reassurances.

  *I'll **be** home in time for tea.*
  *This **won't happen** again, I can assure you.*

- to announce a decision that the speaker has just made.

  *Er, I'll **have** the pizza Margherita and a side salad, please.*
  *Right, I **shall** ask him, and see if his story matches yours.*

- to express negative intention, using **won't**.

  *I **won't go** there again. The service was dreadful.*

– to express refusal.

> I **won't put up with** any more of this silly behaviour.
> I've tried to persuade her but she **won't come**.

– to talk about an event in the future, possibly in the distant future. A time clause may be used.

> People **will be** amazed when they hear about this in years to come.

– to refer to inevitable actions or events that will take place in the future.

> Christmas is past, but it **will come** again next year.

– to express an opinion about a future event after verbs such as believe, expect, hope, know, and think.

> I **expect** he'**ll be** home soon.
> I **hope** you'**ll be** very happy in your new home.

– to express a real possibility in conditional sentences. See p. 277.

> If you phone after six I'**ll tell** you all about it.

2 **be going to**
Future reference can be made with *be* + *going to* + the **base form** of a main verb.

> I **am going to wait**.
> He **is going to wait**.
> I **am not going to wait**.
> He **is not going to wait**.
> **Is** he **going to wait**?
> **Are** they **going to wait**?

Be going to is used in the following ways:

– to express intention about the future.

> Mary **isn't going** to study art; she**'s going** to be a nurse.

– to talk about things that have already been decided.

> Is Jim **going to leave** his job? – Yes, **he is**.
> Where's Mary? She said she **was going to come** early.

– to make a prediction about the future, often the very near future, based on something in the present.

> Watch the milk! It **is going to boil** over!
> Sally never does any work; she **is going to fail** her exams.

If the past tense of *be* is used, a past intention or prediction can be expressed.

> Judy **was going to meet** me, but she was ill and couldn't come.
> She **was** obviously **going to get** blisters with those new shoes.

Note this difference:

Be going to is usually used for future events where the speaker expresses his or her intention.
Will is used to express decisions made at the moment of speaking.

> I**'m going to go** to the pictures on Friday; would you like to come?
> Yes, I**'ll go** if Chris goes.

3 Present continuous

The present continuous tense is used to talk about plans for the future, or specific arrangements that people have made for future events.

*The school **is having** a sale next week; I**'m running** the bookstall.*

It is often used in questions about future arrangements.

*What **are you doing** on Saturday? – I**'m going** to a football match with Peter.*
*When **are you leaving**? – At the end of term.*

If there are two verbs in the sentence, it is normal not to repeat the auxiliary before the second and subsequent ones.

*We **are meeting** at 12.30 p.m., **having** a quick lunch, and **starting** work at 1.15.*

4 Present simple

The present simple tense is also used to talk about events that form part of a timetable or programme.

*The train **leaves** Edinburgh at 10.10 a.m. and **arrives** in London at 3.20 p.m.*
*These are the arrangements for Friday: doors **open** at 7 p.m., the Mayor **arrives** at 7.30 p.m., and the meeting **starts** at 7.45 p.m.*

5 The future perfect (*will have* + the past participle of a main verb)

This form is used to talk about an action that will be complete at a time in the future that you are talking about. It is often used with verbs relating to finishing or completing.

The contracted positive form is *'ll have* or *will've*.

> *Can you come round next Saturday? – Yes, I'll have finished*
>   *my exams by then.*
> *Dad will've made dinner by the time we get back.*

The contracted negative is *won't have*.

> *The essay is due on Tuesday, but I won't have completed it by*
>   *then.*

In questions, the subject comes after *will*. The short answer to a question is *will* without the past participle.

> *Will you have finished dinner by then? – Yes, we will.*

6 *be + about to +* **the base form**

The appropriate form of *be + about to +* the **base form** of a main verb is used to talk about events in the very near future.

> *Turn off the gas – the soup is about to boil over.*
> *Come on! The film's about to start!*

It is sometimes used with *just* following the *be* word to give even more immediacy.

> *Quick, jump in! The train is (just) about to leave.*

Be about to can also be used in the **past** to suggest that someone is *on the point of* carrying out an action when it is interrupted. In this case it is usually followed by *when*.

> *They were (just) about to go to bed when the phone rang.*

7 **The future continuous tense**
This is made with *will* + *be* + the **present participle** of a main verb.
Will be forms negatives, contractions, questions, and short answers
in the usual way.

The future continuous is used in a rather informal way to suggest
that something is about to happen or will happen at some time that
is not clear or precise.

> *I'll **be seeing** you.*
> *We'll **be getting** in touch with you.*
> *They'll **be wanting** us to clean our own classrooms next!*
> *We **won't be seeing** Uncle John while we are in Australia.*

It is also used to talk about an activity that will already be in
progress at a particular time in the future.

> *Will you **be working** here next week?*
> *No, I won't. I'll **be starting** my new job.*
> *Just think! This time next week, we **will be flying** to Sydney.*

8 *be to* + **the base form**
The appropriate form of *be* + *to* + the **base form** of a main verb is
used mainly in fairly formal English to talk about plans, arrangements,
and instructions. It indicates that what will happen is part of an
expected process, and is often found in journalistic texts.

> *Foreign ministers of the NATO countries **are to meet** in Brussels*
>   *next week.*
> *The President has left for Geneva, where he **is to attend** the*
>   *meeting.*

Active and passive

Active sentences

In the following example, the verb is **active**.

> *The postman delivers* hundreds of letters every day.

The subject of an active sentence is also the person or thing that carries out the action. We use the active when the subject of the verb is the doer of the action. The active is used in most English speech and writing, because we usually want to inform our listener or our reader who or what carried out the action of the verb.

> *He hid* the money under the bed.
> *The car knocked over* a pedestrian.
> *I'm sending* the book by express delivery.

Passive sentences

In the following example, the verb is in the **passive**.

> *Thousands of letters are delivered* every day.

The subject in a passive sentence is not the person or thing that does the action of the verb. It is the person or thing that is acted on by the verb.

> *The injured man was helped* by a passer-by.
> *The man was being questioned* by the police.
> *The patient was operated on* by a team of five surgeons.

The passive is made with the appropriate form of *be* + the **past participle** of the main verb.

- We use the passive to direct our listener's attention to the important part of our message. For instance, in the first example of this section we do not need to know who delivers the letters, so all mention of the postman is left out.

- The passive can be used when we do not know who carries out the action expressed by the verb, or when it is not important that we should know. It is sometimes much more important to know what has happened than who or what did it.

> *The money **was hidden** under the bed.*
> *The book **is being sent** by express delivery.*
> *An elderly man **was run over** while crossing the road.*
> *Roger **has been given** his promotion.*
> *The patient **was operated on**.*

The passive allows us to select the parts of a sentence to which we want to draw attention. It can be used when we want to focus on:

- the **agent**, i.e. who brought the action about. We show the agent with *by*.

> *The window was broken **by some boys**.*
> *My brother was given extra tuition **by his teacher**.*
> *The old man was run over **by a careless driver**.*
> *The patient was operated on **by a team of top surgeons**.*

- the **instrument**, i.e. what was used to make the action happen. We show the instrument with *by* or *with*.

> *The sorting is done **by machine**.*
> *The safe was blown open **with dynamite**.*
> *The old man was knocked over **by a bus**.*
> *I was showered **with presents** on my eighteenth birthday.*

– the **means**, i.e. what caused the action to happen. We show the means with *by* or *with*.

> *The window was shattered **by the explosion**.*
> *He was exhausted **with the strain of caring for his elderly parents**.*
> *Spelling errors are marked **with a cross in the margin**.*
> *He was taken to hospital **by ambulance**.*

The subject of a passive verb

The verb in a passive sentence has the word that would normally be its object in the position of the subject. When a verb has two objects, either the indirect object or the direct object of the active verb may become the subject of the passive verb.

> *I've **been offered** a place at university.*
> *We **were given** a second chance.*

If the indirect object is mentioned after the passive verb, the sentence must use *to*.

> *The building **has been sold to** property developers.*
> *The medal **is awarded to** students who have shown academic excellence.*

Some verbs that are often used this way are: *give, offer, lend, promise, sell,* and *tell*.

Form of the passive

Passive verbs are made from a form of *be* + the **past participle** of a main verb. In the passive, the form of the auxiliary verb *be* indicates the tense.

> *They **sell** cheap computer games here.*
> *Cheap computer games **are sold** here.*
> *They **took** him to the police station for questioning.*
> *He **was taken** to the police station for questioning.*

- Some verbs are only or mostly used in the passive, e.g. *be born* and *be deemed*.

  > *The film **was deemed** unsuitable for younger audiences.*
  > *My brother and I **were born** in Wales.*

The impersonal passive

This form of the passive sentence is useful when you want to report what is or was generally understood or accepted by a group of people.

> *The suitcase **was found** to be empty.*
> *The money **is thought** to be missing.*
> *The rumour **is believed** to be true.*

The form *it* + **passive** + **that** can be used when you do not want to mention the source of a report or rumour.

> *It **is reported** that over a hundred people died in the explosion.*
> *It **is said** that his income is over £200 a minute.*

The passive with *get*

In informal English, a type of passive is sometimes made with *get* instead of *be*.

> *How did that teapot **get broken**?*
> *Our cat **got run over** last week.*

Get is also used to form a small set of passive verbs in contexts which are not informal (or 'neutral'), e.g. *get dressed, get married, get lost*.

> *Harriet got lost on the Underground.*
> *When are you two getting married?*

The causative passive with *have*

There is another kind of verbal group that is like the passive, because the person who carries out the action of the main verb is not the person who is the subject of the clause. It expresses the idea that the subject caused or ordered someone to take the action mentioned.

> *We are having the garage door replaced.*
> *She had her hair cut short.*
> *They did not have the carpet cleaned after all.*

It has the form: *have* + **direct object** + **past participle**.

Compare:

Ralph repaired his car = Ralph did the work.
Ralph had his car repaired = He paid someone else to do the work.

Finite and non-finite verbs

In a sentence, there is normally at least one verb that has both a **subject** and a **tense**. When a verb has a subject and a tense, it can be referred to as a **finite** verb.

> *We want Charlie to act as club secretary.*
> *I like taking photographs of insects.*
> *Coming home last night, I saw a deer run across the road.*

Some forms of a verb are referred to as **non-finite**. The **present** and **past participles** and the *to infinitive* are the most common of these. The base form is often used in a non-finite way. Every verb can be used in a clause in either a **finite** or **non-finite** way.

- A verb is finite if it is found in a clause in combination with a subject and a tense.

  > *I walked home.*
  > *We saw a deer.*
  > *They appreciate a little praise now and then.*

- It is non-finite if it is used:

- without the verb having a tense.

  > *To open, tear off the tab.*
  > *Looking around, he noticed a letter on the floor.*
  > *Worn out by the heat, they stopped for a drink.*

- with no agreement between the subject (if there is one) and the verb.

  > *That plan failing, he gave up.*
  > *Our guests departed, we felt a little depressed.*

A compound verb is actually made up of one finite part, which is always the first auxiliary verb, while the remaining non-finite parts are the base form or the participles.

In the following examples the finite part of the verb phrase is in blue italic:

> I **may** have been joking *when I said that.*
> *Helen* **was** running *around screaming.*
> I **had** been living *in a dream for months.*
> *Olivia* **is** coming *round at 6 o'clock this evening.*

The present simple and past simple forms of a verb are always finite.

> I **sing**.
> *We* **tell** *stories at night.*
> *Maya* **laughed**.
> *The shelter* **collapsed**.

- A non-finite verb is sometimes used immediately after a finite verb.

> I **like** to get up *early at the weekend.*
> *Harriet really* **dislikes** cleaning *the cooker.*
> *I certainly* **wouldn't want** to see *him again.*
> *We* **persuaded** *them* to join *us.*

Often a noun or pronoun can come between the finite verb and the non-finite one. See p. 132 and p. 133 for more on this.

> *We* **want** *Charlie* to act *as club secretary.*
> *She* **wanted** *him* to wash *his hands in the bathroom.*
> I don't **like** *you* cleaning *your boots over the sink.*

- When the second verb is an *-ing* form coming after a noun or pronoun, there can be a difference in grammar between two similar sentences. Both sentences below are acceptable, although the first example might seem ambiguous to some people. In the second sentence, the *-ing* form is used as a verbal noun. See also p. 134.

    *She didn't like **him** cleaning his boots over the sink.*
    *She didn't like **his** cleaning his boots over the sink.*

The non-finite parts of the verb

Non-finite parts of a verb are those that do not indicate number, person or tense. The common non-finite forms are:

- the **base form**
- the **present participle** or *-ing* form
- the **past participle**
- the *to* **infinitive**

There are also other non-finite forms, such as:

- the **continuous** *to* **infinitive**: *to be teaching*
- the **perfect** *to* **infinitive**: *to have taught*
- the **passive** *to* **infinitive**: *to be taught*

The base form

As well as serving as the verb form on which most of the other parts of the verb are based, the **base form** is frequently used as a non-finite part of the verb. Because of this it is sometimes called the '*bare infinitive*' or the '*infinitive without to*'.

The **base form** is used as a **non-finite** part of the verb in these ways:

- after modal verbs.

    *You must **stop** at the kerb before you cross.*
    *He should **think** before he speaks.*

- after *let's* (suggestion) and *let* (permission) and *make* (compulsion).

    *Let's **invite** Annette round for dinner.*
    *Let the cat **go**!*
    ***Make** him stop!*
    *Let him **finish** what he was saying!*

- after *feel, hear, see, watch* + an object.

> I *heard* him **run** downstairs.
> Later we *saw* them **leave** the house.

- after a **to** infinitive to which it is joined by *and*.

> I want you to sit and **listen**.
> Just wait and **see**.

- after *would rather* and *had better*.

> I would rather **go** out, but I think we had better **stay** home and finish the painting.

Verbs of perception may be followed either by the **base form** or by the **-ing** form. There is often a change of sentence meaning.

These verbs include: *see, hear, feel, smell, listen to, watch.*

> We watched her **park** the car = we watched the whole event.
> We watched her **parking** the car = we may only have seen part of the event.
> I heard a cuckoo **call** = I heard just one call.
> We heard the birds **singing** = We heard part of the song of the birds.

The *to* infinitive

The *to* infinitive is used as follows:

– after an adjective of quality such as *small*, *tall*, *agreeable*, *pleasant*, *funny* that is used in combination with *too*.

> The child was **too small to reach** the switch.
> The knife was **too blunt to cut** the string.

or (*not*) + adjective of quality + *enough*.

> The child was **not tall enough to reach** the switch.
> The knife was **not sharp enough to cut** the string.
> I was **stupid enough to go** walking in flip flops.

– after adjectives of emotion such as: *angry*, *happy*, *glad*, *sad*, *sorry*, *surprised*, to express the reason for the emotion.

> I'm **glad to see** you.
> I'm **sorry to hear** your news.

– after a 'behaviour' adjective such as: *good*, *kind*, *nice*, *silly*, *wrong*, (sometimes + *of* + another **noun phrase**).

> It was **good** of you **to come**, and **kind** of Jane **to have sent** those flowers.
> It was **silly to go** off like that.
> It was **kind** of you **to ring** me.

– after a **WH-** word such as: *how*, *what*, *where*, *whether*, *which*, *who*, *whom*.

> We have no idea **what to get** for Tim's birthday.
> I don't know **where to go**.
> I can't think **how to do** it.
> They were wondering **who to see** first.

– after a noun phrase such as *a good idea, a good thing, a mistake* (sometimes + *for* + another **noun phrase**).

> *It was a mistake for Jim to buy that motorbike.*
> *It was a good idea to stop here.*

– after an adjective such as *easy, difficult, hard, impossible* + *for* + **noun phrase**.

> *It has never been easy for David to sit exams.*

– after a verb followed by *for*, e.g. *ask, wait* + *for* + **noun phrase**.

> *They are waiting for us to decide.*

• The *to* infinitive can be used to express purpose or necessity after a verb followed by a pronoun or a noun.

purpose: I brought *it to read* on the train = so that I could read it.
necessity: There is *work to do*! = work that must be done.

Sometimes the particle *to* can be used alone, provided the meaning is clear, for example in a short response, when the whole verb form is used in a previous sentence or clause.

> *Did you meet Tina? No, I wanted to, but she was ill.*
> *Are you going to visit the museum? Yes, we hope to.*

The *to* infinitive and the *-ing* form

The *to* infinitive and the *-ing* form (the present participle) can each be used after certain verbs.

Verbs followed by the *to* infinitive include: *agree, arrange, attempt, choose, decide, fail, hope, learn, manage, offer, plan, seem.*

> I *agreed to help* Shona with her homework.
> The driver *attempted to remove* the flat tyre.
> I *hope to see* you again at the next meeting.

Verbs followed by an **object** + the *to* **infinitive** include: *advise, allow, command, forbid, force, invite, order, persuade, remind, teach, tell.*

> Peter advised Ron **to call the police**.
> Esther reminded her teacher **to set some revision**.

Verbs that can be followed *either* directly by the *to* **infinitive** *or* by an **object** + the *to* **infinitive** include: *ask, expect, help, intend, like, love, hate, mean, prefer, want, wish.*

> I certainly intended **to go** to the party.
> We really expected **Sally to pass** the exam.

> Note this difference:
> I want **to have** a cat = It will be my cat.
> I want **her to have** a cat = It will be her cat.
> Dad likes **to wash** the car = Dad washes the car.
> Dad likes **John to wash** the car = John washes the car.

Verbs followed by the *-ing* form include: *avoid, be used to, delay, dislike, escape, finish, forgive, give up, go on, imagine.*

> I usually **avoid going** into town late at night.
> Miriam **hates peeling** potatoes.
> Have you **finished reading** that book yet?

- Some verbs may be followed either by the *to* infinitive or by the *-ing* form with little or no change in meaning. These verbs include: *begin, start, cease, continue, intend, like, love, hate, prefer.*

    *He began **to run** around shouting.*
    *He began **running** around shouting.*
    *She likes **to swim** in the sea.*
    *She likes **swimming** in the sea.*
    *I can't bear **to see** violence.*
    *I can't bear **seeing** violence.*

- Some verbs may be followed either by the *to* infinitive or by the *-ing* form but the meaning of the sentence changes depending on the form that is used. These verbs include: *try, forget, remember.*

    *I **remembered to switch** the lights off before we went out.*
    *I **remember switching** the lights off before we went out.*
    *She **tried to talk** to him, but his secretary wouldn't put the call through.*
    *She **tried talking** to him, but he wouldn't listen.*

Particularly after verbs such as *go* and *come*, the **to** infinitive is understood to express purpose.

    *She has **gone to do** the shopping.*
    *They **came** here **to learn** English.*

Use of the verb followed by the *-ing* form concentrates on what happens. The second verb is really the object of the first one. These verbs include: *remember, forget, try.*

    *I definitely **remember switching the lights off** before we went out.*
    *She **tried talking to him**, but he wouldn't listen.*

Some **set expressions** (idioms) are followed by -*ing*. These include: *it's not worth*, and *it's no fun*.

> It's **no fun going** out alone.
> It's **no use phoning** him; he's gone away.
> It's **worth trying** one more time.

The noun phrase

A noun phrase is a word or group of words that can function as the **subject**, the **object**, or the **complement** in a sentence.

> *The manager interviewed all the applicants on Tuesday.*
> *Lydia was the successful applicant.*

See pp. 22–23 and pp. 234–235 for more information about these functions. A noun phrase must always contain a noun or a pronoun.

A noun phrase may consist of only one word. That word will be either a noun or a pronoun.

> *Mary left late.*
> *She left late.*
> *Cheese is expensive.*
> *It is expensive.*

A noun phrase may consist of more than one word. One of these words, a noun or a pronoun, is the **headword**. The other words describe or modify the headword.

> *the tall girl*
> *the very tall girl*
> *a strikingly beautiful girl*
> *the tall girl with green eyes*

Words that go before the headword are called **premodifiers**. A noun can be premodified by:

– a determiner. See p. 164.

> *the girl*   *that boy*
> *a spider*   *some rice*

– one or more adjectives. See pp. 164–194.

> *tall* girls
> *tall dark* girls
> *tall dark handsome* men

– a number, another noun, or the present participle or past participle of a verb.

> *three* days
> the *railway station* buffet
> an *annoying* habit
> an *overworked* man

Words that go after the headword are called **postmodifiers**. A noun can be postmodified by:

– a prepositional phrase (a noun phrase with a preposition in front of it).

> the person **in the corner**
> the view **across the valley**
> the house **opposite the church**
> creatures **under the sea**

– a subordinate clause (usually one beginning with *who*, *which* or *that*). See p. 268.

> All the women **who had gathered there** finally went away.
> Milk **that has been kept too long** can go sour.

– less commonly, certain adjectives. See p. 164.

> the princess **royal**
> the president **elect**

- Personal pronouns are only rarely premodified or postmodified. See p. 207.

    Silly me.
    Poor old you.

Types of noun

Nouns can be classified according to what they refer to.

- Nouns that are really names are called **proper nouns**. Proper nouns usually refer to a particular named person or thing.

They include:

– the names of specific people.

> *Anna Dickinson*   *John Lennon*
> *Lucy White*   *Mrs Merton*

– geographical items.

> *Spain*   *Mount Everest*
> *China*   *England*
> *The Thames*   *Paris*
> *Covent Garden*   *Balcombe Road*

– days of the week, months, and annual Church festivals.

> *Thursday*   *June*
> *Christmas*   *Easter*

– patented goods and trade names.

> *Hoover*   *Persil*
> *Jaguar*   *Samsung*

– newspaper and magazine titles.

> *The Times*   *Vogue*
> *The New Scientist*   *Time Out*

– shop, cinema, theatre names, buildings.

> *The Odeon* *Next*
> *The Royal Mews* *Abbey National*

– titles (the polite or professional labels that we give to people).

> **Doctor** *Johnson* **Sir** *George Hardie.*
> **Professor** *James* **President** *Sarkozy*

A person's title is usually placed before his or her name. Proper nouns and titles are always written with an initial capital letter.

● All the other nouns that refer to things or species are called **common nouns**.

> *I put the **tennis balls** in that **basket** there.*
> *My **brother** and **sister** visited my **mother**.*
> *The **anger** that John felt was overwhelming.*

Common nouns can be divided into the following groups, according to their meaning:

Abstract nouns. These refer to intangible items.

> *honesty* *anger*
> *idea* *time*
> *ugliness* *behaviour*

Concrete nouns. These refer to tangible items.

> *pig* *granite*
> *table* *butcher*
> *brother* *sugar*

A concrete noun may refer to a living thing (**animate** nouns) or a physical object (**inanimate** nouns).

Collective nouns. These refer to collections of people or animals.

> *a herd of cows*
> *a swarm of bees*

Nouns may also be classified according to the words with which they are used, that is:

– whether or not the noun gives us information about **singular** and **plural number**.

– the other words that can be used in the same noun phrase.

This gives us a useful distinction between **countable nouns** and **uncountable nouns**.

Countable nouns refer to things that we can count: *one cat, two cats, seventeen cats,* and so on. They have singular and plural forms, which are shown by the spelling. They must be used with a determiner if they are singular.

> ***Dogs** ran wild in the streets.*
> ***The dog** is loose again.*
> *Fetch **a chair** for Maddy, will you?*
> *We've bought **six new chairs**.*

Uncountable nouns refer to:

– things that are not normally thought of as countable.

> *John asked me for some **advice**.*
> *Anna gave us some more **information** about her work.*
> ***Homework** occupied much of Sonia's evening.*

– qualities or abstract ideas.

> Our **knowledge** of outer **space** is increasing daily.
> Trevor gave **evidence** at the trial.
> **Anger** is a normal human emotion.

Uncountable nouns do not usually have a plural form. They are followed by a singular verb. They are not normally used with the indefinite article. (You cannot talk about '*an advice*' or '*a money*'.) When it is necessary to think of an item as countable it has to be used with a **partitive noun**. See p. 145.

> He bought seven **sheets of** cardboard.
> Let me give you **a piece of** advice.

Some examples of the commonest uncountable nouns are: *advice, anger, beauty, behaviour, conduct, despair, evidence, furniture, happiness, homework, information, safety, knowledge, leisure, money, news, progress, research, jumble.*

• Verbal nouns (p. 162), which are formed from the present participle of verbs, can also be used as uncountable nouns.

> Why don't you try **walking** to work?
> Brian was told to stop **smoking**.
> The **ringing** in his ears continued.

> Note that nouns that are uncountable in English may be countable in other languages. See p. 146.

Mass nouns

These are nouns that refer to a substance that can be divided or measured but not counted, e.g. *sugar, water*. They do not usually have an indefinite article in front.

> *Meat is usually more expensive than cheese.*
> *Sugar is quite cheap.*

Mass nouns only take a plural in special cases. They can be counted when they refer to:

− a particular type or types of the substance.

> *There was a buffet of bread and rolls, cheese, cold meats*
>   *and tea or coffee.*
> *Ros brought out a tempting selection of French cheeses.*
> *The principal sugars are glucose, sucrose, and fructose.*

− a serving of the substance.

> *Two teas, please.*
> *He went up to the bar and ordered two lagers.*

• Mass nouns are often used together with a partitive noun.

> *There are only two pieces of furniture in the room.*
> *There are three portions of meat in this special pack.*
> *Five pints of lager, please.*

Partitive nouns

Partitive nouns are commonly followed by *of*. They are used when we need to talk about a part of a mass noun or when we need to count the quantity of something that is referred to by an uncountable noun or a mass noun, especially when it is necessary to talk about:

– measurements and quantities with mass nouns.

> *three **pieces** of toast*   *a **slice** of cheese*
> *a **bit** of fluff*   *two **spoonfuls** of sugar*

– individual items with uncountable nouns.

> *Two **pieces** of furniture needed major repairs.*
> *We needed several **lengths** of string.*

– a collection of countable nouns.

> *The road was blocked by a **flock** of sheep.*
> *He has a small **herd** of dairy cows.*
> *There was a **crowd** of football supporters of the bus.*
> *A **couple** of cats were fighting.*

> Many collective nouns can be used as partitive nouns.
> See p. 142.

Nouns that have both countable and uncountable uses

Most nouns are either countable nouns or uncountable nouns, as explained on p. 142. Some nouns, however, behave like countable nouns in some sentences and uncountable nouns in other sentences. They usually have different meanings depending on how they are used. For example *time*, *light*, *history*, *space*, *laugh*, and *grocery* have more than one meaning.

> *Time* passed slowly.
> She did it four *times*.
> *Light* travels faster than sound.
> The *lights* in this room are too bright.
> The rocket was launched into *space*.
> There are plenty of empty *spaces* on the shelves.

Some nouns that are countable nouns in other languages are used only as uncountable nouns in English, e.g. *information*, *advice*.

> He received all the necessary *information*.
> I don't need your *help*.

Some nouns are used only in the plural form, even when we are talking about one item, e.g. *trousers*, *clothes*, *jeans*. We can use a partitive noun with *of* when referring to a single item.

> These *trousers* need cleaning.
> Put the *scissors* back when you have finished with them.
> I need a pair of *pliers*.
> Liz gathered up a bundle of *clothes*.

Gender of nouns

In some languages, nouns have **gender**. This means that a noun causes other words such as adjectives to change their spelling according to certain rules. Grammatical gender has little to do with biological gender. English does not have **grammatical gender** for nouns.

On the other hand, the **biological gender** of the thing or person referred to does affect a few areas of English grammar.

> *a cow... **she** or it*   *a bull... **he** or it*
> *a girl... **she***   *a boy... **he***

Gender distinctions are relevant where personal pronouns (p. 203) and possessive determiners (p. 160) have to be decided on. These distinctions are only noticeable in **singular** nouns.

> ***He*** *found **his** book.*
> ***He*** *had been looking for **it**.*
> ***She*** *found **her** book.*
> ***She*** *had been looking for **it**.*

There are also special cases, such as the association of neuter gender with babies and small animals, or feminine gender with a vehicle.

> *I just saw a **mouse**. **It** was running across the room.*
> *The **spider** was spinning **its web**.*
> *The **beetle** crawled into **its hole**.*
> *The **baby** threw down **its** rattle.*
> *I've got a new boat; **she's** a real beauty.*

Nouns denoting male persons and animals are **masculine** in that they are used with the pronouns and possessive determiners *he, him, his*.

Nouns denoting female persons and animals are **feminine** in that they are used with the pronouns and possessive determiners *she, her, hers*.

*Barry saw Linda. **He** called out to **her** that **he** had found **her** book.*
*Marcia saw Paul. **She** called out to **him** that **she** had found **his** book.*
*Madeleine saw Kim. **She** said 'Hello' to **her**.*

The pronouns and possessive determiners used to refer to common or **neuter** nouns are: *it, its*.

> **The truth** will emerge. **It** always does.

Nouns denoting inanimate objects and abstract notions are also neuter.

- Some nouns denoting people have the same form for masculine and feminine. Nouns used for a group, e.g. *government* or *team*, have **common** or **neuter** gender, even when we know that the group is made up exclusively of male or female members.

> *The **government** has changed **its** policy.*
> *The **team** has won **its** first medal at a major championship.*

With some nouns of common gender it might be possible to specify the gender if we had sufficient information. But if we do not have this knowledge, the choice of pronoun or possessive determiner becomes a problem.

> *a driver...he/she*
> *the cook...he/she*
> *doctor...he/she*

As a way around this problem, in informal and spoken English, **their** is sometimes used after a singular noun or an indefinite pronoun. See p. 206. Many people consider this grammatically unacceptable, but it is widely used to avoid repetitions of *his or her* or *him or her*.

> *Each **student** must apply to **his or her** tutor for an extension.*
> *Everyone must apply to **their** tutor for an extension.*
> *Someone has left **their** coat in my room.*

The specialized terms used to name male, female and neutered animals show a number of gender differences.

horse	mare	stallion	gelding
–	cow	bull	steer
sheep	ewe	ram	–

Gender differences are also shown in the nouns that indicate relationships.

parent	mother	father
child	daughter	son

- Many nouns denoting an occupation have no explicit gender.

engineer	doctor	programmer
mechanic	lawyer	driver

Some occupations and professions have a special feminine form for the noun.

> Call your bank **manager** today.
> Sue is **manageress** of a hairdressing salon.
> **Authors** from all over the UK attended the ceremony.
> Here in the studio to talk about her new book is **authoress** Mary Farrell.

Many people prefer to avoid these forms, regarding the distinction as unnecessary.

> J.K. Rowling is a highly successful **author**.
> Judi Dench is one of our finest **actors**.
> Michelle Stewart has been promoted to Branch **Manager**.

Some speakers prefer to use a different form of the word or an entirely different word in order to avoid a gender-marked noun.

> *the chairman*   *the chairperson*   *the chair*

If necessary, the gender of a common noun can be made clear by adding a descriptive term such as *woman* or *male/female*.

> *Would you prefer to see **a woman doctor**?*
> ***Male staff** should use locker room B.*

If we are discussing a country from an emotional, economic, or political viewpoint we sometimes use feminine gender.

> ***Poland** has made steady progress restructuring **her** economy.*

Showing possession through nouns

Possession can be shown in two ways:

> *The **man** was mending his **car**.*
> *The **car** was being mended by a **man**.*

– by adding -'s to a singular noun, or an irregular plural noun that does not end in -s.

> *one dog*   *one boy*   *several children*
> *the **dog's** bones*   *the **boy's** books*   *the **children's** toys*

– by adding -' to a plural noun.

> *more than one dog*   *more than one boy*
> *the **dogs'** bones*   *the **boys'** books*

There is also the **of possessive** (a phrase with *of* followed by a noun).

> *the side **of the ship***   *the end **of the queue***

The **of possessive** is not just a different way of saying the same thing as the -'s possessive.

> *the **boy's** pencil*   **but not** *the pencil of the boy*

The -'s possessive is generally used only with nouns referring to animate items (e.g. people and animals) and in time phrases.

> *the **driver's** foot*   *the **dog's** nose*
> ***today's** newspaper*   *a **week's** holiday*

The *of* possessive is generally used with nouns referring to inanimate things (i.e. objects) and abstract ideas.

> the leg *of the table*   the arm *of the sofa*
> the wheel *of the car*   the foot *of the bed*
> the world *of ideas*   the power *of thought*

The function of the possessive form in English is to:

– show possession.

> the **boy's** books   the **dog's** blanket

– show a relationship, with a person either as the originator, or the user of the thing named.

> her **parents'** consent   the **student's** letter
> a **women's** club   the **children's** park

– indicate that a place is where someone works or lives.

> a **grocer's**   the **butcher's**
> a **solicitor's**   my **aunt's**

– show that something is a part of a whole.

> the leg *of the table*   the **dog's** nose
> the wheel *of the car*   the **girl's** shoulder

– add a descriptive element which premodifies a noun. It is a type of determiner. See also p. 164.

> **writer's** cramp   A **Winter's** Tale

Rules for the formation of the possessive -'s (apostrophe -s) and -s' (-s apostrophe) are as follows:

– most singular nouns add an apostrophe + -s.

   *a **girl's** ring*   *a **cat's** face*

– most plural nouns add an apostrophe after the plural form -s.

   *the **boys'** football*   *five young **girls'** faces*

There are exceptions for the following:

– common nouns that end in -s in the singular. When these are made plural the choice of -'s or a simple apostrophe is optional.

   a cactus   *the **cactus'** spines*
                                   *the **cactus's** habitat*

– plural nouns not ending in -s, for example those that that have a plural ending in -en. In this case, add an apostrophe + s.

   children's   ***men's***

– proper nouns and common nouns that end in -s. These usually add -'s in the singular unless the final sound of the basic word is [-iz], in which case, a simple apostrophe is sufficient.

   *Mrs **Evans's** car*   *Mr **Jones's** fence*
   ***Keats's** poetry*   *the **Bates's** cat*
   *I like **Dickens's** novels*
   *Peter **Bridges'** car*

Compound nouns (see p. 155) put the -'s or the simple apostrophe at the end of the complete compound.

> *my mother-in-law*　　　*my **mother-in-law's** car*
> *the runner-up*　　　　　*the **runner-up's** trophy*
> *the fire-fighters*　　　　*the **fire-fighters'** efforts*

Noun phrases that are descriptive of someone's role or profession put the -'s on the headword of the phrase.

> *a **stock market analyst's** annual income*
> *the **senior hospital consultant's** weekly visit*

If they use an *of* construction the -'s or simple apostrophe usually goes on the last noun.

> *the **President of Austria's** official car*
> *the **director of marketing's** personal assistant*

Compound nouns

A compound noun is a noun that is formed from two or more words. The meaning of the whole compound is often different from the meaning of the two words on their own. Compound nouns are very common. The main noun is normally the last one.

tea**pot**	head**ache**
washing **machine**	driving **licence**
self-**control**	CD **burner**

Compound nouns are commonly formed from the following word combinations:

- noun + noun,
- verb + noun,
- adjective + noun,
- phrasal verb used as noun,
- particle + noun.

noun + noun:	boyfriend	skinhead
verb + noun:	breakfast	grindstone
adjective + noun:	software	hardware
phrasal verb:	a break-in	a take-over
particle + noun:	onlooker	aftershave

> The term **particle** is used for a word which could be either an adverb or a preposition.

Compound nouns can be written:

– as one word.

bookcase   wallpaper
birdcage   snowflake

– as two words.

post office   fire engine
eye shadow   cough sweets

– with a hyphen.

window-cleaner   air-conditioning
lamp-post   tee-shirt

Consult a dictionary to discover how the word is normally written. There are often alternative forms to be found, for example, *drop down menu*, *drop-down menu*, and *dropdown menu* are all currently acceptable forms of the same compound noun.

Nouns as modifiers

The compound noun *girlfriend* names a special sort of *friend*. Nouns can also be used as **modifiers** without forming a compound noun.

a **concrete** slab   old **oak** beams
a **car** mechanic   a **store** manager

A noun that is used as a modifier has the same function as an adjective. The first noun usually makes the second one more specific, but we do not think of it as part of a combination that forms a new word. See p. 190 for more on modifiers.

Number in nouns

Singular number is used when the noun refers to one item.
Plural number is used when the noun refers to more than one item.

Countable nouns have both singular and plural forms.

Uncountable nouns and **mass nouns** do not normally have a plural form. See p. 140 for more on the types of noun.

The regular plural ending of an English noun is -*s*.

cat	*cats*

These are the exceptions to the normal pattern:

singular noun ending	*plural noun ending*
-s, -ss, -ch, -x, -zz *focus* *princess* *church* *box* *buzz*	**-es** *focuses* *princesses* *churches* *boxes* *buzzes*
-o *hero* *piano* *potato*	**-s** or **-es** *heroes* *pianos* *potatoes*
consonant + y *baby* *hobby*	**-ies** *babies* *hobbies*
vowel + y *key* *ray*	**-s** *keys* *rays*

singular noun ending	plural noun ending
-f hoof dwarf thief roof	–s or –ves hoofs or hooves dwarfs or dwarves thieves roofs
-fe knife life	-ves knives lives

Irregular plurals

Some nouns have two plural forms.

fish	fish or fishes

Some of them have the same form in the singular and plural.

a sheep	ten sheep
a deer	seven deer

A few change a vowel to form the plural.

man	men
woman	women
foot	feet
mouse	mice

Some nouns form the plural with -en.

child	children
ox	oxen

Since it is not possible to give more than a selection of the irregular forms, you should check in a dictionary if you are in doubt. If the dictionary does not show the plural form, then you can assume that it is regular.

Compound nouns normally form the plural by adding -*s* to the last word of the compound.

a games console	*three games consoles*
a bookcase	*two bookcases*
an Indian take-away	*two Indian take-aways*

There are a few exceptions:

A compound noun formed from a noun and an adverb makes the first word plural.

a passer-by	*several **passers-by***

Compound nouns with *woman* as the first word make both words plural.

a woman doctor	*several **women** doctors*
a woman driver	*most **women** drivers*

A compound word which ends in -*ful* normally adds -*s* after -*ful*, but there is an alternative form with the -*s* following the base noun.

a cupful	*three **cupfuls/cupsful***
a spoonful	*two **spoonfuls/spoonsful***

Plural nouns with singular reference

Some nouns referring to clothes and tools where two equal parts are joined together, e.g. *trousers*, *binoculars*, and *tongs*, are treated as being plural and are followed by a verb in the plural.

*My shorts **are** dirty.*
*The scissors **are** on the table.*

To talk about one of these items we can use the expression *a pair of...*

*John bought **a pair of jeans**.*

To talk about more than one we talk about however many *pairs of...*

*Martina bought **five pairs of tights**.*

- When they are used as ordinary numbers, words such as *dozen* and *million* have no plural form.

  nine million stars   **two dozen** glasses

  When they are used to mean a large number, they do have a plural form, which can be used as a partitive.

  *There are **millions** of pebbles on the beach.*
  *I saw **dozens** of children in the playground.*

Foreign plurals

Nouns that have come into English from foreign languages can:

- keep the plural form of the language they come from.

  an axis   *two axes*
  a crisis   *two crises*

- have plurals formed according to the rules for plural in English.

  a thesaurus   *several thesauruses*
                          (instead of thesauri)

– have two plurals: one from the foreign language and the other
  formed according to the rules for plural formation in English.
  The foreign plural is usually kept for scientific or specialized use.

an index	*some indexes/indices*
a formula	*some formulas/formulae*

Verbal nouns

The **verbal noun** is the *-ing* form, i.e. the present participle of the verb, used as a noun. It can be used in all the places that a noun can be used, but still keeps some characteristics of the verb. It is sometimes called the **gerund**.

> The **screaming** of the brakes terrified me.
> **Smoking** is prohibited.

The verbal noun normally functions as an uncountable noun, as above. However, there are some uses of the verbal noun that can be preceded by an indefinite article or used in the plural.

> He gave **a reading** from his latest volume of poetry.
> The **takings** were down this week in the shop.

The verbal noun can be preceded by the definite article, by adjectives, and by possessives.

> Her marvellous **singing** won Helen the scholarship.

Just like any noun, the verbal noun can function:

– as a **subject**.

> **Driving** was impossible.

– as the **complement** of the verb *be*.

> **Seeing** is **believing**.
> His greatest pleasure is **working**.

– as an **object** after certain verbs. See also p. 134.

> Louisa likes **swimming** but Helen prefers **diving**.

- after **prepositions** to make a prepositional phrase.

  *Can you watch them **without laughing**?*

Verbal nouns are also used:

- after some phrasal verbs such as: *be for/against, give up, keep on, look forward to, put off*.

  *She was all for **leaving** immediately.*
  *Linda gave up **swimming** but she kept on **dieting**.*
  *They were looking forward to **writing** home.*

- after certain set expressions such as: *can't stand, can't help, it's no use/good*.

  *I can't stand **waiting** around.*
  *I can't help **getting** cross.*
  *It's no use **crying** over spilt milk.*

The **possessive determiner** can be used with the verbal noun, especially in formal English.

  *Anna left the house without **my knowing**.*

- The verbal noun also has:

- a perfect form: *having ...ed*.

  *Martin was accused of **having cheated**.*

- a passive form: *being ...ed*.

  ***Being asked** did not bother me.*

- a perfect passive form: *having been ...ed*.

  *The car showed no sign of **having been touched**.*

Determiners

Determiners are words that make the reference of nouns more specific. If I say '*this car*' it is clear that I mean a particular car which is near me. If I change it to '*my car*' I am saying something quite specific about ownership.

Determiners can be divided into several kinds according to:

– their meaning.

– what they may go with and where they may come in the noun phrase.

There are eight classes of determiner:

– the indefinite article *a* or *an*. See p. 166.

> *A man came into the shop.*
> *An honest person would return the car to the owner.*

– the definite article *the*. See p. 168.

> *The dog chased the rabbit.*

– the demonstratives *this*, *that*, *these*, *those*. See p. 172.

> *This book is better than that one.*
> *These apples are redder than those ones.*

– the possessives *my*, *your*, *his*, *her*, *its*, *our*, *their*. See p. 213.

> *I gave my share to her sister.*
> *Shona found his book in her car.*

- the quantifiers *some*, *any*, *enough*, *no*, *all*, *both*, *half*, *double*, *several*, *much*, *many*, *more*, *most*, *few*, *fewer*, *fewest*, *a few*, *little* (meaning not much), *less*, *least*, *a little*. See pp. 175–181.

    *I've got **some** coffee but I haven't got **any** sugar.*
    *Have you got **much** money on you?*
    *There were **no** witnesses to the accident.*
    ***Both** girls saw the attack.*
    ***Few** people know the answer to that.*
    *The safety net gives **little** help to those who need it most.*

- the numbers, cardinal (*one*, *two*, *three*...), and ordinal (*first*, *second*, *third*...). See p. 180.

    *There's **one** thing I need to ask you.*
    *The **two** boys grew up together in Manhattan.*
    ***Three** men were found hiding in the building.*
    *Their **second** child is due in October.*
    *She lost in the **third** round of the tournament.*

- the distributives *each*, *every*, *either*, *neither*. See p. 182.

    ***Each** child received a book.*
    ***Every** girl was given a number to wear.*
    ***Either** book should help you with the problem.*

- the exclamatives *what*, *such*. See p. 184.

    ***What** nonsense!*
    ***What** a shame!*
    *They make **such** a fuss over small things!*

Generally, a noun phrase has only one determiner in it, or none at all. See p. 164. A few determiners, e.g. *all*, *both*, and the numbers, can be used together with another determiner. See p. 164.

The indefinite article

The indefinite article is *a* or *an*. The form *an* is used before a word that starts with a vowel sound.

> *a girl*   *a cat*
> *an eight-year-old girl*   *an engineer*

The indefinite article is used with singular countable nouns:

– to refer to a person or a thing that you are mentioning for the first time in a conversation or a piece of writing.

> *A man was seen driving away in a black car.*

– to refer to a person or a thing which you do not want to be specific about.

> *I stopped off at a shop to buy a newspaper.*
> *You go past a petrol station on the left, and then you'll see our house on the right.*

– to refer to a person or a thing which you cannot be more specific about because there is not enough information.

> *A man called to see you this afternoon.*
> *There was a telephone call for you a minute ago.*

– in definitions.

> *An octopus is a sea creature with eight tentacles.*

– when you refer to a person's profession.

> *Her father is a dentist and her mother is a teacher.*

– to express a quantity, unless you wish to emphasize the number, when *one* must be used. The equivalent for plural nouns is *some* or no determiner at all. See p. 164.

> *I want **a** needle and **a** thimble.*
> *Would you like **a** glass of wine?*
> *There is only **one** glass of wine left in the bottle.*
> *Guy has bought **a** skateboard.*
> *We've got three pairs of rollerblades and **one** skateboard.*

It is the sound, not the spelling, that decides where *an* is used. For example, although *unique* begins with a vowel, the sound at the beginning resembles a y- sound.

> *an idiot*   *an awful mistake*
> *a unicorn*   *a unique experience*

There are a few words that begin with a silent *h-*, in front of which *an* should be used. They are: *heir, heiress, honest, honour, hour.*

• Very formal or old-fashioned speakers also use the *an* form with some words beginning with an *h-* that is not silent, especially *historical* and *hotel*.

> *I waited **an** hour.*
> *They joined **a** historical society.*
> *They joined **an** historical society.*   (old-fashioned English)
> *They were staying at **a** hotel.*
> *They were staying at **an** hotel.*   (old-fashioned English)

The definite article

The definite article is *the*.

The definite article is used with singular and plural nouns. It is used both with countable nouns and uncountable nouns:

– to make definite or specific reference to a person or a thing that has already been referred to.

> *There's **the** man I was telling you about!*

– to refer to a person or thing that is already specific because of what those talking already know. In the first example below, '*the children*' would be members of our family and '*the swimming pool*' is the swimming pool we normally go to.

> *Let's take **the** children to **the** swimming pool.*
> *Did you switch **the** heating on?*
> *There were drinks in **the** fridge but **the** beer was soon finished.*

– to generalize about a whole class or species, usually of plants or animals. A singular noun is used for this purpose. The first example means '*The elephant species is hunted.*'

> ***The** elephant is still hunted for its tusks.*
> ***The** snowdrop is the first flower to arrive in the new year.*

– when it is followed by an adjective used as a noun indicating nationality or when generalizing about a whole class of people. *The Dutch* in the first example means '*Dutch people in general*'.

> ***The Dutch** are very skilful engineers.*
> ***The poor** were crowding the streets of the capital.*
> ***The homeless** were sheltered in the church.*

– before the names of rivers, groups of islands, seas, oceans, and mountain ranges.

> **The** *Thames*   **The** *Hebrides*
> **The** *North Sea*   **The** *Pacific*

– before the names of certain public institutions, most newspapers, and some magazines.

> **The** *British Museum*   **The** *Hilton Hotel*
> **The** *Lyceum Theatre*   **The** *Houses of Parliament*
> **The** *Independent*   **The** *Guardian*
> **The** *Listener*   **The** *New Scientist*

– before parts of the body when these are referred to in an impersonal way.

> *A stone struck him on* **the hand**.
> *Martin hit him on* **the head**.

• The definite article is rarely used with titles. Proper nouns that refer to persons, such as *Sue* and *Ron*, and proper nouns used in conjunction with titles, such as *Queen Elizabeth*, *Doctor Thomas*, and *Captain Parry*, only take a definite article if:

– they stand for the name of a thing such as a boat.

> **The** *Queen Elizabeth II is on a long cruise*.

– a distinction is being made between people who have identical names. This use can give emphasis to the noun.

> *Ah, no.* **The David Parry I know** *lives in Manchester*.
> *I saw Paul Kay in town this morning. – Not* **the** *Paul Kay?*

Nouns used without a determiner

Certain noun phrases do not have a determiner at all.

We usually leave out the determiner when we use a noun or a noun phrase in the plural to make a generalization.

> He sells **cars** for a living.
> **Tigers** are nearing extinction.
> **Onions** are good for you.
> **Grassy hills** rise on all sides of the town.

Singular nouns that are uncountable are used without a determiner when you are making a general reference.

> New **information** is now available.
> Do you like **jelly**?
> This shop sells **furniture**.

- This is particularly true when the uncountable noun is used for the first time in a general way in the course of a conversation or piece of writing. They can be used with a determiner when the reference becomes specific. For example, you can ask someone if they like *cake* as a rule, and then ask the person if she would like some of *your cake*.

  > **The** information she gave me was inaccurate.
  > Would you like some of **the jelly** I made for the party?
  > We don't let the dog climb onto **the** furniture.

There are a number of idiomatic expressions that usually omit a determiner. Examples are expressions that refer to:

- travel, when you proceed **by**: *bicycle, car, bus, train, ship, boat, plane*.

  > Anna went **by bicycle** but Lucy went **by car**.
  > He was chased by police **on foot**.

– time with the prepositions *at*, *before*, or *by*, *dawn, sunrise, sunset, noon, midnight, night, supper, dinner, day, night*.

> *Catherine rose **at dawn** and went to bed **at sunset**.*
> *We swam in the pool **by day** and partied **by night**.*

– meals: to have *breakfast, tea, lunch*.

> *Jane had **breakfast** at home.*
> *She met Diana **for lunch**.*

– institutions, with the prepositions *to* or *at*: *church, hospital, prison, school, work*.

> *John was taken **to hospital** with a broken ankle.*
> *Lucy has been kept late **at school** today.*
> *Ruth was **at home** all day.*

– seasons of the year, when you are generalizing, e.g: *in spring, in summer, in autumn, in winter*.

> ***In autumn**, the grapes are harvested by hand.*
> *The place is packed **in summer**.*

However, all of these words are used with the definite article when you are talking about a specific time, place, season, etc.

> *Philip travelled by **the same train** as Mehandra.*
> *Just look at **the wonderful sunset**.*
> *Pam works at **the hospital**.*
> *I can't work well **in the summer**.*

Demonstratives

Demonstratives are used to specify the distance of something in space or time in relation to the speaker.

The **demonstratives** are: *this*, *that*, *these*, *those*.

This and *these* refer to objects near the speaker.

> *This apple looks ripe.*
> *These apples come from Australia.*

The reference may be nearness in time, especially future time.

> *I'll call round this afternoon.*
> *The festival ends this Thursday.*
> *This summer is the warmest I can remember.*

That and *those* refer to objects that are further away from the speaker.

> *I think that boy over there is lost.*
> *Can you see those people up on the hill?*

This and *that* are used before singular countable nouns and uncountable nouns.

> *I can touch this picture, but I can't reach that one.*
> *This book is mine, but that magazine isn't.*

These and *those* are used before plural countable nouns.

> *I'm peeling these potatoes for a shepherd's pie.*
> *Those men are mending the roof.*

Possessives

Possessives are used to specify the ownership of an item, or, if the noun refers to something animate, to specify a relationship.

> *That is **my** car.*
> *Mr Smith was **my teacher** in the sixth form.*

The form of the possessive changes according to the number and gender of the person or thing that possesses the item.

> ***His brothers** all came to the wedding.*
> ***Their aunt** lives in London, but **their cousins** live in Berlin.*
> ***Your shoes** are under **your bed**.*

person	singular	plural
1st	my	our
2nd	your	your
3rd (masculine)	his	their
3rd (feminine)	her	their
3rd (neuter)	its	their

Possessive determiners, which can go into a noun phrase, are not the same as possessive pronouns (*mine, hers, yours,* etc.), which can stand alone. See p. 148.

Another sort of possessive is the **possessive phrase**.

This acts just like a possessive word but is a noun or noun phrase ending in -'s or -s'. A possessive phrase acts as a possessive determiner, but may itself include one of the other determiners.

Robert's mother

the *visitors'* washroom

a good *day's* work

the Prime *Minister's* press secretary

Sally's new job

the *residents'* dining room

my *wife's* cousin

Quantifiers

Quantifiers are used to indicate the amount or quantity of something referred to by a noun. They are different from numbers because they indicate an approximate amount rather than an exact amount. They can be grouped according to their use.

all, some, any, much, enough, no

– You can use *all*, *some*, *any*, or *enough*, before a plural countable noun or an uncountable noun.

> *Can I have some chips, please?*
> *Anna gave me all her money.*
> *Peter never has any time to visit us.*

You can use *no* before a singular or a plural countable noun or an uncountable noun.

> *There were no pictures of the party.*
> *There is no hospital in this town.*
> *No information has been released yet.*

– *Some*, *any*, *much*, and *enough* are used to refer to a part of the item.

> *Would you like some ice cream?*
> *We didn't have much success.*
> *I haven't seen enough evidence to convince me.*
> *I couldn't find any fresh milk at the shop.*

All and *no* refer to the whole of the item.

> *All the milk has been used.*
> *There is no milk in the fridge.*

– *Some* is used in positive sentences.

> *I've bought **some** chocolate.*
> *I saw **some** lovely shoes in town this morning.*

– *Any* is used in negative sentences.

> *I didn't buy **any** chocolate this week.*
> *I haven't seen **any** birds in the garden today.*

• In questions, *any* is used when there is no particular expectation about the answer; *some* is used when the answer is expected to be positive.

> *Have you got **any** fresh bread?*
> *Has Paul heard **any** news about the accident?*
> *Would you like **some** cake, Aisha?*

• The use of *no* with *there is/are* is very common.

> ***There was no post** today.*
> *There are **no jobs** available for electricians at the moment.*

half, double, both

– *Half* can be used with countable nouns and with uncountable nouns.

> ***Half** the time I didn't understand what was going on.*
> ***Half** the students came from overseas.*

– *Double* is used with uncountable nouns.

> *We're going to need **double the present supply** of water.*
> *They want **double the money** they originally asked for.*

– *Both* is used to define two things represented by a plural countable noun.

> ***Both men*** *were given another chance.*
> ***Both dogs*** *had to be put down.*

See p. 165 for more information about quantifiers when they are used with other determiners.

The following quantifiers are used to express **graded** amounts of an item (e.g. whether there is more or less of something).

> *Have you seen **many tourists** in town?*
> *Yes, I've seen **more tourists** than usual.*
> *I think **most tourists** just stay for a couple of days.*

> *I didn't put **much petrol** in the car.*
> *I think we need **more petrol**.*
> *The news caused **much excitement**.*
> ***Most information*** *about our services is available on the Internet.*

– *Many*, *more*, *most* are used with graded quantities of plural countable nouns.

> *Have you seen **many tourists** in town?*
> *Yes, I've seen **more tourists** than usual.*
> *I think **most tourists** just stay for a couple of days.*

– *Much*, *more*, *most* are used with graded quantities of uncountable nouns.

> *I didn't put **much petrol** in the car.*
> *I think we need **more petrol**.*
> *The news caused **much excitement**.*
> ***Most information*** *about our services is available on the Internet.*

- *Few*, *fewer*, *fewest* are used with graded quantities of plural countable nouns.

  > *Few people* know the answer to this problem.
  > *Fewer loans* are being granted than usual.
  > Japanese workers take *the fewest holidays*.

- *Little*, *less*, *least* are used with graded quantities of uncountable nouns.

  > There is *little chance* of rain today.
  > This technique causes *less harm* to the environment.
  > I need to get from one place to another with *the least inconvenience*.

- *A few*, and *a little* are different from *few* and *little* on their own because they have a positive sense. *Few* means 'not many',

  > *Few buildings* survived the earthquake.

  but *a few* means 'several'.

  > *A few kind people* helped the injured man.
  > *A few delays* are inevitable.

  Little means 'not much',

  > The students were given very *little help* with their projects.
  > Edward got *little encouragement* from his parents.

  but *a little* means 'some'.

  > I need *a little help* from my friends.
  > Everyone needs *a little encouragement* now and then.
  > Do you take sugar? – Just *a little*, please.

Few and *little* are often used in a negative sense to suggest disappointment or pessimism, while *a few* and *a little* are used in a positive sense to suggest that things are better than they might have been.

Numbers

There are two common kinds of number:

Cardinal numbers are used in all forms of counting that involve a total.

> *one* chair   *two* chairs
> *a hundred* people   *ten thousand* pounds

Ordinal numbers are used to talk about where something is placed in an ordered sequence. They are often used right after the definite article or after a possessive.

> *The first* horse in was disqualified.
> *He's celebrating **his fifty-first** birthday in August.*
> *The company has just celebrated **its one hundred and fiftieth** anniversay.*

Ordinals are mostly formed by adding *-th* to a cardinal number.

> *fourth*   *twentieth*   *hundredth*
> *fifth*   *forty-ninth*   *millionth*
> *sixth*   *eighty-sixth*   *thousandth*
> *nine hundred and ninety ninth*

Some examples of exceptions are the words *first*, *second*, and *third*, and combinations which contain them, such as *twenty-first*.

Cardinal numbers can be used at the beginning of a noun phrase, like determiners.

> *one* chair   *two* chairs
> *a hundred* people   *ten thousand* pounds

or on their own, like pronouns.

> *And then there were **three**.*
> ***Four** of them came towards us.*
> *The other **two** went to get help.*

- Grammatically speaking, the words *next*, *last*, and *another* can also be regarded as ordinal numbers.

> *It rained on **last** day of our holiday.*
> *The **next** horse in was declared the winner.*
> *Oh no, not **another** birthday!*

Ordinal numbers and the words *next* and *last* are sometimes called **postdeterminers**, since they come after the word *the* or a possessive .

> *The **next** three days are going to be very exciting.*
> *The **last** three years have been difficult for everyone.*
> *We have to get off the bus at the **next** stop.*

- An ordinal, as well as *next*, *last*, and *another*, can be used together with a cardinal number in the same noun phrase.

> *The **first three** correct entries will win a prize.*
> *He scored **another three** goals before the end of the match.*

- To show that a cardinal number is only approximate, the word, *some* is often used before it.

> ***Some two hundred** people gathered in the pouring rain.*

Distributives

Distributives are determiners that are used to talk about how something is shared out or divided.

The distributives are *each*, *every*, *either*, and *neither*. They are used with a singular noun.

> *Each child was given a balloon.*
> *I remember **every detail** of our conversation.*
> *Either child could win the prize.*
> *Neither plan was successful.*

– *Each* and *every* are not used with proper nouns.

– *Each* is used to refer to separate persons or things in a group of two or more.

> *Four girls came and **each one** sang a song.*
> *Each ticket should have a number on the back.*

– *Every* is used to refer to all the persons or things in a group of three or more.

> *Every teacher has a key to the building.*
> *Katrina danced with **every boy** at the party.*

– *Every* can be used in front of ordinal numbers. 'Every second house' means *the second house, the fourth house, the sixth house*, and so on.

> *I have to work **every third weekend**.*
> *Every fourth house has a garage.*

– **Either** is used to talk about one of two people or things.

> They did not appoint **either** man as captain.
> **Either** restaurant would suit me.

– **Neither** is used to exclude both of two people or things that are being referred to.

> They appointed **neither** man as captain.
> **Neither** restaurant is cheap enough.

Exclamatives

Exclamatives are used to introduce an exclamation of surprise, admiration, or a similar emotion.

The exclamatives are: *what*, *such*.

Exclamations introduced by one of these words consist either of:

– the exclamative in a noun phrase alone (usually with *What*...).

> *What a laugh!*
> *What awful weather!*

– the exclamative and its noun phrase in a complete clause.

> *He is **such** a nice man!*
> *You always wear **such** lovely things!*
> *What a pleasant surprise this is!*

Noun phrases with several determiners

Most noun phrases contain only one determiner or none at all, but if there are more, they follow a definite order. Determiners can be divided into four groups, depending on what other determiners they can be used with and the order that they follow.

There are two large groups:

A *the, this, these, that, those, a(n)*, and the possessives *my, your, her, his*, etc.

> *a* ripe orange *my* young sister
> *this* ripe orange *our* young sister

B *another, some, any, no, either, neither, each, enough, a few, a little*.

> *each* ripe orange *another* sister
> *some* ripe oranges *enough* money

The words in groups A and B are known as the **central determiners**. A noun phrase will normally contain only one central determiner.

- The group A and group B words cannot be used together, with the exception that words in group B may be followed by a group A word if *of* is placed between them.

> *some* **of** *those* oranges *neither* **of** *my* sisters

- Words in group A can be used in combination with determiners in groups C and D (below).

> *Both* girls were reading.
> *Both my* young sisters are really naughty.
> *All* visitors must now leave the ship.
> *All the* visitors left the ship.

There are two smaller groups.

C The smallest group consists of the words: *all*, *both*, *half*, *double*, and *twice*. These can be used on their own before a noun or before the group A determiners above. Some speakers of English prefer to insert *of* between *all*, *both*, or *half* and a central determiner.

> *All of the visitors left the ship.*
> *Half of the oranges will have to be thrown away.*

- The words in group C are sometimes called **predeterminers**. The exclamatives *such* and *what* belong to this group. See p. 184 for more details about these.

D The words in the fourth group are, *every*, *many*, *several*, *few*, *little*, *much*, *more*, *most*, *less*, the ordinal numbers *first*, *second*, *third* etc., and *last*. These can be used on their own before a noun,

> *Every move was carefully recorded.*
> *She did many kind things.*
> *She has few friends.*
> *Last orders, please.*

or after the A group of determiners.

> *Your every move is being watched.*
> *The many kind things she did went unnoticed.*
> *Her few possessions had been stolen.*
> *The first thing she did was call her mother.*
> *I would rather forget these last few days.*

Adjectives

Adjectives are used with nouns to make the meaning more specific. If you use the noun '*bear*' it can mean any animal of that species. As soon as you say '*a large, brown bear*' you have given two of its **attributes** (colour and size). A noun is said to be **modified** by its adjectives.

Adjectives have two main features:

– Most adjectives can go before a noun; this is known as their **attributive** use.

> *a **tall** girl*
> ***green** grass*
> *four **badly behaved little** boys*

– Most adjectives can also go after a link verb such as *be* or *seem*; this is known as their **predicative** use.

> *The roses are **yellow**.*
> *The girls are getting **tall**.*
> *These books seem really **interesting**.*

Any word that can go into both of these positions is a normal adjective. When used predicatively (after a link verb), an adjective can either describe the **subject** of a sentence,

> *The roses are **yellow**.*
> *The girls are getting **tall**.*
> *These books are really **interesting**.*

or the **object** of the sentence. See also p. 15.

> *Anna painted the room **green**.*
> *The children drove him **mad**.*

Adjective order

The order is normally:

– adjectives that describe feelings or qualities.

> **pleasant** *childhood memories*
> **beautiful** *brown hands*

– adjectives of size, age, temperature, or measurement.

> *some* **hot** *scones*
> *a* **rectangular** *pie dish*
> *those* **nice young** *girls*
> *a* **lovely big** *smile*

– adjectives of colour.

> *the* **green** *hills of home*
> *smart* **brown** *shoes*
> *her beautiful* **blue** *eyes*

– adjectives of nationality or origin.

> *those friendly* **Spanish** *girls*
> *both the small grey* **Irish** *horses*
> *an elegant* **French** *woman*

– adjectives denoting the substance or material that something is made from.

> *a large* **wooden** *door*
> *an elegant* **silver** *teapot*

It is possible to pile up adjectives in English, but in practice more than four is uncommon.

> *a happy young blonde German girl*
> *beautiful old English half-timbered houses*

- Adjectives before a noun are not usually separated by *and*, unless they are adjectives of colour.

> *a green and white striped shirt*
> *a red and blue flag*

- Adjectives can themselves be premodified by adverbs of degree. See also p. 190.

> *an extremely intelligent student*
> *a very tall man*
> *a fairly untidy flat*

Some adjectives can only be used predicatively (i.e. after a link verb such as *be*). Many of the members of this group begin with *a-*:

> *afloat, afraid, alike, alive, alone, ashamed, asleep, awake.*

> *Our balloon was aloft at last.*
> *Charles is abroad again.*
> *The child is afraid.*
> *The girls were asleep and were not aware of the noise.*

When an adjective is used predicatively it may have to be followed by a particular preposition if the phrase continues.

> *She was glad.*   *She was glad to help.*
> *He was afraid.*   *He was afraid for his life.*
> *I was free.*   *I was free from guilt.*
> *It is devoid of interest.*   *He was intent on revenge.*

There are some adjectives such as *devoid (of)*, *intent (on)* that always have to have a following phrase.

Although attributive adjectives usually come before the noun that they modify, there are some that can go immediately after the noun, particularly when they are used with plural nouns, e.g. *absent*, *present*, *involved*, *concerned*. When these adjectives are used in this position they may have a different meaning from the one that they have when they come before the noun.

> *Everyone **present** was given tea.*
> *The **present government** took over four years ago.*
> *The **people absent** from work were all ill.*
> *Let us toast **absent friends**.*
> *The **dealers concerned** were sent to jail.*
> *There were letters from **concerned parents**.*

- There are some set phrases which always have an adjective immediately after the noun.

> *the **Princess Royal***   *a **lion rampant***
> *the **president elect***   *the **Attorney General***

Premodifiers and postmodifiers

Adjectives, determiners, and other nouns can all be used to describe a noun more specifically; that is, they can be used as **modifiers**. Nouns can also be modified by prepositional groups (groups of words that begin with a preposition) and relative clauses added after the noun. See p. 274 for more about relative clauses.

To make it simpler to talk about any modifying word which comes in front of a noun, we can use the term **premodifier**.

> *a **young** man*   ***these** onions*
> ***my aunt's** house*   *the **elephant** house*

Those modifiers that come after the noun are called **postmodifiers**.

>*the young man **with the guitar***
>*the person **who met me***
>*the girl **I was standing near***
>*the people **involved***

Comparison

The **comparative** form of an adjective is commonly used to compare two people, things, or states, when you want to say that one thing has a larger or smaller amount of a quality than another.

- If the second part of the comparison is mentioned it follows **than**.

  *Anna is **taller than** Mary but Mary is **older**.*
  *Emma is much **slimmer than** when I last saw her.*
  *Online learning is **less expensive than** conventional college courses.*

- Comparison in which you are considering whether two people or things are equal is shown by using **as...as** in the affirmative and **not as...as** or **not so...as** in the negative.

  *Helen is **as tall as** Linda, but **not as strong**.*

The **superlative** form is used for more than two people, things, or states, when one thing has qualities that exceed all the others. Superlative adjectives have **the** in front of them, but it can be omitted in predicative positions.

  *That is **the smallest** camera I have ever seen.*
  *He gave **the least expensive** gift to his sister.*
  *I'll have whichever is **(the) ripest**.*

There are two ways in which the comparative and superlative forms of adjectives are formed:

- You add **-er** (comparative) or **-est** (superlative) to the adjective. Adjectives with one syllable usually take these endings.

	comparative	superlative
bright	brighter	the brightest
long	longer	the longest
sharp	sharper	the sharpest

- If the word already ends in *-e*, the *-e* must be left off. If a word ends in *-y*, it usually takes *-er* or *-est*, and the *-y* changes to *-i*.

	comparative	superlative
wise	wiser	the wisest
pretty	prettier	the prettiest
weary	wearier	the weariest

- You add the word *more* or *most* in front of the adjective. Adjectives with three syllables or more use *more* or *most* in front of the adjective.

	comparative	superlative
fortunate	more fortunate	the most fortunate
relevant	more relevant	the most relevant

Adjectives formed from participles use *more* or *most* as well.

	comparative	superlative
provoking	more provoking	the most provoking
enthralled	more enthralled	the most enthralled

To indicate the opposite of both the *-er/-est* and the *more/most* forms of comparison, *less* or *least* is always used.

	comparative	superlative
sharp	less sharp	the least sharp
fortunate	less fortunate	the least fortunate
interesting	less interesting	the least interesting
involved	less involved	the least involved

> Adjectives with two syllables (including those that already end in -er) can follow either pattern or sometimes both patterns. If you are doubtful about a two-syllable adjective, use the more/most pattern.

	comparative	superlative
shallow or	shallower more shallow	the shallowest the most shallow
polite or	politer more polite	the politest the most polite

A small group of irregular adjectives have quite different forms for the comparative and superlative forms.

	comparative	superlative
good	better	the best
bad	worse	the worst
far	further	the furthest

Adverbs and adverbials

When you want to add information about *how*, *when*, *where*, or *to what extent* something has happened, you can use an **adverbial**. Many adverbials are members of the group of words called **adverbs**, but adverbials are not necessarily just single words. They can also be word groups, prepositional phrases, or even clauses. They are sometimes called **adjuncts**.

Adverbials generally modify the meaning of a verb,

> I *greatly* admire your courage.
> They changed **hurriedly** into their pyjamas.
> Monica hummed **softly** as she washed the car.
> The firework exploded **with a loud bang**.
> He ran **across the lawn** towards the house.

an adjective,

> Harry is **absolutely** terrified of flying.
> You must admit that he can be **rather** boring.
> That is **quite** silly.
> Fears like that are **very** real to the sufferer.

another adverb,

> I thought about it **quite** seriously.
> The children are behaving **remarkably** well.
> Ali objected **very** strongly to the plan.

a whole sentence,

> **Frankly**, I think he is lying.
> **Nevertheless**, we must give him a chance.
> **Honestly**, I didn't mean to be rude to you.

or a prepositional phrase.

> *We are really in a no-win situation.*

Most adverbials are optional parts of a clause or phrase, but there are a few verbs that need an adverb to complete their meaning. See p. 85. Conditional sentences must also have an adverbial clause, usually one beginnining with *if* or *unless*. See p. 271 for more about adverbial clauses.

Adverbials can be divided into:

– adverbials of **manner**, which express *how*: e.g. *slowly, with care, well*.

> *Two men were working their way **slowly** up the hillside.*

– adverbials of **place**, which express *where*: e.g. *there, here, up, in town*.

> *Two men were working their way **up the hillside**.*

– adverbials of **time**, which express *when*: e.g. *now, today, last night, lately*.

> *Two men were lost on the hills **yesterday**.*

– adverbials of **degree**, which express *to what extent*: e.g. *largely, extremely, much, by a whisker*.

> *It was **largely** their own fault.*

– adverbials of **frequency**, which express *how often*: e.g. *rarely, often, sometimes, twice daily*.

> *Search parties went out **every hour**.*

Although adverbials change the meaning of clauses or phrases, they are usually optional parts of the group or clause.

> He coughed **nervously**.
> **Really**, I think you are mistaken.
> **In a fit of temper**, he slammed the door shut.

They stand outside the word, group, or clause that they are associated with. For example, the same adverb can in one sentence be part of the description of a verb, while in another sentence, it may modify the whole clause.

> I think she acted **honestly**.
> **Honestly**, who does she think she is?

The exceptions are that:

– Some verbs must be followed by an adverbial to complete their meaning.

> Alice behaved **wonderfully**.
> Sylvia acted **unlawfully**.
> Justin sped **down the corridor**.

– Some verbs require both an object and an adverbial to complete their meaning. See also p. 32.

> Ranjit put the folder **back**.
> James stood the golf clubs **in the corner**.
> Clare placed the cover **over the cot**.

• New meanings can be made by combining an adverbial with a verb to make a phrasal verb. See also p. 85 for more about phrasal verbs.

> The car **pulled out**.
> Lydia **went away**.
> Things **are looking up**.

Adverbials are classified according to the way they modify a word, group or clause. In addition to the uses given on p. 195, one important use of a special group of adverbials is to show how a sentence relates to what comes before it. An adverb used in this way is called a **sentence adverb**.

> *Nevertheless, we must give him an answer.*
> *However, it's good advice.*
> *On the other hand, we cannot turn him down.*

Another use of adverbials is to let your listener or reader know your point of view about a situation. This is called a **viewpoint adverb**.

> *Foolishly, I gave him my address.*
> *Clearly, he deserves our help.*
> *Actually, I don't mind.*

A further group of adverbials, all of them adverbs of degree, can only be used with adjectives or other adverbs. Examples are *very, rather, quite, really, too, somewhat*. These are sometimes called **submodifiers** because they can weaken or strengthen the descriptive value of the adjective.

> *She seems **rather** nice.*
> *Angus is a **very** good tennis player.*
> *Kim gave me this **really** expensive bag.*

They are used mainly with adjectives of quality. An adverb can also be submodified by another adverb.

> *She began to cry, **quite loudly**.*
> *Sometimes I think you're **too easily** impressed.*
> *It must have been done **extremely recently**.*
> *The car was **almost totally** submerged in the flood water.*

There are certain adverbs (and adverbials) which can only be used with verbs and so cannot modify adjectives.

- Most adverbs are able to come:

- before the verb phrase or the subject

  > *Happily she ran over the sand dunes.*
  > *Tearfully, he told his brother the whole story.*

- after the verb phrase or the object

  > *She ran **happily** over the sand dunes.*
  > *He was telling the whole story **tearfully** to his brother.*

- between the auxiliary and the main verb.

  > *She was **happily** running about over the sand dunes.*
  > *He was **tearfully** telling the whole story to his brother.*

- Some adverbs can only come **after** the verb, e.g. *back, up, down, sideways, clockwise.*

  > *Suddenly the frightened animal ran **back**.*
  > *They hammered the wedge in **sideways**.*

- A few adverbs can come **before** the main verb, e.g. *barely, hardly, little, rarely, scarcely, seldom.*

  > ***Scarcely** had she spoken when it came crashing down.*
  > *He **had hardly eaten** anything.*
  > ***Seldom** have I seen such ridiculous behaviour.*

A subordinate clause that begins with one of these words adopts the same word order as a question. These are called **broad negatives**, because they give a negative meaning to a clause.

Compare:

*They **never noticed** her presence.*
*They **scarcely noticed** her presence.*

> Some speakers take care not to place an adverb between the *to* and the **base form** of the verb in a '*to* **infinitive**'. This is called a 'split infinitive'. There is no good reason to regard a split infinitive as an error; the choice is a matter of personal preference.
>
> *I need to **really** think hard about this.*
> *I **really** need to think hard about this.*

Adverbs with nouns and pronouns

While **adverbs** can modify most parts of speech, they normally do not modify **nouns** or **pronouns**. Much more common is the use of an adverb of degree to modify a whole **noun phrase**.

*Dominic thought that Geoffrey was **rather a good teacher**.*
*Jason is **quite a skilled craftsman**.*

There is a small group of adverbs that can modify nouns and indefinite pronouns.

*the **man downstairs***
*the **example above***
***Almost everyone** brought a bottle to the party.*

Form of adverbs

Most **adverbs** are formed by adding *-ly* to the end of the related adjective.

slow	*slowly*
clever	*cleverly*
annual	*annually*

Exceptionally, words which end in *-ble* drop off the *-e* before *-ly* is added. So do the words *true* and *due*.

sensible	*sensibly*
suitable	*suitably*
true	*truly*
due	*duly*

A common spelling mistake is to add *-ley*. This mistake is often made when the adjective ends in the letter *-e*. Note the correct spelling of adverbs formed from adjectives ending in *-e*.

extreme	*extremely*
divine	*divinely*
free	*freely*

Adjectives that end in *-y* change to *-i* before adding *-ly*, unless, like *sly* or *dry*, they have only one syllable.

happy	*happily*
greedy	*greedily*
sly	*slyly*

Some adverbs keep the same spelling as the adjective to which they are related. It is often difficult to tell at first whether the word is an adjective or an adverb. The general rule is to look at the other words which it occurs with. If it comes before a noun it is probably an adjective.

> *a short way*   *a late meeting*
> *a long pause*   *an early lecture*

If it relates to a verb or an adjective it is probably an adverb.

> *The lesson **was cut short**.*
> *We **met late** at night.*
> *Don't **stay long**.*
> *He **came in early**.*

Some adverbs have the same spelling as a preposition. They can be told apart if you look at the words they are found with. Prepositions are normally used in front of noun phrases, because prepositions must have an object.

> *He rushed **in an attempt** to catch his bus.*
> *She hurried **over her meal** because she was late.*

When the word is found without an object, especially at the end of a clause, it will usually be an adverb.

> *He rushed **in**.*
> *She hurried **over**.*

Just like certain adjectives, some adverbs have comparative and superlative forms and can be used with submodifiers.

Kim treated Sharon **well**, Karen **less well** and Janice
   the least well.
Malcolm walked **the most slowly** of all of them.
Tariq acted **very kindly** towards him.
You must behave **far more sensibly** in future.
This graph shows that girls performed **the best** at maths
   this year.

Superlative forms of adverbs are quite rare.

Pronouns

A **pronoun** is a word that is used in the place of a noun or a whole noun phrase.

Pronouns are commonly used:

– in place of a noun or a noun phrase that has already been mentioned, when the repetition of the noun or noun phrase would be very strange.

> *Sam has to go to the airport. Can you give **him** a lift?*
> *The young prince and his wife came out on to the balcony.*
> *   **They** waved to the crowd.*
> *The mechanic tested the starter motor. **It** would not work.*
> *   **He** tried **it** again.*

– when we know perfectly well who or what is referred to. When, for example, I use the pronoun *I* it is because it would be unusual to refer to myself by name.

> *I'm sorry I'm late.*
> ***We**'d better ring and say **we**'re not coming.*

– when the name of someone or something is not known.

> ***He**'s the man who came to the house yesterday!*
> ***Who**'s she?*

Types of pronoun

There are seven different types of pronoun, classified according to their meaning and use.

The **personal** pronouns can be used as subject or object in a clause.

> *He gave her a box of chocolates.*
> *We saw them both on Friday.*
> *I can see you!*

The **reflexive** pronouns are used in object position when the action of a verb is performed on the subject by the subject. They are obligatory with certain verbs.

> *The puppy entangled itself in the lead.*
> *I've just cut myself on a piece of glass.*

Reflexive pronouns are also used for emphasis.

> *Never mind. I'll do it myself.*
> *The professor himself did not know the answer.*

The **possessive** pronouns indicate ownership.

> *Give it back, it's mine.*
> *Perhaps it really is theirs after all.*

The **demonstrative** pronouns indicate items that are near to or far from us.

> *This is Betty's and that is Peter's.*
> *These are nice. Where did you find them?*

The **relative** pronouns are used to link a modifying clause to a noun phrase or to a clause.

> *I don't know what you mean.*
> *That's the girl who always comes top.*

The **interrogative** pronouns are used to ask a question about the noun phrase they stand in for.

> *What would you like for lunch?*
> *Which is the fresh milk?*
> *Who was responsible?*

The **indefinite** pronouns are used for a broad range of reference when it is not necessary or not possible to use a personal pronoun.

> *Everyone had a compass and a whistle.*
> *Neither wanted to give in and apologize.*
> *Much needs to be done.*

Personal pronouns

Personal pronouns are used as the subject, object, or complement in a clause. They are commonly found taking the place of a noun phrase when it is mentioned for a second time.

person	subject	singular object	subject	plural object
1st	I	me	we	us
2nd	you	you	you	you
3rd masculine	he	him	they	them
3rd feminine	she	her	they	them
3rd neutral	it	it	they	them

We use the 1st person pronoun *I* to take the role of the speaker. The 2nd person pronoun *you* is used to take the role of the listener. In the case of *you*, there is only one pronoun to cover the singular and the plural, so that it is sometimes necessary to use a form of words that will make clear who is being addressed.

> *You should be ashamed.*
> *All of you should be ashamed.*
> *You must all stop writing now.*

When more than one personal pronoun is used with a verb, the order is normally: 3rd or 2nd person before 1st person; 2nd person before 3rd person.

> *She and I do not get on very well.*
> *You and he should buy the boat between you.*

When two pronouns or a personal noun and a personal pronoun are the joint subject of a verb, the subject form of the pronouns must be used. Avoid the common mistake of saying, for example, *Jerry and me are…*

> *Jerry and I are going to paint the house ourselves.*
> *He and I are going to paint it.*
> *Melanie and I are going shopping.*

When either two pronouns or a noun plus a personal pronoun are the joint object of a verb, the object form of the pronoun must be used:

> *They decided to help Jane and me.*

The object form of a pronoun is used after a preposition. Avoid the common mistake of saying, for example, *between you and I.*

> *Between you and me, I don't like this place.*
> *Wasn't that kind of me?*

The object form is usual in everyday spoken usage. In formal and old-fashioned English, the subject form is used:

– after the verb *be*.

> *It's me.*   Informal
> *It is I.*   Formal/old-fashioned
> *I saw at once that it was her.*   Informal
> *I saw at once that it was she.*   Formal/old-fashioned

– after *than* in comparison with *be*.

> *John is smaller than him.* Informal
> *John is smaller than he (is).* Formal/old-fashioned
> *Sylvia is cleverer than me.* Informal
> *Sylvia is cleverer than I (am).* Formal/old-fashioned

Otherwise, *than* + **object** pronoun is necessary.

> *She's probably done more than me.*

• The object form is also used to supply short answers to questions.

> *Who found Gran's watch? – Me. Aren't I clever!*

Reflexive pronouns

Reflexive pronouns are used:

person	singular	plural
1st	myself	ourselves
2nd	yourself	yourselves
3rd masculine	himself	themselves
3rd feminine	herself	themselves
3rd neuter	itself	themselves
General	oneself	

– when the speaker or writer is referring to an action that he or she has caused to happen and of which he or she is also the object.

> I cut **myself** with the carving knife.
> Sometimes I just don't like **myself** very much.

– when the direct object or prepositional object of a sentence has the same reference as the subject.

> John looked at **her**.
> John looked at **himself**.
> John taught **himself** to play the guitar.

The reflexive form **oneself** can be used to refer to people in general.

> The first golden rule is not to take **oneself** too seriously.

It can also be used as a substitute for the 1st person singular. If it is used like this, the subject pronoun should be **one**. In normal direct speech this usage is often felt to be rather pretentious.

> One asks **oneself** whether it is worth the bother.
> One owes it to **oneself** to do something worthwhile.

Some verbs take a reflexive pronoun only in particular uses of the verb.

> *Jeremy introduced **himself**.*
> *The cat washed **itself**.*

The reflexive pronoun can be left out if it is obvious that the subject was performing the action of the verb on him- or herself.

> *Jeremy **washed** and **dressed**, then went out.*

When a preposition is followed by a pronoun, the pronoun is normally in the object form.

> *They all looked at **him** in silence.*

If that pronoun refers to the subject of the main verb, however, it must be a reflexive pronoun.

> *She looked at **herself** in the mirror.*

- The reflexive can be used to make something you say stronger. To make a strong point, we sometimes use a normal subject or object pronoun and a reflexive pronoun as well.

> *He told me **himself** that he was leaving.*
> *I'll do it **myself**.*

- The reflexive can also be used with or without *by* meaning 'alone' or 'without help'.

> *I think you should try and do it **yourself**.*
> *Did she do that all by **herself**?*

The compound pronouns *each other* and *one another* are not true reflexives. They are used when two or more subjects mutually take part in an action. They are sometimes called **reciprocals**.

> *They should stop blaming one another.*
> *We will always love each other.*

Possessive pronouns

Possessive pronouns are used when you want to indicate who owns or is associated with an item.

> *All those books are **hers**.*
> *Those suitcases are **ours**.*
> *Are you selling those books? I'd never sell any **of mine**.*
> *Those awful cousins **of yours** are here.*
> *This TV is really cheap. – Yes, **ours** was a bit more expensive, but better quality.*

There are separate forms for the singular and the plural except in the 2nd person. In the 3rd person singular the form changes to match the gender of the possessor.

> *I'm looking for Helen's trainers. Perhaps these are **hers**.*
> *These are our seats and the ones in front are **yours**.*

possessive determiner	possessive pronoun
my	*mine*
your (singular)	*yours*
his	*his*
her	*hers*
its	*(no form)*
our	*ours*
your (plural)	*yours*
their	*theirs*

Note that none of these words should be spelled with an apostrophe. Avoid the common mistake of writing *it's* for the possessive form. *It's* is a short form for *it is*.

The demonstrative pronouns

The **demonstrative pronouns** are used instead of a noun phrase to indicate distance in time or space in relation to the speaker. They also indicate grammatical number – singular or plural.

	singular	plural
near	this	these
far	that	those

- Note that the demonstrative pronouns have the same spelling as demonstrative determiners. See also p. 164. Usually a demonstrative pronoun substitutes for a noun phrase that contains the same word being used as a determiner.

    Would you like to share some of this pizza with me?
    *Would you like to share **this** with me?*
    I'd like you to put these things away before we go.
    *I'd like you to put **these** away before we go.*

- It is regarded as impolite to use a demonstrative pronoun to refer directly to a person, except when making introductions.

    *John, **this** is Harry Forbes, my colleague.*
    ***This** is my husband, Rob.*
    *Mum, **this** is my form teacher, Miss Evans.*

Relative pronouns

The relative pronouns are the words *who*, *whom*, *which*, and *that*.

	person	thing
subject	**who** or *that*	**which** or *that*
object	**whom** or *that*	**which** or *that*
possessive	*whose*	*whose*

The function of a relative pronoun is to link a subordinate clause to a main clause.

> **He might lose his job,** *which would be disastrous.*
> *She promised* **to give away all the money,** *which was*
>   *a bit rash.*

A subordinate clause introduced by a relative pronoun is called a **relative clause**.

Relative pronouns refer back to a noun phrase or pronoun that has just been mentioned. All relative pronouns must come as near as possible to the start of the clause that they are in. The only words that normally come before them in the clause are prepositions or conjunctions.

The choice of relative pronoun is influenced as follows:

– *That* as a relative pronoun never has a preposition before it.

> *That is* **a kind thought,** *for which I am most grateful.*
> *This is* **the person** *that Annie was talking about.*
> *This is* **the person** *about whom Annie was talking.*

– *Which* is not used for human subjects or objects.

> *That is* **the car** *which she has just bought.*
> *I have found* **a ring** *which you will love.*

– *Who* and *whom* are restricted to human subjects or objects.

> *He introduced me to* **his friend,** *who had just returned from China.*
> *I liked* **the actor** *who was playing Oedipus.*

– In **defining** relative clauses (see p. 274), *that* can be used instead of *which* and is sometimes used instead of *who* or *whom*.

> *I have found* **a ring** *which you will love.*
> *I have found* **a ring** *that you will love.*
> *She is* **the girl** *who was at Sam's party.*
> *She is* **the girl** *that was at Sam's party.*

The **object** form of the relative pronoun is used as the object of a verb or a preposition, but because *whom* is very formal, it is not often used: in everyday English, *who* is usually used instead.

> *The late* **Principal** *of the College,* **whom** *we all remember with affection, left this bursary in her will.*

> *I discovered* **who** *he was visiting.*   neutral
> *I discovered* **whom** *he was visiting.*   formal

• In informal writing and speech, any **preposition** is placed after the verb phrase instead of before the relative pronoun.

> *The girl* **who** *Brian was talking* **to** *seemed nervous.*
> *The people* **who** *he had been working* **for** *that summer had offered him a permanent job.*

- In informal and spoken English, a defining relative pronoun referring to the object of the clause may be left out entirely.

    *He is the **person** (that/who/whom) Annie was talking about.*
    *That is the **car** (which/that) she has just bought.*

Interrogative pronouns

The **interrogative pronouns** *who*, *whom*, and *whose* are used only for reference to people. The interrogative pronouns *which* and *what* are used for reference to things.

	subject	object	possessive
people	who	whom	whose
things	which what	which what	

Interrogative pronouns allow us to build a question around the thing that the pronoun refers to. See p. 241, where they are explained more generally under the heading of **WH-** words.

> **Who** *is dancing with Lucy?*
> **Which** *of these books would you recommend?*
> **What** *do you do when you're on holiday?*
> **Whose** *are these clothes?*

Who is used to ask questions about people in general.

> **Who** *is that man over there?*
> **Who** *did this?*
> **Who** *controls the day-to-day running of the business?*

What is used to ask questions about things in general when the answer is an open one. **What** can be either a subject or an object in a clause.

> **What** *happened next?*
> **What** *did you have for lunch?*

Which is used ask for identification of a particular person or a particular thing in a group.

> *Which do you prefer, working in theatre or film?*
> *Which is your favourite Simpsons episode?*

Whose is the possessive form of the pronoun. It is used when a person is the possessor.

> *Whose is that sports car outside?*
> *Whose side are you on?*

- *Whom* is the object form of *who*. It is a very formal word and one which most speakers avoid using in casual conversation, when *who* could be used instead. When writing, however, it is usual to use *whom*.

  Informal
  > *Who do you have in mind?*
  > *Who were you speaking to?*

  Formal
  > *Whom have you in mind?*
  > *To whom were you speaking?*

- The object forms of the interrogative pronoun are used after a preposition. In informal and everyday usage, you can place the preposition at the end of the clause.

  > *Who does this belong to?*   Informal
  > *To whom does this belong?*   Formal

Indefinite pronouns

The indefinite pronouns are used when you do not know or do not need to say precisely who or what you are referring to. The noun phrase which they substitute for can refer to a person, a thing, or a group of people or things, in which gender and number are not made clear.

> *Someone will have to tell her that she's failed.*
> *Everybody had a wonderful time.*
> *Anything is better than nothing.*
> *Nothing can make up for this loss.*
> *Some people like that sort of thing.* *Others don't.*

The indefinite pronouns can be grouped according to meaning, as follows:

A General amounts and quantities: *most, some, none, any, all, both, half, several, enough, many, each.*

> *Many find it impossible to cope.*
> *Congratulations from all at the club.*
> *Judging by the comments, most wanted her to stay on.*
> *Although we lost a lot of stuff in the fire, some was saved.*
> *Enough has been said on this topic to fill a book.*

B Choice or alternatives: *either, neither.*

> *Could you bring me one of those spanners? Either will do.*
> *Neither was keen on a traditional wedding.*

C Undefined singular or multiple persons and things:

someone	*somebody*	*something*
no one	*nobody*	*nothing*
anyone	*anybody*	*anything*
everyone	*everybody*	*everything*

> Note the form of *no one* or, less usually, *no-one*.

- The pronouns in group C that refer to people can cause problems concerning the **number** and **gender** of a following determiner or pronoun. Traditionally, only the use of a following **singular** form was permitted. Common practice uses the plural form *their* and avoids awkward expressions like *his or her*.

> *Everybody* has **their** ups and downs.
> Has **anybody** finished **their** lunch yet?
> **No one** in **their** right mind goes on holiday there in January.

Many of these pronouns, especially those in groups A and B, have the same form as determiners. See p. 164.

- The way to tell them apart is to see if the word on its own is used as a subject, an object, or the complement of a verb; if it is, it is a **pronoun**. If, on the other hand, it is used in front of a noun, it is a **determiner**.

> As a pronoun:
> **Both** were given life sentences.
> **Several** managed to escape.
> I've found **some**!

> As a determiner:
> **Both men** were given life sentences.
> **Several sheep** managed to escape.
> I've found **some scrap paper**.

- The pronouns in Groups A and B are often used like partitives, with *of* and a noun phrase or a personal pronoun.

    None *of the children were hurt, but* ***most*** *of them were rather upset.*
    Neither *of his parents remarried.*

Prepositions

A preposition is one of a small but very common group of words that relate different items to each other. Most English prepositions have a number of meanings that are particular to each preposition.

Simple prepositions consist of one word, e.g. *in*, *on*, *under*. Complex prepositions consist of more than one word, e.g. *due to*, *together with*, *on top of*, *in spite of*, *out of*.

Prepositions enable us:

– to express movement to or from a **place**.
– to express **location** and **time**.

Prepositions are normally followed by:

– a noun phrase.

> *in **time***   *over **the edge***
> *under **the table***   *together with **my friends***

– an **-ing** clause.

> *Thanks **for looking**.*
> *He picked up some extra cash **by working** in a bar at night.*

– a relative pronoun (**WH-** word).

> *He's married to Rachel, **with whom** he has one daughter.*

In everyday speech a preposition may end a relative clause rather than come before it. See also p. 274.

> *That's the girl we were talking **about**.*
> *That's the man (**who**) I gave the money **to**.*

A preposition needs an object, rather like a transitive verb. A preposition and the noun phrase that goes with it is called a **prepositional phrase**.

A prepositional phrase is used as an **adverbial**.

> *He put the flowers on the table.*
> *She shut the dog in the kitchen.*
> *He found the papers in time for the meeting.*

or a **postmodifier**.

> *The house on the corner has at last been sold.*
> *The flowers on the table are from Tim.*
> *A bird with brilliant plumage roamed the lawns.*

• Prepositions combine with some verbs to make new meanings from the combination. These are one type of **phrasal verb**. See p. 85.

> *I believe in his innocence.*
> *I stand for justice.*
> *She went through a bad patch.*

The list below shows all the common simple prepositions. Some words can be either **prepositions** or **adverbs**, depending on how they are used and what they combine with. The words in *italics* are the prepositions that can also be used as **adverbs**.

> *aboard, about, above, across, after,* against, *along, alongside,*
> amid, among, *around,* as, at, atop, bar, *before, behind,*
> *below, beneath, beside, between, beyond, by,* despite, *down*
> during, for, from, *in, inside,* into, like, *near,* of, *off, on,* onto,
> *opposite, outside, over, past,* pending, per, prior, pro, re,
> regarding, *round, since,* than, *through, throughout,* till, to,
> towards, *under, underneath,* until, unto, *up,* upon, via,
> with, *within, without.*

The example below shows adverbial uses.

> *He went in.*
> *I took it through.*

When a verb is followed by a preposition, there is often little or no choice as to which preposition to use, e.g. *rely on, speak to, give to*.

When there is a choice of preposition, the meaning changes with each:

check for, check on, check over; speak to, speak about; talk to, talk with.

Prepositions allow us to express relationships. These are mostly to do with place and time. Some prepositions can be used with more than one meaning, depending on how we think about the time or place we are discussing.

Prepositions of location

Prepositions can indicate:

–   the direction in which something is moving in relation to another person or thing: *towards, from, to, off.*

> *They ran towards the station.*
> *He took the road from the town to the nearest village.*

–   something or someone being enclosed: *within, in, inside, outside.*

> *The lake can be seen from most positions within the room.*
> *There seems to be something loose inside the control box.*
> *You have to stand outside the room while we make up some questions.*
> *Did you put the cheese back in the fridge?*

- being at a certain point: *on, at, by, near*.

> *Don't stand **on** the beds.*
> *I'll meet you **at** the library.*
> *There is a huge park **near** where I live.*

- movement over or onto a place: *over, across, on, onto*.

> *Graham jumped **onto** the back of the lorry.*
> *He slid the packet **across** the table.*
> *Warms tears flowed **over** his cheeks.*

- location as a line: *along, over, on*.

> *We walked **along** the bank of the river.*
> *Please sign **on** the dotted line.*

Prepositions of time

Prepositions can also indicate:

- a point in time or a date : *at, on, in*.

> *The baby arrived **at** 9 pm. **on** April 1st.*
> *They got married **in** June.*
> *I'll be with you **in** five minutes.*

- a period or point of time which marks a change: *before, after, since, until*.

> *We lived there **before** Mother died.*
> *I went to that school **until** I was sixteen.*
> *I usually go there **after** work.*

- the duration of some event: *for*.

> *Helen stayed there **for** the whole of July.*

Word order in sentences

The order of words in an English sentence is very important. A change in word order often results in a change of meaning.

Many other languages use **inflection**, a change in the form of words, to show how the parts of a sentence function. English has very few inflections, so the place that a word occupies in a sentence, its **syntax**, is the most important feature.

Neutral word order

Most sentences have a subject, and then something that is said about the subject, which is usually the rest of the sentence. This divides the sentence into the **subject** and the **predicate**.

> *John* (subject) *bought the tickets on Saturday* (predicate).
> *The wall* (subject) *was torn down* (predicate).
> *My elderly mother* (subject) *is rather deaf* (predicate).

Most sentences put the information that they carry in this order. This is neutral word order. When this neutral order is changed, the meaning of a sentence also changes.

> *The **cat** killed the dog.*
> *The **dog** killed the cat.*
> *The **child** watched the rabbit.*
> *The **rabbit** watched the child.*

Word order in simple sentences

Simple sentences are those which have only one clause. They are extremely common in all forms of written and spoken English. Simple sentences have a normal word order which varies according to whether the sentence is:

- a **statement**,

> *I saw you at the theatre on Saturday night.*
> *I didn't see you at the theatre on Saturday night.*

- a **question**,

> *Did I see you at the theatre on Saturday night?*
> *Didn't I see you at the theatre on Saturday night?*

- a **command**.

> *You **should buy** a ticket now.*
> *You **shouldn't buy** a ticket yet.*
> ***Buy** a ticket now.*
> ***Don't buy** a ticket now.*

Word order also varies according to whether the sentence is **negative** or **positive**.

Focusing

When we want to focus the attention of a reader or a listener on a particular word or phrase, we can use variations on neutral order, such as putting the subject last, splitting the clause into two, or repeating some part of the sentence.

Some variations on the theme of neutral word order.

> *We used to call him 'Fuzzy'.*
> *'Fuzzy', we used to call him.*
> *Didn't we use to call him 'Fuzzy'?*
> *'Fuzzy' was what we used to call him.*
> *It was 'Fuzzy' we used to call him.*

Declarative, interrogative, and imperative statements

Each sentence in English provides some type of information.
For example, a sentence can be a statement, a question, a request, a command, a denial or a response, etc. In English the choice and order of the parts of a sentence help us express these meanings.

Most statements and denials are in the **declarative**. An important feature of declarative sentences is that they have a subject that comes before the verb.

> *Our dog **eats** any old thing.*
> *Our dog **won't** just **eat** any old thing.*
> *The dog **has** already **been fed**.*
> *The dog **hasn't been fed** yet.*
> *We **have** already **won** several races.*
> *We **haven't won** any races yet.*

Most questions are in the **interrogative**. An important feature of interrogative sentences is that they normally have a subject that comes after an auxiliary verb.

> ***Does** your dog **eat** any old thing?*
> ***Has** the dog already **been fed**?*
> ***Hasn't** the dog **been fed** yet?*
> ***Have** you **won** any races yet?*
> ***Haven't** you **won** any races yet?*

If the subject does come first it will be a special question word.

> ***Who won** the race?*
> ***Which** team **was** it?*

- Exceptionally, we can ask questions using the declarative. We do this by using a special tone of voice.

You're telling me he has a new car? I don't believe it.
It's raining again? That makes three days running.

Many commands are in the **imperative**. Commands in the imperative have no word that acts as a subject, though the subject is understood to be *you*. Commands in the imperative can sometimes sound rude or impatient.

> *Eat up quickly. We have to go!*
> *Leave me alone.*
> *On your marks, get set … go!*

- We can make a **request**, which is a type of command, sound more polite by using the interrogative.

> *Would you feed the dog, please.*
> *Would you mind shutting the door.*
> *Could I have that now, thank you.*

> Not all imperative sentences are orders or commands.
> They can be social expressions.
>
> > *Have a nice day.*
> > *Get well soon.*
> > *Help yourselves to coffee.*

There is also a **subjunctive** form. This is rarely used in English now. It may be used when you want to talk about an improbable or unlikely situation.

> *If I were Prime Minister, I'd spend more money on education.*

The declarative

The **declarative** is used to make statements. A statement is usually the expression of a fact or of an opinion. Statements can be both positive or negative.

> *Kate is not working after all.*
> *Tim wasn't reading your diary.*
> *Helen wasn't talking about you.*
> *I'm not going on holiday this year.*

Declarative sentences always contain a subject and a following verb phrase.

The normal word order for declarative sentences:

subject + verb phrase

> *Kate is working.*
> *Tim was reading.*
> *Helen stared at me in surprise.*

subject + verb phrase + direct object

> *Ross is writing a letter.*
> *Pam borrowed three library books.*
> *Stephen ordered vegetarian lasagne.*

subject + verb phrase + adverbial

> *Dominic was eating very slowly.*
> *Lyndsey was studying in her room.*
> *Mikhail laughed nervously.*

---

subject + verb phrase + direct object + adverbial

> *Dominic was eating his lunch very slowly.*
> *Lyndsey had been reading a book in her room.*

Certain verbs must have following objects, e.g. *see, find, prefer, take*.

> *She saw **her friend**.*
> *He found **a camera**.*
> *They took **a holiday brochure**.*

Other verbs need, or can have, both a **direct** and an **indirect** object, e.g. *give, buy, offer*.

> *Laura offered **me** **another biscuit**.*
> *Scott's uncle bought **him** **a new bike**.*

The word order can be either:

subject + verb + indirect object + direct object

> *Kate gave **the dog** a bone.*
> *Stuart bought **Marie** a birthday present.*

or, with the addition of a word that indicates the recipient:

subject + verb + direct object + *to/for* + indirect object.

> *Kate gave a bone **to the dog**.*
> *Stuart bought a birthday present **for Marie**.*

Another group of verbs must be followed either by an object and an adverbial expression, or an adverbial expression on its own e.g. *put, place, stand.*

> *Richard placed **the computer** on the table.*
> *Diana put **her jeans** in the drawer.*
> *Michael stood* in the middle of the pitch.

A further type of declarative statement has the same basic order of subject and verb as the **subject** + **verb phrase** + **direct object** example on p. 231, but with a **complement** replacing the direct object. See p. 234 for more about complements and p. 15 for more about objects.

> *Elisabeth seems to have been **rather worried** lately.*
> *This dessert is **delicious**.*

Complements

Some verbs such as *be, become, seem*, do not have an object but a **complement**.

The **subject complement** is a word or phrase that tells us more about the subject.

> *Alan is **a nice person**.*
> *Rajiv is **a psychiatric nurse**.*
> *Alison seems **very well balanced**.*
> *Rosamund is **herself** again.*
> *That's **it**!*
> *This is **for you**.*

The subject complement is linked to the subject by a verb, and the order is as follows:

subject + **verb** + **subject complement**

Subject complements may be either noun phrases, pronouns, adjectives, or even prepositional phrases.

- Most adjectives can be used after a group of verbs that includes: *appear, be, become, look, seem, smell, taste*, etc. An adjective that is used in this position is called a **predicative** adjective and it is functioning as a **complement**.

> *The tickets seemed **expensive**, but the show was **excellent**.*
> *These little cakes are **delicious**.*
> *Soon afterwards, Patrick became **ill**.*
> *Jackie appeared **friendly enough** when I first met her.*

Less frequently we find an **object complement**. The object complement tells us more about the direct object. It relates directly to the object and is placed after it.

Verbs that can take an object complement with their direct object include *make*, *call*, and *appoint*. The word order is as follows:

subject + verb + direct object + object complement

> *Peter's phone call made Maureen* happy.
> *She called me* a fool.
> *They appointed him* Director.

Word order in negative statements

In negative statements, the basic word order for subject and object is the same as in positive statements.

> *John has gone to school.*
> *John has **not** gone to school.*

The difference is that negative statements must contain *not*, and must have as part of the verb phrase, either:

– a **primary auxiliary** verb,

> *She **had not** arrived in time for lunch.*
> *Kate **is not** working this evening.*
> *Tim **was not** reading your diary.*

– one or other of the **modal auxiliary** verbs, or

> *I warn you, he **may not** want to come.*
> *Ailsa **could not** see the road clearly.*

– a form of *be* used as a main verb.

> *That **is not** my book.*

The word *not* is added immediately after the first one of these auxiliary verbs. The main verb follows.

The word order is, therefore:
subject + **auxiliary** + *not* + **main verb.**

A negative sentence may contain a modal verb and one or more auxiliaries as well.

>*I* **may** *not* **have** *gone by the time you arrive.*
>*They* **could** *not* **have** *seen her – they were asleep in bed.*
>*They* **should** *not* **have been playing** *in the road.*

In this case the word order is:
   subject + **modal** + *not* + **primary auxiliary** + **main verb**.

If the verb phrase does not already contain one of these verbs, then it is necessary to add the **supporting auxiliary** verb *do*.

The present simple and the past simple tenses of main verbs take the appropriate form of *do*, and then add *not* followed by the base form of the main verb.

>*He runs.*
>*He* **does not** *run.*
>*He ran.*
>*He* **did not** *run.*
>*Lynn* **does not** *work overtime now.*
>*The bus service* **did not** *run on Sundays.*

The word order is, therefore:
   subject + *do*- **auxiliary** + *not* + **main verb**

See p. 239 for more on the supporting auxiliary.

• The contracted form of *not*, which is *n't*, can be used after every auxiliary verb except *am*. This is the most common spoken form.

>*He* **doesn't** *run.*
>*He* **didn't** *run.*
>*Lynn* **doesn't** *work on Sundays.*
>*She* **hasn't** *been to work all week.*
>*He* **isn't** *going to come after all.*
>*Bill went swimming but Ann* **didn't** *fancy it.*

The full form with *not* tends to be used more in writing.

> *can* + *not* is usually written *cannot*.
>
> *She can't come.*
> *She cannot come.*

- Other words with a negative meaning, *never*, *barely*, *hardly*, *scarcely*, *rarely*, do not change the order of words in a statement.

    She doesn't buy Vogue.
    She never buys Vogue.
    He barely earns enough to live on.
    I hardly think that is going to put them off.

The interrogative

The interrogative is normal for many questions. It contains a verb phrase that is followed by a subject.

There are two main types of question: those that can be answered *yes* or *no*, and those that have to be answered with a specific piece of information or a sentence such as *I don't know*. Each type of question has its own special word order.

Yes/no questions

Questions that expect the answer *yes* or *no* are called **yes/no questions** or sometimes, **polar questions**.

The **interrogative** is used to form yes/no questions.

The normal sentence order for the interrogative is:
modal/auxiliary verb + **subject** + **base form** of the **main verb**.

> *Were the dogs barking?*
> *Have you been dieting?*
> *Can Mahmoud come too?*
> *Must you go so soon?*
> *Would you like a chocolate?*

When a sentence does not contain a modal verb or an auxiliary verb, the question is formed by placing a form of the supporting auxiliary verb *do* before the subject and following it with the **base form** of the main verb.

> *Does he enjoy tennis?*
> *Do they he play a lot?*
> *Did that surprise his mum?*

Yes/no questions also have a negative form. **Negative yes/no questions** are almost always contracted. The negative in its contracted form *n't* comes immediately before the subject.

> *Doesn't he like talking about his childhood?*
> *Can't Peter have one too?*
> *Don't you speak French?*
> *Wouldn't you like to know a bit more about this?*

If the full negative form *not* is used, it comes immediately after the subject. The full form is very formal.

> *Does he not like talking about his childhood?*
> *Do you not want to know what it was about?*
> *Can Peter not have one too?*

WH- questions

When you want to get a detailed answer, not just *yes* or *no*, you must use a **WH- question** (or **'non-polar' question**), which allows for many possible answers. The words *who, whom, whose, what, which, when, where, why,* and *how* are used to form this sort of question. These words are referred to as **WH-** words. See pp. 241–244.

> **Yes/no:**
> *Did you ring the school? – Yes, I did.*
> *Was she all right in the end? – No/I don't know.*
> *Have you seen Ali yet? – Yes, I have.*

> **WH-:**
> *Who was that man? – He's my geography teacher.*
> *What did he say when you told him the news? – He was too surprised to say anything.*
> *When did you see Ali? – Last Wednesday.*
> *Where is Peter going? – To work.*
> *When did they arrive? – Yesterday.*
> *Why have you stopped going running? – The doctor told me to.*

WH- words

The **WH-** words are also called **interrogatives**. They are used for **WH-** questions. They can be determiners, adverbs, or pronouns.

WH- determiners

When used as determiners, *what, which,* or *whose* can be used to ask questions:

– about nouns

> *What book are you reading?*
> *Which plane is he catching?*
> *Whose jacket is this?*

– or about the pronoun *one* or *ones.*

> *Which one would you like?*
> *Which ones did Ruth want?*

• The determiner *which* can be used in questions about selecting. It can also be used together with the preposition *of* for the same purpose.

> *Which colour shall we use?*
> *Which book sells the most copies?*
> *Which of these colours shall we use?*
> *Of all your novels,* *which of them* *did you enjoy writing the most?*

• The determiner *whose* asks about possession with reference to a person as the possessor.

> *Whose mother did you say she was?*
> *Whose bag is this?*

WH- adverbs

The adverb **WH-** words, *when*, *where*, *how*, and *why*, always make the sentence follow the interrogative word order.

– *When* asks about time.

> *When will they arrive?*
> *When shall I see you again?*

– *Where* asks about place.

> *Where are you going?*
> *Where have you been?*
> *Where is your coat?*

– *How* asks about manner.

> *How did you get here? – We came by train.*
> *How does this thing work?*

– *Why* asks about reasons and purpose. Questions with *why* are usually answered with a clause containing *because* to express reason, or with the *to* infinitive to express purpose.

> *Why is the baby crying? – Because she's hungry.*
> *Why are you saving your money? – To buy a bike.*

– *How much* implies reference to a quantity; *how many* implies reference to an amount or a countable number of things but may leave out the noun referred to.

> *How much money did they take? – All of it.*
> *How much does it cost? – £4.20.*
> *How many packs do you want? – Twelve, please.*
> *How many do you want? – Twelve, please.*

– *How* can also be used with adjectives such as *old*, *big*, *far*, or with adverbs such as *often*, *soon*, *quickly* to ask about degree, rate, or timing.

> *How far is it to the station? – About five kilometres.*
> *How often does he come? – Not very often.*

WH- pronouns

The **pronouns** *who*, *whose*, *which*, and *what* can be the subject or object of a verb.

> *Who can help me?*
> *Whose is the new sports car outside?*
> *Which was your best subject at school?*
> *What happened next?*
> *What have you got to take with you to camp?*

The interrogative pronoun *whose* is used when the question is asked about a person as the possessor of something. See also pp. 205–206 on interrogative and relative pronouns.

> *Whose is the motorbike parked outside?*
> *Whose is this?*

• The form *whom* is used as the object of a verb or of a preposition in very formal or old-fashioned English.

> *Whom did you talk to?*
> *Whom would you rather have as a boss?*

Modern English usage prefers *who* instead of *whom* in all but the most formal contexts.

> *Who did you talk to?*
> *Who would you rather have as a boss?*

When *whom* is used as the object of a preposition, it normally follows the preposition.

> *To whom did you speak?*
> *With whom did she go?*

When *who* is used, the preposition is placed at the end of the clause.

> *Who did you speak to?*
> *Who did she go with?*

The **WH-** subject pronouns are found in the same sentence order as statements:
WH- subject pronoun + **the main verb**.

> *Who can help me?*
> *Whose is that motorbike parked outside?*
> *Which was your best subject at school?*
> *What happened next?*

The **WH-** object pronouns make the sentence take the word order of a question:
WH- object pronoun + **primary or modal auxiliary** + **subject** + **base form** of the verb.

> *What do you have to take with you to camp?*
> *What has Jonathan done now?*

- The exception to this is in informal spoken English, when the speaker wants to show shock or disbelief.

> *You did what?*

Sentence tags

Tags are short additions that look like questions, used at the end of a declarative sentence. They are sometimes called **question tags**, but many sentences ending with a tag are not real questions. They are usually used to check that the listener agrees with what the speaker has said. Sentence tags are very commonly used in spoken English, but not in formal written English.

The tag is added to the end of a statement. If the auxiliary verb *be* or *have* or a **modal** verb is part of the verb phrase in the sentence, then it is used as the verb in the sentence tag.

> It **isn't** raining again, **is it**?
> You**'ve seen** the programme, **haven't you**?
> Well, we **can't jump** over it, **can we**?
> You **will come**, **won't you**?

If the main verb is in the present simple or past simple tense, the tag is made using *do*.

> He certainly **likes** eating, **doesn't he**?
> I **slipped up** there, **didn't I**?

In negative tags, *n't* is added to the auxiliary. Note that this contracted form is always used.

> He certainly **likes** eating, **doesn't he**?
> I **slipped up** there, **didn't I**?
> They **went** with you, **didn't they**?

- The formal forms such as, *does he not, did I not, have you not*, sound old-fashioned. They are more common in some regional varieties of English.

The pronoun in the sentence tag must match the subject of the main verb.

> *You aren't listening, are you?*
> *He reads a lot, doesn't he?*

Sentence tags can be **negative**

> *They went with you, didn't they?*

or **positive**.

> *Your father doesn't belong to the golf club, does he?*

Normally, when the first part of the sentence is positive, the tag verb will be negative, and vice versa. Sentences in which both parts are positive are less common. These sentences must be used carefully as, with certain tones of voice, they can sound aggressive or judgemental.

> *I see, you think I'm a fool, do you?*
> *So you smoke now, do you?*

- The same sentence tag may have different meanings depending on the tone of voice that is used with it.

> Falling tone: statement
> *She's gone out, hasn't she?*

> Rising tone: question
> *She's gone out, hasn't she?*

The sentence can be a statement of fact or a question, depending on whether your voice rises or falls at the end. However, a question mark is always required.

Sentence tags are used in the following combinations:

- To say something that the speaker expects the listener will agree with. This doesn't always sound like a question:

positive main verb + negative tag

> *Mary will pass her driving test this time, won't she?*
> *Richard seems to have lost interest in everything, doesn't he?*

or **negative main verb + positive tag**

> *Jessica didn't care, did she?*
> *Kerry hadn't done enough preparation, had she?*

- To point out or remark on something, often something that the listener cannot deny. This frequently sounds more like a question:

positive main verb + negative tag

> *You've just bought a new car, haven't you?*
> *Henry has been away already this year, hasn't he?*

or **negative main verb + positive tag**

> *Desmond hasn't been to see you, has he?*
> *Paula wasn't in your class at school, was she?*

- To show interest in something. This often repeats part of what the previous speaker has said:

positive main verb + positive tag

> *You saw him in town, did you?*
> *So, you come from New Zealand, do you?*
> *So you've just come back from skiing, have you?*

When a tag is used to show interest in something, the sentence is often begun with *So*. This type of tag can also be used in a challenging manner.

> *Oh, so you've been here all the time, have you?*

After a command, a tag made with *can*, *could*, *will*, *shall*, or *would* makes an order more polite.

> *Make me a cup of tea, will you?*
> *Just wait a minute, would you?*
> *Let's go to the cinema, shall we?*

The imperative

Commands and orders

The **imperative** is used to give commands and orders. The form of the verb used for the imperative is the **base form** of the main verb, which is used without a subject.

> *Walk* to the corner, *turn* right, and *cross* the road.
> *Open* your mouth and *say* 'Aaaah'.

- Although the main feature of sentences in the imperative is that they have no **grammatical** subject, they do have an **understood** subject, *'you'*.

The basic form of the imperative remains the same whether it is addressed to one or more people.

> *Come on*, **Mary**; I'm waiting.
> *Come on*, **girls**; you're late.

There is also a special type of imperative, using *let's*, that is used when you need to include the speaker. See p. 251.

The word order of a sentence in the imperative is:
verb + **object** (if needed).

The negative imperative is made with *do* + *not* or *don't*.

> *Don't lose* that key.
> *Do not come back* without it!

The uses of the imperative are as follows:

- to give an order.

  > *Go away.*
  > *Stop that.*
  > *Keep quiet.*

- to give instructions.

  > *Don't use this spray near a naked flame.*
  > *Apply the glue thinly and leave it for ten minutes.*

- to give advice or warnings.

  > *Don't forget to take your passport with you.*
  > *Be careful!*
  > *Don't go on the ice.*

- to make an offer or an invitation.

  > *Have a piece of cake.*
  > *Come round and see me some time.*

The imperative of *do* + a **main verb** can be used:

- for polite emphasis.

  > *Do take your coat off.*

- to be persuasive.

  > *Do try to eat a little of this; it will be good for you.*

– to show irritation.

> *Do stop talking! I'm trying to work.*

• Note that the imperative is not the only way to form a command or an order. You can also issue a command when you use a sentence in the declarative or the interrogative.

> *I'm certainly not going to get it – you get it.*
> *Would you get it, then? I'm busy.*

Making suggestions

Let's (*let* + *us*) + **main verb** is used in the 1st person plural only, especially when you are trying to encourage someone to do something with you.

It includes both the speaker and the hearer, so the subject that is understood is represented by the plural *we*.

> *Let's visit Malcolm this weekend.*
> *Please let's go to the cinema tonight.*
> *Do let's have a look at your new computer, Chris.*
> *Let's pool our resources.*

• Suggestions which start with *let's* often end with the sentence tag *shall we?*

> *Let's phone her now, shall we?*
> *Let's go for a walk after supper, shall we?*

In ordinary English the negative is *let's not* + **main verb** or sometimes *don't let's* + **main verb**.

> *Let's not worry about that now.*
> *Don't let's worry about that now.*

In formal English, the negative is *let us not* + **main verb**.

> **Let us not lose** sight of our aims.

Do let's is the emphatic form.

> It's a very good bargain; **do let's buy** it!

* The uncontracted form *let us* + **main verb** is occasionally used in formal and written English.

> **Let us be** clear about this.
> **Let us** hope that this will never happen again.

The answer to a suggestion with *let's* is normally either, *yes, let's* or *no, let's not* or sometimes, *no, don't let's (...)*.

> **Let's phone** her now, shall we? – Yes, let's.
> **Let's phone** her now, shall we? – No, let's not.
> **Let's invite** Malcolm over this weekend. – No, **don't let's** do that.

The vocative

The imperative is often used with a **vocative**. This is where you mention a person's name or some other way of identifying the person to whom a command or request is being addressed.

> *David, come here!*
> *Come here, David.*
> *Hey, you, stop talking!*

The vocative can be a proper noun, the pronoun *you*, or a noun phrase. The vocative can come before or after the main clause. A vocative forms a part of many questions.

> *Peter, do you know where I put the DVD?*
> *Have you seen Chris recently, Jenny?*

A vocative is also combined with an interrogative clause to form a request.

> *Tony, would you pass me the hammer?*
> *Could I speak to you privately for a minute, Sue?*

When a vocative is used with an imperative clause, the sentence is usually a command.

> *Sam, get off there!*
> *You, come back!*

A command can also be phrased as a request.

> *Would you stop talking now, darling, and go to sleep.*
> *Would you get off there, please, Sam.*

A practical reason for using a vocative is to supply the missing but understood subject, so that the right person will understand the command or request, and act on it.

Note the punctuation. There should be a comma between the vocative part of the clause and the remainder.

As part of a command, except for urgent warnings, the use of the vocative is considered rude or abrupt.

The subjunctive

The **subjunctive** was formerly used in English for situations that were improbable or that expressed a wish. It is only rarely used in modern British English. It is, however, found in certain set phrases and in very formal forms of speech and writing.

> God *save* the Queen!
> God *bless* you!
> God *help* us!
> Heaven *help* us!
> Heaven *forbid* that that should happen to me.
> *Suffice* it to say he escaped with only a caution.

The present subjunctive

The form in the present tense is exactly the same as the base form in all persons of the verb. That is, there is no -*s* on the 3rd person singular.

The subjunctive is used, in very formal English, in subordinate clauses that follow verbs expressing a desire, a demand, a formal recommendation, or a resolve.

> I only ask that he *cease* behaving in this extraordinary manner.
> It is vital that they *be* stopped at once.
> Is it really necessary that she *work* all hours of the day?
> I demand that he *do* something to make up for this.

The clause containing the subjunctive is linked to the main clause with *that*.

- This use of the subjunctive is more common in American English than in British English. British speakers usually take advantage of other ways of expressing the same message, especially in less formal speech.

*I only ask that **he should cease** behaving in this extraordinary manner.*
*It is vital that they **are** stopped at once.*
*It is vital **to stop** them at once.*
*Is it really necessary **for her to work** all hours of the day?*
*I demand that **he does** something to make up for this.*

The past subjunctive

In written English and in very formal speech, the past subjunctive form **were** is sometimes used with the 1st and 3rd person singular, in place of the normal past form **was**.

The past subjunctive may be used:

– after *if* or *I wish*, to express regret or longing

*If your father **were** alive he would help you.*
*If I **were** rich I would buy a Ferrari.*
*I wish I **were** taller.*
*If only he **were** here now!*

– after *as if/as though* and similar expressions, to express doubt or improbability.

*You talk to him as if he **were** your slave!*
*Some people behave as though dogs **were** human.*

Many people prefer to use the normal form of the past in this type of sentence. This is quite acceptable in ordinary English.

*If your father **was** alive he would help you.*
*If I **was** rich I would buy a Ferrari.*
*I wish I **was** tall.*
*If only he **was** here now!*
*You talk to him as if he **was** your slave!*

Exclamations

Exclamations are short utterances that you make when you are very surprised or upset. They are not always whole sentences. Sometimes they are more like a noise than a word. In this case they are called **interjections**.

> *Ugh!*   *Phew!*
> *Wow!*   *Huh!*

Many exclamations consist of just one word.

> *Help!*   *Nonsense!*
> *Blast!*   *Rubbish!*

Exclamations can also consist of:

- *what* + **noun phrase**

> ***What*** *a pity!*
> ***What*** *a lovely day!*
> ***What*** *rubbish!*

- or *how* + **adjective**.

> ***How*** *silly!*
> ***How*** *kind of him!*

They may also have the form of a negative question.

> ***Isn't*** *it a warm day!*
> ***Aren't*** *they kind!*

- Another form of exclamation is when the hearer repeats part of the sentence that he or she has just heard. This is used when the hearer finds it hard to believe what has been said or is very surprised. This sort of exclamation is called an **echo**.

  *Richard's passed the exam. – **Richard's passed!** That's brilliant!*
  *Sally's here. – **She's here!** What a relief!*

Responses

Responses are made in answer to a question or a statement by another person in the course of conversation. Like exclamations, they may be full sentences, but can also be phrases or single words.

> *Yes.*
> *On Tuesday.*
> *I certainly will.*

Responses usually do not make sense on their own.

Although a response may not have a subject or contain a main verb, it can be classed as a sentence, because a response uses our knowledge of what has just been said. The subject or the verb will usually be understood from the context.

> *Are you coming to the party tonight? –* **Yes**.
> *When are you going to London, then? –* **On Tuesday**.
> *Will you be doing some shopping? –* **I certainly will**.

- If the verb is in a simple tense you can use the supporting auxiliary *do* as the verb in the response.

  > *Do you like courgettes? – Yes, I* **do**.

- You usually just use the first part of the verb phrase in a compound verb to make a response. That is, the first **auxiliary** verb or the **modal verb** becomes the response form.

  > *Has Tamsin called round yet? – Yes, she* **has**.
  > *Was Andrea crying? – Yes, she* **was**.
  > *Can we leave early? – Yes, you* **can**.
  > *Should I be doing this differently? – Yes, you* **should**.

Some speakers prefer to use the modal and the auxiliary form together.

> *Laurence could be running if it wasn't for his injury.*
> – *Yes, he **could be**.*

Sentences and clauses

A clause is a group of words which contains a verb. The verb in a clause can be finite

> *Use this pan for the pasta*
> *He missed the turnoff.*

or non-finite.

> *To cook pasta, always use a large pan.*
> *Dreaming about Jenny, he missed the turnoff.*

Simple sentences

Simple sentences consist of one clause, in which the verb is finite.

> *Ann went to the bank.*
> *She withdrew £100.*

Two or more clauses can be joined to make a **compound** sentence or a **complex** sentence.

Complex sentences

Complex sentences are those that contain a **subordinate** clause as well as a **main** clause.

> **When he arrives,** *I'll phone you.*
> *He stayed at home* **because he felt ill**.

A **subordinate** clause is one that contains special information about the main clause. It will usually be introduced by a **linking word** such as *when, if, because,* or *that*. The linking words are called **subordinating conjunctions**.

Most subordinate clauses can come before, after, or within the main clause. Usually, when one clause is of principal importance and the other clause gives information about the principal one, we have a complex sentence with one **main clause** and one **subordinate clause**.

• The position that a subordinate clause is placed in is determined largely by what is felt to be the main message of a sentence.

> *Since you seem to have made up your mind*, I'll say no more.
> I stopped seeing her *because she moved to Liverpool*.

Compound sentences

A compound sentence is one that consists of two **main clauses**, joined by a word such as *and*, *but*, or *or*, called a **coordinating conjunction**. Each clause is of equal importance and gives information of equal value. The order of the clauses can be very important for the meaning. For example, the timing of an action can be described by the order in which the clauses follow each other.

> He picked it up *and* ran over to her.
> He ran over to her *and* picked it up.
> I drove to Coatbridge *and* went on to Stirling.

Compound-complex sentences

These have more than one main clause and at least one subordinate clause.

> Angie came over *and* we decided to use my car *because* hers
> was playing up.
> He ran over to Julie, *who* was sitting at the end of the bench,
> *and* grabbed her handbag.

Joining clauses

Coordination

The process called **coordination** joins two short clauses of equal importance with a conjunction. Each clause becomes a **main** clause in the new sentence.

> *Ann went to the bank **and** withdrew £100.*
> *Sally goes to work **but** Ann doesn't have a job.*
> *Ann (**either**) stays at home **or** visits her family.*

The clauses are linked by words called **coordinating conjunctions**, such as *and, but, (either) or, neither, nor,* or *yet.* Conjunctions come at the beginning of a clause.

- If the subject of both clauses is the same, it does not have to be repeated in front of the second verb.

> *She came over **and** ~~she~~ gave me a hug.*

The conjunction *and* is used:

- to join clauses where there is no contrast or choice.

- to join more than two clauses; the earlier clauses can be joined by a comma, but the last two must be joined by *and*.

> *Ann got into the car, drove to the bank, withdrew £100,*
> *   **and** went shopping.*

The conjunction *but* is used to join clauses where there is a contrast.

> *She wanted to buy a new dress **but** she couldn't find one she liked.*

The conjunction *yet* is used, mainly in written English, to join clauses where there is a contrast that is of a surprising nature.

> *He's a quietly spoken man, **yet** he still manages to command attention.*
> *She was suffering from a knee injury **yet** she still won the match.*

- The conjunctions *and, but, or, neither,* and *nor* are also used to join two phrases of the same kind,

> *This book is useful for **planning and carrying out** research.*
> ***The former President and his wife** were there.*

  or two words of the same class.

> *I use this chair when I am **reading and working.***
> *Do you undertake **detailed or intricate** work?*
> ***Jack and Jill** fell down the hill.*
> *This is a **complicated but intriguing** film.*

  In particular, *and* and *but* are used to coordinate pairs of adjectives in a predicative position.

When there is a positive choice between the subjects of two clauses, you use the pair of words *either* and *or* to join the clauses.

> ***Either** you come to my place **or** I'll meet you at work. Which do you prefer?*

If the subject of the joined clauses is the same, the subject is used in the first of the joined clauses only. This is often also true of any auxiliary verbs that may be present.

> *Martin said he would **either** meet them for lunch **or** take them to tea.*

When it is used in this way *either* must come in one of these places:

– before the subject in the first clause of the group.
– in front of the main verb and after any auxiliary verb.

You can use *either...or* to join more than two clauses if you repeat the use of *or*.

> *Colin said he would (**either**) meet them for lunch,*
>   *(**or**) take them to tea, **or** have them over for a coffee.*
> *Ian can (**either**) come with us **or** take a taxi later.*

The use of *either...or* emphasizes that the two clauses are alternatives and cannot both be true. Compare *and/or*.

> *Colin said he would meet them for lunch, **and/or** have them*
>   *over for a coffee.*

The word *either* can be left out if the sentence meaning is clear. Some writers treat all but the final *or* as optional.

> You can use *or* on its own to join two or more clauses,
> but *either* cannot be used on its own.

When there is a negative choice between the subjects of two clauses, you can use the pair of words *neither* and *nor* to join the clauses.

> *It is **neither** possible **nor** desirable that they should be invited.*
> *Jane was **not** a fool; **neither/nor** was she prepared to be blamed*
>   *for the error.*

The word *neither* can be used on its own to connect two clauses if the first clause contains a word with broad negative meaning such as *not*, *barely* or *scarcely*. If there is a subject in the second clause, question order must be used.

There was **barely** enough meat for the children; **neither did they** have any bread.

Eric **hardly** saw the fight; **nor did he** remember much about the incident later.

- The words **either** and **neither** can also be used as a pronoun or as a determiner. Each can then be used on its own; it does not then have a joining function.

  Either book will do. It doesn't matter.
  Neither book is at all suitable, I'm sorry.
  You can have **either**.

- **Either**, **or**, **neither**, and **nor** can be used as conjunctions inside a noun phrase or a verb phrase.

  You can choose to study **either** Shakespeare **or** Keats.
  Neither Vimala **nor** Katie knew the answer.
  She is **either** desperate **or** just silly.
  He didn't know whether **to** stay **or** go.

Subordination

When two or more clauses are joined by a conjunction other than *and*, *but*, *or*, or *yet*, one of the clauses is the main clause; the other clauses are **subordinate** clauses. The different types of subordinate clause include **noun** clauses,

> *What matters most is **that you treat everyone fairly**.*

adverbial clauses,

> *They went outside **as soon as the rain stopped**.*

relative clauses,

> *This is the problem **that we're facing** at the moment.*
> *We stayed in Inverness, **which is in the Scottish Highlands**.*

conditional clauses,

> *Maureen plans to live in Australia **if she can get a job there**.*

and **reported** clauses.

> *She told me **that Philip was in France**.*

Each of the subordinate clauses is associated with an introductory word that signals what type of clause it is that follows.

> ***After** she had read the diary, she returned it to the drawer.*
> ***As** they were going downstairs, the phone rang.*
> *They aren't coming **because** they've had an argument.*

These words are called **subordinating conjunctions**. They include:

– the **WH-** words

– words like *since, if, when, because*

– the word *that*, either on its own or used with another word
   e.g. *so that* or *supposing that*

– a phrase ending in *as*, e.g. *as soon as, as long as*

• Each of the subordinating clauses has a preferred position. For
   example, most adverbial clauses usually follow the main clause,
   although they can also come before the main clause.

> *Shall I do the shopping **when I finish work**?*
> ***When I finish work**, I could do the shopping for you.*

Reported clauses usually follow directly on from the main reporting
clause. See p. 281.

Noun clauses

These are clauses that can be used as either the subject or the object
of a sentence or in other places where a noun phrase is usually found.
They are introduced by *that*

> *What I like about him is **that he always tries his best**.*

or by a **WH-** word, e.g. *who, when, where*.

> *I don't know **where you live**.*
> ***How the thief got in** is a mystery.*
> ***Why she acts like this** is beyond me.*

Word order after a **WH-** word is the same as in a statement.

> The subordinating conjunction *that* can often be omitted.
>
> *I think that he'll succeed.*
> *I think he'll succeed.*

Adverbial clauses

Adverbial clauses generally follow the main clause unless otherwise stated. The following are the main types of adverbial clause:

Time: sets the timing for the main clause.

> *We should go **as soon as you are ready**.*
> *I'll call for you **whenever you like**.*
> ***Since she went away**, I haven't been able to sleep.*
> ***The moment he said it**, I started to feel better.*

– may come before or after the main clause.

– introduced by *after, as, as soon as, before, once, since, till, the moment (that), until, whenever, when, while*.

Place: sets where the action of the main clause takes place.

> *I put it **where nobody would find it**.*
> *He made an impact **everywhere that he went**.*
> ***Wherever you looked**, he was to be found.*

– introduced by *where, wherever*, or *everywhere*.

Manner: sets out how the main clause was carried out.

– introduced by *as, as if, as though, how, just as*, or *the way that*.

> *Mandy looked **as if she had seen a ghost**.*
> *Cameron wandered in, **the way that he does**.*
> *You have to fasten it **as though it was a shoelace**.*
> *The room was decorated **just as he had imagined**.*

Reason: sets out the thinking behind the action of the main clause.

> *I don't want to go because I'm not keen on old movies.*
> *Since no one was ready, I sat down and turned on the TV.*

– may come before or after the main clause.

– introduced by *as*, *because*, or *since*.

Purpose: sets out what it was hoped would be achieved by carrying out the action of the main clause.

> *Put it just there so that it holds the door open.*
> *Leave a bit for Becky in case she's hungry when she gets in.*

– introduced by *so that*, *in order that*, *in case*, or *lest*.

• Purpose can also be indicated by *so as to*, *in order to* followed by the base form of a verb.

> *I'm living with my mum and dad so as to save money.*
> *He put the chair against the door in order to hold it open.*

Result: sets out what happened when the main clause was carried out.

> *Ben was so angry that he kicked the wall hard.*
> *Nina is such a generous person that she's often short of money.*

– introduced by *so* + **adjective/adverb** + *that* or by *such a* + **noun phrase** + *that*.

Contrast: suggests that something else may need to be taken into account regarding the main clause.

> *However much you may want to spend your money*, try to
>   save a little each month.
> *Although it had rained*, the ground was still very dry.
> We must try to do something for the environment, *even if we
>   can't solve all the world's problems*.

– may come before or after the main clause.

– introduced by *although, even though, even if, however, much as*, or *while*.

Relative clauses

Relative clauses tell us more about nouns. They function rather like adjectives, and are found as **postmodifiers** in a noun phrase. The noun that is modified is called the **antecedent**. Relative clauses normally begin with *who*, *whom*, *whose*, or *that*.

These words are called **relative pronouns**. Note that some of them also function as interrogative pronouns. See also p. 215.

A relative pronoun can be the subject

> *The people **who live upstairs** are having a party.*
> *The dog **that bit me** had to be put down.*

or object

> *I don't like the music **that they are playing**.*
> *A man **whom I met on holiday** phoned last might.*

of the verb in the relative clause. If it is the object, it can be left out in ordinary informal speech and writing.

> *I don't like the music **they are playing**.*
> *A man **I met on holiday** phoned lat night.*

Subject and object relative pronouns come at the beginning of the relative clause.

- A relative pronoun can also be the object of a preposition.

> *It was definitely Diana **to whom she was referring**.*
> *It's a great game **at which anyone can excel**.*

In informal English a relative clause can end in a preposition, especially if the relative pronoun is omitted.

> *It was definitely Diana **that she was referring to**.*
> *It's great game **which anyone can excel at**.*

Defining and non-defining relative clauses

There are two sorts of relative clause.

Some relative clauses act rather like an adjective by providing more information about a particular noun.

> *The people **who live upstairs** are having a party.*
> *I don't like the music **that they're playing**.*
> *The girl **who was on the bus with us** is called Sonia.*

These are called **defining** relative clauses or **restrictive** relative clauses. A defining relative clause is never separated from the noun by a comma.

The other type of relative clause adds extra information to the whole of the main clause. These are **non-defining relative clauses** or **non-restrictive** relative clauses. This type of clause is separated from the main clause by commas.

> *The man next door, **who works from home**, kept an eye on the house for us.*
> *Thomas went home early, **which was a relief to us all**.*
> *We stopped in Dryburgh, **which is a good place for a picnic**.*

Compare:

Defining.
My brother who lives in Canada is a lawyer.
(There are several brothers. The Canadian one is a lawyer.)

Non-defining.
My brother, who lives in Canada, is a lawyer.
(There is only one brother. He is a lawyer. He happens to
   live in Canada.)

Conditional clauses

Conditional sentences consist of a main clause and a **conditional clause** (sometimes called an *if-clause*). The conditional clause usually begins with *if* or *unless*. The conditional clause can come before or after the main clause.

> *We'll be late **if we don't leave now**.*
> *We'll be late **unless we leave now**.*
> ***If we don't leave now**, we'll be late.*
> ***Unless we leave now**, we'll be late.*

There are three main types of conditional sentence.

Type 1

The main clause uses *will*, *can*, *may*, or *might* + the **base form** of a main verb. The *if-*clause uses the present simple tense.

> ***If you take the first bus**, you'll get there on time.*
> *She'll be cold **if she doesn't wear a coat**.*
> ***If you need more helpers**, I can try and get some time off work.*

Type 1 sentences refer to the future. They suggest that the action in the main clause is quite likely to happen.

> *They **will** not finish their homework unless they start now.*
> *If you book early, you **will** get a seat.*

The use of the modal verb *may* or *might* in the main clause suggests that there is some doubt whether the main verb action will be achieved.

> *If you book early, you **may** get a seat.*
> *Mary **might** deliver your parcel, if you ask her.*

Type 2

The main clause uses *would*, *could*, or *might* + the **base form** of a main verb. The *if-clause* uses the past simple tense

> *If Jim **lent** us his car, we could go to the party.*
> *We would save £3.50 a day if we **didn't eat** any lunch.*
> *If burglars **broke** into my house, they wouldn't find any money.*
> *Would you be very angry if I **failed** my exam?*

or the past subjunctive.

> *If I **were** you, I'd phone her straight away.*

Type 2 sentences refer to an imaginary situation. They imply that the action in the *if-clause* will probably not happen.

> *If I won the lottery, I would buy a house in France.*
> * (...but I don't think I'll win the lottery.)*
> *If you didn't spend all your money on lottery tickets, you could*
> * afford a holiday.*
> * (...but you do spend all your money on lottery tickets.)*

The past subjunctive is often used when giving advice to someone, especially about what the person should do.

> *If I **were** you, I'd tell them the truth.*

Type 3

The main clause uses *would*, *could*, or *might* + *have* + the **past participle** of a main verb. The *if-clause* uses the past perfect tense.

> *We could have had a longer holiday, if we **hadn't spent** so much*
> * money on the house.*
> *If I **had known** about the exam, I would have paid more*
> * attention in class.*

In Type 3 sentences the speaker is looking back from the present to a past time and event. The speaker is talking about what might have happened but did not, either because the wrong thing was done or because nothing was done. This type of sentence is used when making excuses, showing regret, blaming, or giving an explanation.

Conditional clauses can also be used to talk about consequences, or to give an opinion about a situation in the following ways:

- The **if-clause** uses the present simple tense and the main clause uses the present simple tense. This is used to refer to universal truths.

    *If you **heat** water to 100°C, it **boils**.*
    *Plants **die** if they **don't get** enough water.*

- The **if-clause** uses the present simple tense and the main clause is in the imperative. This is used to give advice or orders for particular situations or sets of circumstances.

    *If the alarm **goes off**, **make** your way outside to the car park.*
    *If a red light **shows** here, **switch off** the machine.*

- The **if-clause** uses the present continuous or present simple tense and the main clause uses a modal verb. This is used to make suggestions and give advice.

    *If you're **thinking of** buying a lawnmower, you **could** try mine first.*
    *You **should** turn down his radio if you **don't want** the neighbours to complain.*

- The **if-clause** uses **will/would** and the main clause uses a modal verb.

This is used to make a request or to give a polite order.

    *If **you'll** wait a minute, the doctor **can** see you.*
    *If you **would** sign here, please, I'll be able to send you the books.*

Note that a *'d* in the main clause is the contracted form of *would*. However, a *'d* in an *if*-clause is the contracted form of *had*.

> *I'd have gone if he'd invited me.*
> *I would have gone if he had invited me.*
> *I would've gone if he'd invited me.*

In the main clause the contracted forms of the modals used in speech and informal writing are:

I'd have	or	**I would've**
I could've		**I might've**

Reporting speech

There are two ways of writing down or reporting what was said on any occasion. We can repeat the actual words used (**direct speech**),

> *Monica said,* '**There's nothing we can do about it.**'

or we can build the words into our own sentences (**reported speech**).

> *Monica said that there was nothing we could do about it.*

The words reported are normally accompanied by a **reporting verb**.

> *Monica **said/declared** that there was nothing we could do about it.*
> *'There is nothing we can do about it,' Monica **replied**.*

Another name for reported speech is **indirect speech**.

Direct speech

Direct speech gives the actual words that the speaker used. It is common in novels and other writing where the actual words of a speaker are quoted.

> *Monica said,* '**There's nothing we can do about it.**'

The **reporting verb** may come before the words that were actually spoken, or after them, or at a natural pause inside the reported sentence.

> ***Monica said,*** *'There is a nothing we can do about it.'*
> *'There is nothing we can do about it,' **Monica said**.*
> *'It's no good,' **Monica said**, 'we'll just have to ask for help.'*

- The comma comes inside the quotation marks, unless the reporting verb is positioned inside a reported sentence that itself does not require a comma.

    There is', Monica said, 'nothing we can do about it.'

- Typical reporting verbs are: *agree, answer, ask, inquire, explain, say, tell,* and *wonder.*

The subject and the reporting verb are sometimes reversed.

    'There is nothing we can do about it,' said Monica.

The actual words spoken always begin with a capital letter, unless the reporting verb comes within a sentence. They are separated from the reporting verb by a comma, unless they are followed by a question mark or an exclamation.

    'Why did you do it?' she asked.
    'Oh, mind your own business!' he snapped.

- The words spoken are enclosed in inverted commas (single or double quotation marks).

    'Have you been to the new shopping mall yet?' enquired Shona.

    "I've already seen it," John replied.

- Single quotation marks are often used to draw attention to a word that is being mentioned for a particular purpose. (See also p. 300.)

    There is no such word as 'fubber'.
    He called me a 'stubborn old goat'.

Reported speech

Reported speech or **indirect speech** reports something that was said, but does not use the actual words that the speaker uttered.

>*Lynn asked whether Pippa had been to the new shopping mall.*
>*Pippa replied that she hadn't, but she had heard that there*
>   *were some really cool shops there.*

Reported speech always has two clauses. The words that are spoken are put in a **reported clause**. There is also a **main clause** that contains a **reporting verb**. The main clause with the reporting verb usually comes before the **reported clause**.

>*Katie told me that Alison is going to resign.*
>*Peter asked whether Mandy was feeling better.*

The reporting verb in the main clause tells us how the sentence was uttered, e.g. *comment, remark, say, tell*. If the reported clause is a **statement**, the main clause is linked to the reported clause by *that*.

>*Mary said **that** her favourite actor was Ben Whishaw.*
>*John replied **that** he preferred Scarlett Johansson.*

If the reported clause asks a question, the main verb will be a question verb e.g. *ask, inquire, wonder, query*. The link between the main clause and the reported clause will be *if* or **whether**.

>*Jamie told Dad **(that)** he had passed his driving test.*
>*Lucy said Alan had been accepted at drama school.*

* The linking word *that* can be left out after most reporting verbs,

>*Jamie told Dad **(that)** he had passed his driving test.*
>*Lucy said Alan had been accepted at drama school.*

but the links *if* or **whether** cannot be left out.

> *Miriam asked if she could borrow Leonie's mp3 player.*
> *Evelyn wondered **whether** the concert would be sold out.*

• Speech in a reported clause is not separated from the reporting verb by a comma, is not enclosed in inverted commas, and does not begin with a capital letter unless it is a proper noun. Reported questions are not followed by question marks.

An alternative position for main clauses that would normally have a linking *that*, is after the reported clause. In this case, the link is left out.

> *Harry Potter was on that night, **Mary said**.*

Reported clauses can also be used to express what is in someone's mind as well as what is actually spoken.

> *Evelyn **wondered whether** the concert would be sold out.*
> *Charlotte **thought that** she had better go and see her family.*

Changes in the reported words

When you use reported speech, the words put into the reported clause do not exactly match the words actually spoken.

> *'I'll leave here at 8.30 on Friday.'*
> *She says **that she will leave** home at 8.30 on Friday.*
> *'I'm looking forward to seeing you.'*
> *She says **she's looking forward to seeing us**.*

Pronouns and **possessive determiners** have to change in reported speech because of the change of speaker, e.g. *I* may become *she*; *you* may become *us* or *him*.

'*I believe you.*'
*She said that **she** believed **us**.*

'*I'm leaving you.*'
*She said that **she** was leaving **him**.*

'*I've finished.*'
*She said that **she had finished**.*

Expressions of place and time may also have to change, e.g. *here* may become *there* or *home*; *Friday* may become *in three days' time*.

'*I've been here before.*'
*She said that she **had been there before**.*

'*I'll see you on Monday.*'
*She said that she would see him **in three days' time**.*

The tense in reported clauses

The verb may also change, e.g. *must* becomes *had to* in reported speech. The most common change is a change of tense.

'*Hello Jake? It's me, Penny. I've arrived here on time, and I'm going to take a bus to your place. There's one coming now, so I'd better run.*'

*She rang to say that **she'd** arrived **there** on time and **was going** to take a bus to **our** place. Then she said that one **was** coming **at that very moment**, so **she had to** run.*

A reporting verb in the present tense can be used in the main clause when you report on a letter or on a recent conversation, e.g. a telephone conversation.

'Hello, Jake? I've arrived here on time, and I'm going to take a
  bus to your place.'
Penny has just phoned. She **says** that she has arrived on time
  and that **she's coming** here by bus.

However, it is more common to use a past tense when reporting speech.

The changes of tense may be summarized as follows:

direct speech	reported speech
present simple	past simple
present continuous	past continuous
present perfect	past perfect
present perfect continuous	past perfect continuous
past simple	past perfect or past simple
future	conditional

Questions

Verb tenses in reported questions undergo the same changes as in
statements. See p. 283.

'Are you ready?'
He asked (us) if/whether we **were** ready.

'What time is it?'
He asked what time it **was**.
'Where has Jim gone?'
He wanted to know where Jim **had gone**.

Reporting verbs for questions include *ask, inquire, want to
know*, and *wonder*.

Direct **yes/no** questions are linked to the reporting clause by *if* or *whether*. **WH-** question words, e.g. *who, when, where*, are used in both direct and indirect questions.

> *'Are you ready?'*
> *He asked (us) if/whether we **were** ready.*

> *'What time is it?'*
> *He asked what time it **was**.*
> *'Where has Jim gone?'*
> *He wanted to know where Jim **had gone**.*

- The word order in a reported question is the same as that of a direct statement. Question order is not used in reported speech, i.e. no part of the verb comes before the subject.

Orders and requests

Orders are reported with *tell* + **object** + *to* **infinitive**.

> *'Stop calling me names!'*
> *She **told him to stop** calling her names.*

Requests for action are reported with *ask* + **object** + *to* **infinitive**.

> *'Please don't leave your things on the floor.'*
> *She asked us **not to leave** our things on the floor.*

Requests for objects are reported with *ask for* + **object**.

> *'Can I have the salt, please?'*
> *He **asked for the salt**.*

- The reporting verb can be used in the passive.

> *'Don't park here, please; it's reserved for the doctors.'*
> *I was **told not to park** there.*

Suggestions, advice, promises, etc.

A variety of verbs can be used for reporting suggestions and similar types of speech. Some of these are:

– *suggest, insist on* + present participle

> '*Let's go to the zoo.*'
> **He suggested going to the zoo.**

– *advise, invite, warn* + direct object + **not** + **to** infinitive

> '*I wouldn't buy that one, if I were you.*'
> She advised me **not to buy** that one.

– *refuse, threaten* + **to** infinitive

> '*I'm not telling you!*'
> She **refused to tell** me.

– *offer, promise* + **to** infinitive

> '*Don't worry; I'll help you.*'
> He **promised to help** me.

punctuation

The apostrophe (')

Misusing or omitting the apostrophe is one of the commonest punctuation errors.

Showing possession

The apostrophe (') is used to show that something belongs to someone. It is usually added to the end of a word and followed by an -s.

– -'s is added to the end of singular words.

> *a baby's pushchair*
> *Hannah's book*
> *a child's cry*

– -'s is added to the end of plural words not ending in -s.

> *children's games*
> *women's clothes*
> *people's lives*

– An apostrophe alone (') is added to plural words ending in -s.

> *Your grandparents are your parents' parents.*
> *We're campaigning for workers' rights.*
> *They've hired a new ladies' fashion guru.*

– -'s is added to the end of names and singular words ending in -s.

> *James's car*
> *the octopus's tentacles*

— -'s is added to the end of certain professions or occupations to indicate workplaces.

> *She's on her way to the doctor's.*
> *James is at the hairdresser's.*

— -'s is added to the end of people or their names to indicate that you are talking about their home.

> *I'm going over to Harry's for tea tonight.*
> *I popped round to Mum's this afternoon, but she wasn't in.*

• Note that if the word is a classical Greek name, or a historical building, an apostrophe only is sometimes preferred.

> *Dickens' novels*
> *St Giles' Cathedral*

-'s can also be added to:

— whole phrases

> *My next-door neighbour's dog was barking away like mad.*
> *John and Cath's house was on TV last night.*

— indefinite pronouns such as *somebody* or *anywhere*

> *Is this anybody's pencil case?*
> *It's nobody's fault but mine.*

— each other

> *We're getting used to each other's habits.*
> *We kept fogetting each other's names.*

When the possessor is an inanimate object (rather than a living thing), the apostrophe is not used and the word order is changed.

> *the middle of the street* (not *the street's middle*)
> *the front of the house* (not *the house's front*)

To test whether an apostrophe is in the right place, think about who the owner is.

> *the boy's books* [= *the books belonging to the boy*]
> *the boys' books* [= *the books belonging to the boys*]

Note that:

– An apostrophe is *not* used to form possessive pronouns such as *its*, *yours*, or *theirs*.

– An apostrophe is *not* used to form the plurals of words such as *potatoes* or *tomatoes*.

With letters and numbers

An apostrophe is used in front of two figures referring to a year or decade.

> *French students rioted in '68* [*short for '1968'*].
> *He worked as a schoolteacher during the '60s and early '90s.*

An apostrophe can be used in plurals of letters and numbers to make them more readable.

> *Mind your p's and q's.*
> *His 2's look a bit like 7's.*
> *She got straight A's in her exams.*

REMEMBER

it's = it is, e.g. *It's a holiday today.*
its = belonging to it, e.g. *The dog was scratching its ear.*

Contracted forms

An apostrophe is used in shortened forms of words to show that one or more letters have been missed out. Contractions are usually shortened forms of auxiliary verbs

be	have
I'm	I/we/they've (have)
We/you/they're (are)	He/she/it/one's (has)
He/she/it/one's (is)	I/we/you/he/she/it/one/they'd (had)

would
I/we/you/he/she/it/one/they'd (would)

or the negative *not*.

not
We/you/they aren't
He/she/it/one isn't
I/we/they haven't
He/she/it/one hasn't

In order to work out what the contracted forms *'s* and *'d* represent, you need to look at what follows it:

– If *'s* is followed by an *-ing* form, it represents the auxiliary *is*.

She's **reading** a book about the ancient Egyptians.
He's **going** to Ibiza for his holidays.

− If **'s** is followed by an adjective or a noun phrase, it represents the main verb *is*.

> *She's **nervous** about meeting my parents.*
> *He's **brilliant** at maths.*

− If **'s** is followed by a past participle, it can represent *is* as it is used in the passive,

> *He's **portrayed** by the media as a kindly old grandfather.*
> *It's often **said** that rock stars are frustrated actors.*

or *has* as it is used in the present perfect.

> *She's **broken** her wrist.*
> *It's **been** ages since we last saw you.*

− If **'s** is followed by *got*, it represents the auxiliary *has*.

> *She's **got** two brothers and one sister.*
> *It's **got** everything you could want.*

− If **'d** is followed by a past participle, it represents the auxiliary *had*.

> *I'd **raced** against him before, but never in a marathon.*
> *She couldn't believe what she'd **done**.*

− If **'d** is followed by a base form, it represents the modal auxiliary *would*.

> *I'd **give up** now, if I were you.*
> *When we were kids we'd **spend** hours out on our bikes.*

− If **'d** is followed by *rather* or *better*, it represents the modal auxiliary *would*.

> *We'd **better** go home soon.*
> *I'd **rather** not talk about that.*

The comma (,)

The comma marks a short pause between elements in a sentence.

Separating main clauses

Main clauses that are joined together with *and* or *but* do not normally have a comma before the conjunction unless the two clauses have different subjects.

> *You go out of the door and turn immediately left.*
> *It was cold outside, but we decided to go out for a walk anyway.*

Separating subordinate clauses from main clauses

Commas are normally used if the subordinate clause comes before the main clause.

> *If you have any problems, just call me.*
> *Just call me if you have any problems.*

Sometimes a comma is used even when the main clause comes first, if the clauses are particularly long.

> *We should be able to finish the work by the end of the week, if nothing unexpected turns up between now and then.*

Separating relative clauses from main clauses

Commas are used to mark off non-defining relative clauses (see p. 275). This is the type of clause that adds to information about a noun or noun phrase.

*My next-door neighbour, who works from home, is keeping an
    eye on the house while we're away.*
*She moved to Los Angeles, where she was immediately signed
    as a singer songwriter.*

Commas are not required in defining relative clauses (see p. 274), since
these simply postmodify the noun.

*Let's make sure the money goes to the people **who need it most**.*
*The computer **(that) I borrowed** kept on crashing.*

Separating items in a list

Commas are used to separate three or more items in a list or series.

She got out bread, butter, and jam (but bread and butter).

Note that the comma is often not given before the final *and* or *or*.

They breed dogs, cats, rabbits and hamsters.
We did canoeing, climbing and archery.

Separating adjectives

Commas are used between adjectives, whether they come before
the noun (i.e. used attributively) or after a linking verb (i.e. used
predicatively).

It was a hot, dry and dusty road.
It's wet, cold and windy outside.

A comma is not usually used before an adjective that is followed by
and.

With adverbials

When an adverbial such as *however*, *therefore* or *unfortunately* modifies a whole sentence, it is separated from the rest of the sentence by a comma.

> *However, police would not confirm this rumour.*
> *Therefore, I try to avoid using the car as much as possible.*

With question tags and short responses

Commas are used before question tags and after *yes* or *no* in short responses.

> *It's quite cold today, isn't it?*
> *He's up to date with all his injections, isn't he?*
> *Are you the mother of these children? – Yes, I am.*
> *You're Amy Osborne, aren't you? – No, I'm not.*

With vocatives

Commas are used to separate the name of a person or group being addressed from the rest of the sentence.

> *And now, ladies and gentlemen, please raise your glasses in*
> *a toast to the happy couple.*
> *Come on, Olivia, be reasonable.*
> *Dad, can you come and help me, please?*

With discourse markers

Commas are used to separate discourse markers like *Well* and *Now then* from the rest of the sentence.

> *Well, believe it or not, I actually passed!*
> *Now then, let's see what's on TV tonight.*
> *Actually, I quite enjoyed it.*

In reported speech

Commas are used to follow direct speech (if there is no question or exclamation mark after the quotation), or to show that it comes next.

> *'I don't understand this question,' said Peter.*
> *Peter said, 'I don't understand this question.'*
> *'You're crazy!' Claire exclaimed.*
> *'What do you think you're doing?' Dad bellowed.*

It is also possible to punctuate reported speech of the type *Peter said,* '...' using a colon instead of a comma. This is a particularly common practice in American English.

> *Peter said: 'Dream on.'*

In dates

A comma must be used between the day of the month and the year, when the two numbers are next to each other.

> *March 31, 2011*

Quotation marks (' ') or (" ")

Direct speech

Direct speech gives the actual words that a speaker used. It is common in novels and other writing where the actual words of a speaker are quoted (see p. 282).

The words spoken are enclosed in single or double quotation marks.

> *'Have you been to the new shopping precinct yet?'*
>   *enquired Shona.*

> *"I've already seen it,"* John replied.

- The comma comes inside the quotation marks, unless the reporting verb is positioned inside a reported sentence that itself does not require a comma.

> *There is'*, Monica said, *'nothing we can do about it.'*

Other uses

Single quotation marks are sometimes used:

– to draw attention to a word

> *The word* **'book'** *can be used as a noun or a verb.*

– to indicate an unusual use of a word

> *She pointed out that websites used for internet voting could be* **'spoofed'**.

– to suggest that the writer want to be distanced from a word.

I don't agree with this **'mercy killing'** *business.*

• Note that the full stop comes after the quotation marks in such cases.

Capital letters

A capital (or 'upper case') letter is used to mark the beginning of a sentence.

> *When I was 20, I dropped out of university and became a model.*

Capital letters are also used for the first letter in proper nouns. These include:

– people's names

> *Jenny Forbes*　　　　*William Davidson*

– days of the week

> *Wednesday*　　　　*Saturday*

– months of the year

> *August*　　　　*January*

– public holidays

> *Christmas*　　　　*Yom Kippur*

– nationalities

> *Spanish*　　　　*Iraqi*

– languages

> *Swahili*　　　　*Flemish*

– geographical locations

> *Australia*   *Loch Ness*
> *Mount Everest*   *The Mediterranean Sea*

– company names

> *Dyson*   *Harper Collins*

– religions

> *Islam*   *Buddhism*

Capital letters are also used for the first letter in titles of books, magazines, newspapers, TV shows, films, etc. Where there are several words, a capital letter is usually used for all the main content words in the title (i.e. not the prepositions or the determiners – unless they are the first word in the title).

> *The Times*   *Hello!*
> *Twelfth Night*   *The Secret Garden*
> *Newsnight*   *Mamma Mia!*

The full stop (.)

Full stops are used:

– to mark the end of a sentence

> *Let's have some lunch.*
> *I have to catch a bus in ten minutes.*

– to mark the end of a sentence fragment

> *Are you cold? – Yes, a bit.*
> *Do you like this sort of music? Not really.*

– in initials for people's names, although this practice is becoming less frequent

> *J.K. Rowling*   *Iain M. Banks*
> *M.C. Hammer*   *Ronald G. Hardie*

– after abbreviations, although this practice is becoming less frequent.

> *P.S. Do pop in next time you're passing.*
> *She's moved to the I.T. department*
> *R.S.V.P. to Helen Douglas on 01234 676240.*
> *The U.S. government reacted strongly to the accusation.*

When an abbreviation consists of a shortened word such as *Re.* or *Prof.*, a full stop is needed.

> *Re. your suggestion that we shorten the lunch hour, could*
> *we arrange a quick meeting to discuss the various options?*
> *Prof. John Johansson will be speaking on the subject of*
> *'Discourse in the Electronic Age'.*
> *Flight BA 345: dep. 09.44 arr. 11.10.*

When an abbreviation contains the last letter of the shortened word, a full stop is not needed.

> *Dr McDonald*   *St Mary's School*
> *41, Douglas Rd*   *Universal Pictures (UK) Ltd*

- Note that full stops are not used in many common sets of initials,

    > *Did you see that programme on BBC 4 last night?*
    > *Millions of people now call the NHS Direct helpline each year.*

  or at the end of headlines, headings and titles.

    > *Fear grips global stock markets*
    > *Teaching grammar as a liberating force*
    > *Wuthering Heights*

Remember that a full stop, and not a question mark, is used after an indirect question or a polite request.

> *He asked if the bus had left.*
> *Will you open your books on page 14.*
> *I wonder what's happened.*
> *She asked him where he was going.*

In American English, the full stop is called a period.

The question mark (?)

The question mark marks the end of a question.

> *When will we be arriving?*
> *Why did you do that?*
> *Does any of this matter?*
> *He's certain to be elected, isn't he?*

Question marks are used in direct questions, i.e. when the actual words of a speaker are used. A reported question should end with a full stop.

> *The lady said, 'Where are you going?'*
> *The lady asked where she was going.*

Note that you put a question mark at the end of a question, even if the words in the sentence are not in the normal question order, or some words are omitted. Care is needed here as such a sentence can look, at first sight, like a statement rather than a question.

> *You know he doesn't live here any longer?*

A full stop, rather than a question mark, is used after an indirect question.

> *I'd like to know what you've been doing all this time.*
> *I wonder what's happened.*

A full stop also replaces a question mark at the end of a sentence which looks like a question if, in fact, it is really a polite request.

> *Will you please return the completed forms to me.*
> *Would you please call my brother and ask him to collect my car.*

The exclamation mark (!)

The exclamation mark is used after exclamations and emphatic expressions.

> *I can't believe it!*
> *Oh, no! Look at this mess!*

The exclamation mark loses its effect if it is overused. It is better to use a full stop after a sentence expressing mild excitement or humour.

> *It was such a beautiful day.*
> *I felt like a perfect banana.*

The colon (:)

The colon indicates a break between two main clauses which is stronger than a comma but weaker than a full stop.

A colon is used:

– in front of a list

> *I used three colours: green, blue and pink.*
> *Make sure you wear clothes made from natural fibres:*
> *cotton, silk and wool.*

– in front of an explanation or a reason

> *Nevertheless, the main problem remained: what should*
> *be done with the two men?*
> *I decided against going away this weekend: the weather*
> *forecast was dreadful.*

– after introductory headings

> *Cooking time: about five minutes.*
> *Start time: 10 o'clock.*

– in more formal writing, between two main clauses that are connected

> *It made me feel claustrophobic: what, I wonder, would happen*
> *to someone who was really unable to tolerate being locked*
> *into such a tiny space?*
> *Be patient: the next book in the series has not yet been*
> *published.*

- in front of the second part of a book title

    Farming and wildlife: a study in compromise
    Beyond single words: the most frequent collocations in spoken
        English.

- to introduce direct speech, especially in American English, or when the quotation is particularly long.

    He said: 'You owe me three dollars and twenty-five cents.'
    The Health Minister said: 'The NHS I.T. programme will mean
        that patients will get access to more comprehensive
        information to help them make choices.'

The semicolon (;)

The semicolon is used to mark a break between two main clauses when there is a balance or a contrast between the clauses.

>Compare:
>
>*The engine roared into life. The propellers began to turn. The plane taxied down the runway ready for takeoff.*
>
>with:
>
>*The engine roared into life; the propellers began to turn; the plane taxied down the runway ready for takeoff.*

A useful test to work out when to use a semicolon is to ask yourself whether the two clauses could be written instead as separate sentences. If the answer is 'yes', then you can use a semicolon.

Note that it is quite acceptable to use a full stop in these cases, but a semicolon is preferable if you wish to convey the sense of a link or continuity between the clauses in your narrative.

>*I'm not that interested in jazz; I prefer classical music.*
>*He knew everything about me; I had never even heard of him.*

A semicolon is also used to separate items in a list, especially if the listed items are phrases or clauses, which may already contain commas.

>*The holiday was a disaster: the flight was four hours late; the hotel, which was described as 'luxury', was dirty; and it rained for the whole fortnight.*

Brackets ( )

Brackets (also called **parentheses**) are used to enclose a word or words which can be left out and still leave a meaningful sentence.

> *The wooded area (see map below) is approximately*
> *4,000 hectares.*
> *This is a process which Hayek (a writer who came to*
> *rather different conclusions) also observed.*

Brackets are also used to show alternatives or options.

> *Any student(s) interested in taking part should e-mail me.*
> *A goat should give from three to six pints (1.7 to 3.4 litres)*
> *of milk a day.*

Note that when the structure of the sentence as a whole demands punctuation after a bracketed section, the punctuation is given *outside* the brackets.

> *I haven't yet spoken to John (I mean John Maple, my boss),*
> *but I have a meeting with him on Friday.*
> *For lunch we had sandwiches (pastrami on rye and so on),*
> *salami, coleslaw, fried chicken, and potato salad.*

Punctuation is given before the closing brackets only when it applies to the bracketed section rather than to the sentence as a whole.

> *He's very handsome (positively gorgeous in fact!) and still*
> *single.*

Square brackets [ ]

Square brackets are used, usually in books and articles, when supplying words that make a quotation clearer or that comment on it, although they were not originally said or written.

> *Mr Runcie concluded: 'The novel is at its strongest when describing the dignity of Cambridge [a slave] and the education of Emily [the daughter of an absentee landlord].'*

The hyphen (-)

The hyphen joins words or parts of words.

Hyphens are used at the ends of lines where a word has been split, to warn the reader that the word continues on the next line. If the word you need to split is clearly made up of two or more smaller words or elements, you should put the hyphen after the first of these parts. Otherwise, you put the hyphen at the end of a syllable.

> *wheel-barrow*   *inter-national*
> *listen-ing*   *compli-mentary*
> *infor-mation*

It is best not to add a hyphen if the word is a short one, or if it would mean writing just one or two letters at the end or beginning of a line. For example, it would be better to write 'unnatural' on the line below, rather than writing 'un-' on one line and 'natural' on the next.

Prefixes that are used in front of a word beginning with a capital letter always have a hyphen after them.

> *a wave of anti-British feeling*
> *a neo-Byzantine cathedral*

A hyphen is used to join two or more words that together form an adjective, where this adjective is used *before* the noun it describes.

> *an up-to-date account*
> *a last-minute rush*
> *a six-year-old boy*

The hyphen is omitted when the adjective so formed comes after the noun or pronoun it describes.

The accounts are up to date.
It was all rather last minute.
He's six years old.

Some common compound nouns are usually written with hyphens.

mother-in-law   *great-grandmother*

Hyphens can be used to split words that have been formed by adding
a prefix to another word, especially to avoid an awkward combination
of letters or confusion with another word.

re-elect
re-covering furniture
re-creation

The dash (–)

A spaced dash (i.e. with a single space before and after it) is used:

– at the beginning and end of a comment that interrupts the flow of a sentence.

> *Now children – Kenneth, stop that immediately! – open your books on page 20.*

– to separate off extra information.

> *Boots and shoes – all shapes, sizes and colours – tumbled out.*

An unspaced dash (i.e. with no space before or after it) is used:

– to indicate a range.

> *pages 26–42*

– between two adjectives or noun modifiers that indicate that two countries or groups are involved in something or that an individual has two roles or aspects.

> *Swedish–Norwegian relations improved,*
> *the United States–Canada free trade pact*
> *a mathematician–philosopher*

– to indicate that something such as a plane or a train goes between two places.

> *the Anguilla–St Kitts flight*
> *the New York–Montreal train*

The slash (/)

The slash separates letters, words or numbers. It is used to indicate alternatives, ratios and ranges, and in website addresses.

> *he/she/it*
> *200 km/hr*
> *the 2001/02 accounting year*
> *http://www.abcdefg.com*

Punctuation in numbers

Dates

Full stops or slashes are often used in dates.

American usage

12.3.09   3/12/09
2.28.11   2/28/11

Scientific usage

Full stops are not used in scientific abbreviations.

12 *kg*   50 *cm*

Times
Full stops and occasionally colons are used in times.

4.15 *p.m*   21.15
3:30 *a.m*   20:30

Long numbers

Commas are used in numbers to mark off units of thousands and millions.

1,359   2,543,678

Decimals

Full stops indicate decimal points.

1.5   25.08

index

2. Spelling

328 contents

the basics
of spelling

The basics of spelling

Spelling is the process of using letters to represent a word. For most words there is one arrangement of letters that is accepted as the correct spelling. Using the correct spelling of a word means that you can be confident of being understood when you write English; getting the spelling wrong can make it difficult to be understood and create a bad impression.

The alphabet

There are twenty-six letters that are used to spell words in English:

a b c d e f g h i j k l m n o p q r s t u v w x y z

Each of these letters can also be written as a capital letter. This form is used at the beginning of a sentence or a name, and in certain other places (see pages 405–6).

A B C D E F G H I J K L M N O P Q R S T U V W X Y Z

Five of these letters (**A**, **E**, **I**, **O**, **U**) are **vowels**. These are used to represent sounds that are made when your mouth is open.

cat   *pen*   *sit*
dog   *cup*

The other letters are called **consonants**. These are used to represent sounds that are made by closing your mouth or using your tongue.

pea   *see*   *do*

> The letter **Y** can act as a vowel in some words, such as *sky* and *crypt*.

Most words are spelt using a mixture of vowels and consonants. This is because in most cases we need to open our mouths between pronouncing different consonants. It is unusual to find more than two vowels or two consonants together.

Typical letter-sounds

Most consonants are strongly associated with a particular sound and represent this sound in virtually every word in which they appear. For example, the letter **B** nearly always makes the same sound.

big	**b**ad	**b**ee
ca**b**	clu**b**	ro**b**in

Some consonants can represent different sounds in different words. For example **C** can have a 'hard' sound like a **K**.

cat	**c**up	pani**c**

But it can also have a 'soft' sound like an **S**.

city	a**c**id	pla**c**e

Combinations of consonants

Some consonants can be combined and still keep their typical sounds. The letters **L**, **R** and **W** can come after some other consonants.

b**l**ob	g**r**ip	d**w**ell
c**l**ip	p**r**od	t**w**in

The letter **S** can come before a number of other consonants.

s*can*	s*kip*	s*lip*
s*mell*	s*nip*	s*pin*
s*quid*	s*top*	s*wim*

Some combinations of letters can appear in the middle of a word or at the end of a word, but not at the start of a word.

doc*tor*	le*ft*	gol*den*
mi*lk*	hel*p*	bel*t*
la*mp*	lan*d*	rin*g*
tan*k*	wen*t*	op*t*

It is unusual, but not impossible, to have three consonants together.

s*crap*	sp*lit*	ex*tra*

Combinations that produce typical sounds

When some letters are combined with an **H**, they do not keep their own sounds but create a different sound. For example:

CH

chip	*chat*	*rich*

PH creates the same sound as the letter **F**.

phone	*phantom*	*graph*

SH

ship	*shop*	*fish*

TH

thin   thank   path

TH can also make a different, slightly softer sound.

this   that   with

Simple vowel sounds

The vowels **A**, **E**, **I**, **O**, and **U** each have typical sounds when they appear on their own in short words.

cat	rat	hat
men	pen	ten
bit	hit	sit
dot	lot	got
but	nut	hut

The sound of a vowel changes from a 'short' sound to a 'long' sound when the consonant after the vowel is followed by the letter **E**.

date	rate	hate
scene	swede	theme
bite	mite	like
note	lone	mole
flute	rule	brute

Combinations of vowels

When two vowels are used together, they usually make a different sound rather than keeping the simple sounds they make on their own.

The letters **AI** have a characteristic sound when they appear together.

raid   *train*   *aim*

The letters **AU** have a characteristic sound when they appear together.

daub   *faun*   *haul*

The letters **EA** have a characteristic sound when they appear together.

read   *tea*   *eat*

When the letter **E** is doubled it produces a characteristic sound. The sound is the same as the one typically produced by **EA**.

feed   *tree*   *bee*

The letters **IE** have a characteristic sound when they appear together.

tie   *fried*   *pie*

The letters **OA** have a characteristic sound when they appear together.

road   *goat*   *toad*

The letters **OE** have a characteristic sound when they appear together. The sound is the same as the one typically produced by **OA**.

toe   *hoe*   *woe*

The letters **OI** have a characteristic sound when they appear together.

coin   *soil*   *oil*

When the letter **O** is doubled it produces a characteristic sound.

food   *moon*   *boot*

The double **O** can sometimes make a different, shorter, sound.

good   *wool*   *hood*

The letters **OU** have a characteristic sound when they appear together.

mouth   *count*   *out*

The letters **UE** have a characteristic sound when they appear together. The sound is the same as the one produced by **OO** in the word *book*.

true   *sue*   *glue*

Vowels followed by R, W, or Y

When the letters **R**, **W**, or **Y** come after a vowel, the letter usually changes the sound of the vowel, but it is not sounded itself.

The letters **AR** have a characteristic sound when they appear together.

car   *park*   *art*

The letters **AW** have a characteristic sound when they appear together. The sound is the same as the one typically produced by **AU**.

paw   *claw*   *straw*

The letters **AY** have a characteristic sound when they appear together. The sound is the same as the one typically produced by **AI**.

day   *stay*   *may*

The letters **ER** have a characteristic sound when they appear together.

her   *term*   *herb*

The letters **EW** have a characteristic sound when they appear together. The sound is the same as the one produced by **OO** in the word *book*.

flew   yew   brew

The letters **IR** have a characteristic sound when they appear together. The sound is the same as the one typically produced by **ER**.

sir   girl   shirt

The letters **OR** have a characteristic sound when they appear together. The sound is the same as the one typically produced by **AU**.

sort   born   for

The letters **OW** have a characteristic sound when they appear together. The sound is the same as the one typically produced by **OU**.

how   growl   down

These letters can also make the sound that is typically produced by **OE**.

grow   flow   own

The letters **OY** have a characteristic sound when they appear together. The sound is the same as the one typically produced by **OI**.

boy   toy   joy

The letters **UR** have a characteristic sound when they appear together. The sound is the same as the one typically produced by **ER**.

burn   turn   hurt

why you
need to work
at spelling

Why you need to work at spelling

If every letter represented one sound and one sound only, you could write out words very easily once you knew which letter represented which sound. Some languages (such as Italian) are indeed quite like this, and present few surprises with regard to spelling once you know how each sound is written.

But English uses about 44 different sounds to make up words, whereas there are only 26 letters to indicate these sounds. This means that some letters have to be used for more than one sound.

Moreover, there are certain other factors that mean that it is not always easy to predict how an English word will be spelt. We shall look at these factors in this chapter.

Some letters can have more than one sound

As we have just seen, there are more sounds in English than there are letters to represent them. This means that some letters have to represent more than sound.

For example, the letter **T** usually makes one sound when it occurs on its own.

    *t*in   *t*ank   pa*t*

But it makes a different sound when it is followed by **H**.

    *th*in   *th*ank   pa*th*

More awkwardly, some letters have more than one sound, even though there are other letters which make one of the sounds. For example, the letter **G** typically has a 'hard' sound when it occurs on its own.

*g*irl   *g*ame   ru*g*

But in some cases it makes the same 'soft' sound as the letter **J**.

*g*erm   *g*inger   pa*g*e

Similarly, the letter **S** has a characteristic 'hissing' sound.

*s*ee   *s*it   ga*s*

But it can sometimes make the same 'buzzing' sound as the letter **Z**.

ha*s*   hi*s*   plea*s*ant

The fact that letters can have multiple uses means that when you see a word you cannot automatically know how it will be pronounced.

Some sounds can be represented by different letters

A more significant issue is that some sounds can be represented by different letters or combinations of letters.

The vowel sound in the following group of words has the same pronunciation, but the letters used to represent the sound are different in each word.

m*ar*ch   *al*ms   cl*er*k   h*ear*t

The same thing can be true of most vowel sounds, as the following groups of words show.

*ai*sle	*guy*	*might*	r*ye*
p*ai*d	*day*	*grey*	*neigh*
bear	*dare*	*stair*	w*here*
z*oo*	*do*	sh*oe*	*you*

Similarly, the consonant sound at the end of the following words has the same pronunciation, but is represented by different letters in each word.

if	*graph*	*rough*

The same thing can be true of other consonant sounds, as the following groups of words show.

gem	*edge*	*jam*
cap	*dark*	*plaque*
sit	*centre*	*scene*

So when you hear a word, you can't automatically work out how it is spelt.

Some words that sound the same are written differently

Because sounds can be represented by different letters, it is possible for two different words to sound the same but be spelt differently. This can lead to confusion between the two spellings.

For example, the words *there*, meaning 'that place', and *their*, meaning 'belonging to them' both have the same sound. Similarly, the words *stare*, meaning 'to look intently', and *stair*, meaning 'one of a set of steps', also share a single pronunciation.

It can be easy to confuse these words and use the correct spelling of one word when you are actually intending to write the other word.

English words come from many different languages

One of the most striking features of the English language is its readiness to accept words from other languages. At the heart of modern English are two completely different languages – Anglo-Saxon and French – which have two different spelling systems, but which both contributed thousands of words to the language. In addition to this, English has borrowed words from many other European languages, such as Italian, Spanish, German, and Dutch. Furthermore, whenever scientists made new discoveries they turned to the classical languages of Latin and Greek to come up with names for the new things they needed to describe.

As communications between different parts of the world have become easier, more and more languages have contributed to English, including Turkish, Arabic, Hindi, Chinese, Japanese, and Urdu.

Each of these languages has its own spelling system – many of which are quite different from the natural English system – and the words that English has borrowed from them often keep the spelling patterns of the original language.

For example, many words that come from French use **CH** where you might expect **SH**.

*ch*alet *ch*ute *ch*auffeur

Words that come from Greek use **PH** rather than **F**.

telephone *ph*ysical *ph*otograph

Words that come from Japanese use **K** rather than **C**.

karaoke   *karate*   *kimono*

So unless you know which language a word comes from, the spelling could reflect any of a number of different systems.

Silent letters

Another thing that can be confusing is that some words contain letters which are not sounded when the word is pronounced.

Often these are letters that were sounded in the original form of a word. Over many years the pronunciation of these words became simplified, but the spelling has not changed to reflect the new pronunciation.

For example, the letter **G** is often silent before **N** or **M**.

gnat   *phlegm*   *sign*

Similarly, **H** is often silent at the start of a word, or after **G** or **R**.

honest   *ghost*   *rhyme*

E is often silent at the end of words.

have   *give*   *love*

> In fact, it has been reckoned that of the 26 letters in the alphabet, only five are never silent. These five are **F**, **J**, **Q**, **V** and **X**.

The presence of single and double letters

All of the letters except **H**, **Q** and **Y** can occur as both single and double letters within a word.

For example, the letter **B** occurs as a single letter in some words.

robin   *habit*   *crab*

But in other words the **B** is doubled.

bobbin   *rabbit*   *ebb*

When consonants are doubled, they are pronounced just the same as a single consonant. So when you hear a word you cannot always tell where a consonant sound is represented by a single letter or a double letter.

Spelling variants

Some words do not have a single spelling that is regarded as correct, but can be spelt in two or more different ways.

For example, most words that end in **ISE** can also end in **IZE** in British English.

*special**ise***	*special**ize***
*emphas**ise***	*emphas**ize***

Some words that come from other languages can be written in different ways in English because the original language uses a different alphabet and there are different systems for representing that alphabet in English.

veranda	*verandah*
czar	*tsar*

Other spelling variations are simply a matter of taste.

barbecue	*barbeque*
judgment	*judgement*

The fact that such variations exist means that there is not always a single correct spelling that you can learn.

American and British spelling

One of the most common sources of variations in spelling is the fact that some words are conventionally spelt differently in American English and British English. Some spellings that are regarded as correct by American speakers are not used in Britain (or in Australia and most other English-speaking countries).

The table below shows some examples of variations between British and American spelling.

British English	American English
aesthetic	esthetic
aluminium	aluminum
anaesthetic	anesthetic
analyse	analyze
axe	ax
behaviour	behavior
breathalyse	breathalyze
catalogue	catalog
centre	center
cheque	check
colour	color
defence	defense
favourite	favorite
fulfil	fulfill
grey	gray
instalment	installment
jewellery	jewelry
kerb	curb
litre	liter
lustre	luster
meagre	meager
mould	mold

British English	American English
moustache	mustache
odour	odor
plough	plow
programme	program
pyjamas	pajamas
sceptic	skeptic
theatre	theater
tyre	tire
vice	vise
[=woodwork tool]	

And now the good news

All of these factors mean that English spelling needs some work before you can become very accurate. The good news, however, is that there are things you can do to help you understand the system better and so become confident about how to spell words. We shall look at these in the next two chapters.

patterns and building blocks

Patterns and building blocks

Some groups of letters crop up in lots of different English words. Often a group of letters will indicate the same thing in every word that it appears. For example, the letters **RE** at the start of a word usually mean 'again'.

Because so many words are made up of these building blocks, you don't need to learn every spelling individually. Often you can spell out a word by adding together the blocks of letters that form the word. So it is important to know what these blocks are, how they are joined on to the rest of a word, and what they mean.

Building blocks at the start of words

A block of letters that regularly appears at the start of words and carries a meaning is called a **prefix**. A prefix can be fixed in front of another word or block of letters to create a new word with a different meaning.

For example, when the letters **UN** are added to another word (called a **root word**), they add the meaning of 'not' to the sense of the other word.

unnatural **un**known **un**holy

Notice that you can spell these words by splitting them into the prefix and the root word, as the spelling of the root word stays the same.

It is not always quite as obvious as this that a prefix is being added to an existing word to make a new word. Many prefixes occur in words that came to English from Latin and Greek. In these cases the blocks to which they are joined are often Latin or Greek forms rather than familiar English words. Nevertheless, it is worth studying these building blocks and noting that they occur in many English words.

The prefix **AB** means 'away from' or 'not'.

> *ab*normal *ab*use *ab*scond

The prefix **AD** means 'towards'.

> *ad*dress *ad*just *ad*mit

The prefix **AL** means 'all'.

> *al*together *al*ways *al*mighty

The prefix **ANTE** means 'before'. Take care not to confuse this with **ANTI**. If you remember the meaning of both these prefixes you should be able to work out the correct spelling of a word that starts with one of them.

> *ante*natal *ante*room *ante*cedent

The prefix **ANTI** means 'against'. Take care not to confuse this with **ANTE**. If you remember the meaning of both these prefixes you should be able to work out the correct spelling of a word that starts with one of them.

> *anti*war *anti*social *anti*depressant

The prefix **ARCH** means 'chief'.

> *arch*bishop *arch*enemy *arch*angel

The prefix **AUTO** means 'self'.

> *auto*graph *auto*biography *auto*mobile

The prefix **BENE** means 'good' or 'well'.

> *bene*fit *bene*volent *bene*factor

The prefix **BI** means 'two' or 'twice'.

bicycle **bi**monthly **bi**focals

The prefix **CIRCUM** means 'around'.

circumference **circum**stance **circum**navigate

The prefix **CO** means 'together'. There is sometimes a hyphen after this prefix to make the meaning clear.

copilot **co**-star **co**operate

The prefix **CON** means 'together'.

confer **con**stellation **con**verge

When it is added before words beginning with **L**, the prefix **CON** is changed to **COL**.

collaborate **col**lateral **col**lide

When it is added before words beginning with **B**, **M**, or **P**, the prefix **CON** is changed to **COM**.

combat **com**mit **com**pact

When it is added before words beginning with **R**, the prefix **CON** is changed to **COR**.

correct **cor**respond **cor**relation

The prefix **CONTRA** means 'against'.

contradict **contra**vene **contra**flow

The prefix **DE** indicates removal or reversal.

*de*frost   *de*throne   *de*caffeinated

The prefix **DIS** indicates removal or reversal.

*dis*agree   *dis*honest   *dis*trust

The prefix **EN** usually means 'into'.

*en*rage   *en*slave   *en*danger

The prefix **EX** means 'out' or 'outside of'.

*ex*it   *ex*port   *ex*ternal

The prefix **EX** also means 'former'. The prefix is followed by a hyphen when it has this meaning.

ex-wife   *ex*-partner   *ex*-president

The prefix **EXTRA** means 'beyond' or 'outside of'.

*extra*ordinary   *extra*terrestrial   *extra*sensory

The prefix **HYPER** means 'over' or 'more'.

*hyper*active   *hyper*critical   *hyper*market

The prefix **IN** sometimes means 'not'.

*in*human   *in*sufferable   *in*credible

The prefix **IN** can also mean 'in' or 'into'.

*in*filtrate   *in*take   *in*grown

When it is added before words beginning with **L**, the prefix **IN** is changed to **IL**.

illiterate **il**legal **il**logical

When it is added before words beginning with **B**, **M**, or **P**, the prefix **IN** is changed to **IM**.

imbalance **im**moral **im**possible

> Note that the word *input* is an exception to this rule.

When it is added before words beginning with **R**, the prefix **IN** is changed to **IR**.

irregular **ir**responsible **ir**relevant

The prefix **INTER** means 'between'.

international **inter**war **inter**ruption

The prefix **INTRA** means 'within'.

intravenous **intra**net **intra**mural

The prefix **MACRO** means 'very large'.

macroeconomics **macro**biotic **macro**cosm

The prefix **MAL** means 'bad' or 'badly'.

malpractice **mal**formed **mal**administration

The prefix **MAXI** means 'big' or 'biggest'.

maximize **maxi**mum **maxi**dress

The prefix **MICRO** means 'very small'.

> *micro*scope   *micro*chip   *micro*wave

The prefix **MINI** means 'small'.

> *mini*skirt   *mini*series   *mini*bus

The prefix **MIS** means 'wrong' or 'false'.

> *mis*behave   *mis*fortune   *mis*take

The prefix **NON** means 'not'.

> *non*sense   *non*fiction   *non*stop

The prefix **PARA** usually means 'beside' or 'parallel to'.

> *para*medic   *para*military   *para*legal

The prefix **POST** means 'after'.

> *post*pone   *post*graduate   *post*dated

The prefix **PRE** means 'before'.

> *pre*arranged   *pre*war   *pre*season

The prefix **PRO** means 'ahead' or 'forward'.

> *pro*logue   *pro*active   *pro*voke

The prefix **PRO** also means 'in favour of'. The prefix is followed by a hyphen when it has this meaning.

> *pro*-choice   *pro*-democracy   *pro*-European

The prefix **RE** means 'again'.

   rearrange   **re**read   **re**heat

The prefix **SEMI** means 'half'.

   semi-final   **semi**tone   **semi**-professional

The prefix **SUB** means 'under'.

   submarine   **sub**soil   **sub**way

The prefix **SUPER** indicates 'above', 'beyond' or 'extreme'.

   superhuman   **super**market   **super**star

The prefix **TELE** means 'distant'.

   telegraph   **tele**vision   **tele**scope

The prefix **TRANS** means 'across'.

   transfer   **trans**plant   **trans**continental

The prefix **ULTRA** indicates 'beyond' or 'extreme'.

   ultrasound   **ultra**modern   **ultra**-careful

Building blocks at the end of words

A block of letters that regularly appears at the end of words and carries a meaning is called a **suffix**. Just like a prefix at the start of a word, a suffix can be fixed onto a root word to create a new word with a different meaning.

For example, when the letters **LESS** are added to the end of a root word, they add the meaning of 'without' to the sense of the root word.

*head**less***   *child**less***   *life**less***

It is worth studying these building blocks and noting that they occur at the end of many English words.

The suffix **ABLE** means 'able to'.

*break**able***   *read**able***   *enjoy**able***

> It is difficult to distinguish this from the suffix **IBLE**, which occurs in many words and has the same meaning. A list of the common words with each suffix is given on pages 361–62.

The suffix **AL** means 'related to'.

*season**al***   *nation**al***   *tradition**al***

The suffix **ANCE** indicates a state or quality.

*accept**ance***   *defi**ance***   *resembl**ance***

The suffix **ANT** indicates an action or condition.

*resist**ant***   *toler**ant***   *dorm**ant***

> It is difficult to distinguish this from the suffix **ENT**, which occurs in many words and has the same meaning. A list of the common words with each suffix is given on pages 363–64.

The suffix **ARY** means 'related to'.

*caution**ary***   *revolution**ary***   *document**ary***

The suffix **ATE** creates verbs indicating becoming or taking on a state.

hyphenate   *elevate*   *medicate*

The suffix **ATION** indicates becoming or entering a state.

hyphenation   *elevation*   *medication*

The suffix **CRACY** means 'government'.

democracy   *autocracy*   *bureaucracy*

The suffix **CRAT** means 'ruler'.

democrat   *autocrat*   *bureaucrat*

The suffix **DOM** means 'state of being'.

freedom   *boredom*   *martyrdom*

The suffix **EE** indicates a person who is affected by or receives something.

interviewee   *evacuee*   *honouree*

The suffix **EN** means 'become'.

dampen   *deaden*   *blacken*

The suffix **ENCE** indicates a state or quality.

residence   *abstinence*   *dependence*

The suffix **ENT** indicates an action or condition.

abstinent   *resident*   *independent*

> It is difficult to distinguish this from the suffix **ANT**,
> which occurs in many words and has the same meaning.
> A list of the common words with each suffix is given on
> pages 363–64.

The suffix **ER** means 'person from'.

villag**er**	North**er**n**er**	London**er**

The suffix **ER** also means 'person who does a job' or 'thing that does a job'.

driv**er**	paint**er**	teach**er**
fasten**er**	scrap**er**	light**er**

The suffix **ESCENT** means 'becoming'.

adol**escent**	obsol**escent**	lumin**escent**

The suffix **ETTE** means 'small'.

kitchen**ette**	cigar**ette**	disk**ette**

The suffix **FUL** means 'full of'.

beauti**ful**	pain**ful**	resent**ful**

The suffix **HOOD** means 'state of being'.

child**hood**	likeli**hood**	priest**hood**

The suffix **IAN** creates nouns indicating a member of a profession.

politic**ian**	magic**ian**	mathematic**ian**

The suffix **IBLE** means 'able to'.

> ed**ible**   terr**ible**   poss**ible**

> It is difficult to distinguish this from the suffix **ABLE**, which occurs in many words and has the same meaning. A list of the common words with each suffix is given on pages 361–62.

The suffix **IC** means 'related to'.

> atom**ic**   period**ic**   rhythm**ic**

The suffix **IFICATION** creates nouns indicating an action.

> not**ification**   class**ification**   clar**ification**

The suffix **IFY** creates verbs indicating an action.

> not**ify**   class**ify**   clar**ify**

The suffix **ISH** means 'fairly' or 'rather'.

> small**ish**   young**ish**   brown**ish**

The suffix **ISH** also means 'resembling'.

> tiger**ish**   boy**ish**   amateur**ish**

The suffix **ISM** means 'action' or 'condition'.

> critic**ism**   hero**ism**   absentee**ism**

The suffix **ISM** also creates nouns indicating a prejudice.

> sex**ism**   rac**ism**   anti-Semit**ism**

The suffix **IST** means 'doer of'.

motorist   *soloist*   *artist*

The suffix **IST** also indicates a prejudice.

sexist   *racist*   *ageist*

The suffix **ITY** indicates a state or condition.

reality   *stupidity*   *continuity*

The suffix **IVE** indicates a tendency towards something.

explosive   *active*   *decorative*

The suffix **IZE** creates verbs indicating a change or becoming.
Words that end with **IZE** can also be spelt **ISE** in British English.

radicalize   *legalize*   *economize*
radicalise   *legalise*   *economise*

The suffix **LET** means 'little'.

booklet   *ringlet*   *piglet*

The suffix **LIKE** means 'resembling'.

doglike   *childlike*   *dreamlike*

The suffix **LING** means 'small'.

duckling   *gosling*   *princeling*

The suffix **LY** means 'in this manner'.

kindly   *friendly*   *properly*

The suffix **MENT** means 'state of'.

      *content**ment***   *enjoy**ment***   *employ**ment***

The suffix **METER** means 'measure'.

      *thermo**meter***   *baro**meter***   *speedo**meter***

The suffix **NESS** means 'state of' or 'quality of'.

      *kind**ness***   *blind**ness***   *selfish**ness***

The suffix **OLOGY** means 'study of' or 'science of'.

      *bi**ology***   *soci**ology***   *music**ology***

The suffix **SHIP** means 'state of' or 'condition of'.

      *fellow**ship***   *dictator**ship***   *horseman**ship***

The suffix **SION** means 'action' or 'state of'.

      *confu**sion***   *deci**sion***   *explo**sion***

> It is difficult to distinguish this from the suffix **TION**, which occurs in many words and has the same meaning. A list of the common words with each suffix is given on pages 364–66.

The suffix **SOME** means 'tending to'.

      *quarrel**some***   *trouble**some***   *loath**some***

The suffix **TION** means 'action' or 'state of'.

      *crea**tion***   *produc**tion***   *calcula**tion***

It is difficult to distinguish this from the suffix **TION**, which occurs in many words and has the same meaning. A list of the common words with each suffix is given on pages 364–66.

The suffix **Y** means 'like' or 'full of'.

watery   *hilly*   *snowy*

ABLE and IBLE

The suffixes **ABLE** and **IBLE** are both quite common (although **ABLE** is more common) and have the same meaning. You should be aware of the possibility of confusing these endings and check if you are not sure which one is correct.

The table below shows some common words with each ending.

Words that end in ABLE	Words that end in IBLE
adaptable	accessible
admirable	audible
adorable	credible
advisable	divisible
agreeable	eligible
allowable	flexible
arguable	gullible
available	horrible
capable	illegible
desirable	inaudible
durable	indelible
enjoyable	inedible

Words that end in ABLE	Words that end in IBLE
enviable	invisible
excitable	irresistible
flammable	legible
irritable	negligible
lovable	plausible
movable	possible
notable	risible
palatable	sensible
probable	tangible
suitable	terrible
tolerable	visible

A useful – but not one-hundred per cent reliable – rule of thumb is that when one of these endings is added to an existing word, the spelling is **ABLE**.

adapt**able**   enjoy**able**   lov**able**

Adjectives ending in **ABLE** will form related nouns ending in **ABILITY**.

cap**able**   prob**able**   suit**able**
cap**ability**   prob**ability**   suit**ability**

However, adjectives ending **IBLE** will form related nouns ending in **IBILITY**.

gull**ible**   flex**ible**   poss**ible**
gull**ibility**   flex**ibility**   poss**ibility**

ANT and ENT

The suffixes **ANT** and **ENT** are both quite common and have the same meaning. You should be aware of the possibility of confusing these endings and check if you are not sure which one is correct.

The table below shows some common words with each ending.

Words that end in ANT	Words that end in ENT
abundant	absent
adamant	accident
arrogant	adjacent
assistant	affluent
blatant	ailment
brilliant	ancient
buoyant	apparent
defiant	argument
deodorant	coherent
dominant	deficient
dormant	dependent
elegant	descent
emigrant	efficient
exuberant	eminent
fragrant	equipment
hesitant	evident
ignorant	fluent
immigrant	implement
important	lenient
incessant	negligent
indignant	nutrient
irritant	opulent
migrant	parent
militant	patient
mutant	permanent

Words that end in ANT	Words that end in ENT
occupant	precedent
pleasant	president
poignant	prominent
radiant	pungent
redundant	rodent
relevant	salient
reluctant	silent
stagnant	solvent
tenant	strident
tolerant	succulent
vacant	sufficient
valiant	turbulent

Words ending in **ANT** will form related nouns ending in **ANCE** or **ANCY**.

defi**ant**	toler**ant**	vac**ant**
defi**ance**	toler**ance**	vac**ancy**

However, words ending **ENT** will form related nouns ending in **ENCE** or **ENCY**.

flu**ent**	opul**ent**	suffici**ent**
flu**ency**	opul**ence**	suffici**ency**

SION and TION

The suffixes **SION** and **TION** are both quite common and have the same meaning (although **TION** is more common). You should be aware of the possibility of confusing these endings and check if you are not sure which one is correct.

The table below shows some common words with each ending.

Words that end in SION	Words that end in TION
adhesion	accusation
admission	ambition
cohesion	assumption
collision	attention
conclusion	audition
confusion	caution
conversion	collection
decision	condition
dimension	congestion
discussion	decoration
division	direction
erosion	duration
evasion	emotion
exclusion	equation
excursion	evolution
expansion	exception
explosion	fiction
illusion	intention
inclusion	invention
invasion	isolation
mansion	location
mission	mention
occasion	motion
omission	nation
permission	nutrition
persuasion	option
possession	pollution
revision	relation
session	separation
television	solution
tension	tuition
version	vacation

Words ending in **SION** are often related to adjectives ending in **SIVE**.

expan**sion**   persua**sion**   permis**sion**
expan**sive**   persua**sive**   permis**sive**

However, words ending **TION** are often related to adjectives ending in **TIVE**.

na**tion**   rela**tion**   atten**tion**
na**tive**   rela**tive**   atten**tive**

Building blocks at the end of verbs

There is a small group of suffixes called **inflections** that are regularly added to the basic forms of verbs. These endings indicate either the time of action or the person performing the action.

The ending **S** is added to verbs to create what is called the **third person singular** form of the present tense – that is, the form used after 'he', 'she', 'it' or a named person or thing when talking about present action.

cheat**s**   cook**s**   walk**s**

The ending **ING** is added to verbs to create the **present participle**, which is used to refer to present action.

cheat**ing**   cook**ing**   walk**ing**

The ending **ED** is added to most verbs to create the **past tense** and **past participle** – forms which are used when talking about action in the past.

cheat**ed**   cook**ed**   walk**ed**

Note that some common verbs have past tenses and past participles which do not end in **ED** but which are formed in an irregular way.

bent	*spent*	*did*
gone	*done*	*fallen*

Building blocks at the end of adjectives

There are two inflection suffixes that are regularly added to the basic forms of adjectives to indicate the degree of the quality indicated by the word.

The ending **ER** is added at the end of an adjective to mean 'more'. This is called the **comparative** form.

*clever**er***	*green**er***	*calm**er***

The ending **EST** is added at the end of an adjective to mean 'most'. This is called the **superlative** form.

*clever**est***	*green**est***	*calm**est***

Note that these suffixes are generally only added to words of one or two syllables. For adjectives with more than two syllables (and some adjectives with two syllables) the most comparative and superlative forms are created by using the words 'more' and 'most'.

more *beautiful*	**more** *interesting*	**more** *loyal*
most *beautiful*	**most** *interesting*	**most** *loyal*

The comparative and superlative forms of the common adjectives good and bad are formed in an irregular way.

Good	*better*	*best*
Bad	*worse*	*worst*

Building blocks at the end of nouns

The inflection suffix **S** is regularly added to the basic forms of nouns to indicate the **plural** form of the word, which indicates more than one example of the thing.

cats   *dogs*   *books*

> The plural form of some words is formed slightly differently, and the rules explaining how plurals are formed are given on pages 395–98.

Spelling words that contain suffixes

Adding a suffix that begins with a consonant, such as **LESS** or **SHIP**, to a root word is usually straightforward. Neither the root word nor the suffix is changed.

help + less = helpless

However, when adding a suffix that begins with a vowel, such as **ED** or **ABLE**, to a root word you need to take more care with the spelling. Depending on the ending of the root word, you may need to add an **E**, drop an **E**, double a consonant, or change a **Y** to an **I**.

cope + ed = coped
fit + ing = fitting
deny + able = deniable

> The rules for adding vowel suffixes are given in full on pages 391–92.

Double suffixes

Sometimes a suffix can have another suffix attached to it to make an even longer word.

> abuse + ive + ness = abusiveness
> accept + able + ness = acceptableness
> avail + able + ity = availability
> care + less + ly = carelessly
> commend + able + ly = commendably
> emotion + al + ism = emotionalism
> expense + ive + ly =expensively
> fear + less + ness = fearlessness

Greek and Latin roots

English has many words that contain Greek and Latin roots. Some of these roots appear in lots of different English words, and are still used regularly to create new words.

If you can get to know these roots, how to spell them and what they mean, you will find it a great help in your reading and writing, as well as in your spelling.

AER comes from Greek *aēr*, meaning 'air'. It is used in a lot of words connected with aircraft or aeronautics.

> **aero**plane   **aero**bics   **aero**dynamics

AMBI comes from the Latin word *ambo*, meaning 'both'.

> **ambi**dextrous   **ambi**valent

ANTHROP comes from the Greek word *anthrōpos*, meaning 'human being'.

>   *anthropology*   *philanthropist*   lyc**anthrop**y

AQUA is the Latin word for 'water'.

>   **aqua**lung   **aqua**marine   **aqua**tic

Sometimes the second **A** in **AQUA** changes to another vowel.

>   **aque**duct   **aque**ous   **aqui**fer

ASTRO comes from the Greek word *astron*, meaning 'star'.

>   **astro**nomy   **astro**logy   **astro**naut

AUDI comes from the Latin word *audīre*, meaning 'to hear'.

>   **audi**ence   **audi**tion   **audi**torium

BIO comes from the Greek word *bios*, meaning 'life'.

>   **bio**logy   **bio**graphy   **bio**technology

CAPT and **CEPT** both come from the Latin word *capere*, meaning 'to take'.

>   **cap**ture   **capt**ivate   **capt**ion
>   con**cept**   inter**cept**   re**cept**ion

CEDE comes from the Latin word *cēdere*, meaning 'to go'.

>   inter**cede**   pre**cede**   re**cede**

Note that some words that sound like these do not have the same ending: pro**ceed**, suc**ceed**, super**sede**.

CENT comes from the Latin word *centum*, meaning 'hundred'. A *cent* is a monetary unit in many countries, taking its name from the fact that it is worth one hundredth of the main unit of currency.

century   **cent**imetre   **cent**ipede

CLUDE comes from the Latin word *claudere*, meaning 'to close'.

con**clude**   ex**clude**   se**clude**d

CRED comes from the Latin word *crēdere*, meaning 'to believe'.

in**cred**ible   **cred**it   **cred**ulous

CYCL comes from the Latin word *cyclus*, which is itself derived from the Greek word *kuklos*, meaning 'circle' or 'wheel'.

re**cycl**able   **cycl**one   bi**cycl**e

DEC comes from the Latin word *decem*, meaning 'ten'.

decimal   **dec**ibel   **dec**ilitre

DICT comes from the Latin word *dīcere*, meaning 'to say'.

dictionary   pre**dict**   contra**dict**

DOM comes from the Latin word *domus*, meaning 'house'.

domestic   **dom**icile   **dom**e

DOMIN comes from the Latin word *dominus*, meaning 'master'.

dominate   **domin**eering   con**domin**ium

DUCE and **DUCT** both come from the Latin word *ducere*, meaning 'to lead'.

intro**duce**	de**duce**	re**duce**
aque**duct**	con**duct**or	via**duct**

DUO is the Latin word for 'two'.

duo	**duo**poly	**duo**logue

EGO is the Latin word for 'I'.

ego	**ego**tist	**ego**centric

FACT comes from the Latin word *facere*, meaning 'to make'.

satis**fact**ion	**fact**ory	manu**fact**ure

FRACT comes from the Latin word *fractus*, meaning 'broken'.

fraction	**fract**ure	in**fract**ion

GEN comes from the Greek word *genesis*, meaning 'birth'.

gene	**gen**etics	**gen**esis

GEO comes from the Greek word *gē*, meaning 'earth'.

geology	**geo**metry	**geo**graphy

GRAPH comes from the Greek word *graphein*, meaning 'to write'.

graphic	auto**graph**	para**graph**

GRESS comes from the Latin word *gradī*, meaning 'to go'.

pro**gress**	di**gress**ion	ag**gress**ive

HYDRO comes from the Greek word *hudōr*, meaning 'water'. The word *hydro* also occurs on its own as a shortened form of *hydroelectric* and *hydrotherapy*.

hydroplane   **hydro**foil   **hydro**therapy

Sometimes the **O** in **HYDRO** is dropped or changes to another vowel.

hydrant   **hydr**aulic   de**hydr**ated

JECT comes from the Latin word *iacere*, meaning 'to throw'.

in**ject**ion   de**ject**ed   re**ject**

KILO comes from the Greek word *chīlioi*, meaning 'a thousand'.

kilometre   **kilo**gram   **kilo**watt

MANU comes from the Latin word *manus*, meaning 'hand'.

manual   **manu**facture   a**manu**ensis

MILLI comes from the Latin word *mille*, meaning 'a thousand'.

millimetre   **milli**gram   **milli**pede

MULTI comes from the Latin word *multus*, meaning 'many'.

multiplication   **multi**cultural   **multi**storey

NOV comes from the Latin word *novus*, meaning 'new'.

novelty   re**nov**ate   in**nov**ation

OCT comes from the Latin word *octō*, meaning 'eight'. The Greek word is *oktō*.

    octagon   **oct**ave   **oct**et

PAED comes from the Greek word *pais*, meaning 'child'. The American spelling is **PED**. In British English it is pronounced to rhyme with *seed*. However, in America and Australia it rhymes with *said*.

    paediatrics   **paed**iatrician   **paed**ophile

PED comes from the Latin word *pēs*, meaning 'foot'.

    pedal   **ped**estal   quadru**ped**

PED is also the American spelling of root **PAED**.

    pediatrics   **ped**iatrician   **ped**ophile

PHIL comes from the Greek word *philos*, meaning 'loving'.

    philanthropist   **phil**osophy   Anglo**phil**e

PHOBIA comes from the Greek word *phobos*, meaning 'fear'. It appears in hundreds of words relating to the fear or hatred of certain people, animals, objects, situations and activities.

    claustro**phobia**   agora**phobia**   xeno**phobia**

PHON comes from the Greek word *phōnē*, meaning 'sound' or 'voice'.

    phonetic   sym**phon**y   micro**phon**e

PHOTO comes from the Greek word *phōs*, meaning 'light'.

    photocopier   **photo**graph   **photo**sensitive

POLY comes from the Greek word *polus*, meaning 'many' or 'much'. The word *poly* also occurs on its own as a shortened form of *polytechnic*, *polyester*, and *polythene*.

    polygon   **poly**styrene   **poly**gamy

PORT comes from the Latin word *portāre*, meaning 'to carry'.

    portable   im**port**   trans**port**ation

POS comes from the Latin word *positus*, meaning 'put'.

    position   im**pos**e   de**pos**it

PRIM comes from the Latin word *prīmus*, meaning 'first'.

    primary   **prim**itive   **prim**e

QUAD comes from the Latin word *quattuor*, meaning 'four'.

    quadrangle   **quad**ruped   **quad**riceps

SCOPE comes from the Greek word *skopein*, meaning 'to look at'.

    micro**scope**   tele**scope**   stetho**scope**

SCRIBE comes from the Latin word *scrībere*, meaning 'to write'. **SCRIPT** comes from the Latin word *scriptus*, meaning 'written', which is related to the word *scrībere*.

    scribe   sub**scribe**   de**scribe**
    script   sub**script**ion   de**script**ion

SECT comes from the Latin word *secāre*, meaning 'to cut'.

    section   dis**sect**   inter**sect**ion

SENT comes from the Latin word *sentīre*, meaning 'to feel'.

sentimental *consent* *dissent*

SOC comes from the Latin word *socius*, meaning 'friend'.

social *association* *sociology*

SON comes from the Latin word *sonāre*, meaning 'to sound'.

sonic *consonant* *resonate*

STAT comes from the Latin word *stātus*, meaning 'standing', which itself comes from the verb *stāre*, meaning 'to stand'.

statue *static* *status*

STRICT comes from the Latin word *stringere*, meaning 'to tighten'.

strictness *constrict* *restriction*

STRUCT comes from the Latin word *struere*, meaning 'to build'.

structure *destructive* *construction*

TACT comes from the Latin word *tangere*, meaning 'to touch'.

tactile *contact* *intact*

TERR comes from the Latin word *terra*, meaning 'earth'.

terrain *Mediterranean* *terrestrial*

THERM comes from the Greek word *thermē*, meaning 'heat'.

thermometer *thermal* *hypothermia*

TRACT comes from the Latin word *tractus*, meaning 'dragged' or 'drawn'.

    *con***tract**   *sub***tract***ion*   **tract***or*

TRI comes from the Latin word *trēs*, meaning 'three'. The Greek word is *treis*.

    tri*angle*   **tri***o*   **tri***athlon*

VEN comes from the Latin word *venīre*, meaning 'to come'.

    ven*ue*   *con***ven***tion*   *inter***vene**

VERT comes from the Latin word *vertere*, meaning 'to turn'.

    *di***vert**   *re***vert**   *con***vert**

VIS comes from the Latin word *vīsus*, meaning 'sight', which itself comes from the verb *vidēre*, meaning 'to see'.

    vis*ual*   **vis***ible*   **vis***ion*
    vis*it*   *super***vise**   *tele***vis***ion*

VOR comes from the Latin word *vorāre*, meaning 'to devour'.

    vor*acious*   *carni***vore**   *omni***vor***ous*

Compound words

Many English words are formed quite simply by adding two existing words together. These are called **compound words**. It can be easy to spell these words if you break them down into their parts.

> book + shop = bookshop
> door + mat = doormat
> summer + house = summerhouse
> tea + pot = teapot
> waist + coat = waistcoat

Some words don't immediately seem as though they are made from two common words but in fact are. These can also be easy to spell if you think of them in terms of their two parts.

> cup + board = cupboard
> hand + kerchief = handkerchief
> neck + lace = necklace
> pit + fall = pitfall

Commonly occurring spelling patterns

Prefixes, suffixes and root forms all can be remembered as having a particular meaning. However, there are some combinations of letters that are useful to remember when learning English spelling but don't have any particular meaning.

The patterns in this section all come up in many different words and are not pronounced in the way you might expect. It is worth remembering these patterns and the common words in which they occur.

Some of these letter blocks were usually sounded in the original language (such as **OUGH** in Anglo-Saxon words or **IGN** in Latin words) but have lost their original sound in English as the pronunciation of the language has gradually become simplified.

The pattern **ALM** occurs in several words representing a sound that is more often spelt as **ARM**.

al**m**ond	ba**lm**	ca**lm**
emba**lm**	pa**lm**	qua**lm**
psa**lm**		

The pattern **AUGHT** occurs in several words representing a sound that is more often spelt as **ORT**.

aught	c**aught**	d**aught**er
distr**aught**	fr**aught**	h**aught**y
n**aught**	n**aught**y	onsl**aught**
sl**aught**er	t**aught**	

It also occurs in these words representing a sound that is more often spelt as **AFT**.

dr**aught**	l**aught**er

The pattern **CH** occurs in many words that come from Greek representing a sound that is more often spelt as **C** or **K**.

a**ch**e	an**ch**or	bron**ch**itis
chameleon	**ch**aracter	**ch**arisma
chasm	**ch**emical	**ch**emistry
chiropodist	**ch**iropractor	**ch**lorine
cholera	**ch**olesterol	**ch**ord
choreography	**ch**orus	**ch**risten
Christmas	**ch**rome	**ch**ronic
monar**ch**	o**ch**re	psy**ch**iatry
psy**ch**ology	stoma**ch**	syn**ch**ronize

The pattern **CI** occurs before endings such as **OUS**, **ENT**, and **AL** in several words representing a sound that is more often spelt as **SH**. The root word often ends in **C** or **CE**.

artificial	atrocious	audacious
capricious	commercial	crucial
deficient	delicious	efficient
facial	fallacious	ferocious
financial	gracious	judicious
malicious	official	officious
pernicious	precious	precocious
proficient	racial	social
spacious	special	sufficient
suspicious	tenacious	vivacious

The pattern **EA** occurs in many words representing a sound that is more often spelt as **E**.

bread	breath	deaf
dead	dread	endeavour
head	heather	heaven
heavy	lead	meadow
ready	steady	sweat
thread	treacherous	tread
treasure	wealth	weather

The pattern **EAU** occurs in several words representing a sound that is more often spelt as **OW**. These words all come from French.

beau	bureau	chateau
gateau	tableau	

It also occurs in these words representing a sound that is more often spelt as **EW**.

beautiful	beauty

The pattern **EIGH** occurs in several words representing a sound that is more often spelt as **AY**.

eight	freight	inveigh
neigh	neighbour	sleigh
weigh	weight	

Less commonly, it can represent a sound that is more often spelt as **IE**.

height

The pattern **EIGN** occurs in several words representing a sound that is more often spelt as **AIN**.

deign	feign	reign

It also occurs in these words representing a sound that is more often spelt as **IN**.

foreign	sovereign

The pattern **GUE** occurs at the end of several words representing a sound that is more often spelt as **G**.

catalogue	dialogue	epilogue
fatigue	harangue	intrigue
league	meringue	monologue
plague	rogue	synagogue
tongue	vague	vogue

The pattern **IGH** occurs in several words representing a sound that is more often spelt as **IE**.

blight	bright	fight
flight	fright	high
light	fight	might

mighty	night	plight
right	sigh	sight
slight	thigh	tight

The pattern **IGN** occurs in several words representing a sound that is more often spelt as **INE**.

align	assign	benign
consign	design	ensign
malign	resign	sign

The pattern **OUGH** occurs in several words representing different pronunciations.

although	borough	bough
bought	brought	cough
dough	enough	fought
nought	ought	plough
rough	sought	though
thought	through	tough
trough	wrought	

The pattern **OUL** occurs in several words representing a sound that is more often spelt as **OO**.

| could | should | would |

The pattern **OUR** occurs in several words representing a sound that is more often spelt as **ER**.

armour	behaviour	clamour
colour	demeanour	enamoured
endeavour	favour	fervour
glamour	harbour	honour
humour	labour	neighbour

| parl**our** | ranc**our** | rig**our** |
| tum**our** | vap**our** | vig**our** |

The pattern **OUS** occurs at the end of hundreds of words representing a sound that is more naturally spelt as **US**. Note that these words are invariably adjectives.

anxi**ous**	cauti**ous**	danger**ous**
fabul**ous**	furi**ous**	gener**ous**
hilari**ous**	joy**ous**	mountain**ous**
nerv**ous**	obvi**ous**	pi**ous**
previ**ous**	seri**ous**	zeal**ous**

The pattern **QUE** occurs in several words representing a sound that is more often spelt as **C** or **K**.

anti**que**	che**que**	criti**que**
grotes**que**	mas**que**rade	mos**que**
opa**que**	pictures**que**	pla**que**
statues**que**	techni**que**	uni**que**

The pattern **SC** occurs in many words representing a sound that is more often spelt as **S**.

ab**sc**ess	acquie**sc**e	a**sc**ent
coale**sc**e	cre**sc**ent	de**sc**ent
efferve**sc**ent	fa**sc**inate	ira**sc**ible
ob**sc**ene	o**sc**illate	re**sc**ind
scene	**sc**ent	**sc**ience
scimitar	**sc**intillate	**sc**issors

The pattern **SCI** occurs before a vowel in several words representing a sound that is more often spelt as **SH**.

| con**sci**ence | con**sci**ous | lu**sci**ous |

The pattern **TI** occurs before endings such as **OUS**, **ENT**, and **AL** in many words representing a sound that is more often spelt as **SH**.

ambi**ti**ous	cau**ti**ous	conten**ti**ous
circumstan**ti**al	essen**ti**al	face**ti**ous
infec**ti**ous	nutri**ti**ous	par**ti**al
pa**ti**ent	poten**ti**al	quo**ti**ent
residen**ti**al	spa**ti**al	substan**ti**al

The pattern **TURE** occurs in many words representing a sound that is often spelt as **CHER**.

adven**ture**	cap**ture**	crea**ture**
cul**ture**	den**ture**	fea**ture**
frac**ture**	furni**ture**	fu**ture**
ges**ture**	lec**ture**	mix**ture**
mois**ture**	na**ture**	pas**ture**
pic**ture**	punc**ture**	tex**ture**
tor**ture**	ven**ture**	vul**ture**

spelling rules

Spelling rules

English has a small number of rules that underpin how words and certain types of word ought to be spelt. If you can learn these rules, you will be on your way to becoming a better and more confident speller. Don't be put off if the rule sounds complicated – look at the examples and you will begin to see spelling patterns emerging.

Although these rules do not cover every word in the language, they can often help you make a good attempt at guessing how an unfamiliar word ought to be spelt.

Q is always followed by U

One of the simplest and most consistent rules is that the letter **Q** is always followed by **U**.

*qu*ick   *qu*ack   *qu*iet

> The only exceptions are a few unusual words that have been borrowed from other languages, especially Arabic: *bur*q*a, Iraqi.*

J and V are followed by a vowel

These letters are rarely followed by a consonant and do not usually come at the ends of words.

If you come across a sound you think might be a **J** at the end of a word or syllable, it is likely to be spelt using the letters **GE** or **DGE**.

page   *edge*   *forage*

If a word ends with the sound represented by **V**, there is likely to be a silent **E** after the **V**.

receive   *give*   *love*

Double consonants don't occur at the start of a word

If a word begins with a consonant, you can be confident that it is a single letter.

> The only exceptions are a few unusual words that have been borrowed from other languages, such as *llama*.

H, J, K, Q, V, W, and X are not doubled

The consonants **B**, **C**, **D**, **F**, **G**, **L**, **M**, **N**, **P**, **R**, **S**, **T**, and **Z** are commonly doubled in the middle and at the end of words, but **H**, **J**, **K**, **Q**, **V**, **W**, **X** and **Y** are not, so you can be confident about them being single.

rejoice   *awake*   *level*

> There are occasional exceptions in compound words (such as *withhold* and *bookkeeping*), words borrowed from other languages (such as *tikka*), and informal words (such as *savvy* and *bovver*).

A, I, and U don't come at the end of words

In general, English avoids ending words with **A**, **I**, and **U** and adds an extra letter to stop this happening.

say   *tie*   *due*

However, there are quite a lot of exceptions to this rule, most of which are words that have been borrowed from other languages.

banana   *ravioli*   *coypu*

The three-letter rule

'Content words' (words that name and describe things and actions) have at least three letters.

Words that do not name or describe things but exist to provide grammatical structure (prepositions, conjunctions and determiners) do not need to have as many letters as this.

This rule accounts for the fact that some content words have extra or doubled letters.

buy   *bee*   *inn*

Note that these extra letters are not found in non-content words with similar sounds.

by   *be*   *in*

> Two important exceptions to this rule are the verbs *do* and *go*.

I before E, except after C

When the letters I and E are combined to make the 'EE' sound, the I comes before the E.

brief	chief	field
niece	siege	thief

When they follow the letter C in a word, the E comes before the I.

ceiling	deceit	receive

There are a few exceptions to this rule.

caffeine	protein	seize	weird

The rule does not hold true when the letters I and E combine to make a different sound from 'EE'.

foreign	surfeit	their

Adding a silent E makes a short vowel become long

As noted on page 333, the vowels A, E, I, O, and U each have a 'short' sound when they appear on their own in short words.

cat	rat	hat
men	pen	ten
bit	hit	sit
dot	lot	got
but	nut	hut

Each of the vowels also has a characteristic 'long' sound, which is created by adding an **E** to the consonant after the vowel. The **E** is not sounded in these words.

date	*rate*	*hate*
scene	*swede*	*theme*
bite	*mite*	*like*
note	*lone*	*mole*
flute	*rule*	*brute*

If there is more than one consonant after a short vowel, adding a silent **E** does not make the vowel become long.

lapse	*cassette*	*gaffe*

C and G are soft before I and E but hard before A, O, and U

The letters **C** and **G** both have two sounds: one 'soft' and one 'hard'.

These letters always have a hard sound when they come before **A**, **O**, and **U**.

card	*cot*	*recur*
gang	*gone*	*gum*

> Note that the word *margarine* is an exception to this rule.

In general these letters have a 'soft' sound before **I** and **E** (and also **Y**).

cent	*circle*	*cycle*
gentle	*giraffe*	*gyrate*

The rule is very strong for **C**, but there are a lot of exceptions for **G**.

gibbon	*girl*	*get*

Note that some words add a silent **U** after the **G** to keep the sound hard.

*gu*ess   *gu*ide   *gu*illotine
*gu*ilty   *gu*itar   fati*gue*

Adding endings to words ending in E

Many English words end with a silent **E**. When you add a suffix that begins with a vowel onto one of these words, you drop the **E**.

abbreviat*e* + ion = abbreviation
appreciat*e* + ive = appreciative
desir*e* + able = desirable
fortun*e* + ate = fortunate
guid*e* + ance = guidance
hop*e* + ing = hoping
respons*e* + ible = responsible
ventilat*e* + ed = ventilated

Words that end in **CE** and **GE** are an exception to this rule. They keep the final **E** before adding a suffix that begins with **A**, **O** or **U** in order to preserve the 'soft' sound.

change + able = changeable
notice + able = noticeable
advantage + ous = advantageous

However you do drop the **E** in these words before adding a suffix that begins with **E**, **I** or **Y**.

stag*e* + ed = staged
notic*e* + ing = noticing
chanc*e* + y = chancy

Adding the ending LY to words ending in LE

When you make an adverb by adding the suffix **LY** to an adjective that ends with **LE**, you drop the **LE** from the adjective.

> *gentle + ly = gently*
> *idle + ly = idly*
> *subtle + ly = subtly*

Adding endings to words ending in Y

When you add a suffix to a word that ends with a consonant followed by **Y**, you change the **Y** to **I**.

> *apply + ance = appliance*
> *beauty + ful = beautiful*
> *crazy + ly = crazily*
> *happy + ness = happiness*
> *smelly + er = smellier*
> *woolly + est = woolliest*

However, in certain short adjectives that end with a consonant followed by **Y**, you keep the **Y** when you add the ending **LY** to make an adverb.

> *shy + ly = shyly*
> *spry + ly = spryly*
> *wry + ly = wryly*

Adding endings to words ending in C

You add a **K** to words that end in **C** before adding a suffix that begins with **I**, **E**, or **Y** in order to preserve the 'hard' sound.

mimic + ing = mimicking
frolic + ed = frolicked
panic + y = panicky

The word *arc* is an exception to this rule.

arc + ing = arcing
arc + ed = arced

When you make an adverb by adding the suffix **LY** to an adjective that ends with **IC**, you add **AL** after the **IC**.

basic + ly = basically
genetic + ly = genetically
chronic + ly = chronically

The word *public* is an exception to this rule.

public + ly = publicly

Adding endings to words ending in a single consonant

In **words of one syllable** ending in a short vowel plus a consonant, you double the final consonant when you add a suffix that begins with a vowel.

run + ing = running
pot + ed = potted
thin + est = thinnest
swim + er = swimmer

This does not apply to words ending in the consonants **H**, **J**, **K**, **Q**, **V**, **W**, **X** and **Y**, which are never doubled (see page 387).

slow + est = slowest
box + er = boxer

In **words of more than one syllable** ending in a single vowel plus a consonant, if the word is pronounced with the stress at the end, you double the final consonant when you add a suffix that begins with a vowel.

> admit + ance = admittance
> begin + ing = beginning
> commit + ed = committed
> occur + ence = occurrence

If the word does not have the stress at the end, the rule is that you don't double the final consonant when you add a suffix that begins with a vowel.

> target + ed = targeted
> darken + ing = darkening

However, when you add a suffix that begins with a vowel to a word that ends in a single vowel plus **L** or **P**, you always double the **L** or **P** regardless of the stress.

> appal + ing = appalling
> cancel + ation = cancellation
> dial + er = dialler
> fulfil + ed = fulfilled
> handicap + ed = handicapped
> kidnap + er = kidnapper
> slip + age = slippage
> wrap + ing = wrapping

The word *parallel* is an exception to this rule.

> parallel + ed = paralleled

Adding endings to words ending in OUR

There are a number of English words that end with the letters **OUR**.

colour   *glamour*   *humour*

When you add the suffix **ANT**, **ARY**, or **OUS** to these words, the **U** is dropped and **OUR** becomes **OR**.

colour + ant = colorant
glamour + ous = glamorous
humour + ous = humorous
honour + ary = honorary

When you add the suffix **ABLE** to these words, the **U** is not dropped.

honour + able = honourable
favour + able = favourable

Making plurals

The most common way to make a plural form of a word (to show that you are talking about more than one example of it) is simply to add an **S**.

dog + s = dogs
house + s = houses
bee + s = bees
banana + s = bananas

When you make a plural of a word that ends with **S**, **X**, **Z**, **SH** or **CH**, you add **ES**.

> *bus + es = buses*
> *kiss + es = kisses*
> *lens + es = lenses*
> *fox + es = foxes*
> *jinx + es = jinxes*
> *buzz + es = buzzes*
> *rash + es = rashes*
> *match + es = matches*
> *ranch + es = ranches*

When you make a plural of a word that ends with a consonant plus **Y**, you change the **Y** to **I** and add **ES**.

> *fairy + es = fairies*
> *pantry + es = pantries*
> *quality + es = qualities*
> *spy + es = spies*
> *story + es = stories*

However, when you make a plural of a word that ends with a **vowel** plus **Y**, you simply add **S**.

> *boy + s = boys*
> *day + s = days*
> *donkey + s = donkeys*
> *guy + s = guys*

When you make a plural of a word that ends with a single **O**, you usually just add an **S**.

> *memo + s = memos*
> *solo + s = solos*
> *zero + s = zeros*

However, there are a number of words that end with a single **O** that add **ES** when they are plural.

> *echo + es = echoes*
> *hero + es = heroes*
> *potato + es = potatoes*
> *tomato + es = tomatoes*
> *veto + es = vetoes*

> Remember: My her**oes** eat potat**oes** and tomat**oes**.

When you make a plural of a word that ends in a single **F** (and some words that end in **FE**), you change the **F** (or **FE**) to **V** and add **ES**.

> *leaf + es = lea**ves***
> *elf + es = el**ves***
> *life + es = li**ves***

There are some exceptions to this rule.

> *belief + s = beliefs*
> *chef + s = chefs*
> *roof + s = roofs*

When you make a plural of a word that ends with **EAU**, you can add either **X** or **S**. Words that end with **EAU** are French words that have come into English. The **X** ending is the French plural, and the **S** ending is the English one. Both forms are acceptable for these words.

> *bureau + x = bureaux*
> *bureaus + s = bureaus*
> *chateau + x = chateaux*
> *chateau + s = chateaus*
> *gateau + x = gateaux*
> *gateau + s = gateaus*

Even when the **X** ending is used, these words are usually pronounced as though they end with an **S**, although the **X** can sometimes be treated as a silent letter (as it is in French).

The suffix FUL

The suffix that means 'full of' is spelt **FUL** – not (as you might expect) **FULL**. When you add the suffix onto an existing word to create a new word, the new word is always spelt with just one **L**.

beautiful	*cupful*	*faithful*
grateful	*hopeful*	*painful*

The prefix AL

When *all* and another word are joined to make an unhyphenated word, you drop the second **L**.

all + mighty = almighty
all + ready = already
all + though = although
all + together = altogether

However, if the word you make by adding *all* to another word is spelt with a hyphen, you keep both **L**'s.

all + important = all-important
all + inclusive = all-inclusive
all + powerful = all-powerful

The prefixes ANTE and ANTI

There are some English words that begin with **ANTE** and other words that begin with **ANTI**. You can usually work out how to spell the word if you think about what it means.

Words that begin with **ANTE** usually have a meaning of 'before' or 'in front of'.

> *ante*cedent   *ante*diluvian   *ante*room

Words that begin with **ANTI** usually have a meaning of 'against' or 'opposite'.

> *anti*septic   *anti*social   *anti*matter

The prefixes FOR and FORE

There are some English words that begin with **FOR** and other words that begin with **FORE**. You can often work out how to spell the word if you think about what it means.

Words that begin with **FORE** usually have a meaning of 'before' or 'in front of'.

> *fore*cast   *fore*father   *fore*shore

If the word does not have this meaning, it is likely that it will be spelt **FOR**, and there will not be an **E** after the **R**.

> *for*give   *for*get   *for*feit

The endings CE and SE

There are some English words that end in **CE** and have a related word that ends in **SE**. Sometimes the two words sound the same, and it can be easy to use the wrong spelling.

A useful general rule is that nouns are spelt with **CE** – think of the nouns *ice* and *advice* to help you remember.

> *a dog licence*
> *piano practice*

However, verbs that are related to these nouns end in **SE** – think of *advise* (where the pronunciation makes it obvious that the word is not spelt with **CE**).

> *licensed to kill*
> *to practise the drums*

The endings IZE and ISE

Historically, both **ISE** and **IZE** have been equally acceptable as suffixes forming verbs in English.

> *organize*   *realize*   *pulverize*
> *organise*   *realise*   *pulverise*

The same is true of related words.

> *organizer*   *realization*   *pulverized*
> *organiser*   *realisation*   *pulverised*

It is perfectly correct to use either a **Z** or an **S** in these words in British English, but you should be consistent and stick to one letter. However, the **IZE** spelling is preferred in American English. (Some people regard **IZE** as an Americanism, and object to its use in British English, but all leading British dictionary publishers show **IZE**, **IZATION**, and **IZER** as the main spelling form for these words.)

Some words are always spelt with **ISE**. These are usually words where the ending is a natural part of the word and has not been added on as a suffix.

advertise	*advise*	*chastise*
comprise	*compromise*	*despise*
devise	*disguise*	*exercise*
improvise	*prise*	*revise*
supervise	*surprise*	*televise*

Some words are always spelt with **IZE**.

capsize	*prize*

Note the difference between *prise*, meaning 'to force open', and *prize*, meaning 'to value highly'.

Rules for using apostrophes

Showing possession

The apostrophe (') is used to show that something belongs to someone. It is usually added to the end of a word and followed by an **S**.

'S is added to the end of singular words.

> a baby**'s** pushchair
> Hannah**'s** book
> a child**'s** cry

'S is added to the end of plural words not ending in **S**.

> children**'s** games
> women**'s** clothes
> people**'s** lives

An apostrophe alone is added to plural words ending in **S**.

> Your grandparents are your parents**'** parents.
> We are campaigning for workers**'** rights.
> They hired a new ladies**'** fashion guru.

'S is added to the end of names and singular words ending in **S**.

> James**'s** car
> the octopus**'s** tentacles

Note, however, that if the word ending in **S** is a historical name, an apostrophe only is sometimes preferred.

> Dickens**'** novels
> St Giles**'** Cathedral

'S is added to the end of certain professions or occupations to indicate workplaces.

> She is on her way to the doctor**'s**.
> James is at the hairdresser**'s**.

'S is added to the end of people or their names to indicate that you are talking about their home.

> I'm going over to Harry**'s** for tea tonight.
> I popped round to Mum**'s** this afternoon, but she wasn't in.

To test whether an apostrophe is in the right place, think about who the owner is.

> the boy**'s** books [= the books belonging to the boy]
> the boys**'** books [= the books belonging to the boys]

> Note that an apostrophe is *not* used to form possessive pronouns such as *its*, *yours*, or *theirs*. Nor is it used to form the plurals of words such as *potatoes* or *tomatoes*.

Showing a contraction

An apostrophe is used in shortened forms of words to show that one or more letters have been missed out. These contractions usually involve shortened forms of common verbs such as *be* and *have*.

> I'm [short for 'I am']
> they've [short for 'they have']
> we're [short for 'we are']

Some contractions involve the negative word *not*.

> *aren't [short for 'are not']*
> *isn't [short for 'is not']*
> *haven't [short for 'have not']*

> Note that the apostrophe is always positioned at the point where the omitted letters would have been.

An apostrophe is also used in front of two digits as a way of referring to a year or decade.

> *French students rioted in '68 [short for '1968'].*
> *He worked as a schoolteacher during the '60s and early '90s.*

Showing a plural

An apostrophe should *not* be used to form the plural of a normal word.

However, there is an exception to this rule. An apostrophe can be used in plurals of letters and numbers to make them easier to read.

> *Mind your p's and q's.*
> *His 2's look a bit like 7's.*
> *She got straight A's in her exams.*

Rules for using a capital letter

A capital (or 'upper-case') letter is used to mark the beginning of a sentence.

> *When I was 20, I dropped out of university and became a model.*

Capital letters are also used for the first letter in proper nouns. These include:

- people's names
  Jenny Forbes   *William Davidson*

- days of the week
  Monday   *Wednesday*   *Saturday*

- months of the year
  August   *October*   *June*

- public holidays
  Christmas   *New Year*   *Yom Kippur*

- nationalities
  Spanish   *Iraqi*   *Argentine*

- languages
  Swahili   *Flemish*   *Gaelic*

- geographical locations
  Australia   *Loch Ness*   *Mount Everest*

- religions
  Islam   *Buddhism*   *Sikhism*

Capital letters are also used for the first letter in titles of books, magazines, newspapers, **TV** shows, films, etc. Where there are several words, a capital letter is usually used for each of the main 'content words' as well as the first word of the title.

The Times   *Hello!*   *Twelfth Night*
The Secret Garden   *Newsnight*   *Mamma Mia!*

tips for
learning
hard words

Tips for learning hard words

You can improve your spelling greatly by studying the rules and familiarizing yourself with the patterns that come up regularly. Nevertheless, knowing the principles of spelling can only get you so far. There are times when you just have to learn how the letters fall in a particular word.

The tips in this chapter can help you learn tricky spellings so that they stay in your mind.

Mnemonics

A **mnemonic** is a saying or rhyme that helps you remember something. The word comes from Greek *mnēmonikos*, which itself comes from *mnēmōn*, meaning 'mindful'. A mnemonic can be a rhyme or sentence that helps you remember anything, not just spelling. You may already know mnemonics for other things, for example *Richard Of York Gives Battle In Vain*, which is often used as a way to remember the colours of the rainbow (because the first letters of each word correspond to the first letters of the colours red, orange, yellow, green, blue, indigo, and violet).

There are various types of mnemonics that can help with spelling.

Initial-letter mnemonics

In some mnemonics, the word you want to remember is spelt out by the initial letters of all the words in a sentence or phrase.

> *Big elephants are useful to Indians for unloading logs.*

This sentence can help you to remember the word *beautiful*.

Partial initial-letter mnemonics

In some mnemonics, a phrase just acts as a reminder of how to spell the tricky bits of a word, but does not spell out the whole word.

You can use this sort of mnemonic to remember how to spell the word *accelerate*.

> *If it can **accele**rate, **a c**ar can **e**asily l**e**ad **e**very r**e**ce.*

A similar device can be used to remember the double letters in the word *accommodation*.

> *The ac**comm**odation has **two c**ots and **two m**attresses.*

Partial mnemonics

Another type of mnemonic uses words or syllables that are contained within the problem word to help you remember it.

You can use this technique to remember the beginning of the word *abattoir*.

> *There may be **a batt**le in an **abatt**oir.*

A similar device can be used to remember the double letters at the start of the word *address*.

Add your **add**ress.

The remaining chapters of this book include many mnemonics to help you remember how to spell tricky words. Use these if you find they help you.

However, the best mnemonics are often ones that you make up yourself. If you base these phrases around words and topics that are especially meaningful to you, you are more likely to remember them. For example, you might use the names of your friends, your pets, or your family members, or you might make up sentences that relate to your hobbies. Try to make up your own mnemonics for words you find hard to remember.

Look, Say, Cover, Write, Check

Another way of learning how to spell a word is to go through five
stages: look, say, cover, write, check.

- **Look** at the word carefully.

- **Say** the word aloud to yourself, listening to how it sounds.

- **Cover** the word and try to remember what it looks like.

- **Write** the word.

- **Check** what you have written to see if you got it right.

Breaking down the word into its parts

Another good way of learning a word is to break it down into its
syllables, and sound them out, pronouncing even the silent letters.

> *dictionary = dic + ti + on + ar + y*
> *ecstasy = ec + sta + sy*
> *handkerchief = hand + ker + chief*
> *material = ma + te + ri + al*
> *separate = se + par + ate*
> *Wednesday = Wed + nes + day*

If you get into the habit of looking at words in this way you will find
them easier to learn.

Word families

Words that come from the same root word tend to preserve the same core patterns in the spelling. If you know that one word is related to another word, it can help you remember how the word is spelt.

The words below are all related to *act*.

act	*action*	*activity*
re*act*	re*action*	re*active*

Sometimes knowing that words are related can help you remember which vowel to use. For example, words related to *irritate* all have an **A** after the **T**.

irritate	*irritant*	*irritable*

Word families are a very powerful way of remembering how to spell a word. However, there are just a few occasions when words that sound as though they might be related are in fact not related, or when words that are related are not spelt with the same core pattern. Some of these 'false friends' that you need to watch out for are listed on pages 477–480.

words with
silent letters

Words with silent letters

Some words are hard to spell because they contain letters that are not pronounced in speech. Often these letters were pronounced in the original language from which the word came into English. Here is a list of words that it is worth learning, including ways of remembering some of them.

abhor
There is a silent **H** after the **B**.

> Remember: You ab**hor** something **hor**rible.

abscess
There is a silent **C** after the first **S**.

acquaint, acquiesce, acquire, acquit
There is a silent **C** before the **Q**.

aghast
There is a silent **H** after the **G**.

> Remember: A**gh**ast at the **gh**osts.

almond
There is a silent **L** before the **M**.

answer
There is a silent **W** after the **S**.

asthma
There is a silent **TH** after the **S**.

autumn
There is a silent **N** after the **M**.

bankruptcy

There is a silent **T** after the **P**.

> Remember that this word comes from *bankrupt* + the ending *-cy*.

Buddhism

There is a silent **H** after the **DD**.

campaign

There is a silent **G** before the **N**.

castle

There is a silent **T** after the **S**.

column

There is a silent **N** after the **M**.

comb

There is a silent **B** after the **M**.

condemn

There is a silent **N** after the **M**.

> Remember that this word is related to *condemnation*.

cupboard

There is a silent **P** before the **B**.

debt

There is a silent **B** before the **T**.

> Remember that this word is related to *debit*.

descend

There is a silent **C** after the **S**.

> Remember: You d**esc**end on an **esc**alator.

diaphragm
There is a silent **G** before the **M**.
doubt
There is a silent **B** before the **T**.

Remember that this word is related to *dubious*.

dumb
There is a silent **B** after the **M**.
environment
There is a silent **N** before the **M**.

Remember: There is **iron** in the envi**ron**ment.

exceed, excel, excellent, excess, excite
There is a silent **C** after the **X**.
excerpt
There is a silent **C** after the **X** and a silent **P** before the **T**.
exhaust, exhibit, exhilarate
There is a silent **H** after the **X**.
extraordinary
There is a silent **A** before the **O**.

Remember that this word comes from *extra* + *ordinary*.

fluorescent
There is a silent **U** before the **O** and a silent **C** after the **S**.
foreign
There is a silent **G** before the **N**.
ghastly, gherkin, ghetto, ghost, ghoul
There is a silent **H** after the **G**.

gnarl, gnat, gnaw, gnome, gnu
> There is a silent **G** before the **N**.

government
> There is a silent **N** before the **M**.

handkerchief, handsome
> There is a silent **D** after the **N**.

honest, honour, hour
> There is a silent **H** at the start.

indict, indictment
> There is a silent **C** before the **T**.

> Remember: **I n**ever **d**abble **in c**riminal **t**hings.

island, isle
> There is a silent **S** before the **L**.

jeopardize, jeopardy
> There is a silent **O** after the **E**.

knack, knee, kneel, knickers, knife, knight, knit, knob, knock, knot, know, knuckle
> There is a silent **K** before the **N**.

leopard
> There is a silent **O** after the **E**.

limb
> There is a silent **B** after the **M**.

listen
> There is a silent **T** after the **S**.

medieval
> There is a silent **I** after the **D**.

miniature
> There is a silent **A** before the **T**.

mnemonic
> There is a silent **M** before the **N**.

> Remember: **M**y **n**ephew **E**ric **m**emorizes **o**dd **n**umbers **i**n **c**lass.

moreover
> There is a silent **E** after the **O**.

mortgage
> There is a silent **T** before the **G**.

muscle
> There is a silent **C** after the **S**.

parliament
> There is a silent **A** after the **I**.

playwright
> There is a silent **W** before the **R**.

pneumatic, pneumonia
> There is a silent **P** before the **N** at the beginning.

psalm
> There is a silent **P** before the **S** and a silent **L** before the **M**.

pseudonym, psychedelic, psychiatry, psychic, psychology
> There is a silent **P** before the **S**.

receipt
> There is a silent **P** before the **T**.

rhetoric, rheumatism, rhinoceros, rhododendron, rhombus, rhubarb, rhyme, rhythm
> There is a silent **H** after the **R** at the beginning.

sandwich
> There is a silent **D** after the **N**.

scissors
> There is a silent **C** after the first **S**.

sheikh
> There is a silent **H** after the **K**.

shepherd
> There is a silent **H** after the **P**.

> Remember that a shep**herd herd**s sheep.

silhouette
> There is a silent **H** after the **L**.

solemn
> There is a silent **M** before the **N**.

sovereign
> There is a silent **G** before the **N**.

spaghetti
> There is a silent **H** after the **G**.

stalk
> There is a silent **L** before the **K**.

subtle
> There is a silent **B** before the **T**.

> Remember: **Sub**marines move in **sub**tle ways.

sword
> There is a silent **W** after the **S**.

talk
> There is a silent **L** before the **K**.

two
> There is a silent **W** after the **T**.

viscount
> There is a silent **S** before the **C**.

> Remember: The v**iscount** gets a d**iscount**.

walk
    There is a silent **L** before the **K**.
Wednesday
    There is a silent **D** before the **N**.
what, when, where, whether, which, why
    There is a silent **H** after the **W**.
wrangle, wrap, wrath, wreath, wreck, wrench, wrestle, wretched, wriggle, wring, wrinkle, write, wrist, wrong
    There is a silent **W** before the **R**.
yoghurt
    There is a silent **H** after the **G** in the usual spelling form.

single and double letters

Single and double letters

Some words present a problem in spelling because it is not obvious whether they have a double or single letter. Here is a list of words that it is worth learning, including ways of remembering some of them.

abattoir
There is one **B** and two **T**'s.

> Remember: There may be a **batt**le in an a**batt**oir.

abbreviate
There are two **B**'s.
accelerate
There are two **C**'s and one **L**.
accessory
There are two **C**'s and two **S**'s.
accident
There are two **C**'s.

> Remember: **A c**lose **c**all can lead to an **acc**ident.

accommodate
There are two **C**'s and two **M**'s.

> Remember: If you think that this word **accommodates** as many letters as possible, it will help you to remember that there are the maximum number of **C**'s and **M**'s!

accompany
There are two **C**'s.
accumulate
There are two **C**'s and one **M**.

accurate
> There are two **C**'s and one **R**.

across
> There is one **C** and two **S**'s.

address
> There are two **D**'s and two **S**'s.

> Remember: **Add** your **add**ress.

affiliate
> There are two **F**'s and one **L**.

aggravate
> There are two **G**'s and one **V**.

aggressive
> There are two **G**'s and two **S**'s.

allergy
> There are two **L**'s.

> Remember: An **allergy** saps **all** en**erg**y.

alligator
> There are two **L**'s and one **G**.

already, although, altogether
> There is only one **L**.

aluminium
> There are no double letters.

appal
> There are two **P**'s and one **L**.

apparatus, apparent, appearance
> There are two **P**'s and one **R**.

appendix, appliance, appreciate, apprehensive, approve, approximate
> There are two **P**'s.

assassinate, assess
> There are two double **S**'s.

associate
> There are two **S**'s and one **C**.

attitude
> There is a double **T** followed by a single **T**.

> Remember: **At ti**mes you have a bad **atti**tude.

baggage
> There is a double **G** – just the same as in *luggage*.

balloon
> There are two **L**'s and two **O**'s.

> Remember: A **ball**oon is shaped like a **ball**.

banana
> There are two single **N**'s.

battalion
> There are two **T**'s and one **L** – just the same as in *battle*.

beginner
> There is one **G** and two **N**'s.

belligerent
> There are two **L**'s and one **G**.

boycott
> There are two **T**'s.

broccoli
> There are two **C**'s and one **L**.

> Remember: Bro**ccoli** **c**ures **coli**c.

bulletin
> There are two **L**'s and one **T** – just the same as in *bullet*.

carafe
> There is one **R** and one **F**.

career
> There is no double **R**.

> Remember: A **car car**eered off the road.

cassette
> There are two **S**'s and two **T**'s.

cinnamon
> There are two **N**'s and one **M**.

collaborate
> There are two **L**'s and one **B**.

colleague
> There are two **L**'s.

colossal
> There is one **L** in the middle and two **S**'s.

> Remember: Co**loss**al **loss**es

commemorate
> There is a double **M** followed by a single **M**.

commercial
> There are two **M**'s.

commiserate
> There are two **M**'s and one **S**.

> Remember: You have to com**miser**ate with a **miser**.

commit
> There are two **M**'s and one **T**.

committee

There are two **M**'s, two **T**'s, and two **E**'s.

> If you remember that a **committee** should have as many members as possible, it may help you remember that this word has the maximum number of **M**'s, **T**'s and **E**'s.

compel

There is only one **L**.

connotation

There are two **N**'s and two single **T**'s.

control

There is only one **L**.

coolly

There are two **L**'s.

correspond

There are two **R**'s.

curriculum

There are two **R**'s and one **C** in the middle.

daffodil

There are two **F**'s but no double **D**.

desiccated

There is one **S** and two **C**'s – which is the same as in **c**o**c**onut**s**!

deterrent

There are two **R**'s but no double **T**.

dilemma

There is one **L** and two **M**'s.

> Remember: **Emma** is in a dil**emma**.

disappear, disappoint, disapprove
There is one **S** and two **P**'s.

Remember: Th**is** **app**le has d**isapp**eared.

dispel
There is one **S** and only one **L**.

dissatisfied
There are two **S**'s after the first **I**.

dissect
There are two **S**'s.

dissimilar
There are two **S**'s, one **M** and one **L**.

earring
There are two **R**'s.

effervescent
There are two **F**'s and one **S**.

eligible
There is only one **L** at the start.

Remember: You must **el**ect the most **el**igible candidate.

embarrass
There are two **R**'s and two **S**'s.

Remember: This word has two **R**'s and two **S**'s, which is an **embarrass**ment of riches!

enrol
There is only one **L**.

erroneous
There are two **R**'s and one **N**.

> Remember that this word is related to *err*.

exaggerate
There are two **G**'s.

> Remember: I am st**agger**ed that you ex**agger**ate.

excellent
There are two **L**'s.

> Remember: My **ex-cell**mate was an **excell**ent friend.

flammable
There are two **M**'s (unlike *flame*).

fulfil
There are two single **L**'s.

fullness
There are two **L**'s and two **S**'s.

giraffe
There is one **R** and two **F**'s.

guerrilla
There are two **R**'s and two **L**'s.

graffiti
There are two **F**'s and one **T**.

hallucination
There are two **L**'s, one **C**, and one **N**.

harass
There is one **R** and two **S**'s.

hazard
There is only one **Z** (unlike *blizzard*).

hideous

There is only one **D**.

> Remember: **Hide** that **hide**ous thing away.

holiday

There is only one **L** and one **D**.

> Remember that a hol**id**ay was originally a holy **d**ay.

horrible

There are two **R**'s – just the same as in *terrible*.

horror

There is a double **R** – just the same as in *terror*.

hurricane

There are two **R**'s and one **C**.

illiterate

There are two **L**'s and a single **T**.

imitate

There are no double letters.

immediate

There are two **M**'s and one **D**.

inaccurate

There is one **N**, two **C**'s, and one **R**.

ineligible

There are no double letters.

innocent

There are two **N**'s and one **C**.

innocuous

There are two **N**'s and one **C**.

intelligence, intelligent

There are two **L**'s.

> Remember: I can **tell** the **gent** is in**tell**igent.

interrogate
> There are two **R**'s and one **G**.

> Remember: In**terro**gation causes **terro**r.

interrupt
> There are two **R**'s.

> Remember: It's **terri**bly rude to in**terr**upt.

irregular
> There are two **R**'s and one **G**.

irrelevant
> There are two **R**'s and one **L**.

irritable
> There are two **R**'s and one **T**.

keenness
> There are two **N**'s and two **S**'s.

limit
> There is only one **M** and one **T**.

literature
> There is only one **T**.

luggage
> There is a double **G** – just the same as in *baggage*.

macabre
> There is only one **C**.

macaroon
> There is only one **C** and one **R**.

marvellous
> There are two **L**'s.

mattress
> There are two **T**'s and two **S**'s.

mayonnaise
> There are two **N**'s.

> Remember: Dip **n**ice **n**ibbles in mayo**nn**aise.

medallist

There is one **D** and two **L**'s.

> Remember that this word is made up of *medal + list*.

Mediterranean

There is one **D**, one **T**, and two **R**'s.

millennium

There are two **L**'s and two **N**'s.

millionaire

There are two **L**'s and one **N**.

misshapen

There are two **S**'s.

misspell

There are two **S**'s and two **L**'s.

misspent

There are two **S**'s.

necessary

There is one **C** and two **S**'s.

> Remember: It is ne**cess**ary for a shirt to have **one c**ollar and **two s**leeves.

obsession, obsessive

There is a single **S** followed by a double **S**.

occasion

There are two **C**'s and one **S**.

occupy

There are two **C**'s and one **P**.

occur

There are two **C**'s and one **R**.

occurrence

There are two **C**'s and two **R**'s.

omission

There is one **M** and two **S**'s.

opinion

There is one **P** and a single **N** in the middle.

opponent, opportunity, opposite

There are two **P**'s.

overrate

There are two **R**'s – just the same as in *underrate*.

paraffin

There is one **R** and two **F**'s.

> Remember: Pa**r**affin **r**eally **f**uels **f**ires.

parallel

There is a double **L** in the middle and a single **L** at the end.

pastime

There is one **S** and one **T**.

penicillin

There are two **L**'s and no double **N**.

> Remember: You take penic**ill**in when you are **ill**.

permit

There is only one **T**.

personnel

There are two **N**'s and one **L**.

porridge

There are two **R**'s.

possess

There are two double **S**'s.

> Remember: You should po**ss**e**ss two s**hoes and **two s**ocks.

possible

There are two **S**'s.

preferred
There is one **F** and a double **R**.
preference
There is one **F** and no double **R**.
procedure
There is only one **E** after the **C**.
profession, professor
There is one **F** and two **S**'s.
profitable
There is one **F** and one **T**.
propel
There is a single **P** and a single **L**.
propeller
There is a single **P** and a double **L**.
quarrel
There are two **R**'s and one **L**.
questionnaire
There are two **N**'s.
really
There are two **L**'s.
rebellion
There is one **B** and two **L**'s.
recommend
There is one **C** and two **M**'s.
recurrent
There is a single **C** and a double **R**.
referred
There is a single **F** and a double **R**.
remittance
There is one **M** and two **T**'s.
resurrection
There is a single **S** and a double **R**.
sapphire
There are two **P**'s.

Remember: You would be ha**pp**y to get a sa**pp**hire.

satellite
There is one **T** and two **L**'s.

> Remember: **Tell** me about the sa**tell**ite.

settee
There is a double **T** and a double **E**.

> Remember: **Sett**le down on the **sett**ee.

skilful
There are two single **L**'s.

solicitor
There are no double letters.

success
There is a double **C** and a double **S**.

succinct
There is a double **C**.

suddenness
There is a double **D** and a double **N**.

sufficient
There are two **F**'s.

suffocate
There are two **F**'s and one **C**.

supplement
There are two **P**'s and one **M**.

suppose
There are two **P**'s.

suppress
There is a double **P** and a double **S**.

surplus
There is only one **S** at the end.

symmetry
There are two **M**'s and one **T**.

taffeta
There are two **F**'s and no double **T**.

tattoo
> There is a double **T** and a double **O**.

terrible
> There are two **R**'s – just the same as in *horrible*.

terror
> There is a double **R** – just the same as in *horror*.

threshold
> There is only one **H**.

toffee
> There are two **F**'s and two **E**'s.

tomorrow
> There is one **M** and two **R**'s.

tranquil
> There is only **L** at the end.

tranquillity
> There are two **L**'s.

tyranny
> There is one **R** and two **N**'s.

underrate
> There are two **R**'s – just the same as in *overrate*.

until
> There is only **L** at the end.

usually
> There are two **L**'s.

vacuum
> There is one **C** and two **U**'s.

vanilla
> There is one **N** and two **L**'s.

Remember: **Vanill**a ice cream from the **van** made me **ill**.

---

verruca
> There are two **R**'s and one **C**.

villain
> There are two **L**'s.

walnut
There is only one **L** and one **T**.
welcome, welfare
There is only one **L**.
withhold
There are two **H**'s.
woollen
There are two **O**'s and two **L**'s.

words with foreign spelling patterns

Words with foreign spelling patterns

Some words present a problem in spelling because they have come into English from another language and have kept a spelling pattern found in the original language. Often these spelling patterns are quite different from the patterns you would expect to find in English words.

If you know a bit of French or Greek, for example, you will find it easier to understand why words that come from those languages are spelt the way they are. Even if you don't, you should soon get used to certain spelling patterns from these languages that come up repeatedly in English, such as **EAU** and **EUR** in French words and **AE** and **RRH** in Greek words.

Here is a list of words that it is worth learning, including ways of remembering some of them.

abattoir
> The ending is **OIR**. The word comes from French.

amateur
> The ending is **EUR**. The word comes from French.

apparatus
> The ending is **US** (not **OUS**). The word comes from Latin.

archaeology
> The second syllable is spelt **CHAE**. The word comes from Greek.

> Remember: Ar**chae**ology discovers **c**urious **h**ouses of **a**ncient **e**ras.

beautiful, beauty
> The beginning is **BEAU**. These words come from French.

> Remember: **B**ig **e**ars **a**re **u**seful.

biscuit

The ending is **CUIT**. The word comes from French (where *cuit* means 'cooked').

> Remember: If you want a bisc**uit**, I will give **u it**.

bouquet

The first vowel sound is spelt **OU**, the middle consonant is **Q**, and the ending is **ET**. The word comes from French.

> Remember: A bou**que**t for the **que**en.

bourgeois

The first vowel sound is spelt **OUR**, the consonant in the middle is **GE**, and the ending is **OIS**. The word comes from French.

braille

The ending is **AILLE**. The word comes from a French name.

brochure

The ending is **CHURE**. The word comes from French.

brusque

The ending is **SQUE**. The word comes from French.

bureau

The ending is **EAU**. The word comes from French.

> Remember: **B**usinesses **u**sing **r**otten **e**thics **a**re **u**seless.

camouflage

The vowel sound in the middle is spelt **OU**, and the ending is **AGE**. The word comes from French.

catarrh

The ending is **ARRH**. The word comes from Greek.

champagne

The opening is **CH** and the ending is **AGNE**. The word comes from a French place-name.

chaos
> The opening sound is spelt **CH**. The word comes from Greek.

> Remember: **C**riminals **h**ave **a**bandoned **o**ur **s**ociety.

character
> The opening sound is spelt **CH**. The word comes from Greek.

chauffeur
> The opening is **CH** and the ending is **EUR**. The word comes from French.

chord, chorus
> The opening sound is spelt **CH**. These words come from Greek.

chute
> The opening is **CH**. The word comes from French.

connoisseur
> The middle vowel sound is spelt **OI** and the final vowel sound is spelt **EUR**. The word comes from French. (Also watch out for the double **N** and double **S**!)

crèche
> The ending is **CHE**, and the word is usually spelt with an accent over the first **E**. The word comes from French.

crochet
> The ending is **CHET**. The word comes from French.

curriculum vitae
> The ending is **AE**. The term comes from Latin.

dachshund
> The middle is **CHSH**. The word comes from German (where *Dachs* means 'badger' and *Hund* means 'dog').

> Remember: Da**chsh**und**s ch**ase **sh**eep through the **und**ergrowth.

diarrhoea
> The middle is **RRHOE**. The word comes from Greek.

etiquette
> The ending is **QUETTE**. The word comes from French.

euphoria, euthanasia
> The opening is **EU**. These words come from Greek (where *eu* means 'well').

Fahrenheit
> There is an **H** before the **R**, and the ending is **EIT**. The word comes from a German name.

fiancé, fiancée
> The ending is **CÉ** when referring to a man and **CÉE** when referring to a woman. The word comes from French.

foyer
> The ending is **ER**. The word comes from French.

gateau
> The ending is **EAU**. The word comes from French.

grandeur
> The ending is **EUR**. The word comes from French.

haemorrhage
> The first vowel sound is spelt **AE**, and the middle is **ORRH**. The word comes from Greek.

hierarchy, hieroglyphics
> The beginning is **HIER**. These words come from Greek (where *hieros* means 'holy').

> Remember: **H**idden **i**n **E**gyptian **r**uins.

hypochondriac, hypocrisy, hypocrite
> The beginning is **HYPO**. These words come from Greek (where *hypo* means 'under').

jodhpur
> There is a silent **H** after the **D** and the ending is **UR**. The word comes from a place-name in India.

> Remember: You wear jo**dh**purs when you ride a **d**appled **h**orse.

karate
  The final letter is **E**. The word comes from Japanese.

khaki
  There are two **K**'s and a silent **H**. The word comes from Urdu.

larynx
  The ending is **YNX**. The word comes from Greek.

lasagne
  The ending is **AGNE**. The word comes from Italian.

lieutenant
  The first vowel sound is spelt **IEU**. The word comes from French
  (where *lieu* means 'place').

liqueur
  The ending is **QUEUR**. The word comes from French.

manoeuvre
  The vowel sound in the middle is spelt **OEU**. The word comes from
  French. The American spelling is *maneuver*.

martyr
  The ending is **YR**. The word comes from Greek.

matinée
  The ending is **ÉE** – just the same as in *fiancée*. The word comes from
  French.

meringue
  The ending is **INGUE**. The word comes from French.

moustache
  The first vowel sound is spelt **OU** and the ending is **CHE**. The word
  comes from French. The American spelling is *mustache*.

> Remember: A **mou**sta**che** is between the **mou**th and **che**ek.

naïve
  The middle of this word is **AÏ**. The word comes from French.

niche
  The ending is **ICHE**. The word comes from French.

nuance
  The vowel after **U** is **A**. The word comes from French.

omelette

> There is an **E** after the **M** and the ending is **ETTE**. The word comes from French.

pseudonym

> There is a silent **P** at the beginning, the first vowel sound is spelt **EU**, and the ending is **NYM**. The word comes from Greek.

psychiatry, psychic, psychology

> There is a silent **P** at the beginning, the first vowel is a **Y**, and there is an **H** after the **C**. These words come from Greek (where *psychē* means 'soul').

queue

> The sequence of vowels is **UEUE**. The word comes from French, where it means 'tail'.

reconnaissance

> The third vowel sound is spelt **AI**. The word comes from French. (Also watch out for the double **N** and double **S** – just the same as in *connoisseur*.)

rendezvous

> The first vowel sound is spelt **E**, the second is spelt **EZ**, and the ending is **OUS**. The word comes from French.

repertoire

> The middle vowel sound is spelt **ER** and the ending is **OIRE**. The word comes from French.

reservoir

> The middle vowel sound is spelt **ER** and the ending is **OIR**. The word comes from French.

restaurant

> The middle vowel sound is spelt **AU** and the ending is **ANT**. The word comes from French.

restaurateur

> There is no **N** before the second **T** (unlike in *restaurant*), and the ending is **EUR**. The word comes from French.

rheumatism

> The opening is **RHEU**. The word comes from Greek.

rhinoceros

> The opening is **RH**, and the ending is **OS**. The word comes from Greek.

schizophrenia
> The opening is **SCH**, and the next consonant sound is spelt **Z**.
> The word comes from Greek (where *schizein* means 'to split').

sheikh
> The vowel sound is spelt **EI**, and there is a silent **H** at the end.
> The word comes from Arabic.

silhouette
> There is a silent **H** after the **L**, the middle vowel is spelt **OU**, and the ending is **ETTE**. The word comes from French.

souvenir
> The first vowel sound is spelt **OU** and the ending is **IR**. The word comes from French.

spaghetti
> There is a silent **H** after the **G** and the ending is **ETTI**. The word comes from Italian (as does *confetti*, which has a similar ending).

suede
> The ending is **UEDE**. The word comes from French (where *de Suède* means 'Swedish').

> Remember: **Sue de**manded **suede** shoes.

surveillance
> The middle vowel sound is spelt is **EI**. The word comes from French.

yacht
> The middle is **ACH**. The word comes from Dutch.

confusable words

Confusable words

When two words have a similar or identical sound, it is easy to confuse them and use the correct spelling for the wrong word. This section lists sets of words that are easily confused and offers some ways of remembering which is which.

accept, except
To **accept** something is to receive it or agree to it. **Except** means 'other than' or 'apart from'.

> Please **accept** my apologies
> The king would not **accept** their demands.
> I never wear a skirt **except** when we go out.

affect, effect
To **affect** something is to influence or change it. An **effect** is a result something gives or an impression something makes.

> Tiredness **affected** his concentration.
> discoveries which have a profound **effect** on medicine

> Remember: To **a**ffect something is **a**lter it but the **e**ffect is the **e**nd result.

aid, aide
Aid means 'help', and to **aid** somebody is to help them. An **aide** is person who acts as an assistant to an important person.

> bringing **aid** to victims of drought
> They used bogus uniforms to **aid** them in the robbery.
> one of the President's **aides**

allude, elude

To **allude** to something is to refer to it in an indirect way. If something **eludes** you, you can't understand or remember it, and if you **elude** something, you dodge or escape from it.

> I never **allude** to that unpleasant matter.
> The name of the tune **eludes** me.
> She managed to **elude** the police.

> Remember: If something **e**ludes you it **e**scapes you.

altar, alter

An **altar** is a holy table in a church or temple. To **alter** something is to change it.

> The church has a magnificent **altar**.
> We may have to **alter** our plans.

ascent, assent

An **ascent** is an upwards climb. To **assent** to something is to agree to it, and **assent** means 'agreement'.

> the **ascent** of Mount Everest
> We all **assented** to the plan.
> You have my whole-hearted **assent**.

aural, oral

Something that is **aural** is to do with the ear or listening. Something that is **oral** is to do with the mouth or speaking.

> a good **aural** memory
> **oral** history

> Remember: An **au**ral examination might involve **au**dio equipment.

base, bass
The **base** of something is the bottom part of it. A **bass** voice or instrument is the one that produces the lowest musical notes.

> the **base** of the table
> a **bass** guitar

baited, bated
If something such as a hook is **baited** it has food attached to it as a temptation. The word **bated** means 'cut short', and is mainly used in the expression *bated breath*.

> The trap had been **baited**.
> I waited with **bated** breath.

berth, birth
A **berth** is a bed on a ship or train, or a place where a ship is tied up. The **birth** of someone or something is the act of it being born or created.

> a cabin with six **berths**
> the date of her **birth**
> the **birth** of jazz

born, borne
To be **born** is to be brought into life. To be **borne** is to be accepted or carried, and when fruit or flowers are **borne** by a plant, they are produced by it. If something is **borne** out, it is confirmed.

> Olivia was **born** in Leicester.
> He has **borne** his illness with courage.
> The trees have **borne** fruit.
> The predictions have been **borne** out by the election results.

bough, bow
To **bow** is to bend your body or head, and a **bow** is an action where you bend your body or head. A **bough** is a branch of a tree.

> *He gave a long **bow** to the king.*
> *overhanging **boughs** of elm and ash*

boulder, bolder

A **boulder** is large rock. The word **bolder** means 'more brave' or 'more daring'.

> *The road was blocked by an enormous **boulder**.*
> *The victory made the soldiers feel **bolder**.*

brake, break

A **brake** is a device for slowing down, and to **brake** is to slow down by using this device. To **break** something is to change it so that it does not work or exist.

> *I slammed on the **brakes**.*
> ***Brake** when you approach the junction.*
> *to **break** a vase*

breach, breech

To **breach** something is to break or break through it, and a **breach** is a break or a gap made. The **breech** is the lower part of a human body, a rifle, or some other thing.

> *a **breach** of the peace*
> *a **breech** birth*

breath, breathe

Breath, without an **E**, is the noun, but **breathe**, with an **E**, is the verb.

> *He took a deep **breath**.*
> *I heard him **breathe** a sigh of relief.*

bridal, bridle

Bridal means 'relating to a bride'. A **bridle** is a piece of equipment for controlling a horse, and to **bridle** at something means to show anger about it.

> *a **bridal** dress*
> *a leather **bridle***
> *I **bridled** at the suggestion that I had been dishonest.*

broach, brooch

To **broach** a difficult subject means to introduce it into a discussion. A **brooch** is an item of jewellery.

> *Every time I **broach** the subject, he falls silent.*
> *a diamond **brooch***

callous, callus

Someone who is **callous** does not take other people's feelings into account. A **callus** is a patch of hard skin.

> *He treats her with **callous** indifference.*
> *Wearing high heels can cause **calluses**.*

canvas, canvass

Canvas is strong cloth. To **canvass** is to persuade people to vote a particular way or to find out their opinions about something.

> *a **canvas** bag*
> *The store decided to **canvass** its customers.*

Remember: If you canva**ss** you **s**eek **s**omething.

caught, court
Caught means 'captured'. A **court** is an enclosed space, such as one used in legal cases or to play tennis.

> *They never **caught** the man who did it.*
> *Silence in **court**!*

cereal, serial
Cereal is food made from grain. A **serial** is something published or broadcast in a number of parts. **Serial** also describes other things that happen in a series.

> *my favourite breakfast **cereal***
> *a new drama **serial***
> *a **serial** offender*

> Remember: A **seri**al is part of **seri**es, but a ce**real** is a **real** breakfast.

cheetah, cheater
A **cheetah** is a kind of wild cat. A **cheater** is someone who cheats.

> *a pack of **cheetahs** at the safari park*
> *He was exposed as a **cheater**.*

chord, cord
A **chord** is a group of three or more musical notes played together. **Cord** is strong thick string or electrical wire. Your vocal **cords** are folds in your throat which are used to produce sound.

> *playing major and minor **chords***
> *tied with a thick **cord***

> Remember: A **chor**d is part of a **chor**us.

chute, shoot

A **chute** is a steep slope for sliding things down. To **shoot** something means to send a missile at it, and to **shoot** means to go very fast.

> *a rubbish **chute***
> ***shooting** at pigeons*
> *to **shoot** along the ground*

coarse, course

Coarse means 'rough' or 'rude'. A **course** is something that you go round, or a series of things you do on a regular basis. **Course** is also used in the phrase *of course*.

> *a **coarse** fabric*
> *his **coarse** jokes*
> *a golf **course***
> *a **course** of lectures*
> *Of **course** I want to go with you.*

colander, calendar

A **colander** is a bowl-shaped drainer. A **calendar** is a chart with dates on it.

> *Strain the potatoes with a **colander**.*
> *a **calendar** with Scottish scenes*

> Remember: A col**ander** has h**and**les and drains wat**er**, while the cal**endar** marks the **end** of the ye**ar**.

complement, compliment

A **complement** is something which goes well with something else or completes it, and to **complement** something is to go well with it or complete it. A **compliment** is a remark expressing admiration, and to **compliment** something is to express admiration for it.

> *She is a perfect **complement** to her husband.*
> *It's always good to pass the odd **compliment**.*

> Remember: A compliment is the opposite of an insult and a complement completes something.

confidant, confident

A **confidant** is a friend you tell secrets to. **Confident** means 'trusting' or 'self-assured'.

> *a trusted **confidant***
> *We are **confident** you will do a good job.*

council, counsel

A **council** is a group of people elected to look after the affairs of an area. **Counsel** is advice and to **counsel** is to give advice.

> *the parish **council***
> *I **counselled** her to forgive him.*

> Remember: The coun**cil** members take minutes with pen**cil**s.

currant, current

A **currant** is a small dried grape. A **current** is a flow of water, air, or electricity. **Current** also means happening.

> *a **currant** bun*
> *an electrical **current***

> Remember: There are curr**a**nts in c**a**kes and curr**e**nts in **e**lectricity.

dairy, diary

A **dairy** is a shop selling milk, cream, and cheese. **Dairy** products are foods made from milk. A **diary** is a small book in which you keep a record of appointments.

> *She worked in a **dairy**.*
> *Make a note in your **diary**.*

> Remember: The d**air**y next to the **air**port.

decease, disease

The word **decease** means 'to die'. A **disease** is an unhealthy condition.

> *my **deceased** father*
> *an infectious **disease***

> Remember that if you are de**ceased** you have **ceased** to be.

defuse, diffuse

To **defuse** something is to make it less dangerous or tense. To **diffuse** something is to spread it or cause it to scatter. **Diffuse** means spread over a wide area.

> *Police **defused** a powerful bomb.*
> *The King will try to **defuse** the crisis.*
> *The message was **diffused** widely.*
> *curtains to **diffuse** the glare of the sun*

dependant, dependent

Dependant is the noun. **Dependent** is the adjective.

> *The child is her **dependant**.*
> *a **dependent** child*

desert, dessert

A **desert** is a region of land with little plant life. To **desert** someone is to abandon them. A **dessert** is sweet food served after the main course of a meal.

> the Sahara **Desert**
> She **deserted** me to go shopping.
> We had apple pie for **dessert**.

> Remember: A de**ss**ert is a **s**ticky **s**weet.

device, devise
Device, with a **C**, is the noun. **Devise**, with an **S**, is the verb.

> a safety **device**
> The schedule that you **devise** must be flexible.

disc, disk
A **disc** is a flat round object. A **disc** can be a storage device used in computers, and also a piece of cartilage in your spine. **Disk** is the usual American spelling for all senses of this word, except in the name **compact disc**, which is always spelt with a **C**. The spelling **disk** is sometimes preferred in British English when referring to the computer storage device.

discreet, discrete
If you are **discreet** you do not cause embarrassment with private matters. **Discrete** things are separate or distinct.

> We made **discreet** enquiries.
> The job was broken down into several **discrete** tasks.

> Remember: When discr**e**t**e** means 'separate', the **E**'s are separate.

draft, draught

A **draft** is an early rough version of a speech or document. A **draught** is a current of cold air or an amount of liquid you swallow. **Draughts** is a popular board-game. A person who draws plans is a **draughtsman**.

> *a **draft** of the president's speech*
> *There is an unpleasant **draught** in here.*
> *a game of **draughts***
> *He worked as a **draughtsman**.*

> Remember: A dr**aft** is **a** first **t**ry, and a dra**ugh**t goes thro**ugh** a room.

elegy, eulogy

An **elegy** is a mournful song or poem. A **eulogy** is a speech praising someone or something.

> ***elegies*** *of love and loss*
> *a nostalgic **eulogy** to Victorian England*

elicit, illicit

To **elicit** something such as information means to draw it out. If something is **illicit** it is not allowed.

> *I managed to **elicit** the man's name.*
> ***illicit*** *drugs*

eligible, illegible

Eligible means 'suitable to be chosen for something'. If something is difficult to read it is **illegible**.

> *an **eligible** candidate*
> ***illegible*** *handwriting*

> Remember: **El**igible means suitable to be chosen, and so is related to the word **el**ect.

emigrate, immigrate

If you **emigrate** you leave a country to live somewhere else. Someone who does this is an **emigrant**. If you **immigrate** you enter a country to live there. Someone who does this is an **immigrant**.

> *Her parents had **emigrated** from Scotland.*
> *Russian **immigrants** living in the United States*

> Remember: Immigrants come **in**.

eminent, imminent

Someone who is **eminent** is well-known and respected. **Imminent** means 'about to happen'.

> *an **eminent** professor*
> *an **imminent** disaster*

emit, omit

If something is **emitted** it is let out. If you **omit** something you leave it out. Similarly, something that is let out or sent out is an **emission**, while something that is left out is an **omission**.

> *cars **emitting** exhaust fumes*
> *She was **omitted** from the team.*
> *a programme to cut carbon **emissions***
> *a surprising **omission** from the list of great painters...*

enquire, inquire

These are alternative spellings for the same word. You can spell this word with an **E** or an **I**, although the form **inquire** is more common. Some people use the form **enquire** to mean 'ask about' and the form **inquire** to mean 'investigate'.

ensure, insure
To **ensure** something happens is to make sure that it happens. To **insure** something is to take out financial cover against its loss. To **insure** against something is to do something in order to prevent it or protect yourself from it.

> *His performance **ensured** victory for his team.*
> *You can **insure** your cat or dog for a few pounds.*
> *Football clubs cannot **insure** against the cancellation of a match.*

envelop, envelope
Envelop is the verb meaning 'to cover or surround'. **Envelope**, with an **E** at the end, is the noun meaning 'a paper covering which holds a letter'.

> *Mist began to **envelop** the hills.*
> *a self-addressed **envelope***

exercise, exorcize
To **exercise** means to move energetically, and **exercise** is a period of energetic movement. To **exorcize** an evil spirit means to get rid of it.

> Remember: You ex**e**rcise your l**e**gs but ex**o**rcize a gh**o**st.

faun, fawn
A **faun** is a legendary creature. A **fawn** is a baby deer. **Fawn** is also a pale brown colour, and to **fawn** on or over someone is to flatter them.

> *a story about **fauns** and centaurs*
> *Bambi the **fawn***
> *a **fawn** jumper*
> ***fawning** over his new boss*

final, finale
Final means 'last of a series', and a **final** is the last game or contest in a series to decide the winner. A **finale**, with an **E** at the end, is the finish of something, especially the last part of a piece of music or a show.

*the World Cup **Final***
*a fitting **finale** to the process*
*the **finale** of a James Bond film*

flare, flair

Flair is ability. A **flare** is a bright firework, and to **flare** is also to widen out.

*She showed natural **flair**.*
***flared** trousers*

flour, flower

Flour is used in baking. A **flower** is the coloured part of a plant.

*self-raising **flour***
*a basket of **flowers***

> Remember: Flour makes bisc**u**its and d**u**mplings.

forgo, forego

To **forgo** means to choose not to have something. To **forego** is a less common word meaning 'to go before'.

*I decided to **forgo** the pudding.*
*I will ignore the **foregoing** remarks.*

fowl, foul

Foul means dirty or unpleasant, and a **foul** is also an illegal challenge in a sport. **Fowl** are certain types of birds which can be eaten.

***foul** play*
*booked for a bad **foul***
*a shop selling wild **fowl***

> Remember: An **owl** is a f**owl** but fo**u**l is **u**npleasant.

gambol, gamble

To **gambol** means to run about friskily. To **gamble** means to accept a risk, and a **gamble** is a risk that you take.

> *lambs **gambolling** on the hillside*
> *to **gamble** on horses*
> *Going there would be an enormous **gamble**.*

gorilla, guerrilla

A **gorilla** is a large ape. A **guerrilla** is a member of a small unofficial army fighting an official one.

> *a documentary about **gorillas** and chimps*
> *ambushed by a band of **guerrillas***

> Remember: King K**o**ng was a giant g**o**rilla.

grate, great

A **grate** is a framework of metal bars, and to **grate** means to shred. **Great** means 'very large' or 'very good'.

> *the **grate** over the drain*
> ***grated** cheese*
> *a **great** expanse of water*
> *the **great** composers*

grill, grille

A **grill** is a device for cooking food, and to **grill** food is to cook it in such a device. A **grille** is a metal frame placed over an opening.

> *Cook the meat under the **grill**.*
> ***Grill** it for ten minutes.*
> *iron **grilles** over the windows*

grisly, grizzly
Grisly means nasty and horrible. **Grizzly** means grey or streaked with grey. A **grizzly** is also a type of bear.

> *grisly murders*
> *a grizzly beard*

hangar, hanger
A **hangar** is a place where aeroplanes are kept. A **hanger** is a device for storing clothes in a wardrobe.

> *a row of disused aircraft hangars*
> *Put your coat on a hanger.*

hear, here
To **hear** is to become aware of a sound with your ears. Something that is **here** is in, at or to this place or point.

> *Can you hear me?*
> *We come here every Summer.*

heir, air
An **heir** is someone who will inherit something. **Air** is the collection of gases that we breathe.

> *His heir received a million pounds.*
> *polluted air*

heroin, heroine
Heroin is a powerful drug. The **heroine** of a story is the main female character in it.

> *addicted to heroin*
> *the heroine of the film*

hoard, horde
To **hoard** is to save things, and a **hoard** is a store of things that have been saved. A **horde** is a large group of people, animals, or insects.

> *a priceless **hoard** of modern paintings*
> *a **horde** of press photographers*

hour, our
An **hour** is a period of time. **Our** means 'belonging to us'.

> *a journey of four **hours***
> ***our** favourite coffee shop*

humus, hummus
Humus is decaying vegetable material in the soil. **Hummus** is a food made from chickpeas.

> *soil enriched with **humus***
> *a lunch of salad and **hummus***

Hungary, hungry
Hungary is a European country. It is spelt with an **A**, unlike **hungry**, which means 'wanting to eat'.

> Remember: **Gary** from Hun**gary** gets an**gry** when he is hun**gry**.

idol, idle
An **idol** is a famous person worshipped by fans, or a picture or statue worshipped as a god. **Idle** means 'doing nothing'.

> *the **idol** of the United supporters*
> *The villagers worshipped golden **idols**.*
> *He's an **idle** layabout.*

> Remember: To be id**le** takes **l**itt**le** **e**nergy.

it's, its

It's, with an apostrophe, is a shortened form of *it is*. **Its**, without an apostrophe, is used when you are referring to something belonging or relating to things that have already been mentioned.

>*It's cold.*
>*The lion lifted its head.*

jewel, dual

A **jewel** is a precious stone. **Dual** means 'consisting of two parts'.

>*a box full of jewels*
>*a dual carriageway*

kerb, curb

A **kerb** is the raised area at the side of road. To **curb** something means to restrain it.

>*The car mounted the kerb.*
>*I tried to curb my enthusiasm.*

In American English, **curb** is the spelling for both meanings.

kernel, colonel

A **kernel** is a seed or part of a nut. A **colonel** is an army officer.

>*apricot kernels*
>*a colonel in the French army*

Remember: The co**lonel** is a **lonel**y man.

know, now

To **know** something means to be certain that it is true. **Now** means 'at this moment'.

>*Do you know the way to the bus station?*
>*I'm just leaving now.*

leant, lent

Leant is the past tense of the verb **lean**. **Lent** is the past tense of the verb **lend**.

> She **leant** back in her chair.
> She was **lent** Maureen's spare wellingtons.

led, lead

Led is the past tense of the verb **lead**. **Lead**, when it is pronounced like **led**, is a soft metal, or the part of a pencil that makes a mark.

> the road which **led** to the house
> **lead** poisoning

licence, license

Licence, ending in **CE**, is the noun. **License**, ending in **SE**, is the verb.

> a driver's **licence**
> a **TV licence**
> Censors agreed to **license** the film.
> They were **licensed** to operate for three years.

lightening, lightning

Lightening is a form of the verb **lighten**, and means 'becoming lighter'. **Lightning**, without an **E**, is bright flashes of light in the sky.

> The sky was **lightening**.
> forked **lightning**

loath, loathe

If you are **loath** to do something, you are very unwilling to do it. To **loathe**, with an **E** at the end, is to hate something.

> I am **loath** to change it.
> I **loathe** ironing.

> Remember: I loath**e** that **E** at the end!

lose, loose

Something **loose** is not firmly held or not close-fitting. To **lose** something is not to have it any more, and to **lose** is also to be beaten.

> *loose trousers*
> *Why do you **lose** your temper?*
> *We win away games and **lose** home games.*

mat, matt

A **mat** is a covering for a floor. A **matt** colour has a dull appearance.

> *the kitchen **mat***
> ***matt** paint*

metre, meter

A **meter**, ending in **ER**, is a device which measures and records something. A **metre**, ending in **RE**, is a metric unit of measurement.

> *the gas **meter***
> *ten **metres** long*

In American English, **meter** is the spelling for both meanings.

miner, minor, mynah

A **miner**, ending in **ER**, works in a mine. **Minor**, ending in **OR**, means 'less important' or 'less serious'. A **minor** is also someone under eighteen. Both of these spellings are also often used by mistake for **mynah**, which is the bird that can mimic sounds.

> *His grandfather was a **miner**.*
> *a **minor** incident*
> *a pet **mynah** bird*

morning, mourning

The **morning** is the first part of the day. **Mourning** is a form of the verb **mourn**, and means 'grieving for a dead person'.

> *morning coffee*
> *a period of* **mourning** *for the victims*

net, nett

A **net** is an object or fabric with holes in it. The **nett** result of something is the final result after everything has been taken into consideration.

> *a fishing* **net**
> **net** *curtains*
> *a* **nett** *profit*

of, off

Of is pronounced as if it ended with a **V** and is used in phrases like *a cup of tea* and *a friend of his*. **Off** is pronounced as it is spelt, and is the opposite of *on*.

> *a bunch* **of** *grapes*
> *They stepped* **off** *the plane.*
> *I turned the television* **off**.

palate, palette, pallet

The **palate** is the top of the inside of the mouth, and your **palate** is also your ability to judge the taste of food and wine. A **palette** is a plate on which an artist mixes colours, and a **palette** is also a range of colours. A **pallet** is a straw-filled bed, a blade used by potters, or a platform on which goods are stacked.

> *a coffee to please every* **palate**
> *a natural* **palette** *of earthy colours*
> *She lay on her* **pallet** *and pondered her fate.*

passed, past
Passed is the past tense of the verb **pass**. To go **past** something is to go beyond it. The **past** is the time before the present or describes things which existed before it.

> He had **passed** by the window.
> I drove **past** without stopping.
> the **past** few years

peace, piece
Peace is a state of calm and quiet. A **piece** is a part of something.

> I enjoy the **peace** of the woods.
> the missing **piece** of a jigsaw

> Remember: a **pie**ce of **pie**.

pedal, peddle
A **pedal** is a lever controlled with the foot, and to **pedal** something is to move its pedals. To **peddle** something is to sell it illegally.

> **pedalling** her bicycle to work
> **peddling** drugs

pendant, pendent
A **pendant** is something you wear around your neck. **Pendent** is a less common word meaning 'hanging'.

> a **pendant** with a five-pointed star
> **pendent** yellow flowers

peninsula, peninsular
Peninsula is the noun. **Peninsular** is the adjective.

> The Iberian **peninsula** consists of Spain and Portugal.
> a **peninsular** city

personal, personnel
Personal means 'belonging or relating to a person'. **Personnel** are the people employed to do a job.

> *a **personal** bodyguard*
> *a change in **personnel***

pore, pour
If you **pore** over something, you study it carefully, and a **pore** is also a small hole in the surface of your skin. To **pour** something is to let it flow out of a container, and if something **pours** it flows.

> ***poring** over a map*
> *The rain was **pouring** down.*

practice, practise
Practice, ending in **CE**, is the noun. **Practise**, ending in **SE**, is the verb.

> *target **practice***
> *In **practice**, his idea won't work.*
> *We must **practise** what we preach.*

> Remember that practi**ce** and practi**se** have the same endings as advi**ce** and advi**se**: **CE** for the noun, **SE** for the verb.

pray, prey
To **pray** means to say words to a god. An animal's **prey** is the thing it hunts and kills to eat.

> ***praying** for a good harvest*
> *a lion in search of its **prey***

precede, proceed
Something which **precedes** another thing happens before it. If you **proceed** you start or continue to do something.

*This is explained in the **preceding** chapter.*
*young people who **proceed** to higher education*

prescribe, proscribe

To **prescribe** something is to recommend it. To **proscribe** something is to ban or forbid it.

> *The doctor will **prescribe** the right medicine.*
> *Two athletes were banned for taking **proscribed** drugs.*

principal, principle

Principal means 'main' or 'most important', and the **principal** of a school or college is the person in charge of it. A **principle** is a general rule, or a belief which you have about the way you should behave. **In principle** means 'in theory'.

> *The Festival has two **principal** themes.*
> *the basic **principles** of Marxism*
> *a woman of **principle***
> *The invitation had been accepted **in principle**.*

> Remember: My **pal** is the princip**al**; you must **le**arn the princip**le**s.

program, programme

A **program** is a set of instructions to a computer, and you can **program** a computer. A **programme** is a plan or schedule, and also something on television or radio.

> *a computer **program***
> *a **programme** about farming*

prophecy, prophesy

Prophecy, with a **C**, is the noun. **Prophesy**, with an **S**, is the verb.

> *I will never make another **prophecy**.*
> *I **prophesy** that Norway will win.*

quiet, quite
Quiet means 'not noisy'. **Quite** means 'fairly but not very'.

> *a **quiet** night in*
> *He is **quite** shy.*

> Remember: A qui**et** p**et** can have qu**ite** a b**ite**.

rain, reign, rein
Rain is water falling from the clouds. To **reign** is to rule a country or be the most noticeable feature of a situation. **Reins** are straps which control a horse or child, and to **rein in** something is to keep it under control.

> *torrential **rain***
> *She **reigned** for just nine days.*
> *Peace **reigned** while Charlemagne lived.*
> *Keep a tight grip on the **reins**.*
> *She **reined** in her enthusiasm.*

rigor, rigour
Rigor occurs in the phrase *rigor mortis*, meaning 'the stiffening of a dead body'. **Rigour** is strictness or thoroughness, and **rigours** are difficult or demanding things about an activity.

> ***Rigor** mortis had set in.*
> *intellectual **rigour***
> *the **rigours** of the football season*

roll, role
A **roll** is something that is bent in a cylinder, and to **roll** something means to make it move like a ball. A **role** is the part that you play.

> *a **roll** of paper*
> *to **roll** the dice*
> *He played a major **role** in the incident.*

sceptic, septic

A **sceptic** is a person who expresses doubts. Something that is **septic** is infected by bacteria.

> *a **sceptic** about religion*
> *The wound turned **septic**.*

> Remember that these words are both spelt the way they are pronounced.

sight, site

Sight is the power to see, and a **sight** is something that you see. A **site** is a place with a special use.

> *an operation to improve his **sight***
> *I can't stand the **sight** of all this mess.*
> *a building **site***

stationary, stationery

Stationary, with an **A**, means 'not moving'. **Stationery**, with an **E**, is paper, pens, and other writing equipment.

> *The traffic is **stationary**.*
> *the **stationery** cupboard*

> Remember: Stationery is envelopes, but stationary is standing still.

stile, style

A **stile** is a step that helps you climb over a hedge or fence. **Style** is the way something is done, or an attractive way of doing things.

> *He clambered over the **stile**.*
> *cooked in genuine Chinese **style***
> *She dresses with such **style**.*

storey, story

A **storey** is a level in a building. A **story** is a description of events.

> *a house with three **storeys***
> *a **story** my grandfather told me*

strait, straight

Strait means 'narrow', and is found in the words *straitjacket* and *strait-laced*. A **strait** is a narrow strip of water. **Straight** means 'not curved'.

> *the **Straits** of Gibraltar*
> *a **straight** line*

symbol, cymbal

A **symbol** is something that represents another thing. A **cymbal** is a musical instrument.

> *a **symbol** of fertility*
> *the clash of the **cymbals***

there, their, they're

Their is the spelling used to refer to something belonging or relating to people or things which have already been mentioned. **There** is the spelling for the word which says that something does or does not exist, draws attention to something, or says that something is at, in, or going to that place. **They're**, with an apostrophe, is a shortened form of *they are*.

> *people who bite **their** nails*
> ***There** is no life on Jupiter.*
> ***There**'s Kathleen!*
> *They didn't want me **there**.*
> ***They're** a good team.*

through, threw

Through means 'going from one side to the other'. **Threw** is the past tense of the verb *throw*.

*They walked **through** the dense undergrowth.*
*Youths **threw** stones at passing cars.*

tide, tied
The **tide** is change in sea level. **Tied** is the past tense of the verb *tie*.

> high **tide**
> a beautifully **tied** bow

tire, tyre
To **tire** means to lose energy. A **tyre** is the rubber ring round the wheel of a vehicle.

> We began to **tire** after a few miles.
> a flat **tyre**

In American English, **tire** is the spelling for both meanings.

two, to, too
Two is the number after one. The word **to** has many uses, such as indicating direction in phrases like *to the house* and forming the infinitive of the verb, as in *to go*. **Too** means 'in addition'.

> I have **two** sisters.
> We went **to** Barcelona.
> I need **to** leave soon.
> Will you come **too**?

tongs, tongue
Tongs are instruments for holding and picking up things. Your **tongue** is part of your body.

> curling **tongs**
> It burnt my **tongue**.

vein, vain

Vain means unsuccessful. **Vain** also means proud of your looks or abilities. **Veins** are tubes in your body through which your blood flows. A **vein** is also a mood or style.

> a **vain** attempt to negotiate a truce
> You're so **vain**!
> the jugular **vein**
> writing in a jocular **vein**

> Remember: To be **va**in is **v**ery **a**rrogant, but a **ve**in is a blood **ve**ssel.

wander, wonder

To **wander** is to walk around in a casual way. To **wonder** is to speculate or enquire about something.

> She **wandered** aimlessly about the house.
> I **wonder** what happened

weather, whether

The **weather** is the conditions in the atmosphere. **Whether** is a word used to introduce an alternative.

> the **weather** forecast
> I'm not sure **whether** to stay or to go.

way, weigh

A **way** is a route or path, or a manner of doing something. To **weigh** something is to find out how heavy it is.

> Is this the **way** to the beach?
> You're doing it the wrong **way**.
> **Weigh** the flour.

which, witch
Which is a word used to introduce a question, or to refer to something or things that have already been mentioned. A **witch** is a woman with magical powers.

> *Which house is it?*
> *the ring **which** I had seen earlier*
> *a story about **witches** and wizards*

whose, who's
Who's, with an apostrophe, is a shortened form of *who is*. **Whose**, without an apostrophe and with an **E** at the end, is used when you are asking who something belongs to, or referring to something belonging or relating to things that have already been mentioned.

> *He knows **who's** boss.*
> ***Who's** there?*
> *a little boy **whose** nose grew every time he told a lie*
> ***Whose** coat is this?*

wrap, rap
To **wrap** something means to put something around it, and a **wrap** is something that is folded round something else. A **rap** is a sharp blow, and **rap** is a style of music.

> *to **wrap** presents*
> *a towelling **wrap***
> *a **rap** on the door*
> *They like listening to **rap**.*

wring, ring

A **ring** is the sound made by a bell, and it is also a circle or enclosure. To **wring** something is to twist it.

> the **ring** of the doorbell
> dancing in a **ring**
> **wringing** out the wet clothes

> Remember: You **wr**ing out something **w**et.

wry, rye

Wry means 'mocking' or 'ironic'. **Rye** is a type of grass or grain.

> a **wry** smile
> a sandwich made with **rye** bread

yoke, yolk

A **yoke** is an oppressive force or burden. A **yoke** is also a wooden beam put across two animals so that they can be worked as a team, and to **yoke** things together is to link them. The yellow part of an egg is the **yolk**.

> a country under the **yoke** of oppression
> They are **yoked** to the fortunes of the Prime Minister.
> I like the **yolk** to be runny.

your, you're

Your, without an apostrophe, is used when you are referring to something belonging or relating to the person or people you are speaking to, or relating to people in general. **You're**, with an apostrophe and with an **E** at the end, is a shortened form of you are.

> **Your** sister is right.
> Cigarettes can damage **your** health.
> **You're** annoying me.

false friends

False friends

Knowing that words are related to each other can be a great help to spelling. For example, when you spell *typical*, it can help to think of the related word *type* so that you know that the letter after the **T** is a **Y**.

But there are a few traps. Sometimes it seems logical that a word should follow a certain pattern or be spelt the same way as a word that sounds like it, but you will find that it doesn't. You will need to be alert when you spell the words listed here.

aeroplane
> The beginning is **AE**. Don't be confused by *airport*.

agoraphobia
> There is an **O** after the **G**. Don't be confused by *agriculture*.

ancillary
> There is no **I** after the **LL**. Don't be confused by *auxiliary*.

bachelor
> There is no **T** before the **CH**. Don't be confused by *batch*.

comparison
> The letter after the **R** is an **I**. Don't be confused by *comparative*.

> Remember: There is no com**paris**on with **Paris**.

curiosity
> There is no **U** after the **O**. Don't be confused by *curious*.

denunciation
> There is no **O** before the **U**. Don't be confused by *denounce*.

deodorant
> There is no **U** before the **R**. Don't be confused by *odour*.

desperate
> The vowel after **P** is **E**. Don't be confused by *despair*.

develop
> There is no **E** on the end. Don't be confused by the ending of *envelope*.

disastrous
> There is no **E** after the **T**. Don't be confused by *disaster*.

duly
There is no **E** after the **U**. Don't be confused by *due*.

extrovert
The vowel before the **V** is **O**. Don't be confused by *extra*.

flamboyant
There is no **U** before the **O**. Don't be confused by *buoyant*.

forty
There is no **U** after the **O**. Don't be confused by *four*.

glamorous
There is no **U** after the first **O**. Don't be confused by *glamour*.

hindrance
There is no **E** after the **D**. Don't be confused by *hinder*.

hypochondriac
The vowel after the **P** is **O**. Don't be confused by the more common prefix *hyper-*.

inoculate
There is only one **N** after the **I**. Don't be confused by *innocuous*.

liquefy
The vowel before the **F** is **E**. Don't be confused by *liquid*.

minuscule
The vowel after the **N** is **U**. Don't be confused by *mini*.

negligent
The vowel after the **L** is **I**. Don't be confused by *neglect*.

ninth
There is no **E** before the **TH**. Don't be confused by *nine*.

obscene
There is a **C** after the **S**. Don't be confused by *obsess*.

offensive
There is an **S** after the **N**. Don't be confused by *offence*.

orthodox
The beginning is **OR**. Don't be confused by *authority*.

ostracize
The vowel in the middle is **A**. Don't be confused by *ostrich*.

personnel
There are two **N**'s. Don't be confused by *personal*.

pronunciation
There is no **O** before the **U**. Don't be confused by *pronounce*.

questionnaire
There are two **N**'s. Don't be confused by *millionaire*.

refrigerator
There is no **D** before the **G**. Don't be confused by *fridge*.

sacrilegious
There is an **I** before the **L** and an **E** after the **L**. Don't be confused by *religion*.

supersede
The ending is **SEDE**. Don't be confused by words like *recede* and *precede*.

truly
There is no **E** after the **U**. Don't be confused by *true*.

wondrous
There is no **E** after the **D**. Don't be confused by *wonder*.

other commonly misspelt words

Other commonly misspelt words

The final chapter of this book includes another list of words that are often spelt incorrectly. These words do not fall clearly under any of the categories covered in the previous five chapters.

Sometimes these words are hard to spell because the sound does not match the spelling. Sometimes the problem comes from the fact that a sound has several possible spellings and you need to know which applies in this particular word. Some of the words have several unusual features about them.

It is worth familiarizing yourself with these words. Helpful ways of remembering the spelling have been provided for some of them.

absence
There is a single **S** at the beginning and a single **C** at the end – just the same as in its opposite, *presence*.
abysmal
The vowel sound after the **B** is spelt with a **Y**.
accede
The ending is **CEDE** – just the same as in *concede* and *recede*.
ache
The consonant sound is spelt **CH** and there is an **E** at the end.

> Remember: An **ache** needs **a che**ap remedy.

acknowledge
The second syllable is spelt **KNOW**.

> Remember: The word is made from *ac + knowledge*.

adequate
The vowel after the **D** is an **E**.
advantageous
There is an **E** after the **G**.

advertisement
There is an **E** after the **S**.

> Remember: The word is made up of *advertise* and the suffix *-ment*.

aerial
The opening is **AE** – just the same as in *aeroplane*.

aesthetic
In British spelling, there is an **A** before the **E**. The American spelling is *esthetic*.

aficionado
The middle is **CIO**. The word comes from Spanish.

amethyst
The second vowel is **E** and the final vowel is **Y**.

anaesthetic
In British spelling, there is an **A** before the **E**. The American spelling is *anesthetic*.

analysis
The vowel after the **L** is **Y** and the final vowel is **I**.

> Remember that *analysis* is related to *analyse*.

annihilate
There are two **N**'s and the middle is **IHI** – just the same as in the related word *nihilism*.

anonymous
The vowel between **N** and **M** is a **Y**, and the ending is **OUS**.

anxious
There is an **I** after the **X**.

apology
The vowel after the **L** is **O**.

> Remember: I will **log** an apo**log**y.

arbitrary
There is an **AR** before the **Y** that is sometimes missed out in speech.

architect
There is an **H** after the **C**.
argue
The ending is **UE**.
atheist
The first vowel is **A**, and the second vowel is **E**.
attendance
The ending is **ANCE**.

> Remember: You **dance** atten**dance** on someone.

atrocious
The ending is **CIOUS** – just the same as in *delicious*.
attach
There is no **T** before the **CH** – just the same as in the opposite word, *detach*.

> Remember: Atta**ch** a **c**oat **h**ook to the wall.

auxiliary
There is a single **L**, which is followed by an **I**.
awful
There is no **E** after the **W**, and a single **L** at the end.
bachelor
There is no **T** before the **CH**.

> Remember: Was **Bach** a **bach**elor?

barbecue
The normal spelling is **CUE**. The word can also be spelt *barbeque*.
because
The vowel sound after the **C** is spelt **AU**, and the ending is **SE**.

> Remember: **B**ig **e**lephants **c**an **a**lways **u**nderstand **s**mall **e**lephants.

beggar

The ending is **AR**.

> Remember: There is a begg**ar** in the g**ar**den.

berserk

There is an **R** before the **S** that is sometimes ignored in speech.

boundary

There is an **A** after the **D** that is sometimes missed out in speech.

breadth

The vowel sound is spelt **EA** and there is a **D** before the **TH**.

Britain

The final vowel is spelt **AI** – just the same as in *certain*.

> Remember: There is a lot of r**ain** in Brit**ain**.

broad

The vowel sound is spelt **OA**.

> Remember: **B-road**s can be quite **broad**.

bronchitis

There is an **H** after the **C**, and the ending is **ITIS**.

bruise

The ending is **UISE** – just the same as in *cruise*.

buoy

There is a **U** before the **O**.

> Remember: A **buoy** is a **b**ig **u**nsinkable **o**bject **y**oked in the sea.

buoyant

There is a **U** before the **O** – just the same as in *buoy*.

bureaucracy
The vowel in the middle is spelt **EAU** and the ending is **CY**.

> Remember that the start of this word is the same as the word *bureau*.

burglar
The ending is **AR**.

business
The opening is **BUSI**.

> Remember: It's none of your **busi**ness what **bus I** get!

caffeine
This is an exception to the rule 'I before E except after C'.

calendar
The vowel in the middle is **E** and the ending is **AR**.

carriage
There is an **I** before **AGE** – just the same as in *marriage*.

catalogue
The ending is **OGUE** – just the same as in *dialogue*.

category
The vowel after the **T** is an **E**.

cauliflower
The first vowel is spelt **AU**.

ceiling
The word begins with a **C** and the first vowel sound is spelt **EI**.

> Remember the rule: **I** before **E** *except after* **C**.

cellophane
The first letter is **C** and there is a **PH** in the middle.

cemetery
All of the vowels in this word are **E**'s.

> Remember: A parking **meter** at the ce**meter**y.

certain

The final vowel is spelt **AI** – just the same as in *curtain*.

choir

Nothing much in this word looks like it sounds: the beginning is **CH** and the vowel sound is spelt **OIR**.

> Remember: **Cho**irs sing **cho**ral music.

claustrophobia

The first vowel sound is spelt **AU**, and there is an **O** before the **PH**.

cocoa

The first vowel is **O** and the second vowel sound is spelt **OA**.

coconut

There are two **O**'s – just the same as in *cocoa*.

coffee

There is a double **F** and the ending is **EE** – just the same as in *toffee*.

competent

The second and third vowels are both **E**.

> Remember: You must be **compete**nt in order to **compete**.

competition

The vowel after the **P** is an **E**.

> Remember: You **compet**e in a **compet**ition.

complexion

The letter after the **E** is **X**.

> Remember: **X** marks the spot!

concede

The ending is **CEDE** – just the same as in *accede* and *recede*.

conference

The vowel after the **F** is an **E** – just the same as in the related word *confer*.

congeal
The letter after the **N** is a **G**, and the ending is **EAL**.

conscience
The sound after the first **N** is spelt **SCI**.

> Remember: The ending is the same as the word *science*.

conscientious
The ending is **TIOUS**. The word is related to *conscience*, but the **C** changes to a **T**.

conscious
The sound after the first **N** is spelt **SCI**.

contemporary
There is an **AR** before the **Y** that is sometimes missed out in speech.

continent
The middle vowel is **I** and the ending is **ENT**.

controversial
The vowel after the first **R** is an **O**.

> Remember the related word *controversy*, where this vowel is sounded more clearly.

convenient
The ending is **ENT**.

counterfeit
The ending is **EIT** – just the same as in *forfeit* and *surfeit*.

courteous
The first vowel sound is spelt **OUR** and there is an **E** before the **OUS**.

criticize
The letter after the second **I** is **C** – just the same as in the related word *critic*.

crocodile
The middle vowel is an **O**.

> Remember: A cro**cod**ile has eaten a **cod**.

crucial
> The letter after the **U** is a **C**.

cruise
> The ending is **UISE** – just the same as in *bruise*.

currency
> The vowel in the middle is an **E**.

curtain
> The final vowel sound is spelt **AI** – just the same as in *certain*.

> Remember: Always buy pl**ain** curt**ain**s.

cycle, cylinder, cynic, cyst
> The opening is **CY**.

decrease
> The ending is **EASE**.

> Remember: Decr**ease** with **ease**.

definite
> The vowel after the **F** is an **I**, and the ending is **ITE** – just the same as in the related word *finite*.

deliberate
> The first vowel is **E**, and the ending is **ATE**.

> Remember the related word *deliberation*.

delicious
> The ending is **CIOUS** – just the same as in *atrocious*.

demeanour
> The ending is **OUR**.

> Remember: Demean**our** can mean **our** behavi**our**.

derogatory
> There is an **O** before the **RY** that is often missed out in speech.

> Remember: She was derog**atory** about **a Tory**.

describe
> The first vowel is **E**.

desperate
> The vowel after **P** is **E**.

detach
> There is no **T** before the **CH** – just the same as in the opposite word, *attach*.

deter
> The ending is **ER**.

different
> There is an **E** after the **F** that is sometimes missed out in speech.

dilapidated
> The beginning is **DI** (not **DE**).

> Remember: A **di**lapidated building is **di**sused.

dinosaur
> The middle vowel is an **O**.

> Remember: There are **no** di**no**saurs **no**w.

eccentric
> There are two **C**'s at the start.

ecstasy
> The ending is **ASY** – just the same as in *fantasy*.

elegant
> The vowel after the **L** is an **E**.

> Remember: El**eg**ant **leg**s.

eighth
> There is only one **T**, even though the word comes from *eight + th*.

> Remember: **E**dith **i**s **g**oing **h**ome **t**o **H**enry.

either

    The **E** comes before the **I** – just the same as in the related word *neither*.

emphasis, emphasize

    The sound after the **M** is spelt **PH**.

encyclopedia, encyclopaedia

    This word can be spelt with either an **E** or an **AE** after the **P**.

    The vowel before the **P** is an **O**.

endeavour

    The middle vowel sound is spelt **EA** and the ending is **OUR**.

exasperate

    The beginning is **EXA** and the vowel after the **P** is an **E**.

exercise

    The beginning is **EXE** and the ending is **ISE**.

expense

    The ending is **SE** – using an **S** as in the related word *expensive*.

extension

    The ending is **SION**.

> Remember that this word is related to *extensive*.

extravagant

    The vowel after the **V** is an **A**.

> Remember: There are an extravagant number of **A**'s in extr**a**v**a**g**a**nt.

facetious

    The ending is **TIOUS**.

> Remember: The word f**acetiou**s contains the vowels **AEIOU** in order.

family

    There is an **I** after the **M** that is sometimes missed out in speech.

> Remember that you should be fam**i**liar with your fam**i**ly.

fascinate

There is a **C** after the **S**.

fatigue

The ending is **GUE**.

favourite

The vowel sound in the middle is spelt **OU**.

> Remember: This one is **our** fav**ou**rite.

feasible

The first vowel sound is spelt **EA** and the ending is **IBLE**.

February

There is an **R** after the **B** which is often missed out in speech.

feud

The middle is spelt **EU**.

> Remember: **F**euds **e**nd **u**p **d**isastrously.

fifth

There is an **F** before the **TH**.

foreign

The ending is **EIGN** – just the same as in *sovereign* and *reign*.

This is an exception to the rule 'I before E except after C'.

forfeit

The ending is **EIT** – just the same as in *counterfeit* and *surfeit*.

This is an exception to the rule 'I before E except after C'.

friend

There is an **I** before the **E**.

> Remember: **I** before **E**, except after **C**.

gauge

There is a **U** after the **A**.

> Remember: **G**reat **A**unt **U**na **g**rows **e**ggplants.

generate, generation

The vowel after the **N** is **E**.

genuine

The ending is **INE**.

gipsy, gypsy

The word can be spelt with either an **I** or a **Y** after the **G**.

glimpse

There is a **P** after the **S** that is sometimes missed out in speech.

grammar

The ending is **AR**.

> Remember that gramm**a**r is related to gramm**a**tical.

gruesome

There is an **E** after the **U** and another at the end.

guarantee, guard, guess, guide, guillotine, guilty, guitar

There is a **U** after the **G** in these words.

gymkhana, gymnasium

The vowel sound after the **G** is spelt with a **Y**.

harangue

The ending is **GUE** – just the same as in *tongue*.

hatred

The final vowel is **E**.

hearse

The vowel sound is spelt **EA** and there is an **E** on the end.

> Remember: I didn't **hear** the **hear**se.

height

The middle is **EIGH** – just the same as in *weight*.

heir

There is a silent **H** and the ending is **EIR**.

> Remember: **H**appy **E**dward **is r**ich.

hereditary
There is an **A** before the **RY** that is sometimes missed out in speech.

holocaust
The vowel after the **L** is an **O**.

honorary
There is no **U** after the second **O**, and there is an **AR** before the **Y** that is sometimes missed out in speech.

horoscope
The vowel after the **R** is an **O**.

hyacinth
The vowel after the **H** is a **Y**, and the letter after **A** is a **C**.

hygiene
The first vowel sound is a **Y** and the second vowel sound is spelt **IE**.

hyphen
The first vowel sound is a **Y**.

hypochondriac
The letter after the **P** is **O** and this is followed by **CH**.

hypocrite
The letter after the **P** is **O** and the ending is **ITE**.

hypocrisy
The letter after the **P** is **O** and the ending is **ISY**.

hysteria
The first vowel sound is a **Y**.

idiosyncrasy
The vowel after the **D** is **I**, the vowel after the **S** is **Y**, and the ending is **ASY**.

imaginary
There is an **A** after the **N** that is sometimes missed out in speech.

incense
The letter after the first **N** is **C**, but the letter after the second **N** is **S**.

incident
The letter after the **N** is **C**, which is followed by an **I**.

incongruous
There is a **U** after the **R**.

independent
The final vowel is an **E**.

input
> The opening is **IN**. This is an exception to the rule that the prefix **IN** changes to **IM** before a **P**.

integrate
> The vowel before the **G** is **E** – just the same as in *integral*.

intrigue
> The ending is **IGUE**.

introduce
> The vowel before the **D** is **O**.

irascible
> There is a **C** after the **S** and the ending is **IBLE**.

issue
> There is a double **S** in the middle – just the same as in *tissue*.

itinerary
> There is an **AR** before the **Y** that is sometimes missed out in speech.

jealous, jealousy
> The first vowel sound is spelt **EA**; the second vowel is **OU** – just the same as in *zealous*.

jewellery
> There is an **ER** before the **Y** that is sometimes missed out in speech. The American spelling is *jewelry*.

journey
> The first vowel sound is spelt **OUR**.

> Remember: How was y**our** j**our**ney?

judgment, judgement
> There is an optional **E** before the **M**.

knowledge
> The opening is **KNOW**.

> Remember that **know**ledge is what you **know**.

knowledgeable
> There is an **E** after the **G**.

labyrinth
> The vowel sound after the **B** is a **Y**.

lackadaisical
> There is a **CK** after the first **A** and the vowel sound after the **D** is spelt **AI**.

> Remember: If you **lack a dai**ly paper you are **lackadai**sical

lacquer
> There is **CQU** in the middle.

language
> The **U** comes before the **A**, which is the opposite of the way the letters fall in *gauge*.

languor
> The ending is **UOR** (not **OUR**).

laugh
> The vowel sound is spelt **AU** and the final consonant sound is spelt **GH**.

league
> The ending is **GUE**.

lecherous
> There is no **T** before the **CH**.

leisure
> The **E** comes before the **I**.

length
> There is a **G** after the **N** that is sometimes missed out in speech.

liaise, liaison
> There are two **I**'s in these words.

> Remember: **L**ouise **i**s **a**lways **i**n **s**ome **o**ld **n**ightdress.

library
> There is an **AR** before the **Y** that is sometimes missed out in speech.

litre
> In British English the ending is **RE** – just the same as in *metre*. The American spelling is *liter*.

lustre

In British English the ending is **RE**. The American spelling is *luster*.

maintenance

The vowel after the **T** is an **E**.

mantelpiece

The letters after the **T** are **EL**.

margarine

The vowel after the **G** is an **A**. This is an exception to the rule that **G** is 'hard' before **A**, **O**, and **U**.

marriage

There is an **I** before **AGE** – just the same as in *carriage*.

massacre

There is a double **S** and the ending is **RE**.

> Remember: A **mass** of crops in every **acre**.

mathematics

There is an **E** after the **TH** that is sometimes missed out in speech.

> Remember: I teach **them** ma**them**atics.

meagre

In British English, the ending is **RE**. The American spelling is *meager*.

medicine

There is an **I** after the **D** that is sometimes missed out in speech.

messenger

The vowel after **SS** is **E** – just the same as in *passenger*.

minuscule

The vowel after the **N** is a **U**.

> Remember: This word is related to *minus*.

miscellaneous

There is a **C** after the **S** and a double **L**.

> Remember: Mis**cell**aneous **cell**s.

misogyny
The ending is **GYNY**.

money
The vowel after the **M** is **O**, and the ending is **EY**.

mongrel
The vowel after the **M** is **O**.

> Remember: A m**o**ngrel from M**o**ngolia.

monkey
The vowel after the **M** is **O**, and the ending is **EY**.

mystery
The vowel sound after the **M** is **Y**, and the ending is **ERY**.

mystify
The vowel sound after the **M** is **Y** – just the same as in *mystery*.

nausea
The vowel after the **S** is **E**.

> Remember you might get nau**sea** at **sea**.

neither
The **E** comes before the **I** – just the same as in the related word *either*.

neural, neurotic, neutral
The opening is **NEU**.

niece
The **I** comes before the **E**.

nuisance
The opening is **NUI**.

onion
The first letter is **O**.

ordinary
There is an **A** after the **N** that is sometimes missed out in speech.

original
The vowel after the **G** is an **I**.

> Remember: I ori**gin**ally ordered **gin**.

ornament
    The vowel after the first **N** is an **A**.

oxygen
    The vowel after the **X** is a **Y** and the ending is **GEN** – just the same as in *hydrogen* and *nitrogen*.

pageant
    There is an **E** before the **A** which makes the **G** soft. There is no **D** before the **G**.

pamphlet
    There is a **PH** after the **M**.

parachute
    The ending is **CHUTE**.

paralyse
    The ending is **YSE** – just the same as in *analyse*.

particular
    There is an **AR** at the beginning and the end.

passenger
    The vowel after **SS** is **E** – just the same as in *messenger*.

peculiar
    The ending is **AR**.

penetrate
    The vowel after the **N** is **E**.

permanent
    The vowel after the **M** is an **A** and the vowel after the **N** is an **E**.

> Remember: A lion's **mane** is per**mane**nt.

persistent
    The ending is **ENT**.

persuade
    The beginning is **PER** and there is a **U** after the **S**.

phenomenon
    The middle part is **NOM** and the ending is **NON**.

pigeon
    There is an **E** before the **O** which makes the **G** soft. There is no **D** before the **G**.

pillar

There is a double **LL** and the ending is **AR**.

plagiarize

There is a **GI** in the middle.

plague

The ending is **GUE**.

pneumonia

There is a silent **P** at the start and the first vowel sound is spelt **EU**.

> Remember: **Pneu**monia **p**robably **n**ever **e**ases **up**.

poignant

The **G** comes before the **N**.

prayer

The ending is **AYER**.

prejudice

The letter after **PRE** is **J**.

> Remember: **Prej**udice is **prej**udging things.

prerogative

There is an **R** after the **P** that is sometimes missed out in speech.

prevalent

The vowel after the **V** is **A**.

primitive

The vowel after the **M** is **I**.

privilege

The vowel after the **V** is **I** and the vowel after the **L** is **E**.

> Remember: It is **vile** to have no pri**vile**ges.

protein

This is an exception to the rule 'I before E except after C'.

provocation

The vowel after the **V** is **O**.

> Remember that this word is related to *provoke*.

pursue
There is an **R** after the first **U**.

pyjamas
In British English, the first vowel is a **Y**. The American spelling is *pajamas*.

pyramid
The first vowel is a **Y**.

rancour
The ending is **OUR**.

recede
The ending is **CEDE** – just the same as in *accede* and *concede*.

rehearsal
The vowel sound in the middle is spelt **EAR**.

> Remember: I **hear** there is a re**hear**sal.

reign
The ending is **EIGN** – just the same as in *sovereign* and *foreign*.

relevant
The vowel after the **L** is an **E**, and the vowel after the **V** is **A**.

religion
There is an **I** before the **O** and no **D** before the **G**.

reminisce
The vowel after the **M** is an **I**, and the ending is **ISCE**.

rhythm
The beginning is **RH**, and the only vowel in this word is a **Y**.

> Remember: **R**hythm **h**elps **y**ou **t**o **h**ear **m**usic.

righteous
The ending is **EOUS**.

rogue
The ending is **OGUE** – just the same as in *vogue*.

sacrifice
The vowel after the **R** is **I**. The ending is **ICE**.

sacrilege
The vowel after the **L** is **E** – just the same as in *privilege*.

sausage
> The first vowel sound is spelt **AU**, and this is followed by a single **S**.

sceptic
> In British English, the opening is **SC**. The American spelling is
> *skeptic*.

schedule
> The opening is **SCH**.

> Remember: The **sch**ool **sch**edule.

science, scientific
> The opening is **SC**.

scissors
> The opening is **SC** and there is a double **S** in the middle.

scythe
> The opening is **SC**, the main vowel is **Y**, and there is an **E** at the end.

secondary
> There is an **A** after the **D** that is sometimes missed out in speech.

secretary
> The vowel before the **T** is **E**, and there is an **A** after the **T** that is
> sometimes missed out in speech.

> Remember: The **secret**ary can keep a **secret**.

seize
> This is an exception to the rule 'I before E except after C'.

separate
> The vowel after the **P** is **A**.

> Remember that this word has the word *par* contained
> inside it.

sergeant
> The first vowel sound is spelt **ER**, and this is followed by **GE**.

series
> The ending is **IES**.

serious
The ending is **OUS**.
several
There is an **E** after the **V** that is sometimes missed out in speech.
shoulder
There is a **U** after the **O**.
sieve
There is an **E** after the **I**, and another **E** at the end.

> Remember: A **sieve** is for **si**fting **eve**rything.

similar
There is an **I** after the **M** that is sometimes missed out in speech, and the ending is **AR**.
simultaneous
There is an **E** after the **N**.
skeleton
The vowel after the **L** is **E**.

> Remember: Don't **let on** about the ske**leton** in the cupboard.

sombre
In British English the ending is **RE**. The American spelling is *somber*.
somersault
The first vowel is an **O**, and the final vowel sound is spelt **AU**.
soothe
There is an **E** at the end.
sovereign
The ending is **EIGN** – just the same as in *foreign* and *reign*.

> Remember: A sove**reign reign**s.

spontaneous
There is an **E** after the second **N**.
squalor
The ending is **OR** (not **OUR**).

stealth, stealthy

There is an **A** after the **E** – just the same as in *wealth* and *wealthy*.

stereo

The vowel after the **R** is an **E**.

> Remember: Ster**eo** **re**cords.

stomach

The first vowel is an **O**, and the ending is **ACH**.

strength

There is a **G** after the **N** that is sometimes missed out in speech.

supersede

The ending is **SEDE**. This word is not related to words such as *accede* and *concede* or *exceed* and *proceed*.

surfeit

The ending is **EIT** – just the same as in *counterfeit* and *forfeit*.

surgeon

There is an **E** between the **G** and the **O**.

> Remember: Surg**eo**ns give **e**ffective **o**perations.

surprise

There is an **R** before the **P**.

susceptible

There is a **C** after the second **S**. The ending is **IBLE**.

sustenance

The vowel after **T** is **E**.

synonym

There is a **Y** after the **S** and one before the **M**.

syringe

There is a **Y** after the **S**. The ending is **GE**.

tacit

The middle consonant is a **C**.

temperament, temperature

There is an **E** before the **R** that is sometimes missed out in speech.

> Remember that these words are related to *temper*.

temporary
> There is an **AR** before the **Y** that is sometimes missed out in speech.

theatre
> The first vowel sound is spelt **EA** and the end is **RE** in British English. The American spelling is *theater*.

thorough
> The final vowel sound is spelt **OUGH**.

through
> The vowel sound is spelt **OUGH**.

tissue
> There is a double **S** in the middle – just the same as in *issue*.

toffee
> There is a double **F** and the ending is **EE** – just the same as in *coffee*.

tongue
> The ending is **GUE** – just the same as in *harangue*.

tragedy
> There is no **D** before the **G**.

> Remember: I **raged** at the t**raged**y of it.

twelfth
> There is an **F** before the **TH** which is often missed out in speech.

typical
> The letter after **T** is a **Y** – just the same as in *type*.

usual
> The letter after the first **U** is **S**.

> Remember: **U**gly **s**wan **u**ses **a** **l**ipstick.

vaccinate
> There is double **C** – just the same as in *access* and *accent*.

vague
> The ending is **AGUE**.

vegetable
> The vowel after the **G** is an **E**.

> Remember: **Get** some ve**get**ables inside you!

vehement
There is an **H** after the first **E** which is often missed out in speech.

vehicle
There is a silent **H** which is followed by an **I**.

veterinary
There is an **ER** after the **T** which is often missed out in speech.

vogue
The ending is **OGUE** – just the same as in *rogue*.

voluntary
There is an **A** after the **T** which is often missed out in speech.

vulnerable
There is an **L** before the **N** which is often missed out in speech.

weird
This is an exception to the rule 'I before E except after C'.

word
The vowel is sound spelt **OR**.

worship
The vowel is sound spelt **OR**.

wrath
There is a silent **W**, and the vowel is an **A**.

yacht
This is a very unusual spelling: the middle part of the word is **ACH**.

zealous
The first vowel sound is spelt **EA**; the second vowel is **OU** – just the same as in *jealous*.

Remember that this word is related to *zeal*.

index of
hard words

3. Writing

526 contents

Preparing
to write

Thinking about your writing

Whatever you are writing, it is important to think about it first.
If you plan your writing well, it will be **clear, logical and effective**.

You may think that planning your writing is just one extra job, and a
waste of time, but in fact good planning will probably **save you time**
as well as making your writing better.

Planning does not necessarily take a lot of time, and you do not always
need to make a **written plan**. For instance, it would be silly to make a
written plan for a text message – the whole point is that texting is a
quick way of communicating. However, even with a text message,
you should plan **in your mind**, so that you know what you want
to say.

For longer pieces of writing, such as essays, reports, and often
even letters, it is very useful to make a written plan. A plan will
help you:

- *organize your thoughts*
- *make sure you are clear about what you want to write*
- *make sure you have all the information you need*
- *make sure you don't leave anything out*

> **Key point to remember**
> Planning will save you time and make your writing more
> effective.

Before you start to write, the most important question to ask
yourself is: **What am I trying to achieve?**

The best way to be clear about this is to ask three questions:

1 **Who** is this writing for?
2 **What** do I want to say?
3 **Why** do I want to say it?

Imagine, for example, that you really like animals, and you need a holiday job, so you decide to write to the local zoo. In this case, the answers to the questions above could be:

1 The manager or personnel officer of the zoo.
2 That you want a summer holiday job. That you love animals and worked on a farm last year.
3 Because you want to get a holiday job in a zoo.

There are important points to remember about each of these questions:

• **Who?** Make sure that you use a suitable style and tone for your audience. Informal language and jokes are fine for your friends, but a job application needs to be more formal.
• **What?** Make sure that what you say is absolutely clear, and that you have included everything you wanted to include.
• **Why?** Make sure the letter achieves what you want it to achieve. For instance, if you write a letter of complaint, be clear about what you want to happen: are you writing it because you want an apology, or do you want your money back?

Before starting to write, it can sometimes be helpful to make a brief summary of what you are trying to achieve. This can help you to concentrate on the most important points of your writing.

When you have finished your writing, you can go back to your summary and check that what you have written achieves what you wanted it to. A good summary will always answer the questions, who?, what? and why?

Here are two examples of this kind of summary:

> *A survey of students' opinions of the food in our school canteen, to be used as the basis of a campaign for better school meals.*

> *A letter of complaint to the manager of the local theatre to say that our recent visit was spoiled by the noise of building work going on in the bar area, and to ask for our money back.*

Your summary can also help you resist the temptation to add too many details or extra points. Remember that many people are busy – if they do not understand your main points quickly, you may not achieve what you hope to achieve.

Key point to remember
Always be clear about the purpose of your writing.

Organizing your ideas

Whatever you are planning to write, you need to organize your ideas, either on paper, on your computer, or in your head.

There are several good things about this stage of writing:

- You do not need to worry about grammar and spelling
- You do not need to write whole sentences: single words, phrases, or even pictures are fine
- You do not need to put your ideas into any kind of order to begin with – that can come later
- The act of writing things down can give you new ideas

It is also fine to write down things that you don't know!

Say, for instance, you are writing an essay about the causes of the First World War, a subject you have been studying in class. You might write down the things you know about, e.g. the Alliances between different countries, the assassination of Archduke Franz Ferdinand, the struggle between Britain and Germany to have military control of the seas.

Then you can add things you do not know, but think you ought to include in your essay. Examples might be: why were these Alliances formed?; who killed Franz Ferdinand and why?; what role did imperialism play in the arguments between countries?

These **questions** will help you to see what **further research** you need to do.

> **Tip for success**
> If you write down your ideas, you will not forget them!

When you have written down all your ideas, you need to put them in some kind of **order**. If you have a very clear idea of what your writing will contain, it may be possible to do this right from the beginning.

One simple way to order your ideas is to list them under different **headings**.

For instance, this writer is planning an article for her student magazine about working holidays abroad:

Reasons to work abroad	Types of work available	Practical issues
chance to travel	voluntary v. paid	legal: work permits, etc.
see 'real' life	teaching	safety
earn money	farm work	cheapest way to travel
make new friends	tourist industry	there
work experience		how much will you earn?

It can be useful to be able to **move your ideas around**.

One possibility is to use **Post-it® notes** (small pieces of paper with one sticky edge) and arrange them on a table or a wall.

Imagine you are writing a party invitation. You want to include the date and time of the party, what it's celebrating, that you need a reply to your invitation, that friends and partners are welcome and that you'd like people to bring drinks.

If you write all those things on Post-it® notes, you can make sure you include all the points you want to, and in the best order.

A very flexible way of ordering ideas is to use **mind maps**, or **spider maps**. In these maps, you start with the most important, central idea, and work out from there, using branches leading outwards. The more detailed the idea, the further the branches are from the central point.

This writer is planning to write a leaflet about what we can do to protect the environment:

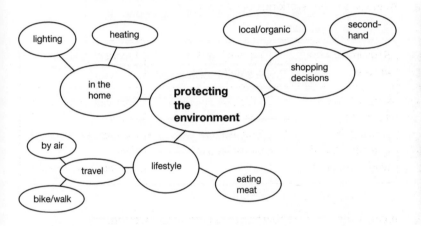

Tip for success
A good mind map will help you structure your writing by showing you how points relate to each other.

Another method that is suitable for some kinds of writing is a flow chart. This writer is planning a letter to the local council to ask for repairs to the public football pitch:

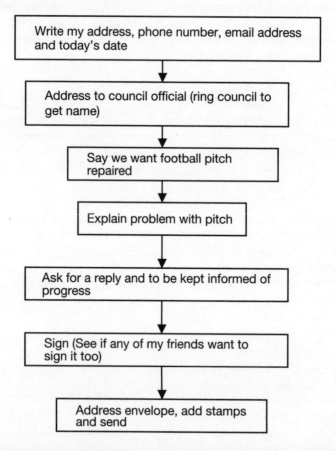

Tip for success

As well as the things you want to write, your flow chart can include things you need to do, for example finding out a name or address, finding information (e.g. a bank account number) or filling in a form you need to enclose.

Research

For some pieces of writing, especially longer pieces, you will need to do some research. How much you need to do will depend on the information you already have and the amount of detail your writing needs.

If you are a student, your **teacher** will be able to help. They may give you a list of books or websites to use.

Think about whether there is **anybody you know** who could give you information, or at least tell you the best place to look. Perhaps you have a neighbour who works at the local museum, a relative who was alive during the Second World War, or a friend who is crazy about sport?

A good place to do research is the **library**. Books will be arranged by subject, so it is easy to find what you want. Many libraries also have computerized systems, which allow you to look for books in several ways, for example:

- by subject
- by keywords in the title
  (important words that give a clue to what the book is about)
- by author
- by date of publication

It is often useful to ask the **librarians** for help. They will know about all the different sources of information, some of which may not be in book form. For example, many libraries have copies of old newspapers in a photographed form, which you need a special machine to read.

Using the Internet is a quick and useful way to research a topic. However, it is important to remember that **absolutely anyone** can put information on a website. You need to make sure that any source you use is suitable.

A good starting point is to ask two questions:

- **Who** wrote the information you are looking at?
- **What** is the purpose of the site where you found it?

Answering these questions will help you to think about two further questions:

- Is this information likely to be reliable?
- Is the information likely to be fair, or does the writer have a particular purpose, such as supporting an opinion or trying to make you buy something?

Using a **search engine** such as Google®, Yahoo® or Alta Vista® can be a start, but there is a danger that you find so many sites that you miss the ones which are really important. Many teachers and lecturers include websites on their reading lists, so if you have been given a reading list, make sure you use it. Otherwise, think about sites that will be reliable. For instance, in the UK you might look for medical information on the National Health Service site. In Australia, you might look for news information on the ABC site.

> **Tip for success**
> If you are using the Internet in a library, the librarian may be able to help you find suitable sites.

Making notes and summaries

When you are doing research, you will want to **make notes**.
Your notes can be in whatever form suits you best. The important
thing is to make sure you will still understand them when you come
to use them!

Do make sure that the notes you take **relate to the subject** you
will be writing about. There is no point adding extra information –
however interesting it is – that you will not be able to use.

Notes should be **short** – do not copy out huge pieces of text.
In order to **summarize**, it is very important to make sure you have
understood the main points. When you have read a chapter or an
article, it can be useful to try to write down the most important
three or four points in it.

Look for clues in what you are reading to help you:

*   Are there any words that are <u>underlined</u> or in **heavy type**?
*   Do the headings summarize the main points?
*   Does the book itself include summaries or lists of main points?

Do use abbreviations, shorten words or miss out words altogether.
'Romans > Britain 55BC' is much more efficient than writing
'The Romans came to Britain in 55BC.'

Key point to remember
Make sure you will be able to understand your notes
when you need to use them.

If you have a good idea of the structure of your piece of writing,
it can be useful to organize your notes.

For example, if you are writing an essay about a book you have read, you may be asked to look at particular things, such as the way the author builds up characters; the style of language used; the way the plot develops; the author's relationship with the reader.

If you divide your paper into **themes** like these, you can order your notes as you take them. This will make it easier to organize your essay, and also help you balance the amounts of material you have on each theme.

You may use your notes to record good **quotations** to use in your own writing, but be careful:

- If you use a direct quotation, you must produce it accurately, and you must say where it has come from.
- If you summarize what someone has said, you must change it into your **own words**. Copying the words of others is called **plagiarizing**. It is not allowed in academic work, and it can be illegal.

Tip for success
While you are making notes, keep a list of **useful words and phrases** to use in your own writing.

Outlines

For longer pieces of writing, it is useful to produce an outline before you start. An outline can have as much or as little in it as you think will be useful for you, but it should at least include a basic list of **headings**. If you have organized your ideas and notes in some of the ways suggested above, you will probably find it quite easy to produce an outline.

Start by picking out a number of main points – these will be the main frame for your writing, and will lead to more detailed points within them.

For some types of writing, such as a report, it may be appropriate to keep these headings in the final text. For others, the headings will simply be a way of organizing your writing and will not appear in your finished work.

You can use your outline to check that everything you want to write is in a **logical order**:

- Make sure that understanding one part does not rely on another part that comes later
- If you move on to a different point, see if it needs some sort of introduction or explanation
- Make sure that all the points connected to a particular theme are treated together

The person who made this outline is writing a report on the use of volunteers in a local charity:

Volunteer report

Introduction

- What this report covers
- Research and methods used
- Purpose of report

Summary of main points

The current situation

- number of volunteers
- what they do
- how they are managed

Problems with the current situation

- not enough volunteers
- volunteers not clear about their role
- lack of communication with paid staff

Suggestions for improvement

- better targeting of recruitment campaigns
- written handbook for volunteers
- regular staff/volunteer meetings

Conclusion

Key point to remember
Use your outline to make sure everything is included and in the best order.

Writing a draft

A draft is a rough version of your finished writing. It can be as close to or as far away from the final text as you like. For instance, you may decide to concentrate on the content and not worry about spelling and punctuation – that is up to you.

If you are writing something very long, or very important, you may write **more than one draft**.

When you have written a draft, it is useful to ask the following questions:

- Does the **order** of what is written make sense?

- Have you **included everything** you wanted to include?

- Is all the material **relevant**? Is there anything you should cut out?

- Is the **tone** right? For instance, if it is a letter of complaint, is it firm and assertive or is it offensive and rude?

- Does any part need **more explanation**, more information or more evidence?

- Is the amount of **space given to each theme** appropriate, or is one part too long or too short?

- Does it **achieve** what you want it to achieve (if you wrote a brief summary at the beginning, you can check against it)?

It can sometimes be useful to give a draft of your writing to **someone else**, and ask if what you have written is clear, interesting, and effective. That person might make suggestions for additions or improvements, or check facts for you.

Key point to remember
Do not expect to produce a perfect piece of writing first time. Many people write two or more drafts of an important piece of writing before they are satisfied with it.

Presentation

General layout

A clear and attractive layout will make your texts both more enjoyable to read and easier to understand.

The use of computers makes it easy for everyone to present their writing in a professional way, and gives us lots of choices about how to do this. One of the most useful things about using a computer is that you can edit text and move it around as you work. You can experiment with different ways of presenting it – you do not have to decide on your layout at the beginning.

Here are some general rules:

- Almost all documents look better if there is plenty of **space** around the words
- Do not make your **sentences or paragraphs** too long
- Do not make the **size of type** too small
- Whatever style you choose for the different parts of your document, make sure you **keep to the same style all the way through**

> **Tip for success**
> Before you finish your document, look at it using the
> **print preview** option, to see how it will look on the page
> when it is printed.

Look at the following piece of text:

> To: all football club members
> Welcome back to football practice after the summer break. Many of you will know that we have a new kit this season. Each player will need a red shirt and shorts for home games and a blue shirt and shorts for away games, white socks with red stripes, shin pads, a tracksuit for practice which doesn't need to be in the club colours, and studded boots, which can be of any type. Please remind your parents that there is a £25 fee to cover coaching and transport to matches. See you at training next week,
> From: Matt (team coach)

Now see how a better layout can make the same information much easier to read:

> To: all football club members
>
> Welcome back to football practice after the summer break.
>
> **New kit**
> Many of you will know that we have a new kit this season. Each player will need:
>
> - red shirt and shorts (for home games)
> - blue shirt and shorts (for away games)
> - white socks with red stripes
> - shin pads
> - track suit (any colour – for practice only)
> - studded boots (any type)
>
> **Fees**
> Please remind your parents that there is a £25 fee to cover coaching and transport to matches.
>
> See you at training next week!
>
> Matt (team coach)

Most pieces of text are divided into paragraphs. Each paragraph discusses one point or idea.

The beginning of a new paragraph can be shown in two ways. The first is to **indent** the first sentence, which means starting it further to the right than the rest of the paragraph, like this:

> Additional research has shown a strong link between smoking and heart disease. In a study of more than 1,000 healthy males, it ...

The second way is to **leave a whole line of space** between paragraphs. If you do this, you do not need to indent the first sentence. Separating paragraphs in this way can help to make the structure of your writing clear by showing where each new point or idea starts and ends.

Try not to leave just one or two lines of a paragraph at the **end of a page**, or to have the last line or two of a paragraph at the **top of a page**. It is better to have a larger space than usual at the bottom of a page than to have a small part of the paragraph on its own.

> **Key point to remember**
> Using plenty of white space will make your document easier to read.

You will need to decide how you want the **edges** of your text to look.

> You can set your computer like this, so that the ends of the sentences do not fall in a straight line. This can look natural, and the spacing between each word looks better.

Alternatively, you can set your computer so that the words form a neat, straight line at both of the edges. For some types of writing, this can look neater, but you may find that you get large gaps between some words in order to make them fit.

You will also have to decide whether or not you want your document to use **hyphens** if a long word comes at the end of a line. If the lines in your document are fairly long, and you are not using extremely long words, it is usually best not to use hyphens. However, if you have short lines, you may need to use them to avoid large spaces between words, especially if you are using straight lines at the edges of your text.

Hyphens must be used at a suitable breaking point in the word. Your computer will do this for you, but if you are writing by hand, you will need to decide where to put hyphens yourself. If you are not confident about this, it is best not to use them at all.

Tip for success
If you do use hyphens, check the line ends when you have finished to make sure there are no word breaks that could cause confusion, such as leg-end, or thin-king.

Fonts and typefaces

A font is the design of the letters that you use to write with. You will be able to choose fonts when you write documents on your computer. They range from standard fonts that you might use for an essay or a letter, to very unusual and dramatic ones that you might use for example for a party invitation:

> Dear Ms Hodges
>   I am writing to enquire about the possibility of work experience in your company ...

> Come to our spooky ghost party!

The **normal font size** for general texts such as essays is 11 or 12 points. You may want to use larger fonts for headings. Sometimes smaller sizes (usually 10 or 11 points) are used for long quotations.

Fonts like this one, which have very small lines at the ends of letters, are called **serif** fonts, while fonts like this one, which have nothing at the ends, are called **sans-serif** fonts. It is best to use a serif font such as 'Times New Roman' for long pieces of text.

You can also choose different ways of writing words, for example using *italics*, **bold (also called heavy) type**, <u>underlining</u>, or SMALL CAPITALS.

> **Tip for success**
> Avoid writing more than a few words in CAPITAL LETTERS because they are difficult to read.

Bullet points

If you want to separate out a list of points from the main part of your text, a simple way to do so is to use bullet points.

Bullet points are often used when the order of the list is not particularly important, e.g.:

> During this exciting week-long course, students will:
>
> - learn how to gather food in the wild
> - spend two nights in a nearby forest
> - learn how to build a shelter from earth and branches

It is not usual to use full stops at the end of bullet points, though if the points themselves are more than one sentence, you may feel it looks better.

You can decide whether or not to use capital letters at the beginning of each bullet point. In the example above, capital letters were not used because each bullet point formed a complete sentence following the introductory phrase 'students will …'.

> **Key point to remember**
> The most important thing to remember is that when you have decided whether or not to use capital letters and full stops, you should do the same for each point.

Bullet points can be introduced by any sort of symbol you think is appropriate:

> - Probably the most common type is a circle like this
> - A dash is also an acceptable way to introduce a point

▶ You may want to emphasize your point more with
a symbol like this
♪ Or even choose something completely different if it is
relevant to your text

It is important to make sure that the bullet points match up
grammatically with the words you use to introduce them. If you use
a phrase such as *'You will need the following:'*, it is simple to follow it by
a list of items.

However, you will often find bullet points introduced by phrases
such as:

To write a successful essay, you should:
Students will have the opportunity to:

In cases like this, make sure you read through the introductory phrase
and the bullet point together, to make certain they form a correct
sentence. Look at the following:

Students will have the opportunity to:

- canoe in the local river
- learn how to cook on a camp fire
- making lots of new friends

The third point does not make a grammatically correct sentence, and
should be 'make lots of new friends'.

Numbered points

Numbered points are used in a similar way to bullet points,
but are often used to show that the order of points is important:

The most common UK girls' names in 2008 were:

1 Olivia
2 Ruby
3 Emily
4 Grace
5 Jessica

You can use numbers or letters to order your points, and in some cases
you may even want to do both, in order to go into more detail about a
particular point:

Here is the agenda for Monday's meeting:

1 Minutes of the last meeting
2 Sales reports
   a Europe and the Middle East
   b Americas
   c East Asia
3 Next year's training budget
   a in-house training
   b external courses

Tip for success
When you want to indent a list of points, always use
a function such as the **Tab key** or the bullet points or
numbers from the **menu bar**. Do not try to indent using
the space bar because the spacing will not be even.

Headers, footers and page numbers

Headers and footers are pieces of text that appear at the top or bottom of the pages of your document but are separate from the rest of the writing on that page.

Typical items that might be put in them include:

- document title
- chapter or section titles
- author name
- copyright information
- date
- document reference

Using headers and footers can make your work look more professional. If you have the same header and footer throughout the whole document, you only need to put the text in once.

It is also possible to use different headers and footers for different sections of a document, for example for each new chapter or section. This can be useful for readers.

Page numbers can also be added automatically, and placed wherever you want them: at the top or bottom of the page; on the right, left or in the centre.

You can also choose the position, size, font etc. of your headers and footers. For example, you may want a chapter heading at the top of each page to be quite large, but a copyright note at the bottom to be quite small.

Using images

Using images can be a great way to liven up your text. Reasons for using images may include:

- helping to explain something – sometimes an image can be clearer than words
- decorating a document such as a party invitation
- emphasizing a brand, for example by using a company logo

A simple way to get images is to use **Clip Art** that is available in your word processing software.

Come to our party!

If you are using images in a more serious document, you should give them captions, and it will often be necessary to number them so that you can refer to them in the text.

Make sure that your images are an appropriate size for your document – it is easy to change the size of an image on your computer.

> **Key point to remember**
> If you use an image, make sure you are legally allowed to do so. Some images have **copyright**, which means you need the owner's permission to use them, and you may have to pay.

Tables and boxes

If you want to present information in rows and columns, it is a good idea to use a table:

Course timetable

	Group 1	Group 2
9.00 –9.30 9.30 – 11.00 11.00- 11.30	Introductions Singing workshop Break	Introductions African drumming Break

You can make tables on your computer, and say how many rows and how many columns you need. You can add more rows and columns later if you need to, and you can change their size.

You can also use tables to set out information neatly and then make the actual lines of the box disappear afterwards.

If you want to separate off one section of text from the rest, you can put a box or border around it.

> You can also put a shade or a coloured tint inside a box to make it stand out, like this.

> There are many different types of boxes and borders to choose from. This one, for example, has a shadow effect.

Charts and diagrams

Charts and diagrams can be a good way to present information, particularly numerical information, which can be much easier to understand when shown in this way.

Charts and diagrams are particularly good for information that needs to be analyzed, for example information showing **comparisons**, **patterns and trends**.

All charts and diagrams should be numbered and have a heading. Make sure there is plenty of space around them, and that there is always a reference to them in the text:

> As we can see from table 1 ...

> Fig. 3.8 illustrates the increase in ...

There are many different types of chart and diagram. Think about which one best suits the information you want to present.

Graphs

Graphs such as this one are a good way of showing trends in numbers:

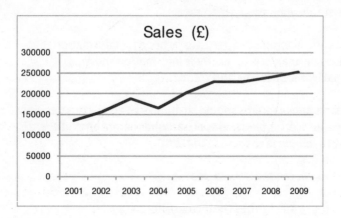

Pie charts

Pie charts are a very clear way of showing the relative size of groups of things:

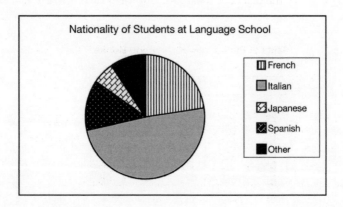

Venn Diagrams

Venn diagrams are used to show overlapping groups:

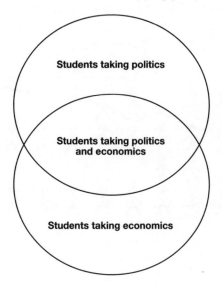

Bar charts

Bar charts also make it easy to compare numbers and amounts:

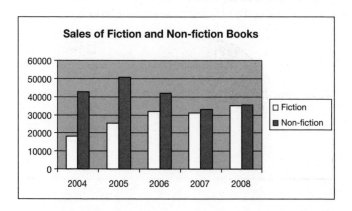

Pictograms

Pictograms are a simple way of showing numbers of people or things. As in this case, each image can represent more than one person or thing:

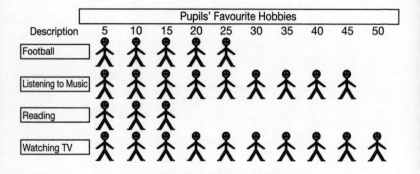

Structure

Logical ordering

If you have planned your writing well, you should have no problem writing it in a logical sequence.

Make sure that your **points lead on to each other** in such a way that your reader is guided through your argument. Remember that you should move from general points to more specific, detailed points.

Never include a point without any necessary **background or explanation**, or one that relies on reading something later in the text. Unless you actually refer to other sources, or unless you know that your reader possesses certain knowledge, the text should include all the information needed to understand it.

Make sure that all points of discussion about a particular area of your text come together – **do not change from one topic to another** and then back again.

An essay should **start with an introduction and end with a conclusion**, and in fact there are many types of writing where this is a useful principle, even if it is not done in such a formal way. For instance, if you are writing a formal letter, it can sometimes be helpful to include a short title after the greeting. This acts as an introduction.

Introductions

When you write an essay, you should start with an **introduction** and end with a **conclusion**.

Your introduction will give your readers the information they need to lead them into the main part of the essay.

The introduction should do the following things:

- **Introduce the topic**: briefly describe what the essay is about, providing any necessary explanation of the background and context of the topic.

- **Explain the purpose of the essay**: say what you will discuss, making sure that it fits exactly with the title of your essay. If you have been given a title, be careful to look for words like 'examine', 'contrast', 'describe' or 'analyze' and make sure that this is what your essay does.

- **Define your terms**: if there is any possibility of doubt, say exactly what you mean by words and phrases, both in the title and throughout the essay. For instance, if your essay is about childhood diabetes, you should say what age range you consider to be covered by the term 'childhood'.

In the same way, if there is any possible doubt about the meaning of the title, you should say very clearly what you understand by it, and how this understanding will form the basis of what follows.

- **Explain how your points are organized**: give a very brief summary of the structure of your essay.

An introduction can be more than one paragraph, if necessary. As a general rule, it should be around 10% of the total length of your essay. Remember though, it should not be a summary of the whole thing – if it is, the reader will not bother reading to the end!

Other points you may want to cover in your introduction include:

- **A statement of why your topic is particularly interesting or important**.

- **An explanation of how your work fits into a wider context**: for example how it relates to research being done by others, or how it is affected by current events or attitudes.

- **A discussion of areas of your topic where there is a lack of knowledge**.

Tip for success
While a short quotation can be an interesting way to start an essay, avoid long quotations or detailed examples in your introduction.

Conclusions

The introduction and conclusion form a frame for your essay. The conclusion brings together all the ideas and information you have discussed. It shows the reader that the essay is complete and that the aims of the essay have been achieved.

When you write your conclusion, always look back at the introduction. Make sure that your conclusion shows your essay has really done what you said it would do.

A conclusion does two main things:

- **Summarizes** the main points and ideas.

- **Reaches conclusions** by saying what the consequences of your evidence are.

By summarizing the main points, you provide your reader with a brief, clear statement of the most important points you have discussed. You should also include a brief reminder of the purpose of this discussion.

Everything that you summarize must be fully covered in the main part of the essay – you should not add any new information here.

As well as summarizing what you have discussed, you should summarize what you have said your evidence suggests.

> **Key point to remember**
> Never add any new points or ideas in your conclusion.

The type of conclusions you reach will depend on the question you were dealing with in the essay. You might:

- **Achieve a task set in the title**: For instance, if you were asked to contrast the characters of the Bennett sisters in the novel *Pride and Prejudice*, you would simply summarize the main differences you had found.

- **Give your opinion**: For instance, if you were asked to say whether or not nuclear power is a good form of fuel, you would express your opinion and explain briefly how the evidence you have presented supports it.

- **Show what you have learned from looking at evidence**: For instance, if you are asked to analyze the results of a research project on the effects of diet on rates of heart disease, you would summarize the main facts you have discovered from the survey.

- **Make recommendations**: For instance, if you are writing a report on the best way to encourage recycling, you would suggest actions that could be taken.

Often you will find that issues you discuss in essays are complicated and you cannot find a simple answer or give a definite opinion. This is fine – you should simply explain why this is the case by summarizing the main points.

Headings

Headings are often used in long documents. They can **make the presentation more effective and attractive** by breaking up long pieces of text.

Headings are **useful for your readers**. They explain the structure of your document and enable the reader to find a particular topic easily.

It is best to **start with headings and then write your text**. If you do it like this, your essay will be better organised than if you simply write it and try to add headings afterwards.

You can use **different levels of heading**. The lower levels are called subheadings. In a long document, main headings mark the major sections and subheadings then divide these sections.

Try not to use too many headings. As a general rule, 2 or 3 headings per A4 page would be enough. Sometimes you cannot avoid having a very short section under a heading – there may simply be very little to say about that particular point. That is fine, but try not to break up the text too much.

> **Key point to remember**
> Start with your headings, then write your text.

If you are using subheadings, it is even more important to plan your heading structure before you write, so that you have a consistent framework for the whole document. Sections of similar importance should have the same level of heading.

It is usually a good idea to number headings, especially if you want to make a table of contents. It is up to you how you number them, but a common way would be to use a system of numbers and points:

> 1. **Main heading**
>> 1.1 **subheading**
>>> 1.1.1 **sub-subheading**

Once you have decided on a structure, you need to choose a style for your headings. Make sure the style is the same throughout the whole document.

You will need to think about the following:

- The **font type and font size** for each level of heading
- Are your headings **numbered**, and if so how?
- Are your headings **bold**, *italic*, <u>underlined</u>, etc.?
- Do they start with a **capital letter**?
- Do they include **punctuation**?
- How much **space** is there before and after the surrounding text?

Tip for success
Computer programs like Word® have headings that you can use. You can change the style if you want, then you can simply choose the heading type when you need it.

Try to make your headings as specific as possible. Instead of the heading 'Background', for example, try to express what sort of background information you are giving in this section. Make sure that your headings do accurately describe the information they include.

Try to think about your headings from the point of view of the reader and the purpose of your document.

For instance, if you are writing an explanation of how to do something, headings with verbs can be effective, e.g.:

- **Planning your vegetable garden**
- **Deciding what to grow**
- **Preparing your soil**

Sometimes it is appropriate to use questions as headings, e.g.

- **What is a carbon footprint?**
- **How can I reduce my carbon footprint?**

The reader should be able to read the text separately from the headings. Do not use pronouns in the first sentence that refer back to the heading. For example, if your heading is 'Principles of the carbon cycle', do not begin the next sentence 'This is the process …'.

> **Tip for success**
> Before you print your document, check that there are no headings on their own at the bottom of pages.

Paragraphs

In a long piece of writing, such as an essay or a report, each paragraph should contain one separate point or idea.

The **first sentence** of each paragraph should usually introduce what the paragraph is about:

* *Smith's views have, however, been challenged by several experts.*
  (continue by explaining what the experts say)

* *This new law gave greater protection to workers.*
  (continue by describing why it did so)

Here are some useful phrases to link your paragraphs:

* ***As a result of*** *this research, scientists have decided …*
* ***Meanwhile****, my brothers had been busy …*
* ***Despite*** *these problems, they carried on trying to …*
* ***Nevertheless****, she was forced to …*
* ***However****, we did not allow ourselves to …*
* ***On the other hand****, many people say that …*
* ***In addition to*** *this work on dolphins, he …*

> **Tip for success**
> Try not to make your paragraphs too long. If they are very long, you will probably find that they can be divided into separate points.

Style

What is good style?

When people write with good style, their writing is clear, interesting, elegant and appropriate for their audience.

The best style to use will vary according to the type of document you are writing: the kind of original, descriptive writing you would use for a piece of creative writing would not be appropriate for a factual report.

There are many aspects to writing with good style, which are discussed in this section.

However, one simple rule applies to all your work:

Avoid repeating words.

Whatever you are writing, it will sound dull and clumsy if you use the same words over and over again. If you read your work aloud, you will notice when you have done this.

Too much repetition	Better ...
Team A discovered ..., Team B discovered ..., Team C discovered ...	Team A discovered ..., Team B found ..., Team C's results showed ...

Sometimes the easiest way to avoid repetition is simply to replace one of the words with a pronoun:

Too much repetition	Better ...
We intend to invite all our friends and ask each friend to bring some food.	We intend to invite all our friends and ask each of them to bring some food.

Writing in sentences

Sentences are the building blocks of our texts. The length of your sentences will depend on who you are writing for, but very long sentences can be confusing, while very short sentences can sound childish. If your sentence is longer than about 15-20 words, see if you can divide it.

The basic rule is that each sentence should have a **verb and a subject**:

> *The vase smashed on the floor.* (vase = subject, smashed = verb)
> *My Mum plays the violin.* (My Mum = subject, plays = verb)

It is best to **avoid starting a sentence with a conjunction** such as 'and', 'but' or 'or', especially in formal writing.

Some people think it is bad style to end a sentence with a preposition such as 'on', 'up' or 'in'. However, avoiding this can sometimes lead to a rather formal style. Compare the following:

> *We were shocked to see the conditions they live in.*
> *We were shocked to see the conditions in which they live.*

As always, think about the purpose of your document and the reader to help you choose the appropriate style and tone.

Tip for success
Try reading your work aloud. If your sentences work well, it will be easy to read. See where you make natural pauses, and think about whether you need to add commas.

Do not try to run lots of sentence parts together using commas. This is a common mistake, and can be confusing.

Look at the following:

> *First we went to the Tower of London, which was fantastic, our tour guide was excellent, and we saw the crown jewels, later we had our picnic on a lawn near the ravens.*

This sentence would be much better using dashes and splitting it into separate sentences, like this:

> *First we went to the Tower of London, which was fantastic – our tour guide was excellent. We saw the crown jewels, and later we had our picnic on a lawn near the ravens.*

However, make sure you use commas where they are needed, as they can help the reader understand your sentences better.

For instance, they are needed if a subordinate clause (less important part of a sentence) comes before the main clause, e.g.:

> *If the train is late, call me from the station.*

They are also needed for adding small pieces of information about someone or something in your sentence, e.g.:

> *My sister, who is a vet, has three children.*

Tip for success
Take care with punctuation. There is a detailed explanation of how to use commas and other punctuation marks in the punctuation section of this book.

Using plain English

It is important to write in plain English. Plain English is easier to write, and certainly easier to understand. This does not mean that you need to write in baby-talk, but try to follow these rules:

- **Avoid unnecessary jargon**. Don't talk about 'interfacing' with someone when you mean 'communicating' with them, or simply 'talking' to them. Don't say 'design solution' – it's just a design.

Of course, there are times when technical and specialist terms *are* appropriate. If you are writing a science essay, you must use the correct terminology. As always, think of your reader.

- **Avoid unnecessary formality**. Ask yourself if there is a simpler word or phrase that would be appropriate for your reader.

very formal	simpler ...
prior to	before
in excess of	more than
in the vicinity of	near

- **Try to use active verbs instead of nouns**. This will make your sentences sound less complex and formal.

noun form	active verb form
give encouragement to	encourage
ensure the completion of	complete
make provision for	provide

Active or passive verbs?

It is usually better to use active verbs in your writing because the structure is simpler. Passives can sound rather formal. Compare these two sentences, for example:

> *New recycling methods have been introduced by the council.* (passive)
> *The council has introduced new recycling methods.* (active)

However, the passive can be useful in certain cases. For instance, you may use the passive if you do not want to appear to be blaming someone or criticizing someone:

> *You have not paid the money.* (active and accusing)
> *The money has not been paid.* (passive and more neutral)

You may also want to use the passive if you do not want your reader to blame you:

> *I'm sorry to report that I have lost your documents.* (active and admitting fault)
> *I'm sorry to report that your documents have been lost.* (passive and implying that it may have been someone else's fault)

The passive is also used when you do not know who carried out an action or it is irrelevant who carried out the action. This will often happen in academic writing in which the slightly more formal style is appropriate:

> *The results were analyzed in the laboratory.*
> *The buildings were knocked down in 1989.*

Avoiding clichés

A cliché is a word or phrase that has been used too often. If you use clichés, your writing will be boring. When readers see them, they may lose interest and miss your main message. They may think that if your writing is not original, your ideas cannot be original either.

You may find that clichés slip into the first draft of your writing – after all, it is because they are so well-known and come so easily to mind that they have become clichés. Read through your document and try to identify any phrases that seem to fit into this category. If English is not your first language, it may be difficult to do this. In this case, it may be a good idea to ask a native English speaker for advice.

Then ask yourself: what does this phrase actually mean? It may not really have much meaning at all, in which case you can probably delete it. Examples of this sort of cliché are:

> *at the end of the day*
> *at this moment in time*
> *with all due respect*

Or it may be that the phrase has been used so much that it has lost all its power, and may well annoy your reader. Examples of this sort of cliché are:

> *moving the goalposts*
> *reinvent the wheel*
> *the best thing since sliced bread*

Sometimes a simple **combination of adjective and noun** can be so overused that it becomes a cliché, e.g.:

> *roaring fire*
> *vice-like grip*
> *long-lost friend*

This does not mean that such combinations should never be used, but try not to use too many obvious combinations, and choose something more original if you can.

One area of language where it is very easy to fall into the trap of using a cliché is the **simile**.

Look at the following similes:

> *as cold as ice*
> *as fresh as a daisy*

They are so overused that they are not powerful descriptions. Now look at the following similes, all found in real writing:

> *as cold as a Siberian winter*
> *as cold as a statue of stone*
> *as fresh as green shoots in the morning*
> *as fresh as a big green shiny cucumber*

Of course, imaginative similes like these are not suitable for all types of writing. In formal writing, it is probably best to avoid similes altogether. In more creative writing, you should aim to be descriptive and original, but your similes should fit into the overall style of the text.

Avoiding redundancy (unnecessary words)

It is very easy to use more words than you need, but too many words will make your writing less effective and may annoy your readers.

Compare the following:

> *Jack and I are of the same opinion on this matter.*
> *Jack and I agree.*

> *Due to the fact that the train was delayed, we were late for the concert.*
> *We were late for the concert because the train was delayed.*

Avoid 'empty' words and phrases that do not add meaning to your sentences, e.g. *in terms of*, *the fact of the matter*.

Avoid saying the same things twice. This is known as **tautology**. Consider the following:

9 a.m. in the morning	a.m. means 'in the morning' – choose one or the other
re-examine again	just say 're-examine' – the 'again' is expressed in the prefix 're-'
my personal opinion	if it's your opinion, it's personal – you don't need to say so
mutual cooperation	you can't cooperate on your own, so it must be mutual

Avoid adding illogical extra words. Consider the following:

in actual fact	if it is a fact, it must be 'actual' – just say 'in fact'
very unique	something unique is the *only* one of its kind – there are no degrees of uniqueness
added bonus	a bonus is something that you get in addition to something else – there is no need to also say 'added'

Avoiding ambiguity

Ambiguity is when something could possibly be understood in more than one way. It is an easy trap to fall into because *you* know what you mean when you write, but try to put yourself in the reader's place and make sure there is no room for doubt.

Be careful with **words that have more than one meaning**. Often the context will be enough to make it clear which meaning is intended. If you write that you are going to the bank, nobody is likely to think you are going to a river bank. However, consider the following:

> *My teacher is really funny.*
> (Is the teacher humorous or strange?)

> *The food was very hot.*
> (Was it a high temperature, or was it spicy?)

Make it clear whether you are using words and phrases in a **literal or figurative** sense:

> *He was in debt to his friend.*
> (Did he owe his friend money or simply feel grateful?)

> *There was a chasm between us.*
> (Was there a hole in the ground, or a big difference of opinion?)

Use pronouns carefully to make sure it is clear who or what they refer to:

> *Rosie had an argument with Sarah, and she started crying.*
> (Who cried, Rosie or Sarah?)

> *I couldn't attach the bird boxes to the posts in the garden because they weren't strong enough.*
> (Was it the posts or the bird boxes that weren't strong?)

Check the structure of your sentence to make sure it is clear how the parts relate to each other. Compare the following:

> *We talked about bullying at work.*
> (Ambiguous – were we at work or not?)

> *We talked about the issue of workplace bullying.*
> *At work, we talked about bullying.*

> *They told us about the murder at 11 o'clock.*
> (Ambiguous – did the murder happen at 11 o'clock?)

> *At 11 o'clock, they told us about the murder.*
> *They told us about the murder that occurred at 11 o'clock.*

Make sure it is clear what your adjectives are describing:

> *a large woman's handbag*
> (Is it the woman or the handbag that is large?)

> *a formal English test*
> (Is the test formal, or is it a test of formal English?)

Be clear about the purpose of your writing. Imagine you are a member of staff receiving a memo from your boss that includes the following:

> *It would be a good idea for all staff to take at least 30 minutes break for lunch.*

It would not be clear whether your boss is saying that you *must* take a 30 minute break or simply that it would be a nice thing if possible.

Register

The word register refers to aspects of language such as how formal or informal it is. Compare the following:

> *They furnished us with the requisite implements.* (very formal)
> *They gave us the necessary tools.* (neutral)
> *They let us have the gear we needed.* (informal)

You should match the register of your language to the type of writing you are doing. Using the wrong register can make your writing sound odd and can even cause offence.

Register can often be shown by the choice of words or phrases:

formal	*neutral*	*informal*
wax lyrical	*speak enthusiastically*	*go on about*
of one's own volition	*voluntarily*	*off your own bat*
in the ascendancy	*becoming successful*	*on the up*

Dictionaries mark words which are formal or informal, so you can check if you are not sure. Many idioms and phrasal verbs are either informal or slightly informal, so take care to use them appropriately.

Informal language is fine for personal letters, emails, texts, etc., but for most forms of writing, a neutral or slightly formal style is more appropriate. Remember, though, that formal does not mean pompous. Do not use very formal language to try to impress – it is more important to put your ideas over clearly.

> **Tip for success**
> Do not use different registers within the same piece of writing.

Sometimes words and phrases with a particular register are needed for specific types of writing. For instance, **legal documents** often contain extremely formal language, such as '*hereunder*' or Latin words such as '*ex gratia*', which would be out of place in most other types of writing.

Similarly, some types of writing need to use very specific **technical terms**. For example, a document for medical professionals might use a word such as '*suprarenal*' instead of saying '*above the kidneys*' because this word will be understood by its readers. In scientific documents, the use of technical terms can be necessary to avoid any ambiguity.

At the other end of the scale, **literary or poetic language** such as '*lovelorn*', '*flaxen*' or '*the gloaming*' may be appropriate in some types of creative writing.

Your choice of **grammar** and the way you **structure** your sentences can also affect register. Compare the following:

> *The man to whom I gave my ticket.*
> *The man I gave my ticket to.*

In the first sentence, the use of 'whom' gives a formal feel to the sentence. In the second sentence, the preposition is used at the end. In the past this was considered incorrect, but it is now widely accepted, and would be appropriate for any but the most formal of documents.

It is not usually considered appropriate to use contractions (e.g. don't, he'd, wouldn't) in formal writing because they make the text sound informal.

Tone

The tone of your writing expresses your **attitude** towards the reader, and it is important that you are careful about this.

For instance, if you are writing to complain about a product or service, you need to come across as being assertive and clear about your facts. You must decide for yourself whether you want to be rude or threatening too – but if you are, make sure it is on purpose and not because you have chosen your words badly!

It can be useful to **imagine that you are talking to your reader**. What sort of tone do you want to take? For example, you might be:

chatty	authoritative	sincere	sympathetic
grateful	serious	assertive	humorous
persuasive	practical	unfriendly	offended
efficient	angry		

If you **think about what you want to achieve** with your writing, it will help you decide what tone to take. For example, if you are writing a letter to accept a job, you will probably want your tone to be friendly yet professional and show that you are pleased to have been chosen.

It is important to use language that is the **right level of difficulty** for your reader. If you use difficult words, you may sound as if you are showing off, but if you use very simple language, your reader might feel you are being patronizing.

An important issue that influences tone is the **relationship of the writer to the reader**. For instance, a suggestion for changes to working practices might have a very different tone coming from a junior employee than if it comes from a senior manager.

You should always take into account **how well you know the person** who will read your document. If you do not know them at all, you must be aware that they may be offended by a tone that is too familiar, for instance by being too informal, or by expressing views that they may not share. Humour can also be difficult – if your readers do not know you, they may be unsure whether you are joking or not.

Compare the following letters:

Dear Emma
*   Tom told me you broke your leg skiing – after I'd stopped laughing, it occurred to me that you must be a bit fed up, so I'm sending you these chocolates to cheer you up. See you when (if???) you can walk again,*
Lizzie, x

Dear Emma
*   I'm so sorry to hear about your skiing accident. Your mother told me you are likely to be in plaster for some weeks, and I know how hard that will be for you. Do take good care of yourself, and I hope to hear some better news of you soon,*
with love from
Aunty Bea

In the first letter, the tone is chatty and humorous, and while it might make Emma smile, if her injury is serious she might be offended that her friend is joking about it. However, if Lizzie is a very close friend, she will probably have judged the tone of the note appropriately. The second letter is much more sincere and serious and the tone shows that the writer is really concerned about Emma.

If you are angry about something, it can be very easy to let it show, sometimes without intending to. For example, look at this email:

> *Thanks for your offer of database training, but I really don't feel it's necessary, and I wouldn't want to distract you from your work, which is already behind schedule.*

The tone of the email makes it clear that the writer was offended by the offer of help and takes revenge by implying that the person offering help cannot manage their own work.

This may be what the writer intends, but if they would prefer to keep a good relationship with their colleague, something like the following would be better:

> *Thanks for the offer of database training, but I think I've managed to get to grips with it now, and I wouldn't want to take up your time unnecessarily as I know you are very busy.*

Key point to remember
The tone you choose is up to you, but if your writing does express your attitudes, make sure this is what you intended.

Emphasis

We use emphasis to draw a reader's attention to the points which are most important. There are several ways of doing this:

- **Order within the document**. It is usual to start with the most important points.

- **Order within a sentence or paragraph**. The first part of the sentence will be seen as the most important. Compare the following:

    A thorough safety assessment is needed urgently, following a number of accidents on the site.
    Following a number of accidents on the site, a thorough safety assessment is needed urgently.

In the first example, the fact that the safety assessment is needed is emphasized by coming first in the sentence. In the second example, the fact that there have been some accidents comes across as the more important point.

- **A summary of main points**. This can be done in the conclusion of a document, or even as a list. For example, a detailed report might start with a section on 'key findings' or 'key recommendations' – simply a list of the main points the author wishes to make.

- **Amount of text**. The more important a point, the more space you are likely to use discussing it. If you add too much detail about minor points, readers may be confused about what is most important.

- **Blank space around a key phrase or sentence**. This is a rather dramatic way of emphasizing one key point:

    The evidence led to one clear conclusion:
    He did not kill his wife.

- **Typeface**. It is very simple to highlight words and phrases by using different forms of typefaces such as **bold**, *italics* or <u>underlining</u>. Italics are probably the most commonly used:

  > Please note that pupils should not bring mobile phones to school *at any time*.
  > Make sure you take *all* your belongings with you.

Fonts can also be made larger or smaller for emphasis, or a different colour may be used to make certain parts of a document stand out.

- **Repetition**. Repetition can be used in several ways to emphasize points. You could make a point and then repeat it immediately, using phrases such as:

  > *In other words ...*
  > *Put more simply ...*

This is a useful way to stress the point you are making and also to explain it in a different way so that you can be certain that your readers will understand it.

If you are writing a long document, you may want to repeat certain points throughout it, using phrases such as:

  > *This demonstrates yet again ...*
  > *Again we see ...*

Repetition can also be a useful stylistic advice, in writing as well as in speech. You might repeat a word, a phrase or part of a phrase:

  > *They said local businesses would close – not true. They claimed jobs would be lost – not true. They claimed traffic would increase – not true.*

- **Headings**. Headings can be used to reinforce the main point that will be made in the parts they refer to.

- **Sudden change of style**. If readers are surprised by a sudden change of style, they may pay more attention to what is being said. One example would be to use a very short, snappy sentence after one or more longer, more flowing sentences:

  > *Architects and engineers had assured officials and residents that the techniques used in constructing the bridge would ensure that it remained solid during an earthquake. It did not.*

- **Emphatic words and phrases**. These can highlight the most important points, e.g.:

  > *Our priority now is ...*
  > *The crucial advantage that this scheme offers is ...*

In a similar way, sentence adverbs such as 'crucially' or 'above all' signal the importance of what follows, as do adjectives such as 'urgent', 'vital' or 'essential'.

- **Punctuation**. The most obvious way to emphasize a sentence is to end it with an exclamation mark:

  > *We won over a thousand pounds!*

Be careful with exclamation marks, though. It is fine to use them in informal letters, emails, etc, but do not use them too often. It is not usually appropriate to use them in more formal writing.

Structuring a sentence with a dash or a colon can also emphasize part of it. See, for example, how the second of these two sentences has more emphasis:

  > *Critics described his performance as terrible.*
  > *Critics had one word for his performance: terrible.*

Avoiding offence

The simple rule for avoiding offence is this:

Treat everyone equally in your writing, regardless of age, sex, race, sexual orientation or physical difference.

Always make sure that you are **aware of current customs and values**. For instance, do not assume that couples, even married couples, consist of a man and a woman: same-sex civil partnerships are legal and common in the UK.

Check that the terms you use for sensitive issues such as race and disability are the **modern**, **accepted terms**, and not old-fashioned terms that might be considered offensive.

Race and religion

It goes without saying that offensive racial or religious insults or stereotypes should never be used.

However, it can sometimes be easy to display discrimination without meaning to, simply because of our cultural background. Make sure you follow these general rules:

- **Only mention race or religion if it is relevant to your writing**. If you mention someone's race or religion, ask yourself if you would have mentioned it if it was the same as yours.

- **Make sure you use accepted modern terms**, not old-fashioned ones which many now consider offensive. For instance, a term such as *Red Indian* belongs only in cowboy movies – for all other writing, use *American Indian*. Similarly, the term *African-American* is the preferred description for black Americans of African origin, not *Negro*.

- **Be aware of different cultures**. For instance, don't assume that everyone celebrates Christmas, or that July and August are always the hottest months of the year.

The accepted current term for people whose parent or ancestors are from different races is *mixed-race*. If you are in doubt about any terms connected with race or religion, check a good dictionary.

Sexism

Here are some rules for avoiding sexism in your writing:

- **Use job titles that refer to both men and women**. For example, use *police officer* rather than *policeman*; *chair* or *chairperson* instead of *chairman*.

- **Avoid the suffix -ess on jobs**. Words like *authoress* and *poetess* are very old-fashioned and patronizing, and should not be used. It is best to avoid the *-ess* suffix for jobs altogether: while the word *actress* is still used, many women in the profession prefer *actor*.

- **Do not mention a person's sex if it is not relevant**. It is usually best to avoid terms such as *male nurse* or *lady solicitor*.

- **Do not make assumptions about the sex of people in a particular profession**. Do not write things like '*businessmen and their wives*'.

- **Avoid stereotypes of roles and characteristics**. It's not necessarily Mum who cooks the dinner and Dad who fixes the car.

- **Avoid using masculine pronouns**. Sentences such as '*Each traveller must present his documents*' sound old-fashioned and sexist. Most people now consider it acceptable to use the pronoun *their* in such cases.

- **If you write to someone whose sex you do not know, do not begin your letter** *Dear Sir/s*. You could use *Dear Sir/Madam* in very formal situations, or choose another form of address altogether, e.g. *Dear Friends/Dear Supporters*.

Disability

When writing about illness and disability, there are several points to bear in mind:

- **Be sure to use current, accepted terms**. Use *bipolar disorder* rather than *manic depression*, for example.

- **Do not describe someone only by their illness**. Remember that they are a person first of all, so say *someone with epilepsy* rather than *an epileptic*.

- **Try not to portray someone with a disability as a victim**. Avoid words like *victim, afflicted with, suffering from*. Say *a wheelchair user* rather than *wheelchair-bound*.

- **Do not refer to people without a disability as** *normal*. Say *nondisabled* or *able-bodied* instead.

Increasing your vocabulary

The best way to increase your vocabulary is to **read a lot**. As you read, notice the words that are being used.

If you find a word you do not know, you will sometimes be able to get a good idea of its meaning from the other words around it. If not, **look it up in a dictionary**. It is not always a good idea to look up every new word as you find it, because it can be distracting, but you could **underline or highlight** some of the words and look them up at the end.

It can be useful to **keep a vocabulary notebook**, to record new words you have learned. You can arrange the words in whatever way is best for you: by alphabetical order or by subject.

Try to develop an interest in words, and ask yourself questions about them. For instance, you can widen your vocabulary by learning **words in groups**. If you know that *canine* means 'referring to dogs', see if you know the word meaning 'relating to cats' (*feline*) or 'relating to cows' (*bovine*). Similarly, if you know that *carnivorous* means 'meat-eating', do you know the word for 'plant-eating' (*herbivorous*) or for creatures that eat anything (*omnivorous*)?

Notice the context that words are in. You can often make your writing more elegant by choosing which words go together, such as the interesting verbs with the common nouns in these examples:

> **abandon** *an attempt*
> **draw** *to a close*
> **adopt** *a method*

Word games such as **crossword puzzles** can help to develop an interest in words and can introduce words you did not know before.

Using a thesaurus

Look at very common words in your writing and see if there are any more interesting or specific words you could use instead. You could use a thesaurus for this. A thesaurus is a reference book which shows lists of words with similar meanings. Some word processing systems have a thesaurus built into them, so that you can click on a word for suggestions of different words with similar meanings:

if you have written ...	consider whether you could use ...
difficult	ambitious, demanding, gruelling, knotty, laborious
eat	bolt, consume, gulp, sample, wolf down
boring	bland, characterless, dreary, insipid, soul-destroying

Using a dictionary

A good dictionary will help a lot with your writing. Try to use a dictionary that is **suitable for you**. For instance, if you are at school, a special **schools dictionary** should have all the words you need for all your subjects, but not be too big to carry around. If English is not your first language, try to use a **learner's** dictionary, which will have simple definitions, lots of example sentences, and all the grammar information you need.

Digital dictionaries

There are many types of digital dictionary available now. Tiny **handheld** ones are easy to carry around, and may be useful for spelling or quick look-ups, but the screens may be too small to show lots of useful information.

A lot of book dictionaries come with either a **CD-ROM** or with a code that gives you access to an **Internet dictionary**. You can use these easily while you are working on the computer. Some of them will even look up words for you if you put the cursor over the word you want.

CD-ROM and Internet dictionaries can be extremely useful because they can do things that are impossible in paper books. For instance, if you don't know how to spell a word, you can just type in the letters you are sure of, and all the words containing those letters will be found. Many of these dictionaries have extra information such as synonyms and antonyms, the ability to search for vocabulary in topics, and extra examples. You can also hear spoken pronunciations, rather than trying to work them out from symbols.

Information in dictionaries

Dictionaries are not just for meanings and spelling, although of course these are very important uses. Dictionaries can give you information on:

- **Irregular inflections**. If words do not have regular patterns, this will be shown. For instance, you can see that the plural of *genus* is *genera* or that the past participle of *sink* is *sunk*.

- **Variant spellings**. You can see which words have more than one spelling, eg. *caftan* and *kaftan*.

- **Regional information**. You can see when words and spelling are used in a particular variety of English, e.g. *courgette* is used in British English, but Americans say *zucchini* for the same vegetable.

- **Example sentences**. Many dictionaries give example sentences, showing how to use a word in context.

- **Etymology**. Large dictionaries often give information about the origins of words and phrases.

- **Register**. A dictionary will tell you if a word is formal, informal, etc.

- **Pronunciation**. This is usually shown using a set of symbols.

Terms used in writing English

The following are important terms that refer to different styles of writing and types of words and phrases. You need to know them for studying literature, and also to be aware of them for using in your own writing.

Antonyms

An antonym is a word with an opposite meaning. *Legal* and *illegal* are antonyms, as are *mature* and *immature*.

Alliteration

Alliteration is the use of the same letter or sound (especially consonants) at the beginning of two or more words that are close together in a sentence:

> *droplets of dew at dawn*

Assonance

Assonance is the repetition of vowel sounds in two or more words that are close together in a sentence:

> *I laughed, but my heart was torn apart.*

Euphemism

A euphemism is a word or phrase that is used to avoid talking directly about something that is embarrassing, upsetting or offensive.

Euphemisms can be used in personal writing to show tact to your reader. For instance, in a letter of sympathy, some people prefer to use the euphemism *passed away* rather than *died*. Euphemisms can be used to avoid embarrassment to readers who are uncomfortable with words connected with sex or bodily functions.

Euphemisms are sometimes used in quite formal writing in order deliberately to disguise an unpleasant truth. For instance, a company press release might talk about *restructuring* or *rationalizing* rather than *sacking staff*. In war, the terms *collateral damage* or *friendly fire* sound much less terrible than the reality of what they describe.

There is no place for euphemism in scientific or technical writing.

Figurative language

Figurative language is where an extra, more imaginative meaning comes from a literal meaning. For instance, the literal meaning of the word *chasm* is 'a large hole in the ground', whereas the figurative meaning refers to a fundamental difference of opinion between people.

Idioms

Idioms are phrases such as *give someone a hand* and *be over the moon*, where the meaning is not the same as the literal meaning of all the words in the phrase.

Metaphor

Metaphor is the use of a particular word or phrase – usually a concrete noun - to describe the characteristics of something else. For instance we might say *She has a heart of ice*, meaning that she shows no sympathy or emotion.

Proverbs

Proverbs are short sentences that many people know, often expressing advice, or something that many people believe to be true. Examples of proverbs are *Marry in haste, repent at leisure* and *Spare the rod and spoil the child*.

Similes

Similes are phrases such *as as dull as ditchwater* or *sing like an angel*, which compare one thing to another. The difference between a simile and a metaphor is that similes say that something is *like* something else, whereas a metaphor says something *is* something else.

Synonyms

Synonyms are words with the same or similar meanings. For instance, *clever* is a synonym of *intelligent*. However, it is important to note that words with similar meanings often have subtle differences in register or tone. *Purchase* is more formal than *buy*, for instance, while *slim* is a much more positive description than *skinny*.

Special
information

Speech

There are two ways of writing about what someone said:

- In **direct speech**, we repeat the actual words used:

    'There is nothing we can do about it,' Mona said.

- In **reported speech** (also called **indirect speech**), we make the words part of our own sentence, usually using a verb such as 'say', 'announce' or 'explain':

    Mona said that there was nothing we could do about it.

Direct speech

Direct speech is common in novels and other writing where the actual words of speakers are quoted. The reporting verb (e.g. *say*, *announce*, *explain*) may come before the words that were spoken, or after them, or at a natural pause inside the reported sentence:

> ***Mona said**, 'There is nothing we can do about it.'*
> *'There is nothing we can do about it,' **Mona said**.*
> *'It's no good,' **Mona said**, 'We'll just have to ask for help.'*

The words spoken must be written inside inverted commas. They can be single (' ') or double (" "). In American English, double quotation marks are usually used.

The words spoken always begin with a capital letter as long as the sentence is not divided by a reporting verb. The comma comes inside the inverted commas unless the sentence is divided by a reporting verb:

> *'**G**ive her a chance,' Jamie begged.*
> *'There is', Mona said, 'nothing we can do about it.'*

If the words spoken are a question or an exclamation, there is no comma but a question mark or an exclamation mark, which comes inside the inverted commas:

> '*Why did you do it?*' *she asked.*
> '*Oh, mind your own business!*' *he snapped.*

The subject and reporting verb can be used either way round:

> '*There is nothing we can do about it,*' **Mona said**.
> '*There is nothing we can do about it,*' **said Mona**.

Tip for success
If you are writing a long stretch of direct speech between two characters, it is not always necessary to use reporting verbs each time. As long as it is clear which character is speaking, you can just start a new line within new inverted commas each time a different character speaks.

Reported speech

When you use reported speech, the words put into the reported clause do not exactly match the words actually spoken. For example, you will need to change pronouns, words like *here* and *there*, or the tense of the sentence:

> *I believe* **you**.
> *She said that she believed* **us**.
> *I've been* **here** *before.*
> *He said that he had been* **there** *before.*
> ***I've done*** *the housework.*
> *He said* **he had done** *the housework.*

Reported speech always has two clauses: the **reported clause** which contains the words that were spoken, usually in a slightly different form, and the **main clause** which contains the reporting verb.

The main clause usually comes first:

>*Katie told me* that Marie is going to resign.
>*Sara asked* whether Hardeep was feeling better.

If the main reported clause is a statement, the main clause is linked to the reported clause by *that*:

>*Monique said **that** her favourite actor was Ben Whishaw.*
>*John replied **that** he preferred Scarlett Johansson.*

The linking word *that* can be left out after most reporting verbs except those that mean 'answer':

>*She told me **(that)** she was going to leave.*
>*I replied **that** I was very sorry to hear that.*

If the main reported clause is a question, the main verb will be a question word such as *ask, inquire, wonder, query*. The link between the main clause will be *if* or *whether*:

>*She asked me **if** I was comfortable.*
>*He inquired **whether** the changes had been made.*

Reported clauses can also be used to express what someone is thinking as well as what is actually spoken:

>*Hussain **wondered** whether **the concert would be sold out**.*
>*Charlotte **thought** that **she had better go and see her family**.*

> **Key point to remember**
> Speech in a reported clause is not separated from the reporting verb by a comma, is not enclosed in inverted commas, and does not begin with a capital letter unless it is a proper noun. Reported questions are not followed by question marks.

Questions

There are three main ways of making questions in English:

- With a **question word**, such as *who*, *why*, *how*:

  Who *won the race?*
  Which *team was it?*

- With an **auxiliary verb** (*do*, *have* or *be*):

  Do *your children like sport?*
  Have *you seen her latest movie?*

- With a modal verb, such as *can* or *may*:

  Can *Mahmoud come too?*
  May *I see the letter?*

Occasionally, we express sentences by our tone of voice, but this would only be appropriate for written English if you are writing direct speech:

  '**She's left her job?** *I thought she was happy there.*'

Negative forms of questions almost always use contractions:

  Doesn't *he like talking about his childhood?*
  Can't *Peter have one too?*

If the full *not* form is used, it comes immediately after the subject. The full form is very formal:

  Does *he* **not** *like talking about his childhood?*
  Can *Peter* **not** *have one too?*

Questions should always have a question mark at the end, even if they are headings. The only time that a question does not have a question mark is if it is written in reported speech:

> *Do you like cats?*
> *He asked me if I liked cats.*

Sentence tags

Sentence tags look like short questions and are used the end of sentences. They are sometimes called **question tags**, but many sentences ending with a tag are not real questions.

They are usually used to check that the listener or reader agrees with what the speaker or writer has said. Sentence tags are used very commonly in speech and in informal writing such as a chatty email, but rarely in formal written English.

If you need to write them, either in a piece of informal writing, or if you are quoting direct speech, remember that they have a comma before them, and a question mark at the end:

> *You've seen the programme, haven't you?*
> *Well, we can't jump over it, can we?*
> *You aren't listening, are you?*

Quotations

There are many reasons to use quotations in your writing:

- To show how the **ideas and research of others** have contributed to your own work.

- To **add evidence** to your arguments, particularly from respected sources.

- To **show different opinions**, sometimes ones which disagree with yours.

- To **add interest or humour** to your writing. If someone has said something particularly clever or witty about your subject, it can liven up your text to quote it.

- In writing about literary works, to give **samples of text for analysis**.

However, do not be tempted to include too many quotations. You are the author, and your ideas and analysis are the most important part of your writing. Your writing should not rely too heavily on quotations – they should be there to support your work but not to form the main part of it.

Make sure that any quotations you do add are there for a good reason – do not put them in simply to make your document longer. Too many quotations can interrupt the flow of your writing and make the text seem cluttered.

Remember that there is a big difference between quoting and **plagiarizing**, which means using the work of others as if it were your own. Even if you use different words rather than quoting directly, if you are using someone else's ideas, you should say so.

Always make sure your quotations are **accurate**. If you have found your quotation as a quotation in someone else's work, you should go back to the original source, if possible, to check it.

It is **not necessary to use whole sentences** in quotes – in fact it is usually best to use only the parts that are relevant to your argument. However, if you take a sentence out of a paragraph, or a word or phrase out of a sentence, make sure that you do not change the author or speaker's intended meaning.

If you use a quote, you must always **explain why you have used it** and what you think its importance is. This can be done very simply. For example, if the quotation clearly backs up a point you have just made, you could use a phrase like:

> *As x says ...*

Other quotations may need more **analysis and explanation**. You cannot assume that your reader will draw the same conclusions from a quotation as you do, so you must make it very clear what you think its significance is. You might start your next sentence with phrases such as:

> *This shows that ...*
> *[The author] is clearly of the opinion that ...*
> *Put more simply, this means ...*

It is often useful to give a **context** for your quotation, for example by explaining when and where it was written or spoken, or the situation the writer or speaker was in.

How to show quotations

For long quotations (around 60 words or more), it is common to use a separate paragraph, indented slightly from the rest of the text and often using a slightly smaller font.

Shorter quotations are usually shown as part of a sentence:

> *Greenshaw argued that 'the upper classes are not capable of*
> *compassion'.*
> *She described the children as 'motivated and alert'.*

Quotations can also follow an introductory clause, using a colon or a comma before the inverted comma:

> *Charles made a pronouncement: 'There will be no more discussion on*
> *this matter.'*
> *Oscar Wilde once said, 'Always forgive your enemies; nothing annoys*
> *them so much.'*

If you are quoting lines of poetry, it is usual to show the ends of lines with /:

> *As an unperfect actor on the stage,/Who with his fear is put beside*
> *his part*

If you want to **omit part of a quotation**, you can use [...]:

> *She described the play as 'racist in a way that was typical of that time,*
> *and deeply upsetting'.*
> *She described the play as 'racist [...] and deeply upsetting'.*

If you want to add something to a quotation, you use square brackets:

> *Giving evidence, then he said, 'I went round to his house with Al*
> *[Albert Flynn, brother of the accused].'*

If a quotation contains an error, for instance of spelling or grammar, or if it contains something that is surprising, shocking or offensive, and you want to stress that this is *really* what the person said or wrote, use [*sic*], which is Latin for *thus*:

> Clarke wrote that he 'could of [sic] done it'.
> (This should be 'could have done it'.)

Quoting or paraphrasing?

Sometimes you may want to use your own words to explain what someone else has said. This is called paraphrasing. There could be several reasons for this:

- The original quote might be too long, so you need to summarize.
- The original quote might be written in language that is too difficult, so you need to simplify it.
- You might not want to break up your own text with too many direct quotes.

Think about the purpose of your quotations. For example, in an essay on literature, it may be necessary to have a lot of quotations so that you can discuss and analyze the actual language of the author. For a science essay, it may be more appropriate to paraphrase most of the ideas you discuss.

If you do paraphrase, you must still make it clear whose work you are using. Make sure that your paraphrase does not change the meaning of the original in any way – if you want to add your own comments, or disagree with it, you must make it clear which are your ideas and which are the ideas of the person you are paraphrasing.

Referencing quotations

If you use a quotation, you should always say who the speaker or author is, and – if at all possible – what the source was.

This can be done **within the text**, using your own words to introduce the quotation:

As Juliet says in Shakespeare's Romeo and Juliet, 'Parting is such sweet sorrow.'
In a speech during his visit to Berlin in 1963, US President John F Kennedy famously said. 'Ich bin ein Berliner'.

In **academic writing**, it is usual to refer to a footnote or a bibliography (list of books you used) to reference a quotation. Styles for this can vary, so it a good idea to ask your teacher if there is a recommended style. A common way would be to show the author and the date of the publication in brackets in the main text, then show the whole source in the bibliography.

In the text:

As ProfWilliams points out: 'There is a measurable difference between the amount people claim to eat and the amount they actually eat.' (Williams, 2007, p.25)

In the bibliography:

Williams, J. (2007) *The Causes of Obesity.* Newtown: Newtown University Press

If you use a **quotation from a website**, you must reference it in a similar way. Again, there are different styles for this, but a common way would be:

Author, A (date) *Title of article or web page.* Available at: article. com. Accessed on 17/04/2010

Proper nouns

Names of people

Names of people should always be written with capital letters:

>   *Ivan Gorecki*
>   *Julia Jones*

Titles, such as *Mr*, *Mrs*, *Ms*, *Dr* can be written with or without full stops:

>   *Ms Hooper*
>   *Prof. McCarthy*

Geographical terms

Remember to use capital letters for all of the following:

- Countries, e.g. *Japan*, *Sweden*
- Nationalities, e.g. *Japanese*, *Swedish*
- Other geographical locations, e.g. *Mount Everest*, *Lake Tahoe*
- Languages, e.g. *French*, *Swahili*

When writing geographical names that begin with *the*, it is more common to use a lower case *t*:

>   *the United States*
>   *the Alps*

Names of companies and products

Names of companies and products usually have capital letters:

>   *Nokia*
>   *Coca Cola*

Be careful to spell the name of companies and products exactly as they are spelled by their owners. For instance, the name of the publisher of this book is *HarperCollins*, with no space before the second capital letter.

In formal writing, or writing that is to be published, you need to find out if a company name or product name is a registered trademark, and if it is, to put a trademark symbol (®) after the word.

Names of books/films, etc

Capital letters are used for the first letter in titles of books, magazines, newspapers, TV shows, films, etc. Where there are several words, capitals are usually used for the main content words, unless they are the first word in the title:

> *The Wall Street Journal*
> *The Merchant of Venice*
> *Gone with the Wind*

If you mention titles such as these in your text, they should be in italic:

> He decided to write a letter to *The Times*.
> Her last book, *Diary of a Wife*, deals with the subject of domestic violence.

The exceptions to this rule are The Bible and The Koran, which remain in ordinary type.

Abbreviations

It can sometimes be difficult to decide when to use full stops in abbreviations. In British English, it is becoming more common to use abbreviations without full stops, while in American English, they are used more often. In both varieties of English, there are some forms of abbreviation where it is more common to use full stops that others.

In some cases, you may make your decision based on the need to avoid ambiguity, e.g. *a.m.* rather than am. Make sure that you treat each form consistently throughout your text.

You must be certain that your readers will understand any abbreviations you use. It is safe to use widely understood abbreviations like *VAT* or *NHS*, though even in these cases, if your audience is not British, you may need to add an explanation. However, less common abbreviations could puzzle your readers, so it is best either to avoid them, or to put the full form in brackets the first time you use them.

There are a few abbreviations which are so much more widely used than their full forms that it is not necessary to given the full forms at all. Examples are *DNA* and *TNT*.

Abbreviations formed from the first letter of all the words can be spelled with or without full stops, though it is now more common in British English to omit them:

> *BBC (British Broadcasting Company)*
> *FBI (Federal Bureau of Investigation)*

Abbreviations formed from the first part of a word are more likely to use full stops:

> *Prof. (Professor)*
> *Oct. (October)*

Abbreviations formed from the first and last letters of a word do not usually have a full stop in British English:

>   *Mr (mister)*
>   *Dr (doctor)*

Abbreviations formed from Latin words often use full stops:

>   *e.g. (exempli gratia = for example)*
>   *i.e (id est = that is to say)*
>   *etc. (et cetera = the other things)*

However, the common Latin abbreviation *AD (anno domini = in the year of the lord)* and its earlier partner *BC (= before Christ)* are more commonly used without full stops.

Abbreviations for metric scientific measurements are often formed from the first letter of each of the parts of a compound word. They do not use full stops, and never add an *s* to form their plurals:

>   *kg (**k**ilo**g**ram or kilograms)*
>   *ml (**m**il**l**i**l**itre or millilitres)*

Abbreviations for imperial measurements are often very irregular, and often do have full stops. Like metric abbreviations, they do not add *s* in the plural:

>   *oz. (ounce or ounces)* Comes from the Italian word *onza*
>   *lb. (pound or pounds, in weight)* Comes from the Latin word *libra*

Acronyms

Acronyms are words formed from the first letters of several words or from parts of words. The difference between acronyms and other abbreviations is that acronyms are pronounced as words themselves, rather than as individual letters:

> NATO *(North Atlantic Treaty Organization)*
> GUI *(graphical user interface)*

Acronyms are not usually written with full stops. In fact, many acronyms make a journey from being abbreviations to becoming words in their own right. For example, an acronym such as *AIDS (acquired immune deficiency/immunodeficiency syndrome)* has become so widely used, that it is often written *Aids*.

Other words have completed the journey – nobody really thinks of words like *laser (Light Amplification by Stimulated Emission of Radiation)* or *scuba (self contained underwater breathing apparatus)* as being abbreviations at all.

Numbers

Numbers can be written using figures or letters:

1	*one*
350	*three hundred and fifty*
1,299	*one thousand, two hundred and ninety nine*

Note that we put a comma or a space between each group of three figures, counting from the right:

3,490

2 350 100

In mathematical and scientific writing, numbers are always written as figures. In general writing, you can use words or figures:

480 coulombs is equivalent to 0.005 faradays.
About two hundred people attended the meeting.
We'll need 50 chairs.

It is quite common to use words for numbers less than 10, and figures for larger numbers. Whatever you decide, be consistent throughout your writing.

However, if you have two numbers together, you may use a combination to avoid confusion:

Three 5-year olds were hurt in a road accident near Leeds.

Very large numbers in the millions, billions or even higher are usually written like this:

> *40 million*
> *3 billion*

Notice that there is no s on the end of *million* and *billion*.

When there has been more than one king or queen with the same name, their name is followed by an ordinal number, usually written in roman numerals:

> *Henry VIII*
> *Elizabeth II*

Tip for success
Take care with spelling the number *forty* – there is no *u* in it.

Dates

There are several accepted ways of writing dates:

> *11th June 1961*
> *11 June, 1961*
> *11 June 1961*
> *11.6.61*
> *11/06/1961*

The style you choose will depend on what you are writing – the longer styles are suitable for essays, polite letters or other formal writing, while the shorter styles are used in quick emails, filling in forms, etc.

Note that in British English, we usually order dates: day – month – year. In American English, it is more common to order them: month – day – year:

> *June 11th, 1961*

If you are writing about centuries, the most common style is:

> *During the 15th century ...*

Remember that the name of the century is always the number above the beginning of the years in it, so for instance 1492 is in the 15th century, and 1997 is in the 20th century.

When we are writing about history, the abbreviations BC and AD are used for dates before and after the birth of Christ.

AH means 'year 1' in the Muslim calendar. It is the equivalent of AD 622.

Tip for success
Note that non-Christian writers often prefer to avoid the abbreviations *BC* and *AD* and use *BCE (before the common era)* and *CE (of the common era)* instead.

Foreign words and phrases

There are many words in English that come from other languages originally, but then become so absorbed into English that we do not think of them as being foreign any more. Examples are *bazaar* from Persian, *karate* from Japanese and *intelligentsia* from Russian. These words are used in just the same way as any other English words.

However, for a word or phrase that is self-consciously foreign, *italics* are often used:

> The same complaint was repeated *ad nauseam*.
> (Latin = until we were sickened)
> *Entre nous*, his finances are in a perilous state.
> (French = between ourselves)
> Her writings displayed a bleak *Weltanschauung*.
> (German = view of life and the world)

Sometimes it can be difficult to decide if a word has entered mainstream English. If you are unsure whether or not to use italics, consider whether your reader is likely to think of the word or phrase as being part of 'normal' English.

For instance, if you know a lot about yoga, terms such as *chi* (vital energy) and *chakra* (one of the points of physical or spiritual energy) will probably be well known to you. If you are writing for an audience which is also knowledgeable about yoga, you can probably use them without italics and without explanation. However, if your writing is for a general audience, it is best to use italics to indicate that these are words of foreign origin (Chinese and Sanskrit), and also to explain them, at least the first time they are used.

Many foreign words and phrases will only be suitable in very formal or intellectual forms of writing.

Checking
your work

General checks

It is important to **leave time to check your work**, so that the finished quality is as high as possible. Checking falls into two main areas:

- **Overall structure and content**.

- **Detailed points of spelling, grammar, punctuation, etc**.

If you have planned your work carefully and written one or more drafts, as described in the section on 'Planning' in this book, your work should already be logical and well structured. However, even for a short piece of writing, such as a letter or work email, it is worth asking yourself the following questions:

- Has my writing achieved what I wanted to achieve?
- Have I expressed my points clearly?
- Do my ideas or pieces of information come in a logical sequence?
- Do I have enough evidence to support my points?
- Is the tone of my writing what I wanted it to be?
- Have I included everything I wanted to include?

It can often be a good idea to **ask someone else** to correct your work – your eyes will see what you *intended* to write, whereas someone else may spot errors more easily.

> **Tip for success**
> Most people find it easier to check their work on paper rather than on a computer screen, so if it is important that it is correct, consider printing it out.

Checking spelling

It is important to make sure your spelling is correct. There is a section on spelling in this book which gives general rules, and also a section on words which are often spelled wrongly.

Use your instinct: if a word looks wrong, check it in a dictionary. You can also use a spellchecker on your computer, but make sure that it is set to the variety of English you want – for example, British or American.

General points to look out for include:

- **Homophones**. These are words which sound the same but are spelled differently, e.g. their/there, witch/which, bare/bear. Remember that the spellchecker on your computer will not be able to correct errors in homophones because they are both correct words.

- **Letters that are the wrong way round**. It is very easy to make this kind of error when you are typing your work, for instance typing '*form*' instead of '*from*'.

- **Missing letters**. Make sure you do not miss out silent letters in words such as 'gover**n**ment', or forget to double the consonant in words such as 'swi**mm**ing'.

> **Tip for success**
> Take particular care with typed writing – it is much easier to make a mistake with fingers on keys than with a pen.

Checking grammar and punctuation

There are sections on grammar and punctuation in this book that give general rules, and also a section on common errors.

General points to look out for include:

- **Apostrophes**. Make sure you have put them in where they are needed and left them out where they are not.

- **Capital letters**. Make sure that all proper nouns have capital letters. It is also a common error to put a lower case 'i' where the upper case pronoun 'I' is needed.

- **Repeated words**. These are often found at the end of one line and the beginning of another.

- **Missing words**. It can be very easy to miss out little words such as 'of' or 'in', and equally difficult to spot that they are missing, since your brain can compensate by adding them in unconsciously when you read.

-
- **Agreement**. This means making sure that all the parts of a sentence relate correctly to each other, avoiding mistakes such as '*We was asked to contribute.*' (Should be: *We were asked to contribute.*)

If you are using your computer to write, you will probably have a grammar checker available. This will pick up some common problems, but you should still check your work yourself.

Tip for success
Do not try to correct huge pieces of text in one go – you need to be fresh to be able to spot errors.

Other things to check

- **Facts and information**. If there is any doubt about the source of your information, for instance if it came from a website you are not sure is reliable, make sure you can confirm it in another, more reliable source.

- **Numbers**. Always check numbers, especially long ones such as telephone numbers. It is very easy to make a mistake when you type these.

- **Dates**. If you tell people a meeting is on Thursday 6th, but the 6th is a Wednesday, you will cause confusion.

- **Repetition of words and phrases**. As you were writing, you may not have realised that you used the same word or phrase over and over again, but when you check at the end, you will notice this, and can vary your words if you want to.

- **References**. If you have referred to another book, paper, etc., make sure you have acknowledged it and referenced it properly. In the same way, if you have used charts, diagrams, etc,. make sure there are references to them all in the text.

- **Cross references**. If you have a long document, with many different, numbered sections, you may want to cross refer from one to another, and it is best to do this at the end, when your section headings will not change. If you are writing on a computer, you will be able to set up your document so that cross references change automatically if the heading numbers change.

Checking work written on a computer

In many ways, computers have made all sorts of writing much easier, especially because we can correct mistakes and move around sections of text without having to write everything out again. However, this does mean that it is very easy to introduce mistakes.

If you correct one word in a sentence or one part of a sentence, take great care to make sure that the whole sentence is still correct. For instance, it is very easy to leave in words that are not needed. Look at the following example:

> *She had an important role in his career.*
> *His mother played had an important role in his career.*

The writer only deleted '*she*' instead of '*she had*' when making this correction, leading to an extra verb in the sentence.

Remember, too, to make sure that agreement within a sentence is not affected by a change to part of it:

> *I gave my passport to the officer, who looked at it closely.*
> *I gave my passport and driving licence to the officer, who looked at it closely.*

In this case, the writer has added the words '*and driving licence*' but has forgotten to change the pronoun '*it*' later in the sentence to '*them*'.

Tip for success
If you decide to move a section of text, do make sure that you have deleted it from where it was originally.

Marking your corrections

It is usually best to **mark up a whole document or section of a document on paper** before you actually make the changes on the computer.

When people do **proofreading** in a formal way, there is a set of standard marks that they use. It is unlikely that you will need to learn formal proofreading marks, but some of them can be useful, as they are a clear way of showing your changes, particularly if you are **correcting someone else's writing**.

For example, the mark ^ shows *where* something is to be added, and the text in the margin shows *what* is to be added. The symbol # shows where a space should be added and the symbol ⌐ in the margin indicates that the words in the text with a line through them should be deleted.

There are several books and websites which explain how to use proofreading symbols.

If you are **correcting someone else's work on screen**, it can be useful to use a system that shows the changes you suggest, rather than simply making the changes yourself. That way, the author can decide whether to accept or reject your corrections. You can also leave explanations, comments and suggestions that the author can delete later.

> **Key point to remember**
> Printing out your work and reading through it on paper
> can be a helpful way of spotting mistakes.

Tip for success
If possible, ask someone else to correct your writing.
Errors that you cannot spot yourself may be very
obvious to a person who is looking at a piece of text
for the first time.

Writing

Formal or work emails

Email is very much faster than writing letters. You can receive a reply to an email within seconds – or minutes – of sending one. In this way, email is more **like conversation** than paper-based writing. This is its great advantage: email communication, like conversation, can be **two-way** and **almost immediate**. It can also be its weakness when people do not take enough care writing emails, especially formal or work emails.

First, here are some general points about email to keep in mind:

- Email tends to be brief.
- Email is generally less formal than communication on paper.
- Email does not communicate emotions as successfully as speech. The reader of your email may not be able to tell from your words if you are serious or joking, angry or just surprised.
- Emails, especially very short emails, can sound angry, unfriendly or rude when this is not intended by the writer.

> **Key point to remember**
> Emails that are written very quickly and carelessly can sound unfriendly and rude.

The **rules are less strict** for writing formal or work *emails* than for writing formal *letters*. People have been writing letters for many hundreds of years so rules have had time to develop. Email, as a recent form of communication, is much less fixed in its rules.

The **rules are** also **different** in different countries and cultures and in different places of work. This point is worth remembering. What is right for one group of people may not be right for all people.

It is also true to say that **everyone** has **their own style** of writing email. Even within the same company, two people may take very different approaches to this form of communication.

The points laid out in this unit are therefore a **guide to writing formal emails**. By following these generally accepted rules, you will get the most out of email. You will also avoid some of the most frequent problems that arise from this form of communication.

> **Tip for Success**
> When you join a new company, notice how your colleagues write their emails and consider changing your style to fit in with the company style.

Salutations for formal emails
(Words or phrases used for saying hello)

It is generally a good idea to **start an email with a greeting** rather than beginning the message immediately. Just like a face-to-face exchange of greetings, email greetings:

- show that you are friendly and pleasant
- show respect for the reader

In addition, a greeting allows the reader to pause for a moment before reading the message itself.

If, however, you and a colleague are writing a series of short emails to each other on a particular subject, the rules are different. It is generally acceptable after the first exchange of emails to include only the information, without salutations.

Note that if you are using **instant messaging**, which is an even faster method of communication, you only need to add a salutation to the first in a series of messages that you send to someone.

There are no fixed rules for the type of greeting that you use. Generally, if you are emailing someone that you work with or even someone that you do not know, it is acceptable to **start the email** with a simple '**Hello**' or '**Hello James**'. (If you know the colleague well, '**Hi**' or '**Hi James**' might also be fine.)

You may want to **show more respect** in your greeting, perhaps if the person is much older than you, has a higher rank than you in the same company, or is from a country or culture that is more formal than yours. If you are in any doubt about this, you could address the person, '**Dear Mr Sanchez**' or '**Dear Ms Sanchez**'.

If you are replying to an email and the sender of the message has used his or her first name only, it is generally **acceptable to use their first name** too.

> **Key point to remember**
> If you decide to use the more formal salutation 'Dear Mr Sanchez' or 'Dear Ms Sanchez' make sure that you use the correct title. If the person you are emailing is a doctor, for example, be sure to include that in the salutation.

Subject lines

People who use email for work often complain that they receive too much email and that it takes up too much of their time dealing with it.

You can help with this situation by **making full use of the subject line**. The subject line gives you the chance to tell the reader of your email **why you are emailing them** before they have even opened your message.

For example, if you are emailing a company to ask for information about a product, in the subject line, write the name of the product and the fact that you need information:

> *Subject: Balance bike (ref: N765) info required*

The subject line gives you the chance to **show the main points** of your email. If you start to type 'Hi' or 'Another thing' in the subject line, think for a moment whether you can replace it with something more useful.

Look at the following subject lines and see how, in only a few words, you can show the main points of an email:

> *Subject: Meeting Room changed to mr5*

> *Subject: Lunch (Fri 9 Oct) cancelled*

> *Subject: REQ: Jan's sales figures*

> *Subject: Reminder: 5-year plan due*

> **Tip for Success**
> Write a useful subject line that says in just a few words what your email is about and what, if any, action you need the reader to take.

Content and length

Before you even start to type your message, make sure you can answer the following two questions:

- Why am I writing this?
- What do I want the reader of this email to do?

Remember that most people receive a lot of email in the course of a working day. For this reason, they do not welcome long emails! Your job is therefore to **tell them your point or points quickly and clearly**. Here are a few tips to help you do this:

- Make the first sentence count. Introduce the topic of the email clearly and in a few words.

- Write in short paragraphs. Separate paragraphs, each relating to a different point, will make the information easier to understand. Do not allow important points to get lost in one long paragraph.

- Consider using headings within the body of your message if the message relates to several different subjects.

- Consider numbering your points. The reader will find this useful when responding to particular points.

- Leave a space between each paragraph.

- Use short sentences. Try to keep your sentences to a maximum of 20 words. These can be quickly read and understood.

- If possible, try to fit your message onto one screen so that the reader does not have to scroll down to see the rest of it.

Read the following email. Consider:

- Is the information presented in the clearest way?

- Did the writer think about the needs of the reader as she wrote her email?

Subject: conference dinner
From: "Hill, Lucy" <Lucy.Hill@bigbooks.co.uk>
To: "Ollie Walsh"

Hi Ollie

Thanks again for offering to help out with the arrangements for the conference dinner. I do appreciate it. I met with David yesterday to finalize details and here's what we decided: The venue (Carmichael Hall) is booked for Dec 18th, 7:00 – 12:00. Your contact there is Julia Winters on 01354 638976. Invitations should go out to all conference delegates the week starting November 3rd. The invitations are currently with the printers, btw, and when they are returned to us (this Friday) will need checking against the original delegate list which I'll get Sujata to send to you. Hallidays, the caterers, will need to know final numbers by Dec. 10th, latest. Please call them to let them know. Last of all, please could you liaise with Sujata over the timing of the speeches and let the relevant people know when their slot is.

Many thanks,
Lucy

Now see how much clearer the same message looks when the writer considers what will be most helpful to the reader and has:

- broken the text up into separate, short paragraphs

- given each paragraph a heading

- allowed plenty of white space

Subject: conference dinner
From: "Hill, Lucy" <Lucy.Hill@bigbooks.co.uk>
To: "Ollie Walsh"

Hi Ollie

Thanks again for offering to help out with the arrangements for the conference dinner. I do appreciate it. I met with David yesterday to finalize details and here's what we decided:

Venue
The venue (Carmichael Hall) is booked for Dec 18th, 7:00 – 12:00.
Your contact there is Julia Winters on 01354 638976

Invitations
The invitations are currently with the printers. When they are returned to us (this Friday) they will need checking against the original delegate list which I'll get Sujata to send to you. Invitations should go out to all conference delegates the week starting November 3rd.

The caterers
Hallidays, the caterers, will need to know final numbers by Dec. 10th. Please call them to let them know.

Speeches
Last of all, please could you liaise with Sujata over the timing of the speeches and let the relevant people know when their slot is.

Many thanks,
Lucy

Tone

Read the following email and ask yourself how the writer was feeling when he wrote it:

Subject: conference dinner
From: "Walsh, Ollie" <Ollie.Walsh@bigbooks.co.uk>
To: "Lucy Hill"

Lucy,

There are problems re the arrangements for the conference dinner:

1. The invitations have only just arrived this morning so I will be late sending them out.

2. Julia Winters called late yesterday. She was under the impression that 150 people were attending. Sujata's list says it's 170. Which of these is right?

3. Re the speeches, Alice and David are fine with 10 minutes each but Michael wants 15 minutes. Is he allowed 15 minutes? Also, you didn't ask Saskia to speak and she's offended. Did you mean not to ask her or is this an oversight?

Ollie

Perhaps the writer of this email was angry or stressed. That is certainly the impression that his email gives. However, it is possible that he was neither angry nor stressed: he simply needed advice from Lucy about how to act. Supposing he was not angry, how might he have written exactly the same questions but in a polite and pleasant way?

Now compare the tone of the previous email with this email:

> Dear Lucy,
>
> I'm afraid[1] there are a few problems re the arrangements for the conference dinner:
>
> 1. FYI, the invitations have only just arrived this morning so I'm afraid I will be a day late sending them out. (This shouldn't make too much difference[2].)
>
> 2. Julia Winters called late yesterday. She was under the impression that 150 people were attending. Sujata's list says it's 170. Do you know[3] which of these figures is right?
>
> 3. Re the speeches, Alice and David are fine with 10 minutes each but Michael would prefer[4] 15 minutes. Is this possible? Also, I have heard that Saskia Winters would like to speak too. This may not be possible but I thought I'd let you know[5].
>
> Best,
> Ollie

Here the writer explains the same problems and asks the same questions without making the reader feel that the problems are all her fault! Notice how:

[1] Before he tells her about a problem, he writes 'I'm afraid ...'
[2] He tells her about a problem but lets her know that it is not serious.
[3] He adds 'Do you know' to the question, which softens it.
[4] He uses the polite phrase 'would prefer' rather than the direct verb 'wants'.
[5] In the previous email he blames the reader, (you didn't ask Saskia to speak and she's offended). Here, he simply lets the reader know that there is a problem. She can then decide what to do.

Generally, people intend their emails to be **polite and pleasant** – or at least neutral. However, because emails are often brief and quickly written, they can sometimes sound slightly demanding, angry or even rude.

Remember that the reader of your email **cannot see you smile** and **cannot hear that your voice is friendly**. Try to be aware of this potential problem and to develop ways of showing that you are polite and friendly through the words that you write. This is *especially* true if the person you are emailing has never met you.

If you are emailing someone that you have spoken or written to before, consider starting your message by saying '**I hope you are well**'. Again, this lets the reader know that you are friendly and pleasant.

It is fine to keep your emails brief, but **not too brief**. You want to communicate quickly and efficiently but you still need to show respect to the reader and to show that you have considered their feelings. This can be difficult, especially when you are in a hurry, but it is important. If, for example, you are giving a piece of bad news, start your sentence with 'I'm afraid ...' or 'I'm sorry ...' rather than just stating the problem.

Be aware that verbs used in **the passive can sound a little formal**. For example 'The sales report that you were sent in February' (passive) sounds slightly formal whereas 'the sales report that I sent you in February' (active) does not. This is fine if you want to write a slightly formal email. If you are emailing a colleague that you know well, and want to write a friendlier email, however, you may want to avoid this structure.

Do not write using all UPPER-CASE LETTERS. People sometimes use upper-case letters to show the difference between their own writing and someone else's. This may make the reader think that you are angry and shouting. Upper-case letters are also more difficult to read than lower-case letters.

Always read an email that you have written before you send it, especially if you are writing to disagree with someone. **Imagine that you are the reader** and try to **read the email as they will read it**. Does it sound angry, aggressive or demanding and, if so, is that *really* what you intended? If you are in any doubt, do not send the email immediately. Save it and read it later in the day when you are feeling calm and can judge whether you need to change it.

> **Tip for success**
> Before you send an email, read it to check that the tone of it is what you intended.

Punctuation and abbreviations

Generally, the rules for spelling, grammar and punctuation that apply to letter-writing also apply to formal or work emails:

- Bad spelling, grammar and punctuation may give the reader a bad opinion of you and of your company, if you work for one.
- In addition, they may make your message unclear or confusing. In particular, emails that lack full stops or commas are difficult to read.

It is generally agreed that **contractions** (I'm, he's, can't, etc.) **are acceptable** in most formal or work emails. In formal *letters*, the full form of the words should be used but, as we have said before, formal emails are less formal than formal letters.

Other abbreviations, such as 'U' for 'you', 'plz' for 'please', and 'tx' for 'thanks', though often used in personal email, are generally not acceptable in formal or work emails.

Likewise, emoticons or smileys ☺ are not generally used in formal or work emails:

- They are considered too informal or 'familiar'.

- There is a risk that the reader will not understand what you mean by these symbols.

> **Tip for success**
> Always read an email before you send it to check for errors.

Ending a formal email

Between the main part of the email and the 'sign-off', (the part that says goodbye), there is often a line linking the two.

What you write at this point will, of course, depend on the purpose of your email, but here are a few typical sentences that are often used here:

- *I hope to hear from you soon.*
- *I look forward to hearing from you.*
- *I look forward to your response.*
- *Many thanks for your time.*
- *Thanks again for this.*
- *Many thanks in advance.*
- *Thank you for taking the time to answer my questions.*
- *I hope this helps.*
- *Please do get in touch if you have any more queries.*
- *Please do not hesitate if you have any questions.*
- *Do let me know what you think.*

Just as it is a good idea to start an email with a greeting, it is also **polite to finish an email with a sign-off**. Not everyone does this: some people end an email by typing their name alone. But an email that ends without a sign-off can sound a little rude, especially if the content of the email has included a disagreement or problem.

A number of sign-offs are commonly used in formal or work emails. Again, there are no fixed rules for the type of sign-off that you use. The phrases below are some of the most common.

- *Many thanks*
- *Thank you*
- *Thanks again*
- *Best*
- *Regards*
- *Best regards*
- *Kind regards*
- *With kind regards*
- *Best wishes*
- *With best wishes*

Below is an example of a slightly formal email. The sender of the email, (an artist), is replying to a person who has made an enquiry about their work. They have never met each other. Notice the tone which is polite and friendly but still slightly formal.

Subject: paintings
From: "Lewis, Lara" <lara.lewis@pnc.co.uk>
To: "Michael Peters"

Hello Michael

Thank you for your enquiry.

I am a studio artist at Holler Arts Centre and am based at Portland, just west of Bristol. You are welcome to visit me there anytime and have a look at the paintings I have available (no obligation of course!).

I also attend events around the country as you can see in my 2010 Events page on my website.

Prices start at £150 for the small paintings (approx. 20 x 15 cm). The larger paintings are about £400 (50 x 40 cm) depending on the piece.

I also undertake commissions if you have something specific in mind.

Please give me a ring on 01209 459825 if you would like to come to my studio and we can arrange a suitable time.

Kind regards
Lara

This email is sent from one colleague to another. This time, as the sender and reader know each other, the tone is slightly less formal, though it is still formal enough to be suitable for work.

Subject: minutes, (meeting 20/03/09)
From: "Rose, Andrew" <andrew.rose@wentworths.co.uk>
To: "Helena Ghiotto"

Hi Helena,

I'm attaching the minutes from yesterday's meeting.

Thanks very much for coming to the meeting. I think we all found it very useful to have your sales perspective on the various issues. Sophia and I agreed that it would be good to have you or Chris present at such meetings in the future. Perhaps we could discuss this over a coffee sometime?

Would you mind emailing me a copy of Jeanne's report? Thanks in advance.

Have a good trip – and please say hi to Carlo from me.

Best,
Andrew

Informal or social emails

The rules for writing informal or social emails are very relaxed.
Generally, when people email their friends, **they write as they speak**.
They use the same words as they would use in speech and they put
those words together in much the same way.

Salutations
(Words or phrases used for saying hello)

People generally **start informal emails with a greeting** in order to
sound friendly. There are no fixed rules for the type of greeting used.
Generally, people write '**Hi**' or '**Hi Julia**' or '**Hello**' or '**Hello Julia**'.
Sometimes there is no greeting and the name of the reader alone
is used.

Tone

As we have said before, email does not communicate emotions very
clearly. The reader of an email cannot see the sender's face or hear their
voice and they may struggle to work out how they are feeling. This is
especially true when an email has been written very quickly or with
little care. One solution to this problem is the **smiley** or **emoticon**,
a typed symbol representing a face. Smileys are used either to show
how the sender feels or to show the tone of an email when the words
alone do not make this clear. The most common of these smileys are
shown below:

☺ or 😃	'I am happy/pleased/friendly.'
☹ or 😕	'I am sad or fed up.'
😳	'I am surprised or shocked.'
😉	'I am joking/being sarcastic.'

Punctuation and abbreviations

Some people take care to punctuate their informal emails correctly but many do not. For example, it is quite common to see informal emails written completely in lower-case letters. Generally, people do not expect perfect punctuation in this type of email.

Emails **often include abbreviations**. Some of the most common abbreviations are shown below. It is worth remembering when you use one of these that not everyone knows what all these abbreviations mean.

AFAIK	As Far As I Know	IOW	In Other Words
AKA	Also Known As	IRL	In Real Life
ASAP	As soon as possible	L8R	Later
B4	Before	LOL	Laughing out Loud
BTW	By The Way	OTOH	On the Other Hand
CUL8R	See You Later	POV	Point of View
CYA	See Ya	ROTFL	Rolling on the Floor Laughing
CYU	See You	SYL	See you Later
FWIW	For What It's Worth	TAFN	That's all for now
FYA	For Your Amusement	TIA	Thanks in advance
FYI	For Your Information	TTYL	Talk to you later
HTH	Hope This Helps	TTFN	Tah tah for now
IMO	In My Opinion	TX	Thanks
IMHO	In My Humble Opinion		

Ending an informal email

As with email openings, there are no fixed rules for how to end informal emails. In a very quickly written email there may be no 'sign-off', (the part before the name that says goodbye), or just the name of the sender. Sometimes, people write only the first letter of their name instead of their whole name. However, **most people like to use a sign-off** as it is friendly. Additionally, between the main part of the email and the sign-off, there is often an extra line linking the two. Below are some examples:

- *Talk to you later.*
- *Hope you're doing okay/well.*
- *Hope you're all well.*
- *See you soon.*
- *Better go now.*
- *Tell you more when we speak.*
- *Have a good weekend.*
- *Hope to see you soon.*

A number of sign-offs are commonly used in informal emails before the name of the sender. The phrases below are some of the most frequent:

- *Love*
- *Lots of love*
- *Take care*
- *Ciao*
- *Later*
- *See you*
- *See ya!*
- *Cheers!*

Texts

Texting (or 'text messaging') between mobile phones is now an extremely popular form of communication. Its great advantage is that it allows people to communicate almost as quickly as spoken language in situations where speech is not suitable.

Texts (or 'text messages') are **short** as there is a limit to the number of characters that can be used in each message. Because of this, a special language of **text abbreviations** has developed. Some of these abbreviations include numbers as well as letters. Here are some of the most common text abbreviations with their meanings:

@	at	gr8	great	tx/thx	thanks
2	to or two	ic	I see	u	you
2day	today	l8	late	w8	wait
2moro	tomorrow	l8r	later	wan2	want to
4	for	lo	hello	wk	week
aml	all my love	m8	mate	wrk	work
b4	before	pls	please	xlnt	excellent
btw	by the way	r	are	y	why
c	see	some1	someone		
cm	call me	spk	speak		
cu	see you	sry	sorry		
cul	see you later	syl	see you later		

Sometimes people also use **smileys** or **emoticons** in their texts. These are typed symbols representing a face. They are used to show how the sender feels or to show the tone of a text when the words alone do not make this clear. Here are some of most common of these smileys:

    ☺ or 😃   'I am happy/pleased/friendly.'
    ☹ or ☺   'I am sad or fed up.'
    ☺   'I am surprised or shocked.'
    ☺   'I am joking/being sarcastic.'

Formal or work letters

Nowadays so much communication is done through email and the telephone that the skill of formal letter writing can get forgotten. However, letters are still used in some situations.

Here is a general layout for a formal letter. Note that the layout of formal letters varies but that this format is generally accepted.

---

7 Molden Rd
Bristol
[1]BR2 4UP

[2]18 November 2010

[3]Ms Harriet Jones
Planning Officer
Bristol City Council
Bristol
BR1 3GY

[4]Dear Ms Jones,

[5]**Planning Application Ref. No. 09/291/XUL**

Thank you for your letter informing us of this application. As the owners and occupiers of no.7 Molden Road, we are concerned that the creation of five new houses will create an unacceptable degree of noise and disturbance in the area.

We are also anxious about the amount of traffic that this development will generate. As parents who cycle on Molden Road with our children, we feel that the extra volume of traffic will make the road unsafe.

For these reasons, we believe that this is a highly unsuitable proposal for development in this area, and hope that the Council will reject the application.

[6]Yours sincerely,

Anthony Johnson   *Sylvie Marks*

[7]Mr Anthony Johnson & Ms Sylvie Marks

---

1. Write your address in the top right corner of the letter. Do not write your name here.
2. Write the date on the right, under your address. Write the month in full as a word.
3. Write the address of the person that you are writing to on the left, under your address and date.
4. If you know the name of the person you are writing to, use the title and the family name to address them. If you do not know the name of the person you are writing to, write 'Dear Sir or Madam'.
5. The heading goes here in bold, giving the subject matter of the letter. This will not be appropriate for all formal letters but is useful in cases where the letter clearly relates to a particular subject.
6. Write 'Yours sincerely' to end the letter if you know the surname of the person you are writing to. Write 'Yours faithfully' if you do not. Remember to start 'Yours' with a capital letter.
7. Write your signature by hand and then type your name under it. Put your given name first and family name second.

> **Key point to remember**
> If you know that the person you are sending the letter to is a woman but you do not know how she prefers to be addressed, use the title, 'Ms'. 'Ms' is used for both married and single women.

Most formal letters have a similar structure, having an introduction, a main part and a conclusion.

In your first paragraph, introduce the reason that you are writing. This should be brief – one line or two is usually enough.

> *On June 20th, 2009, I bought a self-assembly children's scooter (model: XR36) from you for £25 which I paid for with cash.*

In the main part of the letter **give details which explain the reason that you are writing**. Keep this as brief as you can. Say everything that you need to say but no more. Present the facts in a logical order that can easily be understood.

> *The next day I unpacked and assembled the scooter and my son rode it to the park. After half an hour of using the scooter, I noticed that the middle of the rear wheel was cracked. I immediately stopped my son from riding on the scooter as I was worried that it was unsafe.*

In the conclusion to your letter, **tell the reader what you would like them to do** as a result of your letter:

> *I am not at all happy with the quality of this make of scooter and am therefore requesting a full refund.*

The language that you use in a formal letter must be appropriate. It should be polite, whatever subject you are writing about. It does not need to be very formal but it **must not be *informal***. Do not use:

- slang or informal language
- contractions, such as 'I'm' and 'can't'

Make sure that you **spell the name of the person that you are writing to correctly**. People can feel offended when their names are spelled wrongly.

It is helpful to **write a clear heading** before the main part of your letter. This tells the reader exactly what the letter is about. There is a greater chance that the reader will pay attention to your letter if they know from the start what they are dealing with.

Take care over the appearance of your letter. Present the text in short blocks and leave plenty of white space between them. Prepare a letter that looks easy to read.

> **Key point to remember**
> Make sure that you use the reader's correct title. For
> example, do not write 'Mr ...' if the reader is a doctor and
> likes to be addressed with that title.

When you are planning your letter, try to **think of the contents of
that letter from the point of view of the reader**. Most working
people read a great deal of text every day, whether it is email, text
messages or printed matter. Most people are also very busy in their
jobs and have only a limited amount of time to read a message in
whatever form it is sent.

You – the letter writer – must therefore try to help the reader by making
the message of the letter as clear as possible. You can do this by:

* giving the main point (or points) first. Your reader will immediately
  want to know why you are writing to them and may feel impatient
  with your letter if they have to read through a lot of text in order to
  find this out.

* not including too much information. Only write what the reader
  needs to know. Do not include a lot of details or the reader may
  struggle to understand the main point of the letter.

* not including irrelevant information. This might confuse the reader
  or make them impatient.

* keeping your sentences short and simple. Short sentences with
  a simple structure are easier to understand.

> **Tip for success**
> Write a clear letter that can be easily understood.

Look at this letter written by the parent of a child to the child's teacher:

62 Acer Glen
Perth
WA6023

13 December 2009

Carine Glades School
Carine Avenue
Perth
WA6023

Dear Ms Lennon,

I am writing to clarify the situation regarding Millie's nut allergy as I know this has recently caused some confusion and concern. Millie has a slight allergy to almonds and hazelnuts. The allergy is mild and not life-threatening but it does cause swelling of the mouth which Millie finds distressing. Our doctor has recommended that Millie avoids eating all foods containing these nuts. If any of the children brings birthday cake or biscuits into school, please could Millie not be given any in case the food sets off an allergic reaction. In the event of Millie accidentally eating food that contains almonds or hazelnuts, please administer the medicine which the school office now has in their medicine box. This will immediately alleviate the symptoms. The medicine is clearly marked with Millie's name. I hope this clarifies the situation. If you have any questions at all, please call me on 57837 7293045. Many thanks for your help.

Yours sincerely,
Anna Green

Now see how much clearer and easier to read the letter is when:

- a heading is used, giving the reason for the letter
- the text is broken up into short paragraphs
- there is plenty of white space around those paragraphs

---

62 Acer Glen
Perth
WA6023

13 December 2009

Carine Glades School
Carine Avenue
Perth
WA6023

Dear Ms Lennon,

Millie Green's nut allergy

I am writing to clarify the situation regarding Millie's nut allergy as I know this has recently caused some confusion and concern.

Millie has a slight allergy to almonds and hazelnuts. The allergy is mild and not life-threatening but it does cause swelling of the mouth which Millie finds distressing. Our doctor has recommended that Millie avoids eating all foods containing these nuts.

If any of the children brings birthday cake or biscuits into school, please could Millie not be given any in case the food sets off an allergic reaction. In the event of Millie accidentally eating food that contains almonds or hazelnuts, please administer the medicine which the school office now has in their medicine box. This will immediately alleviate the symptoms. The medicine is clearly marked with Millie's name.

I hope this clarifies the situation. If you have any questions at all, please call me on 57837 7293045.

Many thanks for your help.

Yours sincerely,
Anna Green

Letters are sometimes written to make complaints, for example about the quality of goods or services. The following letter is written by a woman who is unhappy with the service that she recently received in a restaurant:

---

101 Richmond Street
Chatham, ON
N7L 1E1

17 June 2010

Maria's
160 King Street West
Toronto, ON
M5H 1J8

Dear Sir or Madam,

[1] I am writing to complain about the poor service I received in your restaurant, where my friend and I had lunch last Saturday (June 13th).

[2] Having requested over the phone a table by the window, we were disappointed to find ourselves seated instead at the back of the restaurant. Our food took over an hour to come and when it arrived, my friend's main course was cold. We complained about this and our waitress returned the food to the kitchen for reheating. Unfortunately, she forgot to bring the food back to us and, when reminded, was visibly impatient. Neither dessert that we chose from the menu was available and, although we asked for our coffees to arrive with dessert, they came ten minutes after it.

[3] As a result of all this, we did not enjoy our evening. Your restaurant had been recommended to us by a friend but I am afraid we were extremely disappointed by what we found.

[4] I am enclosing a copy of the bill and would like to receive a refund of at least half of it.

I look forward to hearing from you shortly.

Yours faithfully,

Carla Sylva

Carla Sylva

1 In the opening paragraph, explain briefly what you are complaining about.
2 In the main paragraph explain the problem, giving particular examples of what you are dissatisfied with. Include relevant details, such as dates and places. Give enough information here but not so much that the important parts are lost.
3 Tell the reader what the result of all these problems was.
4 Tell the reader what you would like them to do about the problem.

Be polite. Keep the tone of your letter polite and as pleasant as possible. You may feel that the reader is to blame for your situation but do not be rude to them. If the reader is offended by what you write, they will probably not want to help you with your problem. In any case, the person reading your letter will probably not have caused your problem.

Stay calm. You may be angry but try not to let this show. Never use an aggressive or threatening tone. Avoid adjectives such as 'terrible' and 'appalling' that cause or show strong emotion and use calmer, more neutral words. If you are openly angry with the reader, it is likely that they will feel angry with you.

People often apply for a job by sending to a company their CV together with a job application letter. With a well-written job application letter you can:

• point out the most important parts of your CV

• show a potential employer that you can write effectively

• show a potential employer that you are a pleasant person

16 Bezuidenhout Street
Troyeville
Johannesburg 2094

18 March 2010

Ms Helena Lewis
Human Resources Manager
Bigbook Publishing
Johannesburg 2094

Dear Ms Lewis,

[1]**Editorial assistant**

[2]I am writing to apply for the above post as advertised in the Evening Standard on March 14. I am enclosing my CV, as requested.

[3]I am currently working in a publishing company that specializes in children's books. [4]I have been working on various aspects of publishing, including editing, liaising with freelance editors and checking manuscripts.

I have worked in this company for two years and have gained considerable experience and knowledge. [5]I now feel that it is time to take my career to the next step. I am looking for a position that will provide new challenges and engage me more fully in the publishing process. [6]I am organized and energetic and I enjoy meeting and working with a range of people.

[7]I would welcome the opportunity to discuss my CV with you.

I look forward to hearing from you.

Yours sincerely,

Thomas van Leeuwen

Thomas van Leeuwen

1. Give the title of the job that you are applying for here.
2. Give details of the job that you are applying for and say how you found out about it.
3. Describe the job that you are doing now, including details of tasks and responsibilities.
4. Tell the reader what skills and knowledge you have gained in your current job.
5. Tell the reader why you want to leave your current job for the new job.
6. Describe the qualities that make you suitable for the new job.
7. Say that you would be pleased to provide the reader with more information.

Do not write too much in your letter of application. The main part of the letter should have two or three short paragraphs only. Ideally, the whole letter should only be one page.

Write a job application letter for each new job that you apply for. Do not assume that a general letter of application will be enough. Write specifically about the job that you are applying for and keep in mind the skills and qualities that are right for that job.

> **Tip for success**
> Always address a letter of application to a particular person. If you know the title of their job but not their name, call the company and ask for their name.

The following is a letter of enquiry, written by a person who is looking for work. It is not a response to a job advertisement. Instead it is the sort of letter that a person who wants work sends to several potential employers, hoping that one of them will require their services:

3 Victoria Street
Wellington 6011

6 August 2009

Hotel Grand
26 Quay Street
Auckland 1021
BR2 4UT

Dear Sir or Madam

I am writing to enquire about the possibility of work in your hotel this summer. I am especially interested in reception duties but would seriously consider any other type of work that you could offer me.

I am a twenty-year-old student and for the last three years have spent every summer working in hotels in Wellington. I have worked as a receptionist, a waitress and a cleaner. This summer I intend staying with relations in Auckland from December 5th till January 31st and am hoping to find employment for this period.

I enclose a CV giving details of my work experience and very much look forward to hearing from you.

With thanks.

Yours faithfully

Sophia Pylas

Sophia Pylas

Informal letters

Again, so much communication is done through email and the telephone these days that informal letters between friends are becoming quite rare. Still, some people like to write letters – or at least notes – to their friends. There are also some occasions when, even between good friends, a letter seems more appropriate than an email.

---

[1] *18th December, 2009*

[2] *Dear Sara,*

[3] *It was great to speak to you last week – thanks for phoning. I'm so sorry I haven't been in touch this year. It's been quite hectic with one thing and another!*

[4] *We're both really excited that you're coming to see us in the new year – it's been far too long. I just thought I'd better remind you to bring your walking boots. There are some fantastic walks we can do round here (if we have the energy!) Also, make sure you bring warm sweaters and coats. The scenery here is gorgeous but it is <u>very</u> cold, especially in January, (and I seem to remember from our college days together that you feel the cold!)*

Did I mention I bumped into Steve Washington in Manchester earlier this year? He looked so different I almost didn't recognise him. Anyway, I'll tell you more when I see you …

[5] *Really looking forward to seeing you both. I'll call you nearer the time with directions.*

[6] *Much love,*
Emma [7] *xxx*

[8] *PS Can't wait to see you with short hair!*

1   You do not need to write your address here, although some people
    do. If you want to give the reader a new or different address, you can
    write it here. If you sometimes write from one place and sometimes
    another, you may show which of these addresses you are writing
    from by putting, for example:

> *London*
> *8th December, 2009*

2   You can use the traditional greeting for an informal letter, which is
    'Dear Paolo/Greta, etc' or you may like to write simply, 'Hi Paolo/
    Greta, etc'.

3   You can start an informal letter by referring to a previous
    communication with the reader. You can also start by asking after
    the health of the reader or by saying sorry for not having written
    to or telephoned the reader recently:

- *How are you?*
- *How are you doing?*
- *I hope you're both well.*
- *I'm sorry it's been so long since my last letter.*

4   The tone of an informal letter is very often conversational. Just as
    in conversation, you can use informal words and phrases freely.
    You can use contractions (e.g. 'I'm', 'won't', etc) too and you do not
    have to write in full sentences.

5   You can end a letter by saying how pleased you are that you are
    going to see the reader soon. You may also encourage the reader
    to write or to call you:

- *It'll be great to see you.*
- *It would be great to meet up one of these days.*
- *Can't wait to see you.*

- *Hope to hear from you soon.*
- *Stay in touch.*
- *Write soon.*

6   If you are writing to a close friend, before you sign your name, you will want to show affection by using a word or phrase such as:

- *Love,*
- *Lots of love,*
- *Much love,*
- *All my love,*
- *Love from,*

If you are writing to a friend that you do not know so well, you may prefer:

- *Best wishes,*
- *All the best,*
- *Kind regards,*
- *Regards,*

7   If you are very close to the reader, you can add a kiss or kisses after your name (X or XXX) or a hug or hugs (O or OOO).

8   If, when you have finished writing you letter, you think of something else that you want to add, you can put it after the letters, 'PS'.

Letters are still sometimes written to mark special occasions. For example, here is a letter congratulating the reader on getting a new job:

Leeds
3rd July

Hi Channa,

How are you doing? I'm just dropping you a line because I wanted to say congratulations on landing your exciting new job!

Dan and I are both very pleased for you. You told us last time we met up that you were looking around but didn't seem very optimistic about the opportunities. I know there are a lot of people out there chasing not many jobs. You must have been pretty impressive in interview!

Anyway, I just wanted to congratulate you. I hope the job is everything you want it to be and that you get to work with a great bunch of people.

Well done, Channa!

Lots of love, Sharmaline and Dan
xxx

Notice that the letter, though informal, follows the basic structure for formal letters. It has:

- an introduction where the writer says why she is writing the letter, i.e. to congratulate the reader on getting her job.

- a main part, where the writer puts background information, writing that she knew the reader was looking for a new job and that she knew finding work was difficult

- a conclusion where the writer congratulates the reader again and adds two specific wishes of her own

Another occasion which often makes people feel that they should write letters is the death of a person loved by the reader. People often feel that the seriousness of the occasion deserves a proper letter and not a quickly written email. A letter, rather than a phone call, also gives the writer time to think about what they want to say and how they are going to say it. This can be a very hard letter to write.

Stratford
13th June 2009

Dear Polly

I'm writing because I've just heard the very sad news about your dad. I just wanted to tell you how sorry I am and to let you know that I am thinking of you.

I have very fond memories of Colin. He was a very kind, warm man and always so welcoming when I came to visit. You enjoyed such a good relationship with him and remained so close throughout your adult life. I know you will be devastated by his death. I am very sorry. I know Ben will be a great comfort to you at this difficult time.

Thinking of you, Polly, and sending you all my love.

Julia

Again, this letter follows the introduction – main part – conclusion format.

- an introduction where the writer says that she has been told that the person has died.

- a main part, where the writer relates good memories of the dead person and says they know how important the person was to the reader. This part also often includes something that the writer hopes will comfort the reader.

- a conclusion where the writer usually says that they are thinking of the reader.

Blogs

A blog is a website where someone regularly writes their thoughts and opinions in the form of a *post*. Blogs usually contain text, images and links to other websites.

Blogs are written for various different reasons. Many people write blogs in order to comment on political issues or stories in the news. Some bloggers write about particular activities and all the issues that relate to them, while other people write blogs in order to sell a product or service. Some blogs, meanwhile, just describe what the blogger does in their daily life.

The style and tone of a blog will depend very much on its content. A cycling blog written by a keen cyclist might have an informative and factual tone. The blog writer, (*blogger*), wants to provide useful information for other cyclists and to share their experiences with them. They may not be so interested in entertaining their readers.

A political blog, on the other hand, might be very funny, using humour in order to criticize politicians.

The blog that someone writes about their daily life will probably have an informal tone and be written in the style of a conversation, 'chatting' to its readers as if they were friends.

Whatever the content or subject matter of the blog that you are writing, there are a few general rules.

The first – and possibly the most important – is to **consider your reader**. **Who** do you intend to read this? What are their interests and opinions, and **what do they want from your blog**? Do they want:

- information on a particular subject?
- entertainment?
- to hear your opinions?
- all of the above?

It is only by providing what your reader wants that you will keep them coming back for more.

It might help to **think of your blog as a *resource*** for the reader. For example, if you are writing a blog about a particular sport, you might like to **share tips** with the reader about techniques that you have discovered that have improved your performance. Or you might **provide links** to websites that sell equipment that you have found useful. Give your reader the advantages of your experience and knowledge.

> **Key point to remember**
> If you give links to other blogs or websites, make sure you have visited them first and are certain of their content.

Talk to your reader. Most blogs are written in a slightly informal, conversational English. This is what readers expect. It gives them the feeling that they have formed a relationship with the writer and are connecting with them. Try to imagine that you are *chatting* to your reader. **Use the sort of words and phrases that you would naturally use in conversation** with a friend. This may include words and phrases that you would not use in other forms of writing.

Be yourself. People want to read blogs with original writing and original ideas. If they come back to your blog, it is because they like reading about what *you* have to say and they want to see how *you* say it. Be confident in your style and never try to write like someone else.

Do not be afraid to start your sentences with 'I'. Generally, people do not expect blogs to read like newspapers. In other words, they do not visit a blog to read a report of facts. Most people read blogs because they give them a chance to learn about other people. They want to know *what the writer has done* and *how the writer feels* about things.

Tell your reader in the first person about your experiences and opinions.

> **Tip for success**
> Once you have developed a style of writing that you are happy with, keep using that style.

Keep your blog short. Most people spend only a few minutes of their day or week reading blogs. They simply do not have time to read a lot, no matter how interesting or amusing the writing is. Do not fill the screen with text. Leave some white space and create a clean, simple screen that the reader knows they can deal with quickly.

Write a post that readers can scan. Remember that many people who visit a blog do not read the whole text word for word. Instead they *scan* the screen, looking for particular words and phrases. They may want to get the general idea of what you have written or they may want only to find particular information. Present your blog in such a way that people scanning the text can get the most from it. You can do this by:

- writing in **short paragraphs**. It is much easier to scan a text that is broken up into many short *chunks* rather than one long block of text.

- providing **lists of information**, introduced by bullet points. Lists are quick and easy to understand.

- providing a number of **relevant titles** to break up your text. Titles naturally attract the eye and can help guide the reader to a particular part of the post.

Communicate your message quickly. Whatever message or information you are trying to communicate in your post, make sure you do it within the first few lines. Do not assume that the reader has the time or the interest to read through a long introduction. Start your point immediately you start writing.

Make use of pictures. Select attractive and relevant images to break up blocks of text. Even if your images are only for decoration, they will still make the screen look more professional and more appealing.

Finally, when you have finished writing your post, **edit your writing**. The tone of your blog might be relaxed and informal but you still need the writing itself to be correct. Some readers will stop visiting a blog because the English is poor even though they are interested in the topic. Take time to:

- remove phrases or words that are not needed
- change the order of paragraphs if this improves the post
- correct errors
- correct punctuation

> **Key point to remember**
> Get your reader's attention by saying what is most important within the first few lines.

Essays

Writing essays is difficult and a lot of people struggle with some aspect of it. However, there are a number of things that you can do to make the task easier.

Give yourself enough time. In order to write the best essay possible you will probably need to read about the essay topic and research it. All of this takes time. Writing an essay hours before you have to hand it in is very stressful and rarely results in an excellent essay. Help yourself by starting your essay well before the deadline.

Learn from others. Read essays that other people have written on a range of subjects. Consider:

- How does the writer introduce the topic?
- What phrases do they use to present their points?
- How have they linked those points?
- Do they present their points in a logical order?
- Does the conclusion successfully bring together all the ideas and points presented in the essay?

Has the writer succeeded in any of the above and, if so, what can you learn from this?

Never plagiarize. If you use someone else's words, always give the name of the person who wrote or said those words and the title of the work in which the words appeared. Never pretend that someone else's words are your own.

Read and then re-read the essay title. Before you start even to plan your essay make absolutely sure that you understand the title and what it is asking you to do. Remember that this is one of the main points on which your essay will be judged. This point may sound obvious but failure to answer the question is one of the commonest reasons for essays being marked down.

As you write more essays, you will notice that certain verbs are used again and again in essay titles. Here are some of the most common of these, together with their meanings. Make sure that you know exactly what each verb means in the context of an essay title:

- **analyse**: to examine something in detail for the purposes of explaining it
- **assess**: to judge how valuable, important or successful something is
- **compare**: to look for similarities between
- **contrast**: to look for differences between
- **evaluate**: to judge how valuable, important or successful something is
- **illustrate**: to explain something by using examples
- **outline**: to describe the most important points
- **relate**: to show how two or more issues are connected
- **summarize**: to describe the most important points

> **Key point to remember**
> No matter how well written your essay is, if you fail to answer the question, you will lose marks.

Take time to **plan your essay**. Proper planning will help you to organize and develop your thoughts so that you are clear about what you want to write. It will also ensure that you do not leave anything out. Planning does not need to take a lot of time, and there are a number of helpful and imaginative ways that you can do it. There is a section on planning your work near the beginning of this book.

Keep to the point. Do not introduce unrelated subjects or aspects of a subject that are not relevant. Even if your points are interesting, you will not gain marks for them! Ask yourself before you make each new point, how does this point answer the essay title?

Make every word count. Write clearly and concisely, avoiding over-long sentences and unnecessary adjectives. You will want to show that you have a varied vocabulary but do not be tempted to use a lot of words where a few well-chosen words will do!

Remember paragraphs. As a general rule, every time you make a separate point, start a new paragraph. Do not make your paragraphs too long. If a paragraph is very long, consider dividing it into separate points.

Remember that the type of English that is right for essays is a **slightly formal English**. It is more formal than the English that we usually use for speaking and writing emails. The English generally used in essays does not:

- include informal or slang words (unless you are quoting someone).
- include contractions, such as 'isn't' and 'won't'.
- generally include phrases that use the words 'I', 'me', or 'my':

Finally, when you have finished your essay, make sure you **read it carefully at least twice**. Be prepared at this point to make changes to it. Consider:

- the order of the points that you make. Is this logical and does the essay 'flow'?
- your choice of language. Is it clear and does it say exactly what you intended it to say?

Look out too for:

- spelling errors
- repetition of particular words. If you find you have used a word many times, consider replacing it with a synonym (a word with a similar meaning).

Tip for success

Use your computer's spellchecker to check your finished work but make sure that you read your essay for spelling errors too. Remember that a spellchecker will not find a typo such as 'from' where the intended word is 'form'.

Essay phrases and words

There are **different stages to an essay** and each stage of the essay requires you to do different things. Under the relevant heading below, you will see a range of words and phrases that can be used at a particular stage or for a particular purpose. Use these words and phrases to express your ideas in a way that is more precise and more varied.

Introductions

The following notes will help you with many of the issues you need to cover in your introduction:

Introducing the topic and purpose of an essay
Here you **say briefly what you will discuss**, making sure that it fits exactly with the title of your essay:

- *This essay will examine/look at ...*
- *This essay focuses on/discusses ...*
- *This essay considers/explores*
- *The aim of this essay is to assess/examine ...*
- *This essay seeks to evaluate/examine ...*

Defining key terms used in the essay
If there is any doubt about the meaning of a word or phrase that is important in your essay, **explain** in your introduction **what *you* mean** by that word or phrase:

- *Throughout this essay the term 'x' will refer to ...*
- *The term 'x' refers here to ...*
- *For the purposes of this essay, the term 'x' is used to mean ...*

Explaining how the essay is organised
You may like to give a very **brief summary of the structure** of your essay. This shows the teacher/examiner that you have arranged your thoughts and arguments in an organized way. It will also make it easier for them to understand exactly what you are saying:

- *This essay has been divided into three parts. The first part looks at ...*
- *There are three parts to this essay. The first part deals ...*
- *This essay has been structured in the following way.*
- *This essay begins by... It then looks at ...*
- *The first part of this essay examines/looks at ...*

Saying why the topic is particularly interesting or important
You may like to **put the topic in context**, especially if the topic is of particular relevance now:

- *It is often said that...*
- *We live in a world in which...*
- *The issue of x is one that affects everyone ...*
- *Recent years have seen an increasing interest in ...*
- *The past decade has seen the rapid growth of ...*
- *One of the most important developments in recent years is ...*

Raising an area of your topic where there is disagreement or controversy
You might like to **offer arguments against** a statement in the essay title, especially if you know of recent findings that seem to contradict it.

- *This is not always true, however.*
- *This is not always the case, however.*
- *However, recent evidence suggests that this may not be the case.*
- *More recently, research has emerged that seems to contradict ...*
- *Concerns have been recently been raised about ...*
- *There is increasing concern about ...*
- *Not everyone agrees with this statement, however ...*
- *Not everyone is in favour of x, however ...*

Mentioning an area of your topic where there is a lack of knowledge
Again, this offers you the opportunity to introduce an argument against a statement in the essay title or to at least to **show that there is doubt about the subject**.

- *Less is known, however, about the effects of ...*
- *So far there has been little discussion of ...*
- *However, very little attention has been paid to ...*
- *We hear a lot about x but we hear less about y.*

The main part of the essay

This is the part of the essay where you **discuss and develop the ideas** that you outlined in your introduction. In this part of the essay, you will need to do several things, for example, give facts and make statements, justify or disagree with statements, give reasons and suggest causes. The following notes will help you with many of the issues you need to cover in the main part of your essay:

Stating what is generally considered to be true
You will probably want to **introduce a statement that everyone** – or most people – **agree is true**. (You might then develop the point or go on to argue against that point.)

- *It is often said that ...*
- *It is certainly true that ...*
- *It is certainly the case that ...*
- *It is undoubtedly the case that ...*
- *No one would argue that ...*
- *Few people would argue that ...*
- *Few would argue that ...*

Stating that something is partly true
You may **only partly agree** with a statement:

- *There is an element of truth in this statement.*
- *There is some degree of truth in this.*
- *This is to some extent true.*
- *This is to some degree true.*

> ### Key point to remember
> When giving personal opinions in academic essays, it is generally better to avoid phrases that use the words 'I', 'me', or 'my':
>
> ✗ *I think that keeping animals in captivity is wrong for the following reasons.*
> ✗ *It's my opinion that keeping animals in captivity is wrong for the following reasons.*
> ✓ *Keeping animals in captivity is wrong for the following reasons.*

Providing facts
You might like to **refer to some new information** or statistics that relate to your topic:

- *Recent research clearly indicates/shows …*
- *Recent research suggests …*
- *A new study confirms that …*
- *A recent report revealed …*
- *It has recently emerged that …*

> ### Useful words and phrases
> The verbs 'seem' and 'appear' can be used to make these claims less definite, for example:
>
> *Government-funded research into this area appears to/seems to confirm this theory.*

Suggesting reasons for something
You might want to **suggest an explanation** – or more than one explanation – for a situation or problem that you have described:

- *Perhaps this is because ...*
- *It might be that this is caused ...*
- *This may be because of/caused by ...*
- *This may be a result/consequence of ...*
- *It is likely/possible that ...*
- *We might assume from this that ...*
- *One possible explanation is that ...*
- *We might deduce from this that ...*

Describing the result of something
If you have stated the cause of something, you might want to **say what the result is**. These words can be used to start sentences that link the cause of something with the outcome.

- *Consequently ...*
- *As a result/consequence ...*
- *The result is ...*
- *The consequence is ...*
- *It follows that ...*
- *Therefore ...*

Adding to a point that you made before
You might like to **add to a previous point**, either by saying something that you think is **equally important**:

- *Besides, ...*
- *In addition, ...*
- *Similarly, ...*
- *In the same way, ...*

or by giving a point that is **even more important**:

- *What is more, …*
- *Furthermore, …*
- *Moreover, …*
- *More importantly, …*

Introducing examples

You will almost certainly want to **provide examples of what you are claiming**. Examples provide proof for your claim and can be introduced with the following words:

- *For example …*
- *For instance …*
- *A good example of this is …*
- *An illustration/instance of this is …*

> **Useful words and phrases**
> Alternatives to the phrase '*good example*' are '*notable example*' and '*prime example*'.

Note that you can vary the structure of your sentences by sometimes using the phrases 'for example' and 'for instance' in the middle of a sentence, with commas before and after:

- *Paper recycling, **for example**, is now common practice in most countries.*

- *Cycling to work, **for instance**, can significantly reduce your carbon footprint.*

You may want to highlight the importance of one particular example, in the following way:

- *Environmental issues, **particularly/in particular** global warming, dominate the news.*

- *Environmental issues, **notably/chiefly** climate change and recycling, are at last being addressed.*

Giving different opinions

Whatever your view on a subject, you will probably need to **show that you are aware of different views**, with phrases such as:

- *It could/might be argued that …*
- *It is sometimes said that …*
- *There are those who claim that …*
- *Some claim that …*
- *Another way of looking at/viewing this is …*

Discussing differences

You may want to **highlight the differences** between two things:

- *There is a marked/sharp contrast between …*
- *x is in sharp/stark contrast to y*
- *There is a clear distinction between x and y*
- *There are significant differences between x and y*
- *This contrasts sharply with …*
- *x differs/varies widely*
- *By/In contrast, …*
- *By/In comparison, …*
- *Conversely, …*

Key point to remember

Remember that the phrases '*in contrast*', '*by comparison*' and '*conversely*' can appear in the middle of a sentence, (with commas before and after), as well as at the start of a sentence, e.g.:

Carlos was clever, handsome and charismatic. His brother, in contrast, was a plain, shy man.
Carlos was clever, handsome and charismatic. In contrast, his brother was a plain, shy man.

Reporting what someone else has said
You will sometimes want to **quote what someone else has said or written**. There are many reasons for doing this. You might want to provide support for own opinion or you may want to introduce an opinion that you can then disagree with.

- *Smith asserts/claims/proposes/suggests that ...*
- *Smith maintains/states that ...*
- *Jones comments/observes/remarks/reports/writes that ...*
- *Jones concludes that ...*
- *According to Jones, ...*
- *As Jones states/points out, ...*
- *In Jones's view/opinion, ...*
- *Jones's view/opinion is that ...*

> **Key point to remember**
> Note that the present tense is usually used in such phrases.

Introducing quotations
Often, you will need to **name not only the author of a quotation, but also the piece of writing** that the quotation comes from. This can be done in a number of ways so it is a good idea to ask your teacher if there is a recommended style:

- *Blake (1998, p. 62) asserts that "Walker hated his mother".*
- *Blake[1] claims that "Walker hated his mother".*
- *As Blake (1998, p. 62) points out, Walker had a difficult relationship with his mother.*
- *Blake (1998, p. 62) maintains that Walker had a difficult relationship with his mother.*

Saying the same thing in a different way
You will sometimes want to **make clear exactly what it is that you are saying** by repeating your point in a way that is briefer and simpler.

- *In other words, ...*
- *To put it simply, ...*
- *To put it more simply, ...*
- *That is to say, ...*
- *To look at this another way, ...*

Conclusions
The conclusion brings together all the ideas and information you have discussed. It shows the reader that the essay is complete and that the aims of the essay have been achieved. In a conclusion, you **summarize the main points** and say what the consequences of your evidence are:

- *In summary, ...*
- *To summarize, ...*
- *To sum up briefly, ...*
- *In conclusion, ...*
- *To conclude, ...*
- *It can be concluded that ...*
- *We can therefore conclude that ...*

Dissertations

A dissertation is a **long piece of writing on a particular subject**, especially one that a student does as part of their university degree. It is usually divided into a series of numbered chapters.

A dissertation is like an essay in that it is **formal in style**. The type of language that is suitable for essays is also suitable for dissertations. It does not:

- include informal or slang words.
- include contractions, such as 'isn't' and 'won't'.
- generally include phrases that use the words 'I', 'me', or 'my':

For help with formal writing, especially phrases and words to use in dissertations, see the part in this book on writing essays.

A dissertation is **very much longer than a normal essay**. It can be anything up to 10,000 words long.

It has a **more complicated structure** than an essay. This is partly because it is so much longer and partly because it examines its subject in greater depth. It is important to note that the exact structure of a dissertation will vary depending on:

- the area of study of the dissertation. Different subjects require different structures.
- the university that you belong to, or the department within that university. Different universities have different rules on how to structure a dissertation.

Key point to remember
Before you even start to plan your dissertation, make sure you have a copy of your university (or university department's) rules on how to structure a dissertation.

As we have said, the structure of a dissertation will vary, depending on the university and the subject. It is your responsibility to make sure you know exactly what your university or subject requires. The general features of the structure that are given here are therefore only a rough guide:

Title Page
Among other details, this page will include:

- the title of the dissertation
- the name of the writer
- the qualification for which the dissertation has been written
- the relevant university or other place of study
- the date that the dissertation was submitted

Table of contents
This is an index of everything that is contained in the dissertation except the title page and the table of contents.

Abstract
This will say in general terms what the dissertation is about. An appropriate length is generally agreed to be about 300-500 words.

Main part of the dissertation
This will be divided into sections or chapters. The sections or chapters will each have an introduction, a main part and a conclusion. However, it is very important that there is a link between these subsections. When you are writing this part of the dissertation, try to remember that the reader must at all times understand how one part relates to another.

Conclusion
This is where you help the reader to understand the significance of your conclusions, rather than just restating your conclusions. It can be a challenging part of the dissertation to write. Some people find it helpful to write this part of the dissertation a little time after the main

body of the text. This allows them to think more clearly about everything that they have written and to make judgements about it.

Bibliography

This should be a complete list of the books and articles, etc. that you have used in your dissertation.

Tip for success
Do not delay preparing your bibliography until the end of your dissertation. Prepare it as you are writing your dissertation.

Dissertations are complicated pieces of work and are not easy to write. You can help yourself with this challenging task by **planning the structure of your dissertation very thoroughly**. You will want to show the plan to your supervisor before you start to write it. Your discussions with your supervisor will very often result in changes to your plan so **allow yourself plenty of time for the planning stage** of the process.

For general help with planning a piece of writing, see the section on planning near the beginning of this book.

When you are ready to start writing, **do not assume that you must start at the first chapter and finish with the last**. Many people find that there is an area of the dissertation that they are more confident about. Consider starting with that area of the subject.

Most universities have a set of rules about how to present a dissertation. These rules concern, for example, the type and size of font used, the type of paper written on and the layout of the page. **Make sure that you have a copy of the presentation guidelines for your university and that you follow them**.

The **rules for good writing apply to dissertations** as they do to any other form of written work. For general help with formal writing, see the chapters in this book on writing essays and writing reports. It is worth repeating some of these rules here as they are especially true of long, complicated pieces of writing, such as dissertations.

Write clearly. You know what you mean by your writing but if you do not express yourself clearly your reader may not. Make sure your reader does not have to struggle to understand your English.

Write concisely, avoiding over-long sentences and unnecessary adjectives. These will make your English difficult to follow.

Avoid repetition. If you find you have used a word many times, consider replacing it with a synonym (a word with a similar meaning).

Remember paragraphs. Text should never appear as a long block. As general rule, every time you make a separate point, start a new paragraph.

Write paragraphs of the right length. They should not be too long or too short. Never write a paragraph of only one sentence.

Tip for success
Remember your reader at all times. Try to write English that is a pleasure to read.

You will almost certainly want to **write more than one draft of your dissertation**. Re-writing is an extremely valuable part of the process. It can be hard to see where the problems are while you are writing a piece of text. It is only when you come back to the text that you see where changes need to be made. You may find at this stage that you need to:

- explain a point more clearly
- remove a point that is not relevant
- change the order of the points that you are making

The above changes all relate to the content of your dissertation. As well as examining the content of your dissertation, you will also need to **check it thoroughly for errors**.

Remember that a supervisor who has read parts of your work will only have commented on its content or structure. They will not have brought to your attention spelling or grammatical errors. Use your computer's spellchecker to check your finished work but make sure that you **read your dissertation for spelling errors too**. Remember that a spellchecker will not find a typo such as 'from' where the intended word is 'form'.

Tip for success
Give your dissertation a separate read-through in order to check for grammatical errors and spelling errors.

Reports

A report is a **written document which presents information about a particular subject** to a particular reader or group of readers. The writer of the report has usually been asked by the reader to prepare the report.

Reports are written by people who work in many areas, for example business, government and education.

All **reports present a number of facts** which the writer examines in detail. The writer then makes judgments based on those facts. Many reports also make recommendations about things that should be done because of the facts that they have described.

Before you start writing a report, make sure that you **know exactly what it is that you want to achieve**. It may help you to form a clearer idea if you write a short paragraph describing the purpose of it.

Make sure too that you **know exactly who you are writing the report for**. You may be writing for readers with the same understanding of the subject and the same interests, or you may be writing for different types of reader. Your report will need to cover everything that your readers are expecting.

Like an essay, a report is a **formal piece of writing**. The type of English that is right for reports does not:

- include informal or slang words

- include contractions, such as 'isn't' and 'won't'.

- include words that show or cause strong emotions, such as 'horrible' and 'atrocious'

- generally include phrases that include the words 'I', 'me' or 'my'. (However, note that if the report includes recommendations, this part of the report may use such phrases.)

Although the English in your report should be formal, it should also be **clear and *readable***. 'Formal' is not the same as 'difficult'. You want your reader to **understand quickly** what you have written without having to make a lot of effort. Although it may not be possible to write a report that your reader actively *enjoys* reading, you do not want the reader to *struggle* to get through it!

Do not use long, difficult words in order to impress the reader. The use of a lot of long words can have the effect of making your writing less readable. Most readers prefer plainer, more direct English. For example, if you find yourself writing the verb 'utilize', consider whether the simpler verb 'use' could be used instead. Likewise, if you write 'dwelling', ask yourself whether 'home' would in fact be better.

Do not write long sentences. Of course you will want to write some longer and some shorter sentences in order to provide some variety in your English. However, you should try to avoid very long, complicated sentences as they are difficult to understand. Look at the following sentence:

> In terms of numbers, this is essentially an increase, albeit a small increase, and we look forward to seeing this trend continue over the forthcoming weeks and months.

Now see how a shorter sentence can say the same thing much more clearly:

> This is an increase, albeit a small one, and we look forward to seeing this trend continue.

Notice in the first sentence, the phrases and words:

- in terms of
- essentially
- over the forthcoming weeks and months

These words and phrases have *little or no meaning* in this sentence. In the second sentence, the writer has removed them without changing the meaning. If you have written a long sentence, examine the various parts of that sentence and consider whether any of the words are not needed.

As we have said, the main purpose of a report is to present facts about a subject. The purpose is *not* to describe the writer's opinions or feelings on the subject. For this reason, **do not use the words 'I', 'me' or 'my' in your writing**. You may need to suggest ideas and give possible explanations for certain facts, but you should not do so with phrases such as 'it seems to me' and 'in my opinion'. Compare the sentences below:

> ✗ *The same quarter saw sales in these markets rise by 13 percent, a development which I am convinced is due to better marketing of these products.*

> ✔ *The same quarter saw sales in these markets rise by 13 percent, almost certainly as a result of better marketing of these products.*

Similarly, the language that you use in your report:

- should not *show* your feelings
- should not *cause* strong feelings in your readers

For this reason, avoid words such as 'appalling', 'terrible' and 'fantastic'. Instead use adjectives which express the same idea but in a calmer, more formal way. Compare these sentences:

✗ *Sales for the last quarter of the year were terrible.*
✓ *Sales for the last quarter of the year were very disappointing.*

✗ *This was a fantastic achievement.*
✓ *This was a remarkable achievement.*

Remember that some people will not want to read the whole report, word for word. Instead they will want to *scan* it, getting the general idea of what you have written or looking for particular information. Present your report in a way that **allows people to read it quickly**. Consider:

- writing in **short paragraphs**. It is much easier to scan a text that is made of many short *chunks* rather than one long block of text.

- giving information in the form of **bullet points**. Bullet points are quick to understand and are an acceptable way of presenting information in reports.

- breaking up your text with **headings**. Headings will guide the reader to the parts of the report that they are interested in.

The main purpose of a report is to present information. Unlike an essay, a report does not always present information in the form of written paragraphs. You can show information very effectively in the form of **bullet points, tables, diagrams and charts**. Label any tables and diagrams, etc. clearly. Information shown in this way should relate to the writing in your report, for example:

> *Figure 1 shows that overall sales increased by 3% in the third quarter.*
> *Overall sales increased by 3% in the third quarter (see Figure 1).*

The structure of a report

The **structure of your report** will partly depend on what is contained in the report. However, most reports have a fairly similar structure:

1. Title page
2. Contents list
3. Executive summary or 'abstract'
4. Introduction
5. Main part of the report
6. Conclusions
7. Recommendations
8. Appendices
9. Bibliography

1 Title Page
Include the following formation in your title page:

- The title of the report
- The purpose of the report
- Your name and the name of the person that you have written the report for
- The date that you sent or gave the report to the reader

2 Contents list
If you have written a long report, you will need to provide a contents list. This gives the main sections and chapters of the report and the pages on which the reader will find those sections and chapters.

3 Executive summary or 'abstract'
In the executive summary or abstract, you need to give a **summary of the report**, describing briefly the most important information that is in it. The summary should not be long – about ten percent of the total report. As a rough guide, write one sentence for every main section of your report.

4 Introduction

Here, you should give the following information:

- Any background information relating to the subject that the reader should be aware of
- The purpose of the report
- Exactly which areas of your subject you deal with in the report

5 Main part of the report

This is the longest part of the report, where you say:

- What you discovered when you examined this subject
- What you decided was true after considering all the facts (the conclusions)

You will probably need to divide this part of the report into sections. Each paragraph or group of paragraphs on the same subject is a section. It is likely that each section will also need dividing into subsections. These sections and subsections will need to be numbered. The system used by most report writers is as follows:

- Each section in the main part of the report is numbered 1,2,3, etc.
- Sections within those main sections (subsections) are then numbered 1.1, 1.2, 1.3, 1.4, etc.
- If there are any subsections of those subsections, they appear as 1.1.1, 1.1.2, etc.

6 Conclusions

This is the stage at which you bring together all the conclusions that you reached in the main part of your report. Present these conclusions in the order in which they appeared. **Do not include any new information** here.

7 Recommendations

Some reports do not include recommendations. They present and examine facts but do not make suggestions about what should be done because of those facts. Some reports do include recommendations and set them out here, in a separate part of the report. Note that some reports include recommendations in the conclusion or even in the executive summary.

8 Appendices

This is the place to put information which is referred to in the report but is too detailed or complicated to include in the main part of the report. The sort of information you would put here includes:

- questionnaires
- long, detailed tables of figures
- any instructions for research referred to in the report

9 Bibliography

If you refer to a book in your report, give the following information here about that book:

- The author's or authors' name(s)
- The book's full title
- The name of the publisher and place where it was published
- The year it was first published or, the number of the edition and the date it was published

Finally, when you have finished writing your report, **read it carefully from beginning to end**. Be prepared at this point to make changes to it. Consider:

- the order in which you have given the facts. Is it logical?

- the conclusions that you have reached. Are they reasonable, considering the evidence that you have given?

- your choice of language. Is it clear and does it say exactly what you intended it to say?

If possible, leave your corrected report and come back to it a day later. Are you still satisfied with every part of it? Is there any part that you now feel you need to change? **Many people write several drafts of a report** before they are happy with it.

While you are re-reading your report, look out too for:

- typos and spelling errors

- repetition of particular words. If you find you have used a word many times, consider replacing it with a synonym (a word with a similar meaning).

- Unnecessary words. Look out for words which mean nothing. For example, a word such as 'basically' may have no meaning in a sentence.

Report phrases and words

There are **different stages to a report** and each stage of the report requires you to do different things. Under the relevant headings below, you will see a range of words and phrases that can be used at a particular stage or for a particular purpose. Use these words and phrases to express your ideas in a way that is more precise and more varied.

Introductions

Introducing the topic and purpose of the report
Here you **explain the purpose of your report** and say exactly which areas of the subject your report deals with:

- *This report will examine/look at …*
- *This report aims to/sets out to examine*
- *This report focuses on*
- *This report considers/explores*
- *The aim/purpose of this report is to assess/examine …*
- *This report seeks to evaluate/examine …*
- *This report begins by … It then looks at …*
- *The first part of this report examines/looks at …*

Defining key terms used in the report
If there is any doubt about the meaning of a word or phrase that is important in your report, **explain** in your introduction **what *you* mean** by that word or phrase:

- *Throughout this report the term 'x' will refer to …*
- *The term 'x' refers here to …*
- *For the purposes of this report, the term 'x' is used to mean …*

Raising an area of the subject where there is disagreement or controversy

You might like to **offer arguments against** something that people generally think is true.

* *This is not always true, however.*
* *This is not always the case, however.*
* *However, recent evidence suggests that this may not be the case.*
* *More recently, research has emerged that seems to contradict ...*
* *Concerns have been recently been raised about ...*
* *There is increasing concern about ...*
* *Not everyone agrees with this statement, however ...*
* *Not everyone is in favour of x, however ...*

Mentioning an area of the subject where there is a lack of knowledge

You might want to **raise an area of your report's subject that little is known about**:

* *Less is known, however, about the effects of ...*
* *So far there has been little discussion of ...*
* *However, very little attention has been paid to ...*
* *We hear a lot about x but we hear less about y.*

Referring to new information

You might like to **refer to some new information or statistics** that relate to the subject of the report:

* *Recent research clearly indicates/shows ...*
* *Recent research suggests ...*
* *Recent findings suggest ...*
* *A new study confirms that ...*
* *A recent report revealed ...*
* *It has recently emerged that ...*

> **Useful words and phrases**
> The verbs 'seem' and 'appear' can be used to make these claims less definite, for example:
>
> *These recent findings appear to/seem to confirm this theory.*

Main part of the report

This is where you describe exactly what you discovered when you examined the report's subject:

Suggesting reasons for something
You might want to **suggest an explanation** – or more than one explanation – for a situation or problem that you have described:

- *Perhaps this is because ...*
- *It might be that this is caused ...*
- *This may be because of/caused by ...*
- *This may be a result/consequence of ...*
- *It is likely/possible that ...*
- *We might assume from this that ...*
- *One possible explanation is that ...*
- *We might deduce from this that ...*

Describing the result of something
If you have stated the cause of something, you might want to **say what the result is**. These words can be used to start sentences that link the cause of something with the outcome:

- *Consequently ...*
- *As a result/consequence ...*
- *The result is ...*
- *The consequence is ...*
- *It follows that ...*
- *Therefore ...*

Adding to a point that you made before

You might like to **add to a previous point**, either by saying something that you think is **equally important**:

- *Besides, …*
- *In addition, …*
- *Similarly, …*
- *In the same way, …*

or by giving a point that is **even more important**:

- *What is more, …*
- *Furthermore, …*
- *Moreover, …*
- *More importantly, …*

Discussing differences

You may want to **highlight the differences** between two things

- *There is a marked/sharp contrast between …*
- *There is a clear distinction between x and y*
- *There are significant differences between x and y*
- *This contrasts sharply with …*
- *x differs/varies widely*
- *By/In contrast, …*
- *By/In comparison, …*
- *Conversely, …*

Key point to remember
Remember that the phrases 'in contrast', 'by comparison' and 'conversely' can appear in the middle of a sentence, (with commas before and after), as well as at the start of a sentence, e.g.:

Group A suffered few colds and infections. Group B, in contrast, reported constant ill-health.
Group A suffered few colds and infections. In contrast, Group B reported constant ill-health.

Reporting what someone else has said
You will sometimes want to **quote what someone else has said or written**:

- *Smith asserts/claims/proposes/suggests that ...*
- *Smith maintains/states that...*
- *Jones comments/observes//remarks/reports/writes that ...*
- *Jones concludes that ...*
- *According to Jones, ...*
- *As Jones states/points out, ...*
- *In Jones's view/opinion, ...*
- *Jones's view/opinion is that ...*

Key point to remember
Note that the present tense is usually used in such phrases.

Introducing quotations
Often, you will need to **name not only the author of a quotation, but also the piece of writing** that the quotation comes from. This can be done in a number of ways:

- *Blake (1998, p. 62) asserts that "Rogers was at fault here".*
- *Blake[1] claims that "Rogers was at fault here".*
- *As Blake (1998, p. 62) points out, Rogers was at fault here.*
- *Blake (1998, p. 62) maintains that Rogers was at fault here.*

Conclusions

Summarizing
You will want to **summarize the main points of your report**:

- *In summary, ...*
- *To summarize, ...*
- *In conclusion, ...*
- *To conclude, ...*
- *It can be concluded that ...*
- *We can therefore conclude that ...*
- *The following points summarize our key findings:*
- *The key findings are outlined below:*
- *It is clear that ...*
- *No conclusions were reached regarding ...*

Recommending
You may want to **advise the reader that something should be done**:

- *We strongly recommend that ...*
- *It is my recommendation that ...*
- *It is essential that ...*
- *It would be advisable to ...*
- *I urge x to ...*

Writing presentations

Why write a presentation?

The process of writing your presentation will help you to **decide** the **key points** of your talk so that you know exactly what you want to say. Deciding what to include – and what *not* to include – is very important and the key to a successful presentation.

As you write your talk, you will think of the most **logical order** in which to present your main points.

You will also make sensible decisions about what **slides** or other **visual aids** you need for your talk.

By writing the whole of your presentation in advance, you can make sure that your talk is the **right length**. It is no use preparing a brilliant talk that you cannot possibly give in the time allowed. On the other hand, you do not want to finish your talk twenty minutes early!

Giving presentations can be stressful and most people feel anxious about talking to large groups of people. If you know that you have **prepared your presentation properly**, it will give you confidence on the day.

> **Key point to remember**
> Don't leave it to the last minute to prepare your presentation. Have your presentation finished at least 24 hours in advance.

Deciding the content

Whatever your presentation is about, before you start writing it, ask yourself the following question: **What am I trying to achieve with this talk?**

The best way to be clear about this is to ask two questions:

1 **Who** is this presentation for?
2 **What** is my key message?

Who?
Always write a presentation that is suitable for your audience. Try to find out in advance as much as possible about the audience and what they will **expect from you**. If possible, speak to someone else who has given a presentation to the same audience, or at least speak to the person who has organized the talk. It will help you to plan your talk if you know the following about your audience:

- How much knowledge of your subject they have
- Their level of education
- How old they are
- How long they are able or willing to listen to a speaker

What?
The **key message** is the main thing that you want your audience to learn from your talk – or very often, the main two or three things. Before you even start to write your talk, decide what your key message is.

While you are thinking of the **purpose of the talk**, consider these questions. Is the purpose of this presentation:

- to **give your audience information?**
- to **persuade your audience to do something, for example to buy something?**
- to **entertain?**
- to **allow the audience to get to know you?**

Most presentations are intended to give the audience information. If this is your main purpose, make sure you **give the right amount of information**: too much and your audience will be unable to take it in; too little and your audience may feel that they have wasted their time.

It may not be appropriate to entertain your audience – this will, of course, depend on the subject that you are speaking about. However, when you are planning your talk, keep in mind that most people find it hard to concentrate when a speaker makes no attempt to keep their interest.

> **Key point to remember**
> Remember that if you entertain your audience, you will be more likely to persuade them or inform them!

When planning a presentation, it is useful to break it down into three parts: **the beginning, the middle and the end**.

In the beginning part of your talk, try to get your audience's attention. You might ask them to do a short activity or perhaps ask them a question. Choose something that will wake them up and involve them. **Make your audience listen to you!**

In the middle part of the talk, **tell them the facts** that they need to know. Keep it simple and limit yourself to what is really important. Do not tell your audience more than they can understand and remember.

Be aware that the last part of your talk is possibly the most important part. The audience are more likely to remember what you tell them at the end of your presentation than in the middle. Whatever your **key message** is, make sure that you **say it – or repeat it – at the end**.

> **Key points to remember**
> Involve your audience.
> Repeat your key message in the last part of your presentation.

Writing notes for a presentation

Make good notes to help you give your presentation. Very few people can give a full presentation without looking at their notes now and then. Audiences do not expect speakers to be able to do this. Write only the **main points** of your talk on **numbered postcards or 'prompt cards'**. Write one or two key points on each card and make the writing bigger and clearer than your usual handwriting. There are several good things about prompt cards:

- They remind or 'prompt' you to say your next point but you do not read from them. Audiences like you to **look at them** and **speak to them**. A speaker who looks down and reads their notes will not keep their audience's attention.

- They allow you to **see your next point very clearly**. (When you have finished saying one point, put the card to the bottom of the pile and you will see your next point.)

- They are **small**. The audience will not notice them, even if you look at them several times.

- You can **write the time** that you should get to each point **on each card**. This way you can make sure that you say everything you want to say in the time that is allowed.

> **Tip for success**
> Number your prompt cards and write the time that you should get to each point on the cards.

Writing slides for a presentation

Always **prepare your own slides**. Do not be tempted to use someone else's slides. There are several reasons for this:

- The process of preparing your own slides will help you to decide on your key points.

- It will also help you to present those points in a logical order.

- If you know exactly what is on each slide you will able to talk about each slide with confidence and authority.

Keep the **text** on your slides **simple and brief**. Do not put too much information on a slide (a very common mistake). Remember that although *you* will know your slides very well, *your audience* is looking at them for the first time. Make sure they can make sense of them very quickly. Remember too that they will only have a short time to understand what they are looking at. Limit the amount of text on a slide to **six or seven words on each line** and to **six or seven lines of text** per slide. The slide below, for example, gives as bullet points the advantages of a new product, in this case a cleaning fluid:

> ## *Keener Cleaner*
>
> - effective
> - economical
> - good for the environment
> - pleasant-smelling
> - pleasant colour
> - practical bottle

It is important also to write the text of your slides **big enough to be seen**. Remember that if you are speaking to a lot of people in a large room, the people sitting at the back will need to be able to read your slides too.

It is a good idea to write a short **title** on each slide. This should be a single word or a short phrase. The purpose is to let your audience see immediately the subject of the slide. Make sure that your **titles** are **large** – larger than the rest of the text.

Edit your slides carefully. Look over them several times, checking the spelling and the phrasing. It is embarrassing to be told by a member of the audience that there is an error on one of your slides!

> **Tip for success**
> Limit the amount of text on a slide to **six or seven words on each line** and to **six or seven lines of text** per slide.

Presentation phrases

There are **different stages to a presentation** and each stage of the presentation requires you to do different things. Under the relevant heading below, you will see a range of words and phrases that can be used at a particular stage or for a particular purpose. Use these words and phrases to express your ideas in a way that is more precise and more varied.

Introducing yourself (and thanking your audience)
If you are new to presentations, it is a good idea to **write your introduction out in full on a prompt card**. Of course, you know this information yourself, but you may be very nervous at the start of your talk. It is easy to forget what you are saying when you are nervous. A written reminder of your first few lines will give you confidence:

- *Thank you very much for coming here today.*
- *First of all, I'd like to thank you all for coming here today.*
- *I'd like to start by thanking x who invited me here to give this talk today.*
- *My name is Paola Sanchez and I'm the marketing manager for Now Systems.*
- *My name is Paola Sanchez and I'm here today to talk to you about …*
- *Let me introduce myself. My name is Paola Sanchez and …*

Introducing your talk
It is a good idea at the start of a presentation to tell your audience in a few words **what you are going to talk about**. If your audience have a clear understanding of what you are talking about from the start, it will help them to understand the whole of the talk:

- *Today/This afternoon I'm going to be talking about …*
- *My subject today is …*
- *The topic of my talk is …*
- *I'm here today to tell you about …*
- *My aim this afternoon is to …*

You might then **tell your audience about the structure of your talk**. Again, this will help with their understanding:

- *First, we're going to take a look at …*
- *After that, we'll be considering …*
- *Finally, we'll be thinking about …*
- *I'm going to divide this talk into four parts. The first part deals with … The second part looks at … etc.*

> **Useful words and phrases**
> Notice that a speaker will often say '**We're** going to consider/look at, etc.' This makes the audience feel *involved* in what the speaker is saying.

'Reminding' people

You will be stating facts in your presentation. Your **audience may already know** some of those facts. It is a good idea to show that you are aware of this:

- *As you know …*
- *You may be aware that …*
- *You may have heard of …*
- *I'm sure many of you will already know …*
- *It's often said …*

Referring to slides and other visual aids

It is likely that you will use slides or other visual aids as a part of a presentation. Try to **make a clear link between the slide and what you are saying**. The following phrases will help with this.

- *If you could just take a look at this slide …*
- *This slide shows you …*
- *This slide represents …*
- *As you can see from this graph …*
- *Looking at these figures, we can see that …*

Giving more details

Often, in a presentation you make one point and then want to **give further details about that particular point**:

- *I'd like to say a little more about this point ...*
- *I'd like to add at this point that ...*
- *Another relevant point here is ...*
- *While we're on the subject of x, it's worth also saying ...*
- *Let's consider/look at this in more detail ...*
- *I'd like us to think about this for a moment ...*

Changing the subject

At various points in your presentation, you will want to make a new point. **Introduce each new point clearly**:

- *I'd like to move on now to the issue of ...*
- *Moving on now to the subject of ...*
- *Turning to the issue of ...*
- *Let's turn now to the subject of ...*
- *The next issue I'd like to think about/focus on is ...*
- *Now we'll move on to the subject of ...*
- *Let's look now at the issue of ...*

Using questions to make a point

You can **introduce a point by asking a question**. This might be a general point or a point that will especially interest the audience:

- *So, how does this relate to us?*
- *So why is this of interest?*
- *So why have I brought this to your attention?*
- *So why is this an advantage/a benefit?*
- *How much will all of this cost?*
- *What does this mean for ...?*
- *And why is this important/significant?*
- *So where does this lead/take us?*

> **Key point to remember**
> Introduce each new point that you make clearly.

Paraphrasing (saying something in a different way)
You may want to make a point clear by **expressing something in a different way**. These phrases will help:

- *In other words …*
- *So what I'm saying is …*
- *To put it another way …*
- *To put it more simply …*
- *Another way of putting this is …*

Returning to a point you made earlier
You might want to **show how a new point relates to an earlier point** in the presentation:

- *As I said before …*
- *Going back to what I said earlier …*
- *To return to a point I made earlier …*
- *Earlier in the talk, I mentioned …*
- *You'll recall I mentioned x earlier …*
- *This relates to a point I made earlier about …*
- *Let's look back at something I said earlier …*

> **Tip for success**
> Linking a new point with something you said earlier will
> help your audience to understand your presentation.

Summarizing your presentation
Towards the end of your talk, you may like to **remind your audience of the main points** you have made:

- *We've covered a lot of ground today. Let me quickly summarize the main points …*

- *Let's summarize briefly what we've looked at today …*
- *I'd like to quickly go over the main points of today's presentation …*
- *If I can just sum up the main points of the presentation …*
- *To finish, I'd just like to remind you of some of the issues we've covered today …*

Concluding

Now is the time to **tell your audience the thing – or the things – that you want them to remember**:

- *I'll conclude very briefly by saying that …*
- *I'll finish by saying …*
- *Let me end by …*
- *I'd like to leave you with this thought …*

Finishing a presentation

Most speakers like to **let their audience know that they have finished their presentation**:

- *I think that's everything I wanted to say today.*
- *I think I've covered everything I wanted to say today.*
- *I think that's about it.*

You will then want to **thank your audience** and, if there is time, **invite them to ask you questions** relating to the subject:

- *Thank you all very much for taking the time to listen to this presentation.*
- *Does anyone have any questions (or comments)?*
- *Would anyone like to ask any questions?*
- *Please feel free to ask questions.*
- *If anyone has any questions, I'd be very happy to answer them.*
- *We have ten minutes left now if anyone has any questions they would like to ask.*

> **Tip for success**
> Always let your audience know that you have finished your presentation and remember to thank them for listening.

CVs

A CV, (curriculum vitae), is a document that you send to someone when you are applying for a job. It gives details of your qualifications and of the work that you have done in the past and are doing now. It also gives your full name and contact details. 'CV' is the word used in British English. In American English, this document is called a résumé.

People usually send a *cover letter* or *letter of application* with their CV. You will find help with this type of letter in the part of this book on writing letters.

CVs vary in length. In the UK, it is generally agreed that **two or three pages of A4** is about the right length. In the US, the résumé tends to be shorter, many people recommending that it should be no longer than **one side of A4**.

Whether you are writing a one-page document or a two- to three-page document, there are a number of things that you must keep in mind. The first of these is that the reader of your CV will probably assess your CV along with *many* others. They will probably have limited time to do this. Therefore, your CV must be:

- quick and easy to read
- clear and concise
- pleasant to look at

> **Key point to remember**
> Keep your CV concise. The reader will not have time to read through five or six pages, no matter how impressive the details.

Remember that if your CV is poorly presented, the reader will be more likely to reject it even if your skills and experience make you the perfect candidate for the job. Your CV must therefore have:

- a **clear structure**. Be sure to organize the information under headings such as *profile* and *experience*.

- **plenty of white space**. A dense page with too much text is difficult and unpleasant to read.

Make sure too that you write your CV on **good quality, clean paper**. Remember that the reader does not know you. The only evidence that they have of your character and your suitability for the job is the CV they have in their hand. Make it look impressive.

Remember that the information you include must be **relevant** to the work. Do not be tempted to include facts that do not directly relate to the job that you are applying for. A reader with little time to assess several CVs might be distracted by this and may not actually see the important information.

> **Key point to remember**
> Presentation is extremely important in CV writing.
> Two CVs with the same information will be judged
> differently by the reader if one CV is very much smarter
> and better organized than the other.

Here is a general layout for a CV. The structure and layout of CVs varies but this format is generally accepted. Notice the clear headings and the white space around the paragraphs.

[1]**Helena Shapur**

[2]12 Green Lane, Brighton, Sussex, BT1 3EY

Mobile 0779 234567   [3]h.shapur@xyz.co.uk

[4]Personal profile

An enthusiastic, self-motivated professional in the field of online team management, I have a passion for the potential of the Internet and an in-depth understanding of a wide variety of web technologies. I am committed to developing the same values and enthusiasm within my team.

[5]Career Summary

1998 – present   Development Team Leader, Getaways.com

I joined this online travel company as a web developer, and in 2000 moved up to the position of Development Team Leader. During this exciting time, traffic to the site multiplied by more than 100 times. Working with a close-knit team, I gained real understanding of the nature of large-scale website management.

1996 – 1998   Web developer, Toprank Recruitment, Brighton

Having gained a taste for web technologies, I joined this small start-up, developing an IT recruitment website. Programming the site's search engine, I learned ASP, Javascript and SQL. I also gained valuable experience of developing a website as part of a team.

1994 – 1996   Junior Programmer, Oakleaf Processing, Manchester

As part of a small team, I developed and coded accounts and customer databases for clients using Delphi. As the Internet started to take off, I taught myself HTML and designed and created the company's first website.

[6]Education and Qualifications
1990–1993 Merseyside University, BSC Computer Science (2:1)
1987–1989 Prince of Wales Sixth From College, Brighton 3 A-levels
1982–1987 St James High School, Brighton 9 O-levels

[7]Hobbies and Interests
I am an avid reader and film-goer. I like cooking, gardening and writing children's stories.

[8]Referees
(professional)   (personal)
Martin Walker   Elizabeth Joachim
Toprank Recruitment   12, Cotswold Ave
Mill Street   Whalleyrange
Brighton BN2 34Y   Manchester MU32 6TF

1   Give your name in full at the top of the CV where it can easily be seen.
2   Give your contact details just below your name.
3   Always provide your email address.
4   Write a personal profile at the top of your CV. In two or three sentences, summarize the skills and personal qualities that make *you* the person for this job. Try to link your skills and qualities directly to what you have recently achieved at work.
5   Always provide details of your most recent employment first and then work backwards.
6   Likewise, provide details of your most recent qualifications first and work backwards.
7   The reader will want to get some sense of what you are like as a person, so do include brief details of your interests, especially if those interests are relevant.
8   Most employers expect to see details for two referees (= people who will give information about your abilities or character).

Instructions

You will see instructions on signs in public places, in recipe books, in operating manuals, on packets of food and a variety of other places.

Instructions are generally **written using the imperative form** of the verb. The imperative is formed by using the infinitive form of the verb without 'to':

> *Keep off the grass*
> *Stop when lights show*
> *Now add the garlic and tomatoes.*
> *Shake before use*
> *Re-connect the plug to the power socket.*

Negative imperatives are generally formed by putting 'do not' or 'never' before the verb:

> *Do not open door while wash is in progress.*
> *Do not leave in bright sunlight.*
> *Never leave small children unattended.*

Notice that sentences that give instructions often leave out words that you would find in ordinary sentences. For example, they sometimes do not include articles, ('the' or 'a'). Sometimes they leave out objects. For example, the sentence above reads, 'Do not leave in bright sunlight'. It does not say 'Do not leave *this item* in bright sunlight'.

Key point to remember
Instructions are generally not written as complete sentences and they do not show who must follow the instruction.

Think carefully about your readers before you start to write your instructions. Consider:

- How much or how little do they know about the task for which you are writing instructions?

- How old are they?

The answers to these two questions will help you to decide:

- The level of your instructions and **how many steps you include**. If the reader knows little or nothing about the task that you are describing, you may need to give instructions for every action that is required, even if some of the instructions seem very simple to you.

- How **simple or difficult the language of your instructions is**. Will they, for example, understand technical terms? If not, you will have to find a way of giving instructions that involves simple language that anyone could understand.

- Whether you need to **add warnings to your instructions** for younger readers. For example, in a recipe you may need to warn the reader that a food is hot at a particular point and they must not touch it. Or you may decide to tell the younger reader to ask an adult for help with a particular action.

When you are writing instructions, make sure that they are **easy to follow**. Make them as **clear** and as **simple** as possible. Remember that the reader will be using your instructions because they have not done a particular task before.

Use **short, simple sentences**. Long sentences are hard to follow and can confuse the reader. Compare the following instructions for making chocolate fridge cake:

Recipe 1

Melt butter in pan and add cocoa, sugar and syrup, bringing to the boil then remove from heat and stir in broken biscuits, mixing well. Press mixture into tin then melt chocolate in microwave, (medium power for 15 seconds), spreading the chocolate when melted evenly over the surface using palette knife and refrigerate before slicing.

Recipe 2

Melt butter in pan.
Add cocoa, sugar and syrup to pan and bring mixture to the boil.
Remove from heat and stir in broken biscuits. Mix well.
Press mixture into tin.
Melt chocolate in a microwave, (medium power for 15 seconds).
Spread melted chocolate evenly over the surface using a palette knife and refrigerate before slicing.

Recipe 1 is confusing and difficult to follow for the following reasons:

- It uses long sentences. It gives you ten instructions in just two sentences. This is too much information for the reader to take in.

- It gives some instructions in a form that is not the imperative. For example, it uses the ing-form of the verb 'bring' in 'bringing to the boil' and not the clearer 'bring to the boil'.

- It relies on words such as 'then' and 'and' to tell the reader the order in which they should do different things. This is hard for the reader to understand and remember.

Recipe 2 is clear and easy to follow:

- It breaks up the ten instructions into seven short sentences.

- The reader can easily see the order of those instructions as each new step starts a new line.

- It uses the imperative form, (melt the butter, remove from heat, press mixture, etc.), for every instruction.

> **Key point to remember**
> Avoid using the passive form, ('be verb-ed') when writing instructions. The active form is clearer:
>
> ✗ The red button is pressed to start the wash cycle.
> ✓ Press the red button to start the wash cycle.

It is helpful to **give instructions as a list** rather than a paragraph. A list clearly separates the different actions that the reader must do and makes the instructions easier to follow. Your list may be numbered, or may have bullet points:

Grill from frozen in 8 minutes
1 Preheat grill to moderate heat.
2 Remove all packaging.
3 Place on the base of a grill pan and grill for 5-7 minutes.

Planting your seeds
- Fill your pot with compost.
- Spread the seed over the compost surface.
- Water the compost generously.

Think about the order of the actions that you are describing. Always give instructions for actions in the order in which you would perform them. This is not always as obvious or as easy as it sounds! Some actions can be performed at different stages of a task. Try to work out the most logical point at which to perform such actions. It can be helpful to write each step of a task on a different Post-it® note. You can then move the notes around until you have decided the most sensible order.

Consider **giving a title to your list of instructions**. The title should explain what the reader will achieve by following your instructions. You may want to make this sound exciting and appealing, especially if you are writing for children:

> *How to make the best chocolate brownies ever!*
> *How to make a mask that will scare your mum and dad!*

You may be writing instructions for a number of different but related tasks, for example, the different functions of a piece of equipment. It is useful here to **give short titles** for the various tasks, explaining what your instructions will help the reader to do. Note that the '-ing' form of the verb is usually used for titles like these:

> *Setting the Programme 'P'*
> *Deleting/Changing the Programme*
> *Cleaning the appliance*

If the reader needs any items in order to perform your instructions, it is useful to **give a list of these items** before the instructions:

> You will need:
> 2 pieces card (20cm x 20 cm)
> glue
> 2 lengths thin ribbon (width 3mm)
> sequins

Use helpful pictures or diagrams. Pictures and diagrams are especially useful:

- If the task for which you are giving instructions needs the reader to use different pieces of equipment or complicated equipment.

- If you are writing for children.

Choose your **pictures carefully**. Pictures or diagrams that are well-chosen and clearly labelled will show the reader immediately what things look like. (It can be difficult to describe in words the appearance of a particular thing or part.) They will also show how big or small one thing is compared with another thing. This can help to make sense of instructions. Make sure that your pictures or diagrams are:

- **clear and large enough** for the reader to see all the important parts.

- **clearly labelled**. If you are using lines to point to different parts of a picture, make sure the reader can see exactly which parts of the picture the lines are pointing to.

> **Tip for success**
> Give the right number of labels. Label the parts that the reader needs to know about but do not label every part.

You may find it helpful to **test your instructions** to make sure that they work. Test your instructions on people who have not seen your instructions before or have not done the task that you are describing. This will show you:

- where your instructions are not clear.

- where you have missed out an important step or piece of information.

Choose the people to test your instructions carefully – they should be typical of the sort of person who will be using your instructions. To learn the most from this activity:

- Ask the person or people to read through your instructions carefully and then ask them if they have any questions or comments.

- Ask questions that will show whether they have understood your instructions.

- If possible, watch the group try to perform the task by following your instructions. Afterwards, ask them how easy they found the task. Were there any instructions that they found confusing?

You can then rewrite any part of your instructions that was not clear or give instructions for any part of the task that was missing.

Leaflets and Flyers

A leaflet or flyer is a printed sheet of paper that gives information about something. Leaflets are given to a large number of people free of charge.

Leaflets do a variety of things. They may simply give information, for example on a particular health problem, or on the refuse collection in a particular area. They may try to persuade people to buy a particular product or service, or they may try to persuade people to have a particular belief.

Whatever the purpose of a leaflet, all leaflets have a few features in common. **Leaflets are small**. Most are just one sheet of paper, sometimes folded in two. (This is necessary as they will be picked up, quickly read, and often then put in a pocket or bag.) Consequently, leaflets generally contain **only the most important facts** on a particular subject and they **communicate those facts in just a few words**.

When you are writing and designing a leaflet, keep in mind that people generally **look at a leaflet very quickly**. Remember:

- Include the most important information
- Do not include information that is not important
- Keep the text – or texts – short
- Express your points clearly so that they are easy to understand
- Include a telephone number/website address or other contact information

Before you start to write your leaflet, **draw a rough sketch** of how you want it to look. Plan where you are going to put the title, the words, and any pictures you are using.

Try to make the leaflet look attractive and choose an image or images that will capture people's attention. **The right image or images** will also **help to communicate your message**.

Do not put too much in your leaflet. Remember that people need to be able to read a leaflet quickly. If they think that your leaflet will take them too long to read, they may not even pick it up! **Leave plenty of white space** around the text and images.

You can design your leaflet in a number of ways, even if it is a single-sheet leaflet. For example, you could put just a title and image on the front of the leaflet and the words themselves on the back. You may decide to put both images and text on both sides of the leaflet. **Make these important decisions before you even start to write the text**.

> **Tip for success**
> Before you do anything else, plan the overall design of your leaflet.

When you have prepared an overall design for your leaflet, it is time to choose the words. The best way to do this is to try to **see those words through the reader's eyes**. Imagine the questions the reader might ask when they pick up your leaflet.

Your first task, therefore, is to work out **who your typical reader is**. It is only when you have worked this out that you can start to work on the words.

For example, imagine you are preparing a leaflet for a company that delivers boxes of organic fruit and vegetables to people's houses. The typical reader is a person who has at some point considered having a box like this delivered. The reader now wants to find out how your particular company would provide such a service. You can assume that the reader is interested in this type of service because one or more of these is true:

- They like good quality food.
- They care about the environment.
- They want to support small, independent companies.

They will therefore probably want answers to the following questions:

- How good is the food?
- Is it truly organic?
- How 'green' is the company?
- Who runs this company?

On the basis of these questions, the facts that you would want to include in your leaflet are:

- The food is of the highest standard – fresh and delicious.
- The food is grown according to strict organic standards, without pesticides.
- The company respects the environment in everything it does, for example in using only crops grown locally and in using very little packaging.
- This is a small, local, family-run company.

Other facts that *any* reader will want to know are:

- How much does it cost? (Are there different prices for different size boxes?)
- How convenient is it? (Can I choose what fruit and vegetables I have in my box?)

What is important is that you **remember to keep the reader's needs in mind**. *Only* include information that is interesting and useful to them. *Do not* be tempted to give a lot of detailed information.

Tip for success

Before you include information in your leaflet, ask yourself these two questions:

Will the reader want to know this?
Will the reader understand this?

When you know what information you want to include in your leaflet, you must decide how you are going to present that information. A list of **bullet points is a very clear way of presenting key information**. Look at the text in the following leaflet:

Greener Gardening – Local Garden Service

We do all types of gardening tasks, including garden design, hedge trimming, garden maintenance, lawn maintenance, flower beds, tree & shrub planting and grass cutting.

Now see how a list of bullet points can make the same information much clearer:

Greener Gardening – Local Garden Service

We do:
· Garden design
· Hedge trimming
· Garden maintenance
· Lawn maintenance
· Flower beds
· Tree & shrub planting
· Grass cutting

Your leaflet may include the type of information that you cannot present in a list. For example, you may need to explain a number of facts, requiring you to write a series of paragraphs. If you are including a lot of information, remember to **break up the text with titles** for the different paragraphs.

Look at the text in the following medical leaflet:

> Symptoms of the virus may include a sore throat, headache, fever, loss of appetite or extreme tiredness. Call your doctor immediately if you are pregnant or your condition suddenly gets much worse. Some people are more at risk of serious illness if they catch the virus. At risk are people with long-term lung disease, heart disease and kidney disease.

Now see how titles can make the same information much clearer:

> **Common Symptoms**
> Symptoms of the virus may include a sore throat, headache, fever, loss of appetite or extreme tiredness.
>
> **Call your doctor immediately if:**
> You are pregnant or your condition suddenly gets much worse.
>
> **High-risk groups**
> Some people are more at risk of serious illness if they catch the virus. At risk are people with long-term lung disease, heart disease and kidney disease.

Get your reader's attention from the start. Make the first line of your leaflet count. For example, rather than starting the text by describing your company, you could present the reader with the problem that your product or service will solve. Look how one home-delivery pizza company starts their leaflet:

> *Sandro's Pizzas*
> *We deliver hot, tasty pizzas within a two-mile radius of Littleport.*

Now see how effective it can be to take a different approach, talking directly to the reader:

> *Paolo's Pizzas*
> *Hungry but had enough of cooking? We deliver hot, tasty pizzas …*

Include quotations. If you are trying to sell a product or service with your leaflet, you may like to include quotations from previous satisfied customers (though first check with the customer that they are happy for this to happen!):

> *"The most delicious, authentically Italian pizzas I've ever eaten in this country!" (K Peters, Littleport)*

Use simple language. Keep the language of your leaflet simple. Never include technical terms that your readers may not know. Make the sentences short so that the leaflet can be read and understood quickly.

Provide the right contact details. Will the readers of your leaflet want to call you or go to your website? Do they need to know where your office is or how to email you? Make sure you provide the contact details that your reader needs.

Make your contact details clearly visible. Write them where the reader will see them. The top or bottom of a leaflet is usually clearer than the middle of a piece of text. Consider writing them on *both* sides of the leaflet.

Edit your leaflet. Remember that your leaflet is going to be read by members of the public and you need to create the best possible impression. The spelling, grammar and punctuation in your leaflet must therefore be perfect. Read and re-read your finished leaflet. If possible, arrange for someone else to check it.

Test your leaflet on a friend or colleague. Show them your leaflet for ten seconds only. Now ask them two questions, (getting the answer for the first question before you ask the second):

1 What was the main purpose of the leaflet?
2 Tell me three things you have learned from the leaflet.

Could your friend/colleague tell you the main purpose of the leaflet? Were the three things they learned from the leaflet the three *key* things that you want your readers to notice? If their answers were not what you were hoping for, consider re-writing parts of your leaflet.

> **Tip for success**
> Take time to prepare your leaflet properly. A badly written leaflet may do more harm than good no matter how many people read it.

Common mistakes and controversial issues

Words that are often confused

Homophones

Homophones are words which sound the same but are spelled differently, and it is easy to become confused by them:

affect Affect is a *verb*: *How will this new law affect me?*	*effect* Effect is a *noun*: *What will the effect of the new law be?*
already Already is an *adverb*. If something has already happened, it has happened before the present time: *I've already called an ambulance.*	*all ready* In the phrase 'all ready', 'all' is a *quantifier* meaning the whole of a group or a thing, and ready is an *adjective*: *Are you all ready to go?*
alter Alter is a verb, meaning 'to change': *Nothing in the house had altered since 1960.*	*altar* An altar is the holy table in a church: *The priest stood in front of the altar.*
anyone Anyone is a pronoun and always refers to people: *Has anyone seen my hat?*	*any one* In the phrase 'any one', 'one' is a pronoun or a determiner that can refer to a person or a thing, depending on the context: *We never spend long in any one place.* *It could have happened to any one of us.*
bare Bare is an adjective meaning 'not covered' or 'not wearing any clothes': *We ran along the beach with bare feet.*	*bear* A bear is a wild animal: *There are bears in the woods.*

board	**bored**
A board is a flat piece of wood: *They nailed a board over the window.*	If you are bored, you are not interested by something: *I was so bored at school today.*

coarse	**course**
Coarse is an *adjective* meaning 'having a rough texture' or 'talking and behaving in a rude way': *The sand was very coarse.* *His manners are coarse.*	Course is a *noun* with several meanings, including 'a series of lessons' and 'a route or path': *The plane changed course.* *I did a course in art history.*

compliment	**complement**
A compliment is a nice thing that someone says about someone or something. Compliment can also be used as a verb: *They paid him a lot of compliments.* *She complimented me on my roses.*	If people or things complement each other, they have different qualities that go well together: *The dry wine complements this rich dish perfectly.*

counsellor	**councillor**
A counsellor gives people advice, often on personal matters, as a job: *They went to see a marriage counsellor.*	A councillor is an official in a local council: *She was elected as a councillor last year.*

dependent	**dependant**
Dependent is an *adjective*. If you are dependent on someone or something, you rely on them: *Their economy is very dependent on oil.*	Dependant is a *noun*. Your dependants are the people you are financially responsible for: *He has a large income and no dependants.*

discreet	**discrete**
If you are discreet, you are careful to avoid attracting attention or revealing private information: *I made a few discreet inquiries about her.*	If things are discrete, they are not joined or connected in any way: *I met him on three discrete occasions.*

draft A draft of a piece of writing is a first, rough version of it: *He showed me the first draft of his story.*	***draught*** A draught is a current of air: *There's a draught coming in through that window.* Note that in American English, this is spelled 'draft'.
draw Draw is a *verb* meaning to make a picture with a pencil: *Shall we draw a picture?*	***drawer*** A drawer is part of a desk, cupboard, etc.: *I put the papers away in a drawer.*
everyone Everyone is a pronoun and always refers to people: *Everyone enjoyed the show.*	***every one*** In the phrase 'every one', 'one' is a pronoun or a determiner that can refer to a person or a thing, depending on the context: *They have talked to every one of my classmates.* *We have eaten every one of the biscuits.*
hoard If you hoard things such as food or money, you save or store them for yourself: *She hoarded jars of fruit in the cellar.* Hoard can also be a *noun*: *We found a hoard of guns under the floorboards.*	***horde*** A horde is a large crowd of people: *Hordes of shoppers crowded outside the store.*
hole A hole is an opening or a hollow space in something: *There's a hole in my shoe.*	***whole*** Whole is a quantifier meaning 'all of something': *He ate the whole loaf.*

its Its means 'belonging to it': *The dog wagged its tail.*	**it's** it's means 'it is' *It's going to be difficult to fit in all this work.*
led Led is the past participle of the verb 'lead': *He led me into a small room.*	**lead** Lead is a *noun*, meaning 'a soft, grey metal': *The roof is covered with lead.* Lead is also a *verb*, but it has a different pronunciation.
licence Licence is a *noun*: *I showed him my driving licence.*	**license** License is a *verb*: *We are not licensed to serve alcohol.* Note that in American English, *licence* is used for the verb and the noun.
pedal Pedal is a *noun* meaning the part of a bike you press with your foot, or a *verb* meaning to press that part: *Put your foot on the pedal.* *You'll have to pedal harder.*	**peddle** If you peddle something, you sell it: *He was caught peddling drugs.*
practice Practice is a *noun*: *I did my piano practice.*	**practise** Practise is a verb: *I practised the piano.* Note that in American English, *practice* is used for the verb and the noun.

principle Principle is a *noun* meaning 'a belief about what is right or wrong' or 'a basic rule': *Eating meat is against my principles.* *We learned the basic principles of yoga.*	***principal*** Principal is an *adjective* meaning 'most important': *Bad weather was the principal reason for the failure of the expedition.* Principal can also be a noun meaning 'the person in charge of a school or college': *She was sent to the principal's office.*
site A site is an area that is used for a particular purpose or where something happens: *He works on a building site.* *This is the site of the explosion.*	***sight*** Sight is the ability to see, and a sight is something you can see: *She lost her sight in an accident.* *I faint at the sight of blood.*
stationery Stationery is a *noun* meaning 'paper, envelopes and writing equipment': *Envelopes are kept in the stationery cupboard.*	***stationary*** Stationary is an *adjective* meaning 'not moving': *I drove into a stationary vehicle.*
story A story is something you read in a book: *I bought a book of fairy stories.*	***storey*** A storey is a level of a building: *My office is in a six storey building.*
whether Whether is a *conjunction* used to talk about a choice or doubt between two or more alternative: *I can't decide whether to have soup or salad.*	***weather*** Weather is a *noun* we use to talk about rain, snow, sun, etc.: *The weather was great in Portugal.*

whose	**who's**
Whose is a *pronoun* and a *determiner* used to ask questions about who something belongs to, or to talk about things connected to a particular person: *Whose shoes are these?* *He helped a woman whose face was covered with blood.*	Who's means 'who is': *Who's going to do the washing up?*
witch	**which**
Witch is a *noun*, meaning an evil magic woman: *We painted a witch on a broomstick.*	Which is a *pronoun* and a *determiner* used to ask questions when there are two or more possible alternatives, or to talk about things connected to a particular person: *Which is your cabin?* *I took the coat which looked warmest.*
your	**you're**
Your is a *pronoun* showing that something belongs to you or relates to you: *Where is your car?*	You're means 'you are': *You're late again.*

Other words that are often confused

These words do not sound the same, but they are spelled in quite a similar way, and often cause confusion:

accept Accept is a *verb* and means 'agree to have': *I cannot accept money from you.*	**except** Except is a *preposition* and a *conjunction* meaning 'not including': *Everyone was invited except Flora.*
adverse Adverse is a formal *adjective* meaning 'bad' or 'negative': *Do not attempt the climb in adverse weather conditions.*	**averse** If you are averse to something, you do not like it: *I'm not averse to a sing-song now and then.*
advice Advice is a *noun*: *Can you give me some advice about growing roses?*	**advise** Advise is a *verb*: *I advised him to wait a bit longer.*
beside Beside means 'next to': *Put the chair beside the window.*	**besides** Besides means 'as well' or 'in addition to': *I don't need any help. Besides, I've nearly finished.* *He designed houses, office blocks, and much else besides.*
censure Censure is a formal verb, meaning 'to criticize strongly'. It is also a noun meaning the criticism: *They were censured for their failure to implement safety measures.* *The company received censure for its poor safety record.*	**censor** Censor is a verb meaning 'to cut out parts of speech or writing'. It is also a noun meaning the person who does this: *His letters home from the war were heavily censored.* *Government censors cut out much of what he wrote.*

continual Continual is used to mean that something happens without interruption, and also that something happens repeatedly: *I'm fed up with this continual noise.* *There have been continual demands for action.*	**continuous** Continuous is only used for things that happen without interruption and do not stop at all: *He has a continuous buzzing sound in his ear.*
definite If something is definite, it is firm and clear and not likely to be changed: *Do we have a definite date for the meeting?*	**definitive** Something that is definitive provides a firm, unquestionable conclusion: *No one has come up with a definitive answer.*
dessert A dessert is the sweet dish you eat at the end of a meal: *Shall we have a dessert?*	**desert** A desert is a large, dry sandy area: *We travelled through the Sahara Desert.*
elder Elder is used when you are saying which of two people was born first. It is not used with *than*: *I live with my elder sister.* *He is the elder of the two.*	**older** Older simply means 'more old', and can be used of people or things, and can be followed by *than*: *My car is older than yours.*
flout If you flout a law or a rule, you do not obey it: *He accused the president of flouting international law.*	**flaunt** If you flaunt something, you show it off in an obvious way: *I saw her at the party, flaunting her jewellery.*

infer If you infer something, you draw a conclusion from what you have seen, heard or read: *From his resignation letter, I inferred that he had been forced to leave.*	**imply** If you imply something, you say it in an indirect way: *She implied that he owed her money.*
lay Lay is a *transitive* verb meaning 'to put something somewhere carefully', and must have an object: *Mothers often lay babies on their backs to sleep.* It is not correct to say 'I'm going to lay down' – you should use *lie* for this. Lay is also the past tense of *lie*: *We lay on the floor.*	**lie** Lie is an *intransitive* verb meaning 'to be in a horizontal position': *I want to lie down.*
loose Loose is an *adjective* meaning 'not firmly fixed': *The bolts had worked loose.*	**lose** Lose is a *verb* meaning 'to not have something any more' or 'to be defeated': *I'm always losing my keys.* *I think we're going to lose the match.*
personal Personal is an *adjective* meaning 'private' or 'relating to a particular person': *He asked me some very personal questions.* *She has her own personal helicopter.*	**personnel** Personnel is a *noun* meaning 'the people who work in an organization': *All military personnel must report to base.*

quite	quiet
Quite is an *adverb* and used to mean 'very' in a less emphatic way: *It was quite expensive.*	Quiet is an *adjective* and describes things or people that do not make much noise: *She had a very quiet voice.*

These groups of three words are among the most commonly misused words in English. They are all extremely frequent, so it is important that you are confident about using them correctly.

they're	They're means 'they are': *They're going to come on the train, I'll be angry if they're late again.*
their	Their is the possessive pronoun from 'they': *They forgot to bring their coats.* *Their faces were white and tear-stained.*
there	There is a pronoun and adverb used to show position or direction, to show that something exists, and at the beginning of many sentences and phrases: *There's your jacket.* *Can you see the lion over there?* *The old buildings are still there today.* *There must be another way of doing this.* *There are three churches in our town.*
too	Too is used before adjectives to mean 'more than is good': *It's too hot in here.* It also means 'as well': *I want some too.*

to	To is a preposition that is used in many ways, but the main ones are showing direction, showing who receives something, and forming the infinitive: *We went to the zoo.* *I gave it to John.* *I need to buy a new coat.*
two	Two is the number 2: *I have two brothers.*
we're	We're means 'we are': *We're having a party.* *I'll phone you when we're there.*
were	Were is the past tense of *be* when the subject is plural: *We were very happy.* *They were going to tell you.*
where	Where is used to talk about the location of things or to ask questions about the location of things: *Where do you live?* *I left the keys where Kabelo would be sure to find them.*

Words that are often spelled wrongly

These are words which people often misspell. A few of them are difficult words, but most of them are quite common, and it is important to spell them correctly.

accidentally	Don't forget -*ally* at the end, not just -ly.
accommodation	Double *c* and double *m*. This is one of the most commonly misspelled words in English.
acquire	Don't forget the *c* before the *q*.
advertisement	Don't forget the *e* after the *s*.
apparent	Double *p* but only one *r*.
beautiful	Learn the group of vowels – *eau* – at the beginning.
because	Remember *au* after the *c*.
believe	Remember *ie*, not *ei*.
Britain	Don't forget the *i* in the second syllable.
Caribbean	Only one *r*, but double *b*.
catastrophe	Unusually for English, the final *e* is pronounced, but remember it is only one *e* – don't be tempted to write y or ee.
category	Remember it's *e* in the middle, not i or a.
definite/definitely	Remember that there are two *i*'s and no *a*'s in this word.
different	Double *f* and don't forget the *e* after them.

discipline	Don't forget the *c* after the *s* or the *e* at the end.
embarrassing	Double *r* and double *s*.
encyclopaedia or *encyclopedia*	Formerly, British English used the first of these spellings, but the second is now used commonly. American English uses *encyclopedia*.
environment	Don't forget the *n* in the middle of this word.
especially	Remember that this word starts with *e*.
existence	This word ends *-ence*, not *-ance*.
favourite	Don't forget the *u* in the middle of this word. However, in American English, this word is spelled *favorite*.
foreign	Remember *ei* in the second syllable, and don't forget the *g*.
forty	Unlike *four*, there is no *u* in this word.
gauge	Remember the vowel sound is *au*.
government	Don't forget the *n* in the middle of this word. Remember that it comes from the word 'govern'.
grammar	Remember that this word ends *-ar*, not *-er*.
guarantee	Remember the *u* in the first syllable of this word.
independent	Remember that this word ends *-ent*, not *-ant*.
island	Don't forget the *s*.

leisure	Remember that in this word, *e* comes before *i*, which is the other way round from the usual rule.
library	Don't forget the *r* after the *b*.
lightning	Do not be tempted to add an e after *light*.
manoeuvre	The British spelling of this word (both the noun and the verb) has the complicated set of vowels *oeu* in it. The American English spelling of this word is *maneuver*.
mediaeval or *medieval*	Formerly, British English used the first of these spellings, but the second is now used commonly. American English uses *medieval*.
millennium	Double *l* and double *n*.
miniature	Don't forget the second *i*.
minuscule	Note that the second vowel is *u*, not i. Try to think of it as beginning with *minus-*, not mini-
occurrence	Double *c* and double *r*.
opportunity	Double *p* and don't forget the *r* before the *t*.
possess/possession	Two lots of double *s*.
privilege	Remember that the middle vowel is *i*, and the last vowel is *e*. There are no a's in this word.
profession/professional/ professor	Remember there is only one *f* in these words.

pronunciation	Do not be tempted to add an *o* in the second syllable.
questionnaire	Remember to write double *n* in the middle.
receipt	Remember *ei* in the second syllable, and don't forget the silent *p*.
receive	Remember *ei* in the second syllable.
recommend	Only one *c* but double *m*.
relevant	Remember that the second vowel is *e*, not a.
restaurant	Remember to write *au* after the first *t*.
seize	Remember *ei*, here not ie.
separate	Remember that the second vowel is *a*, not e.
truly	Do not be tempted to add an e after *tru*.
weird	Remember *ei*, not ie.

Common mistakes and controversial issues

The English language arouses strong emotions. Many people have very fixed ideas about what is 'wrong' and what is 'right'. It is important when you write – apart from in very informal texts, emails, etc. – that you use a correct, standard form of English.

If you make mistakes such as putting apostrophes in the wrong place, or using the wrong form of a verb, your readers might be distracted from your message, and even take it less seriously.

It is important to remember that there are different customs for written and spoken English. While it might be acceptable in some situations to say something like, '*Jane and me are going to the shops*', non-standard uses should be avoided in writing.

Several customs of English grammar have come about as a result of people applying the grammar of Latin to English. However, many people are inconsistent about this. For instance, someone who objects to the use of the word *data* as a singular noun (because it is plural in Latin), may be quite happy to use the words *agenda* and *stamina* as singular nouns, even though they are Latin plurals too.

Another important thing to bear in mind is that language changes. The language used by EM Forster writing in the 20th century is very different from that of Shakespeare writing in the 16th century, but nobody would say that Forster's English was incorrect.

New words and phrases come into the language all the time, and even the grammar and structure of our sentences changes. Of course, British English is influenced by American English, and although some people dislike this, others pick up new usages with enthusiasm. For instance when asked '*How are you?*', many British people would now say '*Good, thanks*', or even '*I'm good*', which would not have been heard even five or ten years ago.

In the notes that follow, you will find guidance on what is acceptable and what is not acceptable in current British English. However, there are many issues where people disagree, and as always, it is important to think of your audience. For instance, many people do not care about split infinitives – in fact most people do not know what a split infinitive is! Nevertheless, if your writing is very formal, very important, or will be read by someone you know has very strict views on grammar, it may be best to avoid them.

All right or alright?

Some people consider that *alright* is not a 'real' word, and that *all right* should always be used. However, *alright* is very commonly used, particularly when representing speech. It may be best to avoid it in very formal writing.

Among or amongst?

Some people make the distinction that *among* is used when there is no movement and *amongst* when there is movement:

> *I stood among the crowd.*
> *We walked amongst the sand dunes.*

However, in modern English, is it not usual to make this distinction.

Among or between?

If we are talking, for example, of dividing or sharing things, *between* is usually used when there are only two people or things, and *among* when there are more than two:

> *Noma and Doyin shared the bread between them.*
> *We distributed leaflets among the crowd.*

Between is used after the verb *choose* no matter how many things there are:

> *It is difficult to choose between all the different styles.*

Amount and quantity

In formal writing, it is best to use these nouns only with uncountable or mass nouns:

> *There was a large amount of mud on the carpet.*
> *We bought a small quantity of gold.*

It is not good style in formal writing to say things like: *I've got a huge amount of apples*. For countable nouns, it is best to use *number*, or to re-phrase the sentence, for example: *I've got a lot of apples*.

Comprise

Comprise is a rather formal word, and should not be used with the preposition *of*, even though the similar words *consist* or *be composed* are followed by *of*:

> *The grounds comprise a large lawn and 20 acres of woodland.*
> *My cold remedy consists of lemon, honey and garlic.*
> *The committee is composed of members of the legal profession.*

Concerning

It is common to see concerning used as an adjective meaning 'worrying'. However, this use of concerning is not shown in most dictionaries, and must be considered non-standard. Concerning should be used only as a preposition:

>	*She wrote to me concerning the new building work.*

Could of/should of, etc.

It is a very common error to use *of* after modal verbs such as could, might, should or would. This is because in speech, it sounds as if that is what we are saying. However, the sound is really a weak form of the verb *have*, and this should always be used in writing:

>	*We could have helped you if you had asked.*
>	*You should have called for a taxi.*

Dangling participles

Dangling participles occur when the subject of the main clause is not the subject of the modifying clause that contains a participle (usually a word ending in -*ing* or -*ed*).

Look at the following sentence:

>	*Coming home from work, my hat blew off.*

Coming is a dangling participle here because its subject is not *my hat*. In formal writing, it would be better to say something like:

>	*As I was coming home from work, my hat blew off.*

Here is an example of a dangling past participle:

> *Loathed by his colleagues, we understood why he had been sacked.*

This is incorrect in formal writing, because the subject of the main clause is 'we', but the subject of the participle is 'he'. It would be better to write something like:

> *He was loathed by his colleagues, so we understood why he had been sacked.*

It is fine to use clauses with participles as long as the subject of the main clause matches:

> *Having seen the play before, I was keen to go again.*

Data

Strictly speaking, data is the plural form of the Latin *datum*. Some people insist that it should be used with a plural verb:

> *The data were collected over several years.*

However, data is increasingly being used as a singular noun, and most people would accept that as a valid modern use. There is some logic to this too, since data is often used as a synonym for *information* or *evidence*, which would take singular verbs:

> *All the data was uploaded to the new server.*

Data tends to be used as a plural more commonly in scientific or academic writing. Whether you decide to use a singular or a plural verb with data, make sure that you are consistent throughout your document.

Decimate

This word originated from the Roman custom of killing one in ten of a group of soldiers guilty of crimes such as mutiny. A few people, therefore, prefer to use decimate very specifically to mean 'to reduce by one tenth'.

However, in modern English, decimate is used to mean 'to destroy a large amount or number of something', and this is widely acceptable:

> *Troops were decimated by illness.*

Note that it is best not to use decimate – as many people do – to mean 'to destroy completely'. It is better to use a word like *destroy* or *annihilate* for this.

Different

The safest preposition to use with different is *from*, which is the same use as the related verb *differ from*:

> *These biscuits taste different from the other ones.*

It is also considered acceptable in British, but not American English to use *to*:

> *Your circumstances are different to mine.*

In American English, but not British English, *than* can be used:

> *He has a different job than me.*

Dilemma

The word dilemma comes from the Greek prefix *di-* meaning 'two'. Therefore, purists argue that it should only be used to describe a situation where there are two alternatives, and not where there are a wider range of alternatives:

> *To support my husband or my son: that was my dilemma.*

In formal writing, dilemma should not be used simply as a synonym of 'problem', but only for situations where some sort of choice or decision is to be made.

Because the original Greek word referred to two unpleasant alternatives, some people also believe that it should still only be used in this way, and not for a choice between two pleasant things.

Disinterested or uninterested?

In formal, modern English, uninterested is used to mean 'not interested' and disinterested to mean 'unbiased' or 'impartial':

> *The audience seemed completely uninterested in what she had to say.*
> *We need a disinterested person to make a decision for us.*

However, in reality, the two words are used so interchangeably that even if you try to make the distinction, it is probably best to avoid 'disinterested' altogether to avoid ambiguity, and use *unbiased* or *impartial* instead.

Double negatives

A double negative is the use of two negative words in the same sentence. These are common in some dialects of spoken English, but should never be used in writing.

> *I haven't got no money.* (double negative)
> *I haven't got any money.* (standard English)
> *She didn't tell me nothing.* (double negative)
> *She didn't tell me anything.* (standard English)

Due to or owing to

Some people make a distinction between these two because *due* is an adjective and should therefore be used with a noun, and not a verb or a clause, where it is better to use *owing to*. A simple way to remember the difference is that *due to* can be replaced by *caused by* and *owing to* can be replaced by *because of*:

> *His illness was due to stress at work.*
> *Owing to the weather, the plane could not take off.*

Equally

It is common to see sentences such as the following:

> *Their work was equally as good.*
> *His house is equally as large as Ava's.*

However, in formal English, you should not use the word *as* with equally. Equally should come directly before the adjective:

> *Their work was equally good.*
> *His house and Ava's house are equally large.*

Farther/farthest or further/furthest?

The simplest rule is to use further/furthest all the time. A few people prefer to use farther when they are talking about literal distances:

> *We travelled farther into the mountains.*

However, very few people make that distinction nowadays, and further is almost always used in more figurative senses:

> *We agreed to race to the furthest tree.*
> *Let's pause to reflect before going any further with our discussion.*

Fewer or less?

For people who are strict about grammar, fewer should be used before plural nouns and less before uncountable nouns:

> *There are fewer pupils in her class than last year.*
> *I hope you'll have fewer problems this time.*
> *I'm trying to use less butter in my cooking.*
> *I had even less information about it than you.*

In formal writing, it is best to stick to this rule, but in more informal contexts it is common to see less used before plural nouns:

> *There were less people there than I expected.*
> *This checkout is for people with 10 items or less.*

It is acceptable even in formal English to use less before numbers:

> *I had seen him less than five times in my life.*

Hopefully

In current English it is extremely common to see the word hopefully used to mean 'it is hoped', usually at the beginning of a sentence:

> *Hopefully we won't have to wait long.*
> *Hopefully they'll pay us for the time we spent.*

However, some people object to this, saying that hopefully should only be used to mean 'in a hopeful way':

> *He looked at her hopefully.*
> *We waited hopefully to see if she would appear.*

It is best to stick to this second use in very formal writing.

I or me?

You should avoid writing sentences such as *Tim and me cooked a meal*.

When you use two pronouns or a personal name and a pronoun together, think about whether they are the subject or the object of the sentence:

> *Tom and I went to the football match.* (subject)
> *He asked Jo and me to sweep all the floors.* (object)

If you are not sure whether to use I or me, imagine you were only writing about yourself and not the other person. For instance, you would say *I went to the football match*, so that is the form to use when you add the other person too.

Irregardless

This is not a word in standard English, so do not use it in your writing. The word you need is *regardless*.

Lend or borrow

If you lend someone something, you let them use it for a while. If you borrow something, you take it from someone else to use for a while:

> *Can you lend me a pen?*
> *Can I borrow your pen?*

Literally

This word should be used only to emphasize that what follows is exact fact, and is not being said in an exaggerated or figurative way:

> *The waves were literally as high as a house.*
> *She was literally penniless.*

It is common for literally to be used simply to emphasize what follows, but examples like this should be avoided in formal writing:

> *I literally jumped out of my skin.*
> *Their eyes were literally out on stalks.*

Media

Strictly speaking, media is the plural form of the Latin *medium*. Some people insist that it should be used with a plural verb:

> *The media were guilty of invading her privacy.*

However, media is often used as a singular noun in current English:

The media is making the most of this scandal.

However, if you want to talk about one particular form of communication, you should use the singular *medium*:

She is of the view that television is a dangerous medium.

Off

The preposition off should not be followed by of:

It fell off of the table. (incorrect)
It fell off the table. (correct)

In other cases where 'off of' is used in spoken or non-standard English, the preposition *from* should be used:

I got it off of a friend of mine.
I got it from a friend.

Ought

Unlike with the other modal verbs (can, might, must, etc.), when you make questions and negatives with ought, it is necessary to add *to*. The use of ought in questions and negatives sounds quite formal:

Ought he to have gone?
Oughtn't we to see if he's all right?
You ought not to leave your keys in the door.

Out

The word out is an adverb:

> *I dropped my bag and all my money fell out.*
> *I'm not going to go out today.*

In standard, written English, if you want to use it as a preposition, you have to add *of*:

> *She threw the bag out of the window.*
> *I walked out of the room.*

Phenomena

Remember that phenomena is the plural of phenomenon. Do not use phenomena as a singular:

> *Lightning is a natural phenomena.* (incorrect)
> *Lightning is a natural phenomenon.* (correct)

The reason being

Do not use the verb 'is' after this phrase, because it does not relate grammatically. You should use **that**:

> *We had to sell the business, the reason being that my husband was ill.*

Refute

This word is often used simply to mean 'deny', but this is not correct, standard use. Refute means to prove something wrong with evidence.

> *With these documents, he was able to refute the allegations.*

Sat

Avoid sentences such as *I was sat on the floor*. This is not a grammatically correct tense because we do not use a past participle after *was* or *were*. Instead, you should write:

> *I was sitting on the floor.*

Split infinitives

A split infinitive is where you write an adverb between *to* and a verb, e.g. *to finally agree*.

A lot of people do not like this, although plenty of great writers such as Donne, Eliot and Browning have used it. In very formal writing, it is best to re-order your words:

> *We were asked to carefully look inside the box.* (split infinitive)
> *We were asked to look carefully inside the box.*

In a few cases, a split infinitive is necessary to avoid a change in meaning:

> *He failed to completely understand my point.*
> (split infinitive, but means that he did not understand everything about the point)

He completely failed to understand my point.
(this has a different meaning – that he was unable to understand the point at all)

He failed to understand my point completely.
(this could have either meaning, and is therefore ambiguous)

Try

In British English, it is acceptable to use *and* or *to* after try, though *and* is slightly less formal:

Try and find the coin.
We will try to help you.

In American English, *try and* is not considered correct.

Used to

Note that when using the negative and question forms with used to, you need to drop the *d* from *used*:

Years ago, children used to be more polite.
I used to hate broccoli, but now I like it.
Children didn't use to have TVs in their bedrooms.
Did you use to play football when you were a child?

In a very formal style, we could write:

I used not to have a car.
I usedn't to need glasses.

While or whilst?

These two words are used in the same way in British English.

> *I read a book while I was waiting.*
> *Whilst she slept, I cooked a meal.*

In American English, while is used.

Who or whom?

Who is now commonly used as the object where in the past it was only considered correct to use whom:

> *Who do you work for?*

If you use whom in sentences like this, your writing will sound extremely formal:

> *For whom do you work?*

However, you must use whom directly after a preposition:

> *The woman to whom I spoke was a local nurse.*
> *There were twenty masked prisoners, many of whom were armed.*

Index

notes

notes

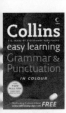

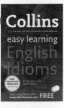